second edition

CASE STUDIES in
CHILD and
ADOLESCENT
PSYCHOPATHOLOGY

second edition

CASE STUDIES in CHILD and ADOLESCENT PSYCHOPATHOLOGY

DeDe Wohlfarth
Spalding University

Robin K. Morgan
Indiana University Southeast

WAVELAND

PRESS, INC.
Long Grove, Illinois

For information about this book, contact:
Waveland Press, Inc.
4180 IL Route 83, Suite 101
Long Grove, IL 60047-9580
(847) 634-0081
info@waveland.com
www.waveland.com

10-digit ISBN 1-4786-2663-1
13-digit ISBN 978-1-4786-2663-3

Printed in the United States of America

7   6   5   4   3   2   1

Quick Reference Guide

Contents

Preface

Psst. Hey you. Yes, you. We'd like to talk with you for a moment. First of all, thank you for buying our book, although you probably didn't feel like you had much of a choice in the matter since the book is probably a required text for a class. Nevertheless, you did buy it, so thank you. Bonus: You're reading the introduction. Most people don't, so your willingness to do so tells us a great deal about you, and all of it is good.

When we taught courses in abnormal psychology, family therapy, and introduction to counseling, we realized that a giant gap existed that even the best of our students were struggling to successfully cross. On one side of the gap is the idyllic, ivory tower of dense and expensive textbooks, the drilled-in-your-head importance of research and evidence-based practice, and the sometimes contradictory and often jargon-filled theories of psychology. On the other side of the gap is the real world, where clients are complex human beings with messy lives, where budget shortfalls in mental health agencies mean high caseloads for providers, and where theory and research are often disregarded. Even if you know the current best-practice treatment approach to a problem, you'll often find yourself asking how you can apply these ideas to *this* client in *this* family with *this* cultural background, as you work in *this* organization with *this* set of challenges.

We understand. We get it. We're both clinical psychologists who, between the two of us, have practiced in the field for fifty years, focusing on children and families. We're also professors of psychology who consume and produce some of the aforementioned research that you might dread reading at times. Thus, we live in the gap between research and practice. We intend this book to be a bridge. We believe that the best way to help you bridge the gap is by practicing—by applying your knowledge to actual cases. We didn't want these cases to be like so many of those idealistic scenarios presented in most textbooks, where clients are predominately culture-free, have one designated and simple problem, always get evidenced-based treatment, and always improve. Who lives in that world? Accordingly, our cases contain ethical lapses, clinical mistakes, confusing diagnostic problems, unevenly applied evidence-based approaches, and sometimes, unhappy endings.

We designed this book around two key educational ideas: problem-based learning and a case study/story approach. The first approach, problem-based learning, helps develop your critical thinking skills. This is important because

ix

the answers to real-world questions are often nuanced, contextual, and tentative. That's why good answers often begin with "It depends. . . ." Students learn more when challenged to solve complex problems. The second key teaching method we used is a case study/story approach. Why did we do this? Because people often struggle to remember facts, but we're much better at remembering stories. Our ultimate goal is to help you learn. We know that one of the best ways to achieve this goal is to get you to care enough about the children and families in our book that you'll be willing to do the hard work of learning that involves remembering, applying, and integrating ideas. We hope we're successful in helping you attain this goal.

The stories of the children are completely fictional, and any resemblance between a case and a real-life child is completely coincidental. We tried to create stories about children who represent a wide variety of races, ethnicities, and cultural backgrounds. We also tried to portray mental health providers who demonstrate that same amazing breadth of diversity. Given the current lack of diversity in the mental health field, we recognize that our representation of diversity among psychologists and therapists was more aspirational than accurate. Nevertheless, we hope their portrayal in this book will help our field move closer to this ideal.

We avoided the s/he/they conundrum by using the pronoun that reflects the gender of the main character in that chapter throughout the entire chapter, even when we discuss the literature. We don't have a chapter representing a transgender person, or gender dysphoria, for two reasons: First, we didn't have an expert to consult in this area and we strove to make each chapter real without being stereotypical. Second, because the research, and even the language, concerning transgender people is in its infancy, we didn't want to write a chapter that would be outdated before the book was even published. Additionally, we attempted to use person-first language out of respect for people struggling with mental illness. A "person with a disorder" instead of a "disordered person" conveys respect for individuals as being more than the sum of their diagnoses.

Because this book is different from a typical textbook, we organized it in a markedly different manner than the usual format. The cases presented in the book are divided into two parts. Each case follows the same outline:

Part I: Case Studies
Introduction

Part II: Diagnosis and Conceptualization
ICD-10/DSM-5 Diagnosis
Diagnostic Discussion
Case Conceptualization
Evidence-Based Treatment

Part I, which contains the introductions for each case, is presented sequentially. Part II, containing the *diagnosis and conceptualization,* for each case, is presented separately. We designed this unusual organizational style deliberately—to get you to slow down and think about the cases presented in Part I before we divulge the "answers" in Part II.

The *introduction* does exactly what you would expect it to do. It introduces you to a child, his or her family, the family's cultural background, and a presenting problem. We tried to talk about the things that make families strong, not just about their problems. Sadly, the field of psychology has become almost exclusively focused on ameliorating people's problems instead of proactively encouraging their health and resilience. We wanted to present a more balanced view of clients, recognizing that all people are complex beings with a mix of strengths and weaknesses. People are not easily categorized as "good" or "bad," and the boundaries of humanity are not sheared as cleanly as if by a knife.

Part II of each case begins with the *ICD-10/DSM-5 Diagnosis*. In this brief section, the clinician diagnoses the child with a mental health disorder (or, sometimes, does not). The ICD-10 and DSM-5 are complementary diagnostic systems created to code mental health problems by using an intricate number system. In a manner similar to the library's Dewey Decimal system, these dual diagnostic tools are used by clinicians to identify (and bill for) the behavioral, mental, and emotional challenges faced by their clients.

The *Diagnostic Discussion* explains how the child meets the criteria for the diagnosis that s/he has been given. Although somewhat research-based, this section is usually pretty straightforward—depending, of course, on the child's presented symptoms and the level of objectivity in the diagnostic criteria.

The *Case Conceptualization* section is the most dense and research-based part of each child's case, so you may find it to be the most difficult to read. However, the work you put into understanding a client's case conceptualization section will pay off for you later. A case conceptualization considers all available data about a client as well as the research on the client's disorder for the purpose of explaining etiology and its impact on treatment. In other words, we try to answer the question, "Why does this person do what they do?" A good case conceptualization should integrate the research behind a disorder with information about a client's culture, the context in which the disorder occurs, and the client's strengths and preferences for treatment. The purpose of a case conceptualization is to organize complex and diverse information with the goal of better understanding a person. Because every person is a unique human being embedded in unique social and cultural systems, the amount of information we have to consider in order to understand just one person can easily be overwhelming. Consequently, we did our best to write case conceptualizations that were neither overly simplistic or mind-numbingly challenging.

A good case conceptualization is vital to creating a good *evidence-based treatment* plan. Thus, the more carefully you read the case conceptualization section, the more thoroughly you'll be able to understand the treatment section. This last section in each chapter is designed to help you answer questions about why clinicians select particular interventions for particular clients. In this section, you'll get to discover how treatment did—or didn't—work for the child.

Embedded throughout each case are critical thinking questions. We hope you will pause and thoughtfully answer these questions, either in a group context or as an individual. Ideally, you will write down your answers, because the sheer act of writing promotes deeper levels of thinking. (We recommend against superficially answering the questions and sprinting through each case—because, frankly, you'll learn more if you really immerse yourself in the cases and the questions they elicit.) You'll find that you must do a little research to answer some questions. You'll also find that some of the questions have definitive correct answers, while others just open up a "hornet's nest" of more questions. Don't be discouraged if answering one question leads you to ask many more. That process is called learning. We want you to be active learners as you read, so highlighting, note taking, and bookmarking will greatly benefit you. The best learning happens when you get messy, so please dog-ear pages and use numerous paperclips or "sticky notes"—whatever aids you in the learning process.

Finally, we wrote this book not just to enhance your learning experience, but also to give a voice to the many clients and families we've served over the years. Too often, the stories of people with mental health problems are neither heard nor told. If these stories are shared, they're sometimes seen from the perspective of an outsider looking in at another's life, like a rubbernecker looking at a train wreck. All people, including clients and therapists, have complicated lives, make mistakes, possess remarkable strengths and almost impossible weaknesses, endure great setbacks and unexpected challenges, and still have hopes, dreams, and goals for their lives. No one is simply defined or described. This book is dedicated to everyone who does their best to get through the day, even the hard days—including you.

DeDe Wohlfarth, PsyD
Robin K. Morgan, PhD

Acknowledgements

Writing may be a solitary activity, but writing well takes a team. I would like to acknowledge my co-author, Robin Morgan, for her high standards and infatigable work ethic, as well as always having the courage to tell me when I was wrong. I appreciate the expertise and work from our contributing authors from Spalding University's doctoral program in clinical psychology who shared the vision for this project, including Zack Thieneman, Claire Horton, Gabriela Alshafie and Andrea Araujo-Talledo, Paul Morgan and David Lairmore, Kathryn Ball and Katerina Stratigis, Meena Kumar, Danniella Jones, RoShunna Lea, Jonathan Bauman and Anna Grace Cooper, and Emily Bullock. Thanks also to others who contributed their cultural or other expertise, including Matt Schooler, Tim Martin, and Sarah Burgher. My greatest appreciation for Dr. Steve Katsikas, Chair of the School of Professional Psychology, for his flexibility and support in all things big and small.

Special appreciation to our editors: Gayle Zawilla, who loved our book enough to read stories and not just count pages, as well as the brilliant nitpicking of Dave Wohlfarth, Cathy Martindale, Claire Horton, and especially Dr. Marlena Woodmansee, who fixed numerous grammar mistakes that made me realize I should have paid more attention in high school. On a more personal note, I appreciate my best friends and running buddies, Martha, Rhonda, and Jana, who were patient even when I talked about fictional characters in mind-numbing detail. Thank you to Terry, mom, and my sisters for being the glue that held everything together the past two years. A shout-out to our four children, for the times you made the cookies for the school bake sales, found the missing soccer socks, and didn't complain when we had chicken nuggets (again) for dinner. To my clients, who help me keep things real, as well as my students who make learning matter. And most importantly, with unending gratitude to God for making the impossible possible.

—DeDe

As with every writing project I have attempted, this book would have never come to fruition without the determination of others. First, and foremost, my co-author, DeDe insisted that we continue working on this book when I was ready to quit. It is her inspiration and heart that speaks from every case in this book. I would also like to thank Sarah Hunter, Rosezona Bowden, Darlene Gehring, Chuck Gehring, Sarah Morgan, and Zach Morgan. To my husband, Dave, thank you for putting up with me. And, finally, I would like to sincerely thank my students, who clamor for better cases (and tell me all of the problems with prior cases), and to the many clients who have allowed me to gain the perspective I have today.

—Robin

SECTION 1

Case Studies

CASE 1

Enrique Dominguez

The cultural values discussed in Enrique's case are broad generalizations of the beautifully diverse Mexican culture. Mental health professionals should always be careful when generalizing cultural information, as each family is unique. Diagnosing mental health disorders in children with a Latino background is complicated. Factors that should be considered include the level of information available to practitioners about the family's mental health disorders, level of English proficiency, the family's view and fears about using government resources, the family's immigration status as documented or undocumented immigrants, and their access to educational and financial opportunities and resources. The family's level of acculturation also may affect their receptiveness to services. Second-generation Mexican Americans often are drastically different (and frankly more similar to Anglo-Americans) than immigrant families or first-generation Latino families. Furthermore, Latino Mexicans are different than Latinos from South American countries and the Caribbean. Discrepancies broaden further depending on whether the family is from el rancho *(the country),* el pueblo *(a town), or* la ciudad *(the city) in Mexico.*

The family in this case study uses the term "Kiké" as a nickname for Enrique, as it is frequently used as a term of endearment among Latinos. (This term is not related to the derogatory term used against members of the Jewish community.) Also, the dialogues between the characters in this story occur in Spanish but are recorded here in English.

Sarah Gonzalez was born and raised in Watonga, Oklahoma, as one of three close-knit siblings. During her childhood, Sarah always saw her mother helping people in need. Her mother was a homemaker who always made time to help a neighbor, no matter how busy she was or how limited the family resources were. Sarah's mother had dreamed of becoming a social worker ever since she moved to the United States from Mexico as a child. Financial and familial situations interfered with Sarah's mother achieving her dream.

When Sarah was a teenager, she promised herself that she would achieve her mother's dream, which had since become her own. Sarah earned her bachelor's and master's degrees at Oklahoma State University and became a Licensed Clinical Social Worker (LCSW). Sarah's mother had supported Sarah in reaching this goal and had sent her money whenever she could. Sarah's father was proud of Sarah's educational achievements but had tried to discourage her from entering the field of social work. His Latino heritage didn't value mental health services. Sarah's father thought a social work

3

degree was a waste of time, and he felt that she should settle down, marry, and have a family. Sarah respected her father's opinions but, nevertheless, pursued her education. Both mother and daughter tiptoed around the subject of school with Sarah's father. Sarah was certain that a career in social work would enable her to help many people as well as eventually provide financial support to her parents. Sarah also hoped to support her younger brother, who still lived at home. Sarah's sister was married and lived nearby with her husband and children. Sarah was 36 years old, her sister was 35, and her brother was 32.

As Sarah gained knowledge and experience at OSU, she was dismayed to learn about the high number of Spanish-speaking families who weren't receiving adequate mental health care because of language barriers. Being *Chicana* herself, of Mexican descent, Sarah became determined to work with Spanish-speaking families in the growing Latino community in Watonga.

Sarah also had a soft spot for people with Autism Spectrum Disorder (ASD). Her younger brother was diagnosed with ASD in elementary school, after declining grades and frequent referrals for disruptive behavior. Sarah's father initially didn't agree to psychological testing for her brother. Over time, however, Sarah's mother wore him down by her insistence that such testing might help. Sarah's brother was officially diagnosed with Autism Spectrum Disorder when he was 10. Unfortunately, Sarah's parents never wholeheartedly implemented the recommended supports for her brother as the changes seemed too overwhelming. Over the years, her brother slowly became "stuck in his ways." He achieved almost no meaningful level of independence and still needed help in daily living skills including hygiene, communication, and cooking. Her brother had a vocabulary of perhaps 50 words and relied on temper tantrums to get his needs met.

In her graduate training, Sarah took a class on individuals with developmental disabilities. For the first time in her life, she recognized that had her brother received early intervention services, the course of his life might have been very different. She was simultaneously filled with hope for people with severe disabilities and disappointment regarding the life that her brother had led. As Sarah watched her aging parents have increasingly more problems physically managing and providing for her brother, she wished she had known as a teenager what she now knew. However, even armed with knowledge of best-practice treatment for individuals with ASD, Sarah doubted that her parents would have had the resources to implement a home-based, comprehensive intervention, given their financial struggles. As an adult, Sarah tried to help her parents put simple interventions in place that might help her brother, but with limited success. Instead, as she earned her degree and license, she became determined to work with all Latino families to help improve their lives. Just as she had promised herself to become a social worker, she also made a promise to herself to help families affected by ASD.

1. How might Sarah's own experience impact her work with clients?
2. What are some possible challenges to working with Latino families given their cultural views of mental health? How might you convince Latino clients of the benefits of therapy while respecting their cultural values?

Sarah became a respected LCSW who worked at a local community mental health center. She often received referrals from Watonga City Schools, as the school system had many Latino students. Because Sarah was the only Spanish bilingual mental health provider in Watonga, other professionals, including teachers, doctors, and nurses, often directly called her when they had a referral for a Spanish-speaking family. That direct referral process is what led to Enrique becoming one of Sarah's clients.

Enrique Dominguez was referred by his kindergarten teacher, Mrs. Miller, who had referred several children to Sarah and trusted the quality of her work. Mrs. Miller wasn't sure, however, if Sarah had the skills to work with Enrique, as his behavior was quite different from that of the other children whom Mrs. Miller had referred to Sarah.

It was late November, and school had been in session for several months. Mrs. Miller had become seriously worried about Enrique's behavior. She told Sarah that Enrique was a dark-haired, bright-eyed Latino kindergartener in her class of 26 children. The students were mostly Latino and white, with a good number of Native American children as well. Enrique lived with his parents, Francisco and Rosa María Dominguez, his maternal grandmother, and three siblings. Enrique was five, his brother Jaime was six, his sister Isabella was eight, and his brother José was 10. Enrique did not attend preschool and had only rarely been away from his family. He was constantly cared for by his mother, grandmother, and older siblings.

On Enrique's first day of kindergarten, Rosa María accompanied Enrique and his three older siblings on the short walk from their house. When they arrived at school, Enrique's hand gripped his mother's arm with increasing intensity, unintentionally but painfully driving his fingernails into his mother's forearm. The school parking lot was bustling with cars coming and going, parents hugging their children goodbye, and teachers welcoming students with bright smiles, vibrant waves, and cheerful greetings. Enrique's siblings were excited to be back at school, quickly spotted some friends, and departed from their mother and Enrique. As Enrique and his mother grew closer to the crowd, Enrique's grasp on his mother's arm became a death grip, with his nails digging deeper under her skin. Rosa María ignored the pain, looked down at Enrique and said in Spanish, "Kiké, you're going to have fun! School is fun!"

Rosa María instantly recognized Mrs. Miller and walked up to her, introducing Enrique. Mrs. Miller had enjoyed teaching Enrique's older siblings when they were in kindergarten, and she was eager to meet him. Mrs. Miller happily welcomed him: "Hi Enrique! I'm Mrs. Miller. We're going to have so much fun today. Mom will pick you up this afternoon."

Immediately, Mrs. Miller noticed something unusual about Enrique. Initially, he refused to let go of his mother's arm. When he did let go, he began rapidly flapping his hands up and down. He said nothing to Mrs. Miller despite her warm welcome and made absolutely no eye contact with her. He began to yell, but instead of words, the sounds were just frantic howls. Enrique survived that first day of kindergarten only because of the patient and caring responses from Mrs. Miller.

Over the next few months, the behavior Enrique had displayed that first day of school intensified. He often flapped his hands, especially when he was stressed or worried. He didn't do well with any changes of routine and quickly began to yell as he had that first day of school whenever anything unusual happened. The slightest change in his routine bothered him—a fire drill, an assembly, a change in the regular breakfast menu, different seasonal decorations on the bulletin board, an unexpectedly colored dry erase marker, or worst of all, any change in seating arrangements. Enrique always wanted to have the same seat in the back corner of the classroom, and he wailed if his seat were moved anywhere else.

One month into the school year, children usually had calmed their first-day jitters and were making friends. Enrique, however, rarely interacted with his peers. He kept to himself at play time and recess, the times that his behavior was most obviously different from his peers. Instead of playing with toys, balls, swings, and slides, Enrique tucked himself into a corner of the room or playground. He hunched over to make himself into a little ball, and then he'd line up blue cars or blue crayons in a perfectly straight line. He only chose to play with things that were blue and methodically avoided non-blue-colored items. As he played, he worked hard to ensure that the gaps between his cars or crayons were perfectly even and the items were positioned in exactly parallel lines. When Mrs. Miller called his name, Enrique never responded. Instead, he'd focus intently on his cars or crayons, never even glancing in her direction. Mrs. Miller would then walk over to him, gently put her hands on top of his hands to pause his playing, and talk to him about the activity he should be doing. This redirection happened frequently, as Enrique was often off-task. Every time Mrs. Miller touched Enrique's hand, he became quickly agitated and frantically moved his hands in an effort to get her keep her distance. Mrs. Miller realized that Enrique was not comforted by her touch, so she stopped touching him and instead used a calm voice to redirect him. Unfortunately, this strategy also did not work well for Enrique, who seemed to ignore her or not hear her.

When Enrique's peers tried to interact with him, he yelled or roughly grabbed a toy from their hands if it were something he wanted, such as a blue crayon or car. Mrs. Miller tried to intervene and explain to Enrique why grabbing a toy was wrong. However, he never seemed to understand. Mrs. Miller knew that the Dominguez family exclusively spoke Spanish at home, yet the problems she noticed in her attempts at communication with Enrique were qualitatively different than what she experienced with a Spanish-speaking or bilingual child. Although she was white, Mrs. Miller had worked many years in a multiracial school and had learned some key Spanish phrases to help students who weren't yet proficient in English. When she spoke with Enrique, she often tried both English and Spanish words.

However, it wasn't the English language that was a problem for Enrique. Instead, it seemed to be the whole idea of language itself. Enrique had problems with his *receptive language*, or understanding what others were saying to him. He also had trouble with *expressive language*, or speaking his thoughts and feelings. This combination of receptive and expressive language difficulties made interaction with his classmates extremely difficult and interfered with his learning as well. Mrs. Miller noted that she'd only heard Enrique speak three- or four-word sentences, which were often robot-like demands such as, "Need blue crayons! Need blue crayons!" In fact, the only time Mrs. Miller had heard Enrique speak a sentence with more than four words was when he said, "Thomas is a useful engine!" a phrase he often repeated at seemingly random times.

Mrs. Miller also noticed that sometimes Enrique would sit alone and flap his hands up and down as he'd done that first day of school, while he rocked or bounced in his chair. Mrs. Miller found it most difficult to redirect Enrique at these times. It was as if he were in his own little world. He tended to flap his hands most often when the classroom was noisy or unsettled.

Mrs. Miller's concerns grew as Enrique made little progress over the first few months of school. She decided to ask Rosa María how Enrique was doing at home. Rosa María said that he was "the same" and doing fine. Mrs. Miller asked if Rosa María would be willing to share any information from his medical checkups with her. Rosa María agreed. The next day, she brought to school the original copies of all of Enrique's medical records. Mrs. Miller was hoping for a thick folder of information, but Rosa María instead brought three sheets of paper. The paper work she brought was from two doctor's visits over the past five years. The first sheet of paper was from a medical clinic in Mexico where Enrique had seen a doctor at age six months. The second sheet of paper was a standard physical form of mostly check boxes from a pediatrician in the United States when Enrique was five. A physical was a requirement for all five-year-old children to begin school in Oklahoma. The third sheet of paper was a brief immunization record, also a required document. The medical checkups contained information about his height, weight, and blood pressure. Mrs. Miller was disappointed by the lack of information. She had hoped to discover more about when Enrique met his developmental milestones, as she was concerned that he might have intellectual problems.

3. What are your thoughts about Enrique's minimal medical file? Given the lack of medical information, will you ethically be able to definitively diagnose Enrique?

4. If you were Mrs. Miller, what would you do? What would be your next step?

Mrs. Miller asked Enrique's parents, Francisco and Rosa María, to come in for a meeting to discuss Enrique's progress. During the meeting, Mrs. Miller expressed her concerns about Enrique and explained the odd behaviors she had seen him exhibit in school. She asked if the Dominguez family had witnessed any atypical behavior from Enrique at home, but they just shrugged in response and denied serious problems. Francisco and Rosa María were quiet during the meeting, though Rosa María began to tear up as Mrs. Miller explained Enrique's struggles. Mrs. Miller encouraged them to meet with Sarah Gonzalez, an LCSW. Francisco agreed that they'd talk with Ms. Gonzales, mostly because her last name signaled to him that she was Latina. However, Francisco was certain that nothing was wrong with Enrique. He was hoping that Ms. Gonzales would let Mrs. Miller know that Enrique was just fine.

When Francisco, Rosa María, and Enrique arrived at Ms. Gonzales's office, they sat, embarrassed, in the crowded waiting room for a few minutes before Sarah came out to greet them. She spoke in Spanish and asked them to call her Sarah. Her bright smile, soft voice, and Chicana features calmed Francisco and Rosa María, whom she initially addressed formally as *Señor* and *Señora* as she invited them into her office. Her small office consisted of toys and games on one end and a compact sofa and chair on the other. The walls were adorned with Mexican tapestries and paintings. Francisco and Rosa María relaxed as Sarah conducted the entire interview in Spanish. Francisco had never before met a mental health professional, let alone been to the office of one. However, he was unexpectedly convinced that Sarah would understand his family. After some warm introductory conversation, Sarah discussed the limits of confidentiality and informed consent.

5. Knowing what you know about Sarah's background and experience, how do you think this session will go?

6. If you're not Latino and don't speak Spanish, what specific behaviors could you do or what things could you say to put the Dominguez family more at ease?

7. The Dominguez family is bilingual, yet Spanish is their native language. How might an intake interview be different for them if conducted in English instead of Spanish? What does the research suggest about the use of a translator in therapeutic settings?

As the adults began to talk, Enrique immediately ran to the train table in the corner of the office and began playing. *He's a cute kid*, Sarah thought, as she watched Enrique play. He was cleanly dressed in shorts and a matching blue T-shirt with an image that she immediately recognized as the popular cartoon character *Thomas the Tank Engine*. She noticed that Enrique didn't play with the toy trains in the same manner as most children do, connecting the magnets on the individual train cars to make a long train and then driving it around the track, often with exciting mock accidents caused by the hills and tunnels. Instead, Enrique carefully lined up the engines, beginning with the two blue ones, Thomas and Edward. He didn't play with James, the rebellious red engine, or Percy, the little green engine. He didn't play imaginatively at all, ignoring the inviting countryside of the little train table and focusing solely on the two blue engines, shuffling them back and forth without ever letting the magnets on the trains touch.

Francisco and Rosa María frequently glanced at Enrique. Sarah quietly studied their faces. Rosa María's face looked concerned, with her furrowed brow and wrinkled dark brown skin around her eyes—the face of tired and worried mothers everywhere. Francisco appeared more stoic and stern, as if he wanted to ensure his son was behaving appropriately. Although Sarah had paperwork from Mrs. Miller about Enrique, she asked what the parents' perspectives were regarding their son.

Enrique's parents were uncertain how to begin. They said they weren't too concerned about Enrique until a few months ago, when he began kindergarten. Rosa María described Enrique's first day of school but noted that she wasn't overly worried about it because she knew he was nervous. Over the next several weeks, however, Enrique began coming home with notes in his backpack about his problematic behavior. Rosa María shared some of the comments that Mrs. Miller had written about Enrique, including how he yelled, had trouble communicating, didn't pay attention, and rarely interacted with other children. They acknowledged that they liked Mrs. Miller and that her notes often were accompanied by smiley-faces or little encouraging sentences such as, "I know Enrique can do it!"

However, despite Mrs. Miller's kindness, Francisco was certain that she was overreacting to Enrique's negative behavior. Francisco thought that Enrique was just being the same headstrong boy he always had been. "You see him now, Sarah," Francisco said, gesturing to his son. "There's nothing wrong with our boy, right?"

> 8. How would you answer Francisco's question in a way that didn't alarm him or break the rapport you've gained with him?

"It sounds like Mrs. Miller has some concerns about Enrique, and that can be hard to hear. I don't know enough about Enrique right now to give my opinion, but as I learn more about him and your family, I'll be honest and tell you what I think," Sarah gently responded.

Rosa María spoke next: "Kiké is fine. We are here because we didn't want to be in trouble with the school. Mrs. Miller told us to come. I told my cousin about you—about everything with Enrique—and she said we should come. She always thinks something is wrong with Enrique. But he's just different. Every child's different. My uncle, he agrees with me. Enrique's fine. He says that schools make big problems out of little ones."

Francisco added, "This must be one of those times."

Sarah remained patient and encouraging but unmoved. "Maybe. We don't know. But anyway, I'm glad both of you are here today. My goal is for us to work together to help Enrique."

Francisco talked with Sarah about the school situation. Sarah noticed that Rosa María grew increasingly quiet as the conversation continued. Sarah looked for opportunities to bring Rosa María into the conversation, as she assumed Rosa María was responsible for most of the childcare in the family, as is common in Latino culture. Sarah asked Rosa María about Enrique's early development. This single question provided Sarah with a great deal of information from both Rosa María and Francisco, who discussed not only Enrique's early years, but the Dominguez family and their immigration history.

The entire Dominguez family moved from Mexico to the United States when Enrique was less than a year old. Enrique was always the quiet one of their four children. He babbled some as a baby and toddler but didn't begin to speak until he was four years old. Even then, he said only a few words and phrases. Rosa María thought that Enrique's slow language development was due to their move to the States and that he might have been confused with hearing Spanish and English. They described how José (age 10), Isabella (age 8) and Jaime (age 6) were talkative and outgoing, but how Enrique had always been quiet except when he had a tantrum, which he did far more often than his siblings.

"He was a wild boy when he was little—he had big tantrums when me and *mi ami* (my mom) couldn't understand what he wanted. He's hard to understand, but me and mom can do it. He points at things. My mom sees and she knows. Isabella understands Kiké, too. She knows what he wants to say. Even when he is quiet, she knows," Rosa María shared. She then described the special bond between Enrique and his only sister. "I don't know how, but Isabella just knows. He's not always nice to her, but she's always nice to him. She adores him. He's good when she's around. She helps a lot. *Mi ami* is deaf and cannot speak or hear, but she understands Enrique."

Rosa María continued to describe Enrique's language. "When Enrique learned to talk, he just repeated things. He heard something on TV—repeat it. Heard something in the family—repeat it. He said 'Thomas is a useful engine!' again and again. Only that. For a year, only that! That's what he says when he's happy. And the trains. He loves trains. He always loves trains. They cost a lot of money, so we only have three trains we got at a yard sale. Look! He loves your trains! He will stay here forever if we say it's OK," she said as she gestured toward her son, who was now crashing the trains off the side of the train table, laughing with glee, and flapping his hands up and down as the trains fell to the floor. As he played, he flatly repeated his favorite phrase that his mother had just said, "Thomas is a useful engine."

Rosa María continued to talk about Enrique's play. He never played with his siblings or neighborhood kids, and no one wanted to play with him except Isabella. Rosa María wanted her son to have playmates and relationships. Tears welled up in her eyes as she described the relationship she'd like to have with her son.

Rosa María noted, "I want to play with him but he just sits there and flaps his hands. Or he gets mad and yells and hits. Sometimes he's OK. Sometimes he'll play. Sometimes, he just gets mad. He has to have the trains be perfect. He gets mad if the trains are not his way. Isabella is good. She is patient. She just lets him play whatever he wants."

Rosa María kept talking as Sarah kept listening. No matter what Rosa María said, Sarah talked about how hard things must be with Enrique, not what bad parents Rosa María and Francisco had been. The more they were confident that they wouldn't be judged, the more freely they spoke. Rosa María discussed how Enrique's tantrums impacted the family. His brothers and sister helped their mother with Enrique by assisting with dinner and getting Enrique to bed. Jaime and José, Enrique's brothers, often described him as *esta chiquiado o es un poco raro* (he's been babied a lot). Enrique's needs were not only straining the siblings' relationships with him and with each other, but Rosa María's relationship with her children as well.

Rosa María added, "Our children are little. I want to be with them. Kiké makes it hard. I'm so pulled. José, Jaime, and Isabella need me, too. They come home from school and want to talk. Or do homework. I can't help them when Kiké needs so much." Rosa María began to cry as she said, "I hate when Kiké has tantrums at the grocery. *La gente me mira bien feo* (people give me ugly looks). I'm failing at my job. My job as a mother. My most important job."

9. What would you say to Rosa María in response to her comment? What could you do to ensure that she truly hears you, given her layers of shame concerning Enrique's behavior?

10. The family seems to rely on help from Enrique's siblings. How might this affect the family?

Francisco and Rosa María continued talking, explaining that many of their extended family members and neighbors think that Kiké's problems are because of the family's move to the United States. Sarah asked Francisco to describe the circumstances regarding their immigration, and Francisco did so matter-of-factly.

Francisco moved to the States with his brother 15 years ago, when he was 17 years old. He and his brother found work at their uncle's car repair shop in town. Francisco traveled back and forth between Mexico and the United States to visit his parents and siblings. On one of these visits, he met Rosa María. They became romantically involved and Rosa María got pregnant with José, so they married. Francisco continued to work in the United States while Rosa María lived in Mexico. José was born and Isabella quickly followed. Francisco continued to work in the United States to earn money while Rosa María lived in Mexico with the children and her mother, who helped her care for them. Francisco visited his family three times a year for weeks at a time, but the traveling and the distance between them were exhausting for the family. Rosa María got pregnant again, this time with Jaime, and then quickly thereafter with Enrique.

With Rosa María's fourth pregnancy, the family decided that they would all move to the United States. Moving was a big decision, especially because Enrique was less than a year old. Francisco began the arduous process of petitioning for residency for his family five years ago, right after Enrique was born, as he knew the paperwork would take a long time. Unfortunately, the residency paperwork took even longer than expected to be approved, and they felt they couldn't wait any longer. The family decided to go ahead and move, despite being afraid that Enrique might not survive the dangerous trip. Francisco and Rosa María had to leave behind their two sons, Jaime and José, with Francisco's parents for three years. They couldn't afford to bring the older boys with them. They paid *coyotes*—human smugglers—to move the family across the border. Rosa María came to the United States with Enrique, Isabella, and Rosa María's mother, Otilia. Otilia was financially dependent on her daughter's family since Rosa María's father had passed away. Otilia didn't want to leave Mexico but felt she had no choice since she was deaf and couldn't find work. Rosa María wanted her mother to move in with her as Otilia was a help with the grandchildren and a support to her. After saving for three years, they were able to bring José, who was then nine, and Jaime, who was then five, into the United States. The older boys just rejoined the family last year. The Dominguez family is still waiting for their paperwork to be approved by the U.S. Citizenship and Immigration Services Department.

"I pray for help to pass this test. God will bless us. I know He's testing our family. I keep trying to be a good mom. *Yo se que al ultimo todo va estar bien* ("I know that at the end everything is going to be okay"), Rosa María sobbed after Francisco finished describing the family's move. Francisco put his arm around his wife to comfort her. Rosa María nervously looked back at Sarah, then at Francisco. Rosa María then rose and went to sit by Enrique, who continued his game with his trains, too absorbed in his play to pay any attention to her presence near him. Then, he showed a train to his mother and said, "Thomas is useful engine!" oblivious to her tears.

11. How might the family's separation and move have impacted the members of the Dominguez family? Who are you most worried about in this family and why?

12. How might the Dominguez's immigration status affect their access to mental health treatment?

Throughout Rosa María's and Francisco's candid descriptions of their family situation, Sarah provided *active listening* cues, such as nodding, making empathic facial expressions, having open body language, and providing short prompts that encouraged them to continue their story. When they finished,

Sarah softly expressed gratitude for their willingness to share. She recognized the difficulty in being so open with someone they'd just met. As she empathized with Francisco and Rosa María, Sarah was cut off by a sharp scream from Enrique.

Rosa María had put the trains back onto the table because the meeting was finishing, but Enrique wanted to continue his game of dropping the trains onto the floor. Rosa María told Enrique, *"Ay hijo no pasa nada"* ("Calm down! Everything is going to be OK."), but Enrique began screaming repeatedly, *"El tren va bien rápido!"* ("The train goes really fast!"). Enrique tried to grab the trains from his mother as she attempted to return them to the train table where they belonged. Rosa María tried to defuse the situation by calmly rubbing Enrique's back and speaking softly to him. Unfortunately, her attempts didn't seem to be helping. Enrique was inconsolable.

Both Sarah and Francisco got up to help, as Enrique had quickly become violent. He threw a toy train at his mother, kicked her, and was trying to pull her long hair because he couldn't reach the trains she was holding above her head. Suddenly, Rosa María stopped, dropped the trains, and asked Francisco to help her control Enrique. Francisco turned to Enrique and handed him a train. Without hesitation, Enrique quickly returned to giggling as he continued to play his game of dropping trains on the floor.

Francisco consoled Rosa María, who was both visibly upset from being assaulted by Enrique and embarrassed by his behavior. Francisco said, "I'm sorry you had to see that, Sarah. Kiké has trouble moving from one thing to the next, especially if we leave him too long. If we leave the remote on the table, he watches the same part of the movie many, many times. If he plays with trains too long, he gets too excited. He tries to hurt us if we tell him it's time to stop. But sometimes, he doesn't. It's impossible to know."

"Sarah, why is God testing us?" Rosa María asked. Sarah looked at Rosa María's timeworn and worried face. *My goodness,* she thought, *she looks like my mother, so exhausted in caring for my brother.* Sarah's response to Rosa María was particularly gentle and kind. She leaned in and touched Rosa María lightly on her hand as she said, "I'm sorry it's so hard. It's tough enough to be a mother, but it's even more difficult when your child can't tell you what he needs. You can't read his mind."

Both Francisco and Rosa María nodded, as Rosa María cried openly and her normally stoic husband teared up beside her, but he quickly wiped away his unshed tear, as if he had a piece of dirt in his eye.

Sarah took a deep breath and carefully considered her next move. She said, "As we finish up our meeting, I have two things to tell you. First, I appreciate your courage today. You came to see me. And you told me your story so honestly. Second, I'm hoping that you might consider a referral for Enrique to get psychological testing to help us figure out what's going on with him."

Sarah then explained the process of psychological testing. Francisco wanted Sarah to perform the psychological testing, but she explained that she wasn't qualified do so. Rosa María nodded her head slowly, her face blotched and swollen from the tears she'd shed. She agreed that a thorough evaluation of Enrique was a good idea. Francisco hesitantly agreed, too, but added that he didn't think it would help. Francisco only agreed to allow testing for Enrique when he asked Sarah if she'd refer Enrique for testing as if he were her own son. When Sarah said that she would, Francisco agreed.

13. Francisco doesn't seem to be completely on board with treatment. How might you persuade him that an assessment will be helpful for Enrique?

14. What are the pros and cons regarding the high level of similarities between Sarah's family and the Dominguez family? Do you think Sarah should have told the Dominguez family about her brother? Explain your answer.

15. Was it ethical for Sarah to touch Rosa María on her hand? Why or why not? Is touching clients ever ethical and, if so, under what conditions?

16. Rosa María is justifiably upset by the situation with her son. However, she appears to be crying more frequently than might be expected. Do you think that Rosa María is depressed? What additional information would you need to make this determination?

CASE 2

Benjie Savat

Benjie Savat, an 11-year-old boy of Filipino descent, is a fifth grader at Merseyside Academy, a prestigious private school in Pittsburgh. Benjie lives with his mother, father, and 15-year-old sister, Pia. As is true for all children, understanding Benjie requires thoughtfully considering his family and culture. Benjie's interesting family story is rooted in his grandparents.

Benjie's father, Rafael, grew up in rural Mindanao, the southern-most province of the Philippines, an island nation in the far reaches of the western Pacific Ocean near China's coast. The Philippines are influenced by both Spanish and Chinese cultures. Benjie's paternal grandfather, Rudy Savat, owned and farmed a banana plantation. Benjie's paternal grandmother Maria helped around the farm, but she also managed the household, including watching Rafael, his two brothers, and four sisters. Maria never had the opportunity to attend school but she wanted better for her children. The Savat family strongly believed in the value of education, and they pushed their seven children to excel academically. The Savats believed that a college education was the single best gift they could give to their children, so they lived off almost nothing and saved money for years. Saving enough money for college tuition for seven children utilizing earnings from a small banana plantation was difficult, but they didn't complain.

Rafael not only completed college but also acquired a doctorate degree in chemistry. While in graduate school in Manila, the large capital of the Philippines, he met his wife, Aurora. Aurora's middle-class family lived in Manila. Aurora's parents valued education as strongly as Rafael's family. They saved all the money they could for their six children to attend college, but found it difficult to save money in the city despite being government employees with decent jobs. Aurora's parents both hated their jobs. They often spoke in frustration to their children about the broken Philippine government, but they were careful with their complaints outside of their home so as not to create any trouble. Because they did not have sufficient funds to pay for a college education for their children, Aurora worked as a city tour guide in Manila, then as a customer care representative for a telecommunications company, and finally as a receptionist for a Filipino airline to put herself through school. Aurora was always an excellent student, and her family expected her accomplishments to bring honor to the family.

Rafael and Aurora met in the graduate school science library. They became acquainted with one another, as they were the last two students to leave the library every night as it closed. They decided to go out for coffee one night and realized they had much in common. They quickly fell in love, attracted primarily to the strong work ethic and intelligence that they saw in each other, and married within the year after defending their dissertations. After they graduated, they immigrated to the United States to accept joint positions as professors in the chemistry and biology department at the University of Pittsburgh. They liked Pittsburgh's many parks, rivers, and trees but didn't care much for its winters.

Soon after Rafael and Aurora moved to the United States, Rafael's mother died. Rafael's father, Rudy, immigrated to Pittsburgh to be closer to Rafael and several of his siblings who had also immigrated. Although several of Aurora's siblings had moved to the United States, her parents remained in the Philippines. As Rafael and Aurora were establishing their professional reputations by churning out scholarly articles, Aurora got pregnant and gave birth to their daughter, Pia. Four years and several publications later, Benjie was born.

The pregnancy, labor, and delivery for Benjie were effortless. Although he weighed only five pounds at birth, both Rafael and Aurora were petite people, so his small size was expected. Benjie reached all of his developmental milestones on time. He had a tonsillectomy when he was seven, after multiple bouts of strep throat. Benjie also once broke his finger when he accidentally shut it in a car door and broke his toe when he tripped over his own feet and fell onto a curb. Benjie was always a little clumsy, and his legs typically were covered with bruises and scrapes from his carelessness.

Rafael and Aurora have high expectations for Benjie to continue the family legacy of academic and professional success. The problem is that Benjie is struggling in school. Although Benjie's parents had pushed for him to enter a specialized academic program for advanced students, he struggled to keep pace with his classmates. Last year, he was dropped back into mainstream classes. With the transition to middle school on the horizon, Benjie's parents are again lobbying hard for advanced academic placement. They met with the school principal, Mr. Magnus, to advocate for a reconsideration of Benjie's case for his placement into advanced classes. Rafael and Aurora gave written permission for Merseyside employees, including the school-based therapist, to review Benjie's case. However, they were unwilling for Benjie to participate in academic, intellectual, or behavioral testing as a part of this process. Mr. Magnus wanted Benjie's case to receive "high-priority" consideration, as Rafael had regularly donated to the school and had a professional relationship with several school board members.

1. What are your hypotheses to explain Benjie's struggles?
2. What cultural factors are most relevant in Benjie's case?
3. If Rafael and Aurora agree to therapy for Benjie, what are the pros and cons in treating Benjie in a school vs. an outpatient setting?

Mr. Magnus, the school principal, is a tall, bald man whose quick-paced and goal-focused walk was a regular sight throughout Merseyside's halls. He was accused of running a tight ship, and indeed, he took pride in this allegation, although it was often said unfavorably. After the meeting with Rafael and Aurora, Mr. Magnus immediately ordered the school-based therapist, James Wojtkiewicz, to follow up on Benjie's case. James was a Caucasian male in his early 30s with several years of experience in the mental health field. He had a master's degree in clinical psychology and had chosen school-based mental health work because of its flexible hours. James loved sports and hiking, and he led the hiking club at school. He was into running and weight lifting, and his physique showed it. The students at Merseyside saw "Mr. Dub" (short for W, or "Double U") as a cool celebrity, although many of them didn't actually understand his role as a school-based therapist.

James's first step was to arrange a meeting with Benjie, his parents, and his teachers. The goal of the meeting was to determine what barriers were interfering with Benjie's progress and how the school might help him reach his full academic potential. Benjie had never received any formalized testing, so his teachers could only estimate his intellectual and achievement skills. At the meeting, Benjie's teachers noted that he struggled to stay on pace with the other students in his class. It took him longer to master basic concepts, and he often forgot important instructions or steps. Not a single teacher recommended that Benjie should move forward into the advanced program, noting that he struggled to keep up in the mainstream classroom and likely would fall even further behind if moved to an accelerated program.

James decided to review Benjie's educational file, which included five years of report cards and teacher's notes, as well as a portfolio of his work.

Kindergarten: Benjie shows average academic performance. He's a sweet boy and very kind but doesn't talk much with his classmates as he prefers more solitary activities like playing with blocks and drawing. I worry about Benjie because he often forgets important steps in a procedure and struggles to focus at times. He's bright but a little absent-minded professor!

A grades/A conduct grade

—Mrs. Katie Majestro

First Grade: Benjie's a good kid with no behavioral problems. He sometimes gets frustrated when he makes mistakes or forgets his work at home, which happens often. He told me that he "doesn't want to make mom and dad upset" when he gets poor grades. Mr. and Mrs. Savat would like for Benjie to be in the advanced track, but I told them that I don't agree due to Benjie's difficulties following instructions. He's shy and quiet, but he can be very talkative if he's interested in the subject matter.

B grades/A conduct grade

—Mrs. Mariel Munoz

Second Grade: At the beginning of second grade, Benjie was moved to advanced classes, but he's struggling in these classes. He daydreams often and doesn't seem to be motivated to learn the class lesson. He's easily distracted and makes numerous careless mistakes. Benjie's also very "pokey" and moves slowly. On a more optimistic note, he's creative and a good artist. He's a good kid, though, and other kids like him. I really enjoy having Benjie as a student but am worried that he's not mastering the basics.

C grades/A conduct grade

—Ms. Jenny Wolfe

Third Grade: Benjie was returned to the mainstream track in the middle of second grade and began third grade in these regular classes. He was upset about the move, but it's a better fit for him. Benjie sometimes calls himself "stupid" when he struggles to learn, and he is sensitive to criticism from others. Benjie often seems lost in his own world. Other kids report that when he's playing with them, he sometimes forgets what he's playing! He often forgets or loses materials such as books or worksheets, but he always has his colored pencils and comic books near so he can draw. Benjie has no behavioral problems other than his difficulty paying attention, and he is a nice young man.

Low B grades/B conduct grade

—Mrs. Julie Crandall-Montgomery

Fourth Grade: Benjie continues to struggle with learning new material except when he's interested in the topic. He's self-conscious of his inability to grasp concepts. Does well with peer-instructed activities and participates well in labs and school group work. Does poorly with large group instruction and lectures, where he mostly just draws. Top-notch imagination, but struggles with organization. Needs improvement, especially in reading. Request for tutor submitted on 10/1/16.

C grades/B conduct grade (due to lack of social interaction)

—Mr. Stan Weston

As James leafed through Benjie's educational file, he also found a portfolio of his classroom work. Every paper included in his portfolio, across a variety of subjects, had one thing in common. Each test, quiz, page of notes, and worksheet had detailed drawings filling the margins of the pages and extending onto the main page until the actual assignment itself was buried under intricate drawings of curlicues and spirals, trees and spiders, comic book heroes and villains, spaceships and planets, and banana plantations and boats. *Well,* thought James, *Benjie's a very good artist.*

James decided to observe Benjie in the classroom to see firsthand why he was struggling and what teaching styles might work best for him. In his observation, James utilized a structured observation form, but he also took notes as he watched Benjie across three different subjects: math, reading, and science. James had never met Benjie, so his teachers quietly pointed him out to James, so that Benjie wouldn't know that James was observing him. James found Benjie to be a handsome boy, short for his age, with dreamy eyes and straight black hair styled in a bowl cut.

James took the following notes as he watched Benjie:

> I arrived before the morning bell as students were entering the classroom. Benjie's quiet and doesn't interact much with his classmates. When spoken to, he smiles and responds but rarely initiates interactions with others. Benjie's homeroom/math teacher, Ms. Bryant, asked the students to turn in their homework folders. Benjie looked through his backpack, and then his desk (which was a mess) and then searched again in his backpack for his work, but he couldn't find it. When his teacher asked him about his homework, he lowered his head and told her that he couldn't find his folder and believed that he left it at his grandfather's house. His teacher asked if he completed the homework, and he confirmed that his grandfather helped him and the worksheet was done. Ms. Bryant asked that he bring the folder on the following day. She told him that he would miss some points for lateness, but he would still receive partial credit.
>
> Ms. Bryant began teaching math at the board. Benjie immediately began drawing in his notebook. Ms. Bryant began calling on students to answer questions, and asked Benjie, "What is 49 divided by 7?" Benjie looked up, dazed and surprised to hear his name. He was completely absorbed in drawing. He shrugged, and Ms. Bryant called on another student. Benjie immediately returned to drawing. He rarely looked up from his notebook, even during work that involved copying problems from the board. He particularly struggled to pay attention during large class lectures.
>
> In reading class, Benjie took out his primer and opened it like everyone else. However, he didn't appear to hear the teacher as she told everyone to turn to page 38. Benjie instead asked a classmate sitting next to him for help. The classmate turned Benjie's book to the correct page. Benjie initially seemed to follow the reading assignment. However, he often didn't turn the page with others. He stared off into space frequently, and then would give a start and return his attention to his primer, trying to find his place. After approximately 10 minutes, Benjie quietly slid out his notebook from his desk and began drawing. Benjie was lost in the world of X-Men, carefully detailing Wolverine's long fingernails and Gambit's dangerous playing card. Benjie's teacher noticed his distracted behavior and immediately questioned him, asking, "Benjie, are you paying attention?" Benjie looked at his teacher wide-eyed as if he had no idea where he was or what she might want. Benjie nod-

ded his head automatically. The teacher asked him to answer the third question on the reading review worksheet. The worksheet was sitting on Benjie's desk, and Benjie had written the correct answer to the third question. Despite having the correct answer right in front of him, Benjie said nothing. The teacher called on another student who correctly answered the question. Benjie immediately returned to drawing in his notebook. He appeared to daydream for the remainder of class.

In science class, the teacher asked the students to conduct simple laboratory experiments in small groups. Benjie was attentive and interested in the experiment, which involved measuring precipitation in 2-liter bottles under various conditions. When the experiment concluded and the students returned to their regular seats, Benjie had already taken out his notebook and begun drawing before the teacher started talking.

Before the final morning bell rang for lunch, Benjie looked absolutely defeated and dazed, surprised by the bell. The other children quickly lined up for lunch, but Benjie was still at his seat, trying to cram his books into his messy desk.

Before lunch began, I introduced myself and asked Benjie to show me his notebook, which contained pages and pages of detailed drawings. I asked Benjie what he was thinking about during the science class that had just finished. He immediately answered, "Comic books." Benjie then shared that he loved comic books more than anything else and that his cousin had just introduced him to the coolest superhero group in the world, called The Triumph Division. The Triumph Division was in the Marvel Universe, already one of his favorite comic book series, but the best part was that the group consisted entirely of Filipino heroes. Benjie excitedly confided that he wished he could be part of The Triumph Division and knew that if he were, he wouldn't have to go to boring school and could instead fly around with Red Feather, and wrestle bad guys with Fighter One. Benjie breathlessly continued that these heroes couldn't ever die, even in the stories. "Well," Benjie added, "they could die, but then a new generation would be born to take their place. I wish I could join them in the fight against evil!"

I asked Benjie to show me what he had drawn in math class from earlier this morning. Benjie flipped backwards through his notebook several pages before finding another page of elaborate drawings. "Well," Benjie explained, "I was waiting for class to start, so I started drawing a picture of St. George (another member of The Triumph Division). He's easy to draw, but I had trouble with his helmet. Then the teacher started talking, so I was trying to finish my drawing. But then I forgot that I was trying to pay attention and just started to draw. St. George is really a hero. See, the original members of The Triumph Division were killed in a terrorist attack, so St. George was just a regular guy who became a hero to protect the Philippines. Iron Man—the real Iron Man—even visited St. George!"

James spoke to Benjie's morning teachers while the students were at lunch. They confirmed that what James had observed that morning was typical for Benjie. Often he would forget his homework folder, but when he did manage to bring it to school, his homework was always completed. However, he often failed to demonstrate mastery of the homework on the following day, suggesting to his teachers that someone else might be doing his homework for him. He also frequently forgot directions, lost his place during lectures, and asked peers for help instead of asking his teachers.

James asked the teachers whether they recommended the advanced program for Benjie. None did. They noted that he took longer than other students to master basic concepts, and they were concerned he would fall even further behind if moved to advanced classes because his grasp on the fundamentals, especially reading, was not strong. His teachers also noted that they thought Benjie was smart, although no formal testing on his intellectual or academic skills had been completed. Every teacher commented on his creativity, drawing skills, and great imagination. His teachers noted that he rarely interacted with classmates. All agreed that he wasn't a behavioral problem, except for his distractibility.

The following day, James had a more formal meeting with Benjie. When he walked slowly into James's office, Benjie had his head down and seemed embarrassed. James generally considered rapport building as one of his strongest clinical skills, but he found himself faltering with Benjie, who remained quiet through much of the session. James was surprised because Benjie had so freely discussed comic books with him the previous day.

Despite his overall reluctance to talk, Benjie was willing to share some information. He told James that he lived with his mother, father, and older sister, Pia, who had been an excellent student at Merseyside. He said both of his parents worked at the university so he and Pia often went to Grandfather Rudy's house after school. He liked living at home except for chores, which he said were "too hard." When James asked Benjie about school, Benjie said that schoolwork was hard, but he wanted to do well to make his parents and grandfather proud of him. When asked what was the hardest part of school, he simply replied "everything . . . except art class." He said he knew that he wasn't a good student and that he was dreading the harder work of middle school. He mentioned that teachers always talked faster than he could think, and the other students always worked quicker than he did. Benjie added that he also liked P.E. class, because he pretended that exercises and games were part of his training to save the world from the bad guys. Benjie wanted to be special in a good way, but instead he always just felt regular.

Benjie shared that his favorite activities were reading comic books, drawing, watching TV shows about superheroes, and playing video games that featured superheroes. Whenever the topic turned to superheroes, Benjie became very animated. He showed James a picture he had drawn in art class of his favorite super hero, Fighter One. Benjie said that drawing helped him pretend that he was a member of the Triumph Division, like Fighter One, protecting the Philippines.

James asked Benjie what worked for him in school, other than art and P.E. classes. Benjie shared that he liked doing experiments in science with other kids. He liked to learn new things when he was interested in the topic, such as the history of Marvel Comics. Benjie said that he had an encyclopedia of comics, including the history of the X-Men and the Silver Surfer, another one of his favorite characters "because he's made of metal and travels in space on a surfboard."

4. Does Benjie strike you as a typical 11-year-old boy, or is he atypical? Is his focus on comic books excessive or normal?

5. What should James's next step be? Explain your answer.

James's next step was to arrange a meeting with Benjie and his parents. Setting up this meeting was harder than James expected. As he called to introduce himself, he shared that he was the school-based counselor and was working to help determine the best academic interventions for Benjie.

Aurora was confused about James's role and about what a "counselor" had to do with determining appropriate school placement for Benjie. She was reluctant to schedule an appointment with James. James explained that in his role as the school therapist, he worked closely with teachers to determine placement for children, including regular and accelerated track placement. He clarified that Benjie was not in counseling, and that Benjie's parents would need to sign for permission if they chose to pursue therapy for Benjie.

Later in the day, the principal, Mr. Magnus, stopped by James's office, something that he'd done so rarely that he had to be given directions. James, a stocky, well-muscled man, and Mr. Magnus, a tall, large man, sat uncomfortably knee-to-knee in James's tiny office.

Mr. Magnus asked James not to use the word "counselor" when describing himself to the Savat family because it made Benjie's parents "uneasy." He explained that Rafael Savat, Benjie's father, had called him this afternoon and was concerned that having a "counselor" involved in Benjie's review would negatively impact Benjie's chances of moving to advanced classes in middle school. Mr. Magnus also advised James to be cautious about putting too much focus on working with families. He reminded James that his wife, Mrs. Magnus, worked closely with the Savats at the university and that their families were close friends. Mr. Magnus narrowed his eyes, looked directly at James, and stated that the Savat family had good relationships with the school board members and had been big donors to the school. "James," he added, "I just want to make sure that none of this stuff with Benjie goes downhill, if you know what I mean." On his way out the door, Mr. Magnus added that he was able to "work my magic" and that Aurora Savat would see James tomorrow morning at 9 AM, but that this would be her only meeting with James.

6. How would you respond to Mr. Magnus if you were James?
7. In future contact with the Savats, if you were James, would you identify yourself as a counselor to the family or change your job title?
8. How do you manage the dual relationship of working with the Savats?
9. Would you involve Benjie's paternal grandfather in educational interventions given his role in Benjie's life?

Aurora Savat, a tiny, impeccably dressed woman in her mid-40s, met with James the following morning. Her presentation was formal yet polite, and James knew without asking that he should address her as Dr. Savat, not Aurora. Aurora began the interview by asking James exactly what his role was in Benjie's education and how much influence he had on the ultimate decision of whether to place him in advanced classes.

10. If you were James, how would you have answered these questions?

After James explained more about his role as a "supporter in Benjie's educational progress," Aurora seemed to relax. James clarified his role in Benjie's placement and outlined that he would meet with Benjie once or twice as a part of this process, but he would not provide counseling to Benjie unless the family approved. James asked Aurora how Benjie was doing at home. Aurora explained that Benjie loved to "disappear" into his bedroom at home and read comic books, draw at his desk, or watch videos on his TV. Benjie was quiet at home, which Aurora noted was uncommon in the Filipino culture. She added that his 15-year-old sister Pia more than made up for his reticence, as she was "born to debate" and should be a lawyer. Aurora added that Pia was receiving straight As in her high school honors classes. She offered that although she knew that Benjie was bright, he always seemed distracted by something or other. For example, he would often fail to do his assigned chores, misplace important notes and school papers, and forget to share important information. Sometimes, even when he was doing an activity that he enjoyed, such as watching a superhero movie, he would start drawing because he was "bored."

Aurora shared a recent example that she said epitomized Benjie. "I asked Benjie to take out the kitchen trash. He didn't, so I asked him again. Finally, he did—sort of. When he walked outside with the trash bag, I watched him from the kitchen window as he put the garbage bag right outside the back door, not in the trash can where it belongs. He ran off to go chase a firefly. He caught the firefly, and then looked for a jar for it so he could keep it. He found a jar Rafael uses to hold nails in the basement, took the jar outside, and emptied the nails from it into the garden—just dumped them. Then he went back into the basement to look for a hammer so he could make air holes in the lid of the jar for the firefly, which he'd already lost. He brought out a swimming noodle and set it aside. Apparently he was planning to do something with it later. I don't know. Benjie cut his finger while he was nailing, just a little scrape, and he came inside to get a bandage. He couldn't find the bandages in the medicine cabinet. When he heard Rafael watching a documentary on the Siberian Express, Benjie walked away from the bathroom, leaving the medicine cabinet door wide open. He sat down to watch the program with his father, got himself a bowl of ice cream, got bored a minute later, and then started drawing. I went outside later and saw the bag of trash by the back door, the empty jar sitting by the basement stairs, the swimming noodle in the middle of the driveway, and a pile of nails in the garden. I went back inside and saw the medicine cabinet door wide open, the dirty ice cream bowl by the TV, his drawing supplies everywhere in the TV room, and no sign of Benjie anywhere. When I saw him later, up in his room, I asked him about taking out the trash and he said that he already did. He didn't lie—he really did think that he finished the job. That story is all Benjie. That's how he spends his day. Chasing things the rest of us can't see."

James asked a few additional questions about the Savat home. He learned that the family spoke both English and Filipino at home, that the Savats' jobs at the university were very demanding, and that Benjie's grandfather helped out with child care in the afternoons. James asked how it worked to have Grandpa Rudy provide child care, and Aurora reported that it worked well for the most part, except she was convinced that Grandpa Rudy did Benjie's homework for him. She also got frustrated with Rudy because he doled out rewards, such as candy, for any homework Benjie completed, and now Benjie was expecting the same rewards at home. Aurora and Rafael didn't believe in rewarding children for good behavior. However, they said nothing to Rudy out of deference to him as Rafael's father.

James thanked Aurora for their meeting. He also thanked her for her acute observations about how Benjie conducted himself at home and explained that Benjie's teachers had seen similar behavior at school. He asked for her permission to request psychological testing for Benjie, as a comprehensive battery of tests can help inform educational placement decisions. Aurora explained that she needed to consult with Rafael before a decision was made regarding permission to test Benjie, and she was disinclined to agree to such testing herself. Aurora did agree to complete some structured behavioral rating forms, and for Benjie to do so as well.

11. Benjie's grandfather and his parents have opposite philosophical approaches to parenting. Apply the terms authoritative, authoritarian, and permissive to describe their parenting styles.

12. Would you follow up on the possibility that Grandpa Rudy is doing Benjie's homework for him? If so, how?

13. What diagnosis do you think best captures Benjie's problems? How important is the testing that James recommends to help determine Benjie's diagnosis?

CASE 3

Zynthia Miller

Interviewing a client for the first time on the psychiatric ward of a hospital can be an intimidating and unsettling experience, especially for a novice therapist. During one of my rotations on my internship year while finishing my doctoral degree, my clinical assignment involved providing psychological services at our local hospital. I was responsible for conducting brief mental health evaluations for patients in the emergency room who showed signs of a mental health problem, and also for interviewing new patients admitted to the hospital's psychiatric ward. Some of these psychiatric patients would be assigned to me for long-term therapy. Zynthia was such a case. When you read this case, imagine yourself as me, a novice clinician with very limited experience in the field.

At my internship, my work began when I received a *consult*—a request from a physician for expertise from a colleague in another field—to assist with a case. Physicians often consult with psychologists to request a mental-status exam, brief psychological assessment, or neuropsychological assessment. Depending on the results of these evaluation measures, a patient might be referred for ongoing psychological services.

I'd been at the hospital for two months and was starting to gain my "sea legs," although I wasn't yet very confident in my skills. When I arrived at work one day to begin my shift, I received an electronic consult which simply stated:

CONFIDENTIAL
Psychological Services Consult
Patient Name: Zynthia Miller
Demographics: 15-year-old Caucasian female
Presenting Problem: Suicide attempt in school bathroom
Reason for Consult: Provide recommendations and therapy
Referring Physician: Dr. MaryAnn McGuire

As I read the consult, I expected to meet a scared and depressed teenager, most likely upset about breaking up with her boyfriend or doing poorly in school. In the two months I'd been at the hospital, most of the suicide attempts that I'd seen had been adolescent girls with these precipitating factors as reasons for their suicide attempt. I looked at Zynthia's hospital chart for any additional information that might be helpful and read this brief background information:

Zynthia Miller was admitted to Mercy General Hospital yesterday. She is from a small town near the Georgia/Alabama state line. She was transported by ambulance and admitted to Mercy General, as no closer hospital services to her hometown are available. Ms. Miller was admitted to the psychiatric ward after being treated in the emergency room. She had been found by a fellow student in the school bathroom, unconscious and bleeding. She apparently had brought a kitchen knife from home to school and had slashed her wrists. In the emergency room she received 24 stitches in her left wrist and 11 stitches in her right wrist. Her medical situation is stable.

When I entered Zynthia's room, I saw her lying on her bed, both wrists wrapped in bandages. She looked much younger than a girl of 15. Zynthia's small frame was dwarfed by the hospital bed, and her skin looked as pale as the hospital sheets upon which she lay. Her shoulder-length blonde hair was disheveled, dirty, and tangled. Zynthia had pulled the sheet up to her nose so that only her bandaged arms and the top half of her head, dominated by large blue eyes, could be seen. She looked frightened and wary. Besides her child-like appearance, two things struck me as odd about Zynthia's situation. First, although she'd been admitted the previous afternoon, she had no flowers or cards in her room, nor had anyone brought her a bag of clothes or personal belongings. Second, no family members were in her room. In every other consult I'd done for a teenager, at least one parent had been present.

Zynthia spoke in a whisper throughout the initial interview. I repeatedly had to ask her to speak up as I couldn't hear her, despite the quiet setting of her hospital room. Although she attempted to answer all my questions, her answers were frequently illogical and rambling. She reported that she was in the ninth grade and enjoyed her art class but didn't like any other classes. She also reported that she didn't have any friends at school because all of the other kids were "stupid." Zynthia explained that the kids hadn't always been stupid but that, ". . . after the invaders took over the school," they'd become that way. She added, "I lost all of my friends because of the invaders."

When I questioned her about the invaders, Zynthia indicated that the invasion took place the previous summer, but that the "troops" were still trying to take over the town. Zynthia cowered under her sheets, asking me if I heard the helicopter outside the hospital window. After I confirmed that, indeed, the sound outside was a helicopter landing at the hospital, Zynthia looked frantically around the room. She hid her face entirely under the sheet, so that her entire body was now covered. Speaking through the sheet, her voice was even quieter and almost inaudible. The sheet rose and fell with her breath, but otherwise she lay motionless. She insisted that the landing of the helicopters was further evidence that the invading "troops" were still being brought into town and that she needed to hide in order to be safe. I gently challenged her on this idea and suggested that I thought the helicopter was bringing injured patients to the hospital.

At this, Zynthia began crying. She insisted, "That's what they *want* you to believe!"

1. Would you ask Zynthia to remove the sheet that is covering her face? If not, would you talk to her even though you can't see her?
2. Do you think the clinician should have challenged Zynthia on her belief that the helicopters were bringing more troops?

Fortunately, the noise from the helicopter outside of her window stopped. Zynthia cautiously moved the sheet off of her head.

"Are they gone?" she asked warily.

I nodded yes. At this point in the interview, Zynthia's comments became increasingly difficult to follow due to her tears and *pressured speech*—speech that is unusually fast. Indeed, Zynthia was almost hyperventilating between her tears and her urgent need to tell me what was happening. She was obviously very upset about "the troops" in the helicopters, to the point of panic. She was extremely afraid that she wasn't safe in the hospital, nor would she be safe at home or school.

Although her train of thought was extremely difficult to follow, I pieced together what Zynthia was trying to tell me—that she believed "the troops" would learn that she hadn't become stupid like the other kids. She feared that once this was discovered, the troops would take her to their camp, located in the woods at the edge of town, which was very close. There, they would remove her brain and replace it with a washing machine motor. She was concerned that if this happened, she'd no longer be herself and her "bearings would be broken."

Zynthia's voice trailed off into a whisper as she said, "Bearings, bearing down, bare. Big bears. Little bears. Berries and berries. Blueberries and strawberries. Bears eating berries. The berries are gone! The berries are gone. The bearings are broken, broken down, bare." I jotted down what she'd said, wanting to ensure that I wrote down her comments verbatim.

I asked Zynthia if she ever heard voices or sounds that other people couldn't hear. She denied hearing voices but told me that she was very religious. She believed that God talked with her on a daily basis. She was grateful for these conversations with God; otherwise, she feared she would "go crazy." She whispered that it was God Himself who had told her it was safe to talk with me. She said, "God told me you'd understand."

3. How would you respond to Zynthia's comment that "God told me you'd understand?" What exactly would you say to her?
4. What topic would you cover next in the interview? What do you think is most important to assess?

Zynthia reported no changes in her sleeping or eating behavior. She reported that she slept seven to eight hours each night. No matter what question I asked Zynthia, she repeatedly discussed "the troops" in her answers. For example, in response to her sleeping habits, she said, "The troops are worse at night. They move more in the dark. But if you lie very still, they can't see you. So, when I sleep, I just hold perfectly still. Then I disappear—pop! Like a lollipop."

I was having some trouble following Zynthia's rambling replies, but I was worried that if I asked her what she meant by disappearing like a lollipop, her conversation would become even more *tangential,* or disorganized and difficult to follow.

Zynthia continued to talk about "the troops," insisting that they were everywhere. She reported that she had difficulty concentrating on her schoolwork because she was afraid she'd be discovered by the troops. She said that if she thought too much, it would alert the troops to her presence, to her not being one of the dumb kids, saying again that they would come for her to remove and replace her brain with a washing machine motor. She repeated that the troops had their camp on the edge of town, which was very close. In fact, this entire monologue was repeated almost verbatim from her previous explanation about the troops.

Zynthia never did address whether she had any changes in her eating behavior, although I asked her directly about this topic again.

5. How do you think the clinician should proceed with the remainder of the interview?

I decided to focus the interview on the present, in hopes of keeping Zynthia more grounded. I also recognized the importance of assessing for safety, because I was concerned about how serious Zynthia's suicide attempt had been and that she was at high risk of trying to kill herself again.

"Zynthia, do you know why you are in the hospital?" I asked her.

"Yes, I know. I tried to kill myself at school. I don't really want to die. I don't. I don't. But I can't be caught by the troops. Death by my own hand is better than being taken to camp. You don't know what happens at camp. What they do to you. Nothing is worse than the troops. I had to die that day. God told me that my math teacher and school principal were in on it. The troops had taken over their minds. Don't you see? They are part of the enemy now. So, I had to die. It's the only way to stay safe from the troops," Zynthia answered.

Zynthia continued, "I chose the best place I could find to die. I didn't think anyone would find me at school. School was better than home because it's more of a private place. Private places are safer. The troops can't find you so easy."

I asked Zynthia if she was safe here in the hospital and if the troops could find her here.

She quietly asked, "I don't know. Do you think I'm safe here? Can they find me?"

6. How would you answer Zynthia's question about her safety from the troops?
7. How would you proceed next?

I told Zynthia that she was safe in the hospital and that she didn't need to die to protect herself. I thanked Zynthia for the interview and left her room.

Given the seriousness of the situation, Zynthia's lack of coherent answers, and the numerous outstanding questions I had regarding her safety, I decided to contact Zynthia's parents. I also decided to review her chart for any additional information and talk with the nurses to see what they'd observed. I wanted to ensure that Zynthia wasn't using any medications or other substances that could cause hallucinations. I also wanted to ensure that she had no medical problems that could cause such unusual behavior. Finally, I called my supervisor because I knew I would need her help on this difficult case.

According to Zynthia's chart, her mother, Rabeckah Miller, had been contacted by the school after Zynthia was rushed to the emergency room. Rabeckah had arrived at the emergency room approximately two hours later. After completing insurance papers and signing for Zynthia to be admitted to the psychiatric ward, Rabeckah had left the hospital without visiting her daughter. When I talked with the nurses on Zynthia's floor, they reported that neither Rabeckah nor Zynthia's father, Beau, had called or come by to see Zynthia in the roughly 24 hours since she'd been at the hospital.

I decided to call the Miller household, but the call resulted in more confusion. The phone was answered by someone who was obviously a child and immediately asked me why I wanted to talk with her parents. When I told the child that I was calling from the hospital in reference to Zynthia, the girl responded, "Who cares?" I asked the child to please find her mom or dad and get one of them to come to the phone. The child yelled directly into the phone for her mother, and Rabeckah picked up another phone, while the child apparently stayed on the line to listen in to our conversation.

I introduced myself and then asked Rabeckah if she knew that someone was listening in to our conversation. Rabeckah said that she knew Zynthia's younger sister, Seraphina, was listening, but she was not concerned about her listening to our conversation.

8. What were the clinician's obligations regarding confidentiality given that Seraphina was listening to the call?

I explained that I had met with Zynthia and was concerned about her safety and unusual behavior. I hoped that I might meet with at least one, if not both, of her parents, to help shed some light on what was going on with Zynthia. Rabeckah reluctantly agreed to meet with me, warning that she'd have to bring her other two children to the meeting and that she couldn't guarantee her husband, Beau, would be there. She explained, "Beau's awfully busy and doesn't like dealing with Zynthia's crap."

After scheduling a meeting for the following day, I hung up the phone with Rabeckah and immediately called my supervisor to explain the situation, seeking guidance on how to proceed. My supervisor recommended that, given Zynthia's unstable condition and the potentially unsupportive situation with the Miller family, I meet with Rabeckah, and Beau if possible, without Zynthia present. My supervisor also recommended that I carefully note all that I had observed in Zynthia's chart. Finally, she suggested that I document my frustrated attempt to conduct a suicide assessment with Zynthia and alert the hospital staff that Zynthia should remain on close supervision for a possible suicide attempt.

The next day both Rabeckah and Beau arrived for a scheduled interview, accompanied by their two children: Seraphina, age 13, and Nixon, age 4. These children were full siblings to Zynthia. Rabeckah began the meeting by stating that she didn't trust babysitters and that she was sure that the children would be no problem. Rabeckah was approximately 40 years old, with graying black hair that was shabbily cut, but clean. Likewise, her clothing was threadbare, but clean. Beau was approximately the same age as Rabeckah. He was dressed in army fatigues, army boots, and had a military-style crewcut. Seraphina wore designer jeans, expensive tennis shoes and jewelry, and a designer polo shirt. Nixon was dressed in a patched pair of jeans and a ripped T-shirt. I immediately noticed that Nixon's clothing and face were quite obviously filthy with dirt and food stains on his clothing as well as drink and food crusted on his face. The whole room reeked of body odor, but I couldn't be sure which of the family members was the source of the smell.

Beau immediately took control of the session. He began talking as soon as everyone was seated. He didn't wait for me to ask any questions or to explain my role or the purpose of the interview. He angrily stated that he was annoyed with the hospital because they wouldn't release Zynthia. He was upset at having to take a day off from his real estate business to visit the hospital as well as having to pay for his family to eat out for lunch. I tried to calm Beau by using active listening skills and empathy, but he waved me off and continued his rant as though I weren't even in the room. His eye contact was hostile and intense. He disregarded social convention, staring at me constantly without blinking much, and he never looked away, no matter who was talking.

Beau explained that he was sure Zynthia's suicide attempt was just another one of her "stupid, manipulative tricks" and that "the best thing for Zynthia would be a good swat on the butt." He stated that coddling Zynthia, as he was sure was happening in the hospital, would just lead to more of her "attention-seeking BS." Therefore, he was not about to go visit her or let anyone else in the family visit her while she was in the hospital. Beau explained that ever since Zynthia was a baby, she had "acted up in one way or another" just to get attention. He added that he believed that Zynthia was jealous of her sister Seraphina, who was very popular, a natural athlete, a good student, and "just darned cute."

While Beau was saying this, Seraphina placed her hand on his arm and smiled broadly at him. When Beau finally paused in talking, Seraphina immediately began, "Beau's right. Zynthia is just jealous of me. She's such a loser. No one wants to be around her."

> *That's odd, I thought. Seraphina just called her father by his first name instead of "Dad." And why is everyone in this family attacking Zynthia? Why doesn't her mother step in to protect her?*

I noticed that Rabeckah had nodded in agreement with Seraphina's assessment of her sister as a loser. I turned to Rabeckah to ask her to share her opinions about Zynthia. Rabeckah added that Zynthia was exactly like Rabeckah's mother, who'd died some years ago after spending more than 15 years at the state psychiatric hospital.

Rabeckah continued, "Don't ask me what my mom was diagnosed with, because I don't know. I just know she took a lot of medication and had those electric shock treatments." Rabeckah reported that her father had died of alcoholism when she was 16, right after she married Beau. She mentioned that she was an only child and that ever since her parents died, it had just been "me and Beau."

When asked about his family history, Beau initially refused to discuss it as he did not see "how it had any bearing on the present situation." Finally, Beau shared that his parents had died in a car crash shortly before Seraphina was born. His childhood was "perfectly normal"—his mother had been a stay-at-home parent and his father had worked in a car factory. Like Rabeckah, Beau was an only child. He said that his parents' death really pulled him and Rabeckah closer together. Beau quickly changed the subject back to Zynthia.

He finished by saying, "It's a good thing that my parents died before they could see just how messed up one child can get. Especially since we named Zynthia after my mom—except her name was Cynthia, so we changed it to Zynthia, with a Z, so it would be a name nobody else had. Plus, then she'd always be at the end in alphabetical-order stuff." This struck me as odd, since most alphabetizing had to do with last names, not first names, but I let it pass.

> 9. What are your impressions of the Miller family thus far? What do you think is the most important information for the clinician to cover in the rest of the interview?

I wanted to get a better understanding of Zynthia, so I followed Beau's lead about how he chose Zynthia's name, letting him know that it was a unique and beautiful name, and indeed, I'd never known anyone else who had the name. Beau and Rabeckah both smiled, and Rabeckah added, "My name is beautiful, too. It's pronounced Rebecca, but it's not spelled that way. It's spelled "R-A-B-E-C-K-A-H. I changed it legally and all. Isn't that just too cute?"

I outwardly agreed that Rabeckah's name was "cute," although I was wondering if anyone in this family felt any warmth or love towards Zynthia, since no concern had been expressed about her. No one had even inquired about the extent of her injuries.

I intentionally turned the focus of the conversation back to Zynthia and asked about her early years. Beau began intentionally tapping his foot and staring at the ceiling, conveying both his impatience and his boredom with my questions. In a tremulous voice, Rabeckah began answering my questions. She reported that Zynthia was a sickly baby who had frequent ear infections and spit up most of her food. She walked at about eighteen months of age but did not begin talking until she was almost three. I asked Rabeckah if she had been concerned that Zynthia was late meeting her developmental milestones, as children usually walk by age 12 months and say their first words about the same time.

Rabeckah said that she hadn't been too concerned about Zynthia and immediately changed the subject to Seraphina. Seraphina was a full two years younger than Zynthia, Rabeckah noted, but "You wouldn't believe what she could do. She talked before Zynthia. She was more coordinated than Zynthia. She could throw a softball when she was only a year old! Seraphina always had more friends than Zynthia. She's just way more social than her sister."

I'm getting frustrated with this family and feel like I'm swimming upstream.
I know I have to manage my own feelings in a therapy session, but
it worries me that no one is even slightly concerned about Zynthia.

I began again, patiently redirecting the conversation by asking, "I was hoping we could talk a little more about Zynthia. What does she like to do?"

Rabeckah reported that Zynthia preferred to spend her time alone, day-dreaming and drawing in her sketchbook. She noted that Zynthia's school performance had been poor. She repeated kindergarten because her teacher did not believe Zynthia was socially or academically prepared for first grade. In third grade, the school also decided to hold Zynthia back a year, which meant that she would be in the same grade as Seraphina.

Just as I was beginning to say that it must've been difficult on Zynthia to be in the same class as Seraphina, Beau interjected and told me that it was Zynthia's fault for failing school twice because she was "just lazy."

Seraphina chimed in, "Well, I can tell you from being in classes with her all these years that she's terrible at school. She's terrible at drawing, too. She has no talent. Her drawings all look crazy, just like her!"

For the first time in the interview, someone took a softer stance when describing Zynthia. Rabeckah said that Zynthia always seemed to "march to the beat of her own drummer" but that this was the first time Zynthia had been in any "serious trouble."

I stopped Rabeckah and said, "It sounds like you're a little worried about her, since she is really struggling right now." Honestly, I was relieved that someone had made a comment that even hinted of concern for Zynthia.

Rabeckah immediately retreated from any appearance of concern. "Of course I'm worried about her! I can't have her living off of me the rest of her life. She's 15! She's old enough to get married or get a job. I'll be glad when I don't have to be responsible for her anymore!"

> 10. Write down two or three possible statements as to how the clinician should respond to this statement and how she should proceed, going forward in the interview.

I decided that conversations about Zynthia likely would result in more disparaging remarks, so I changed my focus.

I asked, "Could you tell me a little bit more about your family?"

Rabeckah described herself as a full-time homemaker and stated that her husband owned his family's real estate office. Beau had been discharged from the military. He spent most of his free time as part of a militia group that trained for imminent war with the government. He noted that he believed in being prepared and had built a concrete fallout shelter in their backyard, with steel reinforcements that could "withstand artillery fire."

Beau continued to stare right at me as he noted, "The time's coming when all of us are going to have to make a choice: you either protect yourself and your family or the government is just going to take away all your rights. And by God, I will be ready to protect my family!" Beau added that he had a training mission in South America this coming weekend. Before I could ask more questions about what the training mission entailed, Rabeckah chimed in, "Rog loves his guns."

The minute she said the word "guns," Nixon looked up from playing on the floor and said, "Daddy guns!" Nixon then used his fingers as mock guns and began "pretend shooting" me while making shooting noises. Seraphina said that Beau really did have cool guns and that she loved shooting guns with him (again calling him Beau instead of Dad). Beau responded to Seraphina, "And Daddy loves shooting guns with you, baby doll. More than anything in the world."

At this point in the interview, Seraphina commented that she wished she could accompany her father on his South American mission so that she could have fun, too. Beau hugged his daughter and kept his arm around her waist. He promised Seraphina that she could accompany him on his next mission after she turned sixteen, as it was a militia rule that everyone had to be sixteen or older. As Beau hugged Seraphina, Nixon climbed into his mother's lap and started to pull at her blouse, exposing her bra. Rabeckah said, "Well, we need to finish up because I need to breast feed the baby."

11. If you were the clinician, what would be going through your head right now as you worked to (a) conceptualize this family and (b) decide how to manage the rest of the interview?

12. What is your reaction to a mother breast feeding a four-year-old child? How is your reaction affected by your background and culture? How would your reaction, whether negative or positive, affect your ability to build rapport with Rabeckah?

13. Do you have any concerns about Beau's relationship with Seraphina? Explain your answer.

I told the family that we would finish the interview in a few minutes. I asked a question that seemed obvious to me but hopefully wasn't too directly challenging to the family's values. "What does Zynthia think of the family's guns and militia involvement?"

Rabeckah answered this question, "Obviously, she hates it. The past year or so, she is more and more upset by Beau's guns. She said that she thinks Beau is one of *the troops,* whatever that is, and that God doesn't approve of his fighting. When the rest of us go outside to shoot, she just wants to stay inside alone. She complains about it all the time, but I don't have time to listen since my other two children need attention. And she doesn't make any sense."

I tried again to get some information about when Zynthia's troubles began. "So, Rabeckah, when did you first notice that Zynthia wasn't making much sense?"

Rabeckah answered, "I don't know. Maybe about a year ago? Zynthia had one friend, Sarah, and they . . ."

Seraphina promptly cut off her mom, saying, "Yeah. Sarah was just as weird as Zynthia."

Rabeckah continued, "Well, they used to go to weird cult movies and art shows in the city near us. Sarah's parents would take them. But, then, well, somehow they just drifted apart."

Seraphina added cruelly, as a taunt, "Or broke up, you mean."

I asked, directly and nonjudgmentally, "Is Zynthia gay?"

Rabeckah answered, "Who knows what she is, other than just weird?"

The afternoon following my visit with the Miller family, I returned to Zynthia's hospital room to see if she were behaving and speaking more coherently than she was when first admitted to the hospital. Unfortunately, during this second interview, she continued to exhibit the same level of disorganized thinking and unusual behavior that she had during her first interview. A week later, Zynthia was still at the hospital and could not be discharged due to ongoing concerns about her safety. The psychiatrist working at the hospital prescribed some antipsychotic medication, which she'd been taking as prescribed. However, even after taking the medication for three weeks, Zynthia's behavior was just as worrisome as the day she was first admitted to the hospital, with disorganized and fearful references to the troops in almost every conversation. The challenge now was that the hospital could no longer treat Zynthia due to insurance limitations for a maximum stay of 28 days as an inpatient.

14. What relationship issues do you see in the Miller family? How might these dynamics affect Zynthia's current symptoms?

15. Would you recommend individual or family therapy for the Millers? Explain your rationale and the advantages and disadvantages of both types of therapy.

16. When the interview turned negative against Zynthia, would you have intervened to stop the family, or would you have ignored the negative comments for the sake of building rapport?

17. You are a student working under supervision. How would you determine whether or not you were competent to treat this case?

CASE 4

Carly Prochaski
Shandiin Begay

Carly Prochaski, 15-year-old daughter of Glen and Helen Prochaski, was referred to an outpatient therapist by her school mental health counselor, Ms. Lisa Hammett. Ms. Hammett had been contacted by the school's computerized automated alert warning system, which identifies children who are struggling with grades, attendance, or behavioral referrals. Ms. Hammett thought it odd that no teachers had contacted her directly about Carly's behavior. Usually, both the automatic alert warning system and referrals from teachers let her know that a child was struggling.

Ms. Hammett reviewed Carly's school records to see what had triggered the automatic alert. Carly was a sophomore at a large, urban high school in Michigan. Prior to the last grading period, Carly, an excellent student, had consistently earned As in her honors courses. This semester, however, Carly was failing all of her courses, with straight Fs on her quarterly progress report. Carly was also skipping classes regularly, something she had never done in the past. Ms. Hammett reviewed the absence records for the last two months of school and saw that Carly had missed eight class periods in the last 41 days of school. She was shocked by Carly's truancy, as she had previously received a certificate for perfect attendance in her freshman year of high school.

1. What are some of your hypotheses as to what is going on with Carly?

Ms. Hammett decided to follow up on the alert and meet with Carly. Prior to the meeting, Ms. Hammett had never talked to or even seen Carly before.

When Carly entered the room, Ms. Hammett quickly made an initial appraisal of her. She was a very thin 15-year-old with dark brown eyes, equally dark brown long, straight hair, and high cheekbones. She wore faded jeans, a cropped T-shirt covered with a denim jacket to comply with school dress code, high-top tennis shoes, and large silver hoop earrings. Her appearance was unremarkable and she looked like most of the other girls at school, but with a little more care given to her attire. Ms. Hammett observed that Carly was unusually thin, even for a 15-year-old girl. She estimated her to be approximately a size 0.

Ms. Hammett introduced herself and briefly explained the purpose of their meeting. As a way of making a connection with Carly, Ms. Hammett asked her about the origins of her unusual last name of Prochaski. Carly explained that Prochaski was Polish, but that she actually was a Navajo Native American and had been adopted as an infant by her parents, Glen and Helen Prochaski, a white couple from Michigan. Ms. Hammett wondered about the story behind the adoption, since Navajo families are rarely willing to have their children adopted outside of the Native American community, even in cases of extreme poverty or other serious problems. However, she decided not to ask Carly about the circumstances of her adoption since she had just met her.

Ms. Hammett clearly explained the limits of confidentiality and told Carly that her parents had a right to know everything they discussed. Carly explained that she understood about confidentiality and noted that it didn't bother her to talk, as she had nothing to hide from her parents. Casually, Ms. Hammett asked Carly what was going on and how life was treating her. Carly was initially vague about her current situation. She admitted that she was skipping classes regularly but said that school had become really "boring" this year and that she didn't like her teachers. When she cut classes, she mostly just walked around the neighborhood near the school. Carly added that she'd always been a good student. Ms. Hammett concurred, having seen her grades, adding that she'd characterize Carly as an "excellent" student, not just good. Carly looked away from Mrs. Hammett and quietly added that she just wasn't "feeling it" this year.

Ms. Hammett asked what she meant by not "feeling it." Carly said that about a month ago, it was as if something inside of her just snapped and that she was tired of pretending that everything was OK.

When Ms. Hammett asked for clarification, Carly responded with, "I don't know. Everything I used to care about, I just don't anymore. Like school. I used to like to learn about stuff, but now it's just stupid. Like, we aren't really gonna use that stupid algebra stuff in our life. And American History is boring. All of those people are dead. Who cares about people after they're dead?"

Despite her increasing dislike of school, Carly denied feeling sad or hopeless and noted that she mostly felt good about herself, her life, and her future. She mentioned that learning was harder for her this year. When Ms. Hammett asked Carly why she thought that was, Carly just shrugged, saying that she didn't know. Carly added that it took more energy than it used to take for her to learn, perhaps because her classes were "boring." She said that it seemed harder for her to think through things and write essays because she felt "foggy" about schoolwork. Instead, she said, she just liked to look out the window and think about life. She said she really enjoyed daydreaming and liked to imagine herself as being born in another place and time.

"Wouldn't you like to time travel, Ms. Hammett?" Carly asked.

"Oh. What a great question, Carly. I certainly would. Where would you go if you could time travel?"

"Maybe the future. Like, when they have electric, self-driving cars and we finally solve global warming. And everyone works from home. And everyone is biracial so nobody can put you down anymore because of your race. So, we would have no wars, or walls, or terrorism or anything."

"Carly, that is a great vision of the future. I like your optimism. Which of those things from the future would make you happiest?" Ms. Hammett wondered.

Carly answered, "I dunno. Probably just no more wars."

Ms. Hammett asked Carly if she thought such a future was possible.

"Maybe," Carly answered cautiously. "If people quit messing up so much and hating on each other."

Ms. Hammett asked if people hated on Carly, but Carly said that they didn't and that she had quite a few friends at school.

Ms. Hammett asked Carly what she liked to do for fun. Carly shared that she had played soccer throughout middle school and high school. However, she had decided not to play this year because she didn't make the travel team. When Ms. Hammett asked Carly for more information, Carly explained that students can play on the school team, which she described as "easy," but that top players try to play on a club team that travels to tournaments throughout the Michigan and Ohio area. Carly had been a solid school-team soccer player. She even made All-Conference honorable mention as a forward her freshman year. However, she tried out for the local travel team this year and did not make the team. Carly mentioned that since colleges mostly recruit team players for scholarships, not school players, she saw no reason to continue playing soccer. As a result, she decided not to play this fall.

Ms. Hammett challenged Carly's thinking about quitting something that she did so well, noting that earning All-Conference honorable mention was impressive for a freshman. Carly shrugged and said, "You know, the thing is, there is always going to be somebody better than you. Somebody faster. Or stronger. Or with better foot skills. So, at some point, you gotta decide if it's worth it. I just decided that it wasn't. That's it. I didn't really love it anyway— I mean, I liked my teammates and the games, but not the practices. So, one day, I just came home and said, 'That's it. I quit.'"

When asked if Carly missed playing soccer, Carly shrugged and said, "Some days. I mean, if I see all the girls running in practice, I'm glad I'm not out there running in the heat because I hate it when it gets really hot and humid. And I'm glad to have more free time. But I miss it sometimes, like when I hear on the morning announcements that our team won a game or something."

Ms. Hammett wondered if Carly was still getting any exercise, such as running, after having quit the soccer team, but Carly said that she wasn't. She said that she didn't really like running and didn't have the energy it took to motivate herself to go for a run without her teammates. Ms. Hammett asked Carly directly about her weight, noting that Carly was quite thin and asking her what she thought about her body build and shape. Carly reported that she was fine with the way she looked and being thin didn't bother her. She noted that she liked buying jeans and cool T-shirts online.

Almost as an afterthought, she added, "You know, it's weird, though. When I quit soccer, I just mostly quit eating. I mean, I still eat food. It's just . . . I don't know. It's just that everything tastes kind of blah. Like it needs spice, or sugar, or salt. I'm so sick of meat and potatoes, which we have every night at home."

When questioned about friends, Carly reported that she had plenty of them, and mentioned a few soccer players by name. She stated that her best friend was Diane, who also played soccer. Since quitting the team, however, she had not seen Diane very much. Carly noted that they used to enjoy going out to drink espresso at an outside café and shop for clothes or jewelry at the mall, but the last time they had done either of these activities was two months ago. Ms. Hammett asked Carly whom she was hanging out with these days, to which Carly answered, "Not really much of anyone." Ms. Hammett asked if Carly had ever had feelings of being bored, experiencing a low energy level, and "not feeling it" before the last month. Carly said that she hadn't, and that all of the changes came on suddenly and "out of the blue" about a month ago.

Ms. Hammett also asked Carly about her relationship with her parents. She responded, "My parents don't understand me. They just don't get me. They expect me to be perfect, and I'm not. Look, can I go back to class? I don't mean to be rude, but I don't really have anything else to say."

Ms. Hammett listened carefully to Carly, who was getting increasingly agitated and irritable as she sat in the cramped school counselor office.

2. What are the topics you think are most important for Ms. Hammett to discuss before Carly leaves?

3. What do you think is going on with Carly? What other potential diagnoses did you consider?

"Sure, Carly. We can finish up in a few minutes. I know this is tough," Ms. Hammett offered. "I just have a few more questions. First, I need to talk to you about drugs, which is sometimes hard for kids to talk about."

Carly interrupted Ms. Hammett. "I'm not doing drugs, if that's what you're going to ask me."

Ms. Hammett responded, "Thanks for being honest with me. Are any of your friends doing them?"

Carly answered, "I don't think so. I mean, I hear about people smoking marijuana sometimes, but it's not really the people who I hang out with."

Ms. Hammett wondered to herself:

I wonder who she means when she talks about the people she hangs out with. She just told me a few minutes ago that she wasn't hanging out with anyone. Does she have anyone who she feels close to at all?

4. How would you phrase the question about friends without sounding like you are accusing Carly of lying?

Carly asked plaintively, "Can I go now? Please?"

Ms. Hammett acknowledged again how difficult it was to talk to a stranger and then thanked Carly for being patient with her. She apologized for being slow in interviewing Carly, but said that she wanted to give Carly the care and consideration she deserved.

Then Ms. Hammett added, "Carly, I just wonder who you are closest to in the world?"

Carly shrugged. "It used to be Diane. Now, I don't know. She is so into soccer that we aren't as close as we used to be, but we'll probably get close again when she has time after the season ends. For now, maybe my cats, Gypsy and Gingko."

Ms. Hammett came out from behind her desk, pulling her chair around so that she was sitting side by side with Carly. "Carly, I'm worried about you. You've given me quite a few reasons to be concerned. And I suspect, if you're honest with yourself, you're a little worried about yourself as well. I'm just wondering if you ever get so worried about things that you think about hurting yourself or killing yourself. Sometimes people do think about it, you know, and it's OK to talk about it."

Carly answered, "No, I promise. I'd never do that."

"I believe you. But could we talk about suicide a little more, please?" Ms. Hammett said.

Carly nodded.

Ms. Hammett asked if Carly would be willing to fill out a form, and Carly agreed. The form that she used was the CAMS Suicide Status Form (Jobes & Linehan, 2016). After Carly completed the form, Ms. Hammett and Carly openly discussed what she had written.

When discussing the results, Ms. Hammett asked, "Carly, on a scale of 1 to 10, could you tell me how much you want to live?"

Carly answered, "Maybe a 7 or 8."

Ms. Hammett asked, "And how much do you want to die?"

Carly thought for a minute and answered, "Maybe a 2—or a 3."

Carly was getting visibly agitated and eyed the door.

"I know you want to leave, Carly. Please give me five more minutes," Ms. Hammett pleaded.

"What is the main reason you want to die? In other words, why did you give wanting to die a 2 or 3 instead of a 1 or 0?"

"I don't know. I don't really want to die."

Ms. Hammett responded, "OK. Fair enough. What's the main reason you want to live?"

Carly sighed. "I don't know. I guess I'm just in a funk right now, but I know things'll get better. They always do. Maybe after soccer season I can hang out with Diane more again."

Ms. Hammett thanked Carly again for her time as well as her honesty. She ended their conversation by saying, "Carly, I'm still worried about you. As we're finishing up, I have two things to tell you that I want you to hear directly from me. First, I'm going to recommend that you see a counselor. I think it would really help you to have someone on your side, someone who is pulling for you, and someone who understands you, at least as well as Gypsy and Gingko anyway."

Carly smiled at the reference to her cats, pleased that Ms. Hammett remembered their names.

"Second," Ms. Hammett continued, "I'm going to call your folks to meet with them. I'd like to share everything you said with them. Is there anything you said that you don't want me to share?"

Although Ms. Hammett's words made Carly look anxious, she shook her head no and quickly departed Ms. Hammett's office.

5. What is your overall impression of Ms. Hammett as a therapist? What could Ms. Hammett have done better during the interview?

6. How concerned are you about Carly's suicidal intent? Why?

7. How would you begin the meeting with Mr. and Mrs. Prochaski? What would be the very first things that you said?

While she was waiting to hear from Carly's parents so she could arrange a meeting, Ms. Hammett decided to visit Carly's advisory teacher, who had known her the first two years of school and would remain her first-period teacher for all four years of high school. The advisory teacher was glad that Ms. Hammett had dropped by to talk about Carly. The teacher was concerned about Carly's recent behavior but had been too busy to follow up with Ms. Hammett. The teacher noted that most of Carly's failing grades were primarily due to Carly no longer submitting any homework assignments. She also noticed that Carly had not seemed like her usual friendly and engaged self. During times between classes, she seemed to walk through the hall in a daze and didn't even greet her friends as she always used to do. The teacher also mentioned that Carly was only cutting one class, American History. Ms. Hammett and the teacher both rolled their eyes and chuckled, as they knew the American History teacher was viewed by students as both boring and boorish. "No wonder she's cutting history, since she has Mr. Davis," the teacher joked.

Ms. Hammett was able to arrange for a meeting with Glen and Helen Prochaski the following day. Upon meeting them, she immediately was struck by how different in appearance they were from Carly, even as she understood that Carly was not their biological child. Mr. Prochaski was portly, pink-skinned, and bald. He wore reading glasses that he was perpetually peering over or adjusting on his upturned nose. He was dressed in a business suit that was too short in the legs, despite his short stature. Mrs. Prochaski looked like the female version of her husband: heavyset, short, pink-skinned, and bespectacled. Both were in their late fifties—older than most parents of young teenagers. Mr. Prochaski worked for a publisher as a copy editor. Mrs. Prochaski worked as a medical transcriptionist in a busy doctor's office. Ms. Hammett was struck by how similar the two looked and acted, down to their matching wristwatches and their similar habit of playing with their glasses.

Ms. Hammett explained to the Prochaskis her role as a mental health school counselor, the limits of confidentiality, and other important information about protected health care information. She then filled in Glen and Helen on her meeting with Carly. The Prochaskis were attentive to Ms. Hammett and listened carefully to her. They were both friendly and outgoing, and they shared information freely. Ms. Hammett used the interview to gather more information about Carly's current situation at home as well as her developmental and family history.

Regarding Carly's history, the Prochaskis were evasive surrounding the details of Carly's adoption. They noted that after college they tried to conceive a child with no success. After years of expensive and exhaustive fertility treatments, they learned that their odds of conceiving were slim and getting slimmer with their advancing ages. They decided to abandon their dream of having a child. Instead, they sought a change that would give their life meaning. They signed up to work as missionaries at a Navajo Indian reservation in Arizona.

The Prochaskis were working as missionaries at the reservation when Carly was born to two teenage Navajo parents. The Prochaskis knew Carly's parents and told Ms. Hammett that they were confident that Carly's mother did not drink alcohol when she was pregnant with Carly. Before committing to adopt Carly, Helen wanted to make certain that Carly's mother was not an alcoholic, since she "had known too many Indians with alcohol problems." Glen and Helen reported that Carly's birth parents were too young and too poor to care for a baby, and the Prochaskis knew they needed to help. They approached Carly's parents three days after Carly was born and offered to adopt her. The exhausted parents agreed to an informal adoption, with papers quickly signed and notarized. After they adopted Carly, the Prochaskis thought it best that they leave the reservation so that "things would be less awkward and people would have no ill feelings about the situation."

They moved off of the reservation and returned to Michigan, which was their home. After the move, they abruptly decided that the missionary lifestyle was not for them. They decided to re-enter the business world. Glen found work as a copy editor and Helen stayed at home with Carly. She went back to work last year, when Carly began high school. Helen was worried that her return to work was causing Carly's current struggles, but Ms. Hammett told her not to blame her return to work for what was happening with Carly right now. Ms. Hammett explained that teenagers get stressed for multiple reasons and that one single event rarely explains an adolescent's struggles.

Helen reported that Carly was the "perfect baby" and was just as easygoing as a child. Carly attained her developmental milestones at appropriate ages. She was always extremely healthy, although thin. She had no major or even minor medical problems, other than an allergy to sulfa. The Prochaski family had no history of substance abuse or mental illness. Carly had never been abused or neglected. She had not been exposed to any major traumas. In fact, the opposite was true. Carly had always done well in school and had earned As in every subject since first grade. She was always well-behaved and had been the Prochaskis' pride and joy. They reported that she was also an excellent soccer player and that they had enjoyed watching her play, trying to attend most of her home games. They were surprised when she quit the school team this year, since she'd been a leading scorer. They added that her soccer coach, a woman Carly liked and respected, was greatly disappointed in Carly's decision not to play. Ms. Hammett asked if the Prochaskis knew why Carly had quit the soccer team this year. The Prochaskis shared that her decision seemed impulsive, as she just came home from soccer practice one day and announced that she was quitting. When the Prochaskis asked her why, Carly gave the same answer that she gave Ms. Hammett, that she "just wasn't feeling it."

The Prochaskis were unaware that Carly's grades had plummeted this semester and that she'd been cutting classes. Semester grades wouldn't be out for a few weeks, and they generally ignored the school's automated alert system for parents, since Carly had always done so well in school and had never given them any reason to worry. They were visibly upset by the drastic changes in Carly's grades.

Other than her quitting the soccer team, Glen and Helen reported no changes in Carly's behavior. They had noticed no changes in her appetite or sleep and did not think she was using drugs or alcohol. She still talked to her parents about school and her friends. Carly took good care of the family's pets and seemed to be in a good mood most days. The Prochaskis had not noticed Carly to be any more irritable, hopeless, anxious, or easily frustrated than usual. She still joined them for their weekly Sunday night game of Scrabble.

The one change that the Prochaskis had noticed is that recently Carly had begun asking them more and more questions about her Native American ancestry. Carly had always known that she was adopted. The Prochaskis had always told her, "You were lucky that we adopted you, because your birth family was so poor—who knows what might have become of you?" Ms. Hammett thought this response sounded negative towards Native Americans, so she carefully inquired about how the Prochaskis had helped Carly develop her identity as a Native American.

The Prochaskis explained that they wanted to expose Carly to Native American ideas, but in a careful way. They bought her books about Native Americans and tried to made sure that she got to play the part of the "Indian" in any school plays. They recalled that in fifth grade, she was able to play the part of Pocahontas in the class play and noted that she made a beautiful Indian princess.

Recently, Carly had been asking her parents to take her to the reservation where she was born, just so she could see it, but they were unwilling to take her because it might devastate Carly to see "how many Indians don't work and just live off of our government." Carly also asked her parents what her birth name was. At first, neither of them remembered, but then Helen recalled it was something like "Shandiin." Carly had looked up the meaning of the name

Shandiin online and was excited to learn that it meant "rays of light in rain." Carly thought her given name was beautiful, and asked her parents if she could start using Shandiin instead of Carly, but Glen and Helen both thought that would be "confusing." Instead, they told her that she could change her name when she was 18 if she wanted to do so. Carly asked what her last name was as a child, and the Prochaskis said that they weren't comfortable sharing that information with Carly yet, but would do so when she became an adult. Carly then told her parents that she decided to choose the last name "Begay" for herself as it was a common Navajo name. Again, the Prochaskis discouraged her from this choice, explaining to her that she was *their* daughter, they loved her, and they wanted her always to be Carly Prochaski.

When asked how Carly fit in with her classmates, the Prochaskis felt that she did well relating to all kids—white, black, Latino/a, and Native American. This last comment struck Ms. Hammett as odd, since she knew that their school had very few Native American students.

As Ms. Hammett concluded her visit with the Prochaskis, she told them that she was worried enough about Carly's behavior to recommend outpatient counseling for her. She specifically discussed the possibility of Carly committing suicide with them, although both Glen and Helen were certain that Carly would never do anything like that. The more they talked with Ms. Hammett, however, the more concerned they became about Carly. They both said that they loved Carly and would do anything to help her. They agreed to schedule an intake interview with a local psychologist who specialized in work with teenagers. They both teared up in Ms. Hammett's office, with Helen voicing what Glen was thinking: "We had no idea it was this bad."

The next morning, Ms. Hammett arrived at school to find frantic email, text, and voice mail messages from Helen Prochaski. The previous night, Carly had picked at her dinner and then said she was tired and was going to bed early. Carly went upstairs for a long shower and apparently had taken an entire bottle of aspirin. When her parents went to check on her before turning in for the night, she was unresponsive. They found the empty bottle of aspirin and had called for an ambulance. Carly was admitted to a local hospital and was in fair condition. According to Helen, the admitting physician had indicated that Carly had tried to commit suicide but had not taken enough aspirin to kill herself.

8. Were you surprised that Carly tried to kill herself? Which of her symptoms made you most concerned that she might do so?

9. How might Carly's adoption and search for her ethnic identity connect with her current struggles?

10. Do you think that Carly really wanted to die, or was her intention in taking the aspirin more of a "cry for help?" Explain your answer.

11. What do you think Carly's diagnosis should be?

CASE 5

Maria Hadjipavlou

> People **think** they know me, but they don't. They **think** I am Greek, but I
> am Cypriot. They **think** I am lucky to be Papou's granddaughter and
> Andreas's daughter. I am lucky, but they don't know how stressful it is to
> be me. They **think** I am smart and nice, but they don't really know the
> real me. They know the "m" but not the "e". Sometimes, I think **I** don't
> know me, but how am I supposed to figure out who I am when every-
> body keeps telling me who I am **supposed to be**?"
>
> —from Maria's Journal

It's not easy being Maria Hadjipavlou. Among the pressures of school,
work, and family, she feels that she has no time to just hang out and be a regular teenager. Weekdays are filled with school and work at her family's restaurant. Weekends are filled with more work at the restaurant and extended
family events, such as christenings, weddings, baptisms, funerals, and holiday
get-togethers. Maria worries about many things, but she believes that no one
understands why she's so worried—which makes her feel more stressed. She
writes in her journal about her worries every night, but it doesn't seem to
help, and she's a tangled ball of nerves.

Maria is a lanky, 17-year-old girl with brown eyes that match her dark
curly hair. Her face is angular and, although not traditionally beautiful, her
features work together somehow. Maria's family emigrated from Cyprus, an
island off the coast of Greece, to Toronto, Canada. She lives with her maternal grandparents, parents, two brothers, and a maternal aunt. Her family left
Northern Cyprus during the War of 1974 as refugees, with only the clothes on
their backs. They chose to settle in Toronto, a city with a large community of
Cypriot and Greek immigrants as well as a thriving Greek Orthodox Church.

Maria lives with her parents, Andreas and Eria, who are both in their
40s; her paternal grandparents, Petro and Maria (who everyone calls Papou
and Yia); and her maternal Aunt Angelieka (better known as Angel), who is
32. Maria's older brother, also named Petro after his grandfather, is 19 and in
his first year of college at a prestigious liberal arts school a few hours away
from Toronto. Her younger brother, Sotiri, is 16 and still lives at home. When
her older brother is home from college for the summer, that makes eight Hadjipavlou family members who live in a modest but immaculate four-bedroom
house. Surrounding the house is a big garden where they grow flowers, herbs,
and vegetables. They have a bunkhouse they built in the back of the garden

for afternoon naps, but no one seems to take them. Maria shares a bedroom with her Aunt Angel, who is well-named because she's sweet and kind, but Maria would really like a room of her own. Every night, she writes in her journal by the light of her cell phone flashlight app, buried under blankets so as not to disturb Aunt Angel.

The Hadjipavlou family owns a popular Greek restaurant that requires everyone to work long hours. Although they used to be more active members of the Greek Orthodox Church, running the restaurant has meant less time for church involvement. They still attend important ceremonies and celebrate the twelve great feasts of the high holy days, but they have less time for church youth groups, which Maria used to enjoy. Instead, the Hadjipavlou family is busy cooking, cleaning, washing dishes, waitressing, hosting, and running the cash register. Maria's earliest memory is of washing dishes in the restaurant and accidentally breaking a vase. Maria guesses that she was about five years old at the time. She was cleaning tables by age six and helping fill orders by age eight. By age ten, she was hosting; by age twelve, she was waitressing; by age fourteen, she was running the cash register. Working at such close quarters in the narrow restaurant kitchen was often the source of conflicts—heated exchanges that boiled over suddenly and simmered down just as quickly. Andreas, Maria's father, especially tended to explode and verbally lash out at others when things didn't go right. But then, fifteen minutes later, no one remembered any of the arguments—except Maria. She carried the weight of angry words with her, mulling them over endlessly in her mind.

Maria's days are summed up in three words: school, family, and work. When she is in school, she worries about the restaurant:

Did father plan ahead for the dinner reservation for that party of 16?
Did Papou remember they were almost out of sour cream when he placed
the grocery order? Will mother be angry with me if I don't have time
to arrange the fresh flower bouquets?

When Maria is at work, she worries about school:

Will I have enough time to study for the big French exam if we close late?
What if I didn't do well on my English paper because Mrs. Cartier is such a difficult
grader? Will my grades be good enough for me to be accepted to college?

When Maria is with her family, she worries about her friends.

Do my friends understand why I'm too busy to go to the movies with them?
Will Trey notice that I smell like onions if I sit too close to him in math
class tomorrow? Will Holly ever forgive me for forgetting her birthday?

Maria always runs out of daylight hours before she runs out of worries.

Regarding school, Maria really doesn't need to worry. She's beginning her senior year in high school. She's a bright girl and an excellent student, earning almost all As and a smattering of Bs throughout high school. Despite how important working in the restaurant is to the Hadjipavlou family, education also is important. They have prioritized Maria's and Sotiri's educational costs as a non-negotiable expense. Andreas and Eria ensure that both children attend an academically rigorous, private high school despite the hefty tuition. They did the same for Maria's older brother, Petro. They also demand that Maria study and complete her homework every afternoon before working in the restaurant. Although Maria appreciates their support, she also feels pressure to excel academically to make her family proud. The pressure weighs down on her every day. Every part of her life feels like it belongs to someone else, and she cannot carve out even the smallest piece of an hour to claim as her own.

Maria hides her worries well at school, and most of her friends are unaware of how anxious she is. Even her closest friends don't really know her that well. Nevertheless, she's one of the most popular girls in school. Her classmates voted her to be Student Council vice-president because she's so responsible and conscientious. Maria's reputation isn't built around being the most athletic girl in school (she's never really cared about athletics and just played sports because everyone else did), or the brightest (although she's plenty smart), or the prettiest (although she wishes she were) or the thinnest (although Maria is at a healthy weight for a girl her age, she never feels thin enough). Her reputation is mostly built around being nice. Being one of the nicest girls in school is a burden as well. She feels like she can never have a bad day or just be herself. She feels that others will judge her if she doesn't live up to her reputation. The expectations of being Maria Hadjipavlou are high. Colossal failure perpetually feels like it's one small misstep away from the narrow path that she feels she must walk. Maria is burdened by the conviction that she must keep her problems and concerns hidden from everyone. Problems should stay in the family. In some ways family boundaries are drawn loosely, and the boundary line for who is considered family is both expansive and expanding. In other ways, however, family boundaries are restrictive, as in the careful consideration of everyone in Maria's family to make sure that negative traits about the family are never discussed beyond household walls: "What will the neighbors think?"

Every day after school, Yia (Maria's grandmother and namesake) supervises Maria while she does her homework, checking carefully to ensure that it's finished. Maria finds this funny for two reasons. First, Maria is 17 years old and a straight-A student. She learned many years ago how to check her own homework. Second, Yia neither speaks nor reads English. She would have no idea if what Maria wrote while doing her homework was just gibberish. Instead, Yia focuses on Maria's penmanship, encouraging her to write her letters in careful and beautiful script, even if Yia can't understand a word that Maria has written.

Maria gets along well with Yia, and being with her is the best part of her days. Yia reminds Maria of a friendly, chattering little bird. While Maria does her homework, Yia gives nonstop advice, dispensing pearls of wisdom and telling long-winded stories about the family. Yia speaks in Greek because she and Papou never learned much English. Yia's chatter is relaxing, like playing a song heard so many times before that it takes no energy or thought to listen to the words as they merge into a familiar background. Yia sits close to Maria as she does her homework, each perched on a tall stool only inches apart from each other in their bright yellow kitchen. Yia is so short and Maria so tall that when Maria sits on her stool, Yia barely comes to Maria's waist. Yia never sits on her stool for very long. Like a bird, she's always in motion— cooking a stew, baking a pastry, sewing a hole in a shirt, braiding Maria's hair, and touching Maria every chance she can get.

Yia can always see the stress that's present in Maria, even when she's relaxing with her grandmother. She constantly tells Maria to sit up straight and not to be so hunched over with worry, clucking that Maria carries the weight of the world on her slender shoulders. Maria's worries always seem to Yia to be lurking just beneath the surface, and unlike the others in Maria's family, she notices that Maria seems perpetually tense. Yia tries to rub Maria's back to get her to relax, but Maria practically jumps out of her skin when touched, even by her loving grandmother. Yia often reminds Maria to "slow down," but she doesn't know how to contain her restlessness. Even now, while sitting on the stool, Maria can't keep her foot from jiggling. Yia asks if her granddaughter is getting enough sleep, and Maria nods yes, because it seems too difficult to explain to Yia how hard it is to actually fall asleep.

Maria begins her homework every afternoon by creating daily to-do list so long that it is impossible to complete. The number of items on her list is often so long that they would take her a week to finish. A typical list might read:

Finish forty math assignments
Read *Beowulf*
Translate ten pages of French into English

Although Maria knows all these goals aren't attainable in a day, she's still disappointed in herself when she can't complete them. She worries that her grades will tank, that she won't get into college, and that she'll always work at the restaurant and never find true love. When Yia notices Maria's distraction, she brings her a homemade pastry to help her refocus on her schoolwork. Maria laughs because Yia is so certain that food can cure every ailment, and dessert can solve every world problem. Maria's exuberant younger brother Sotiri often bursts into the kitchen while Maria and Yia are working together, eating several of Yia's pastries in quick succession and affectionately chiding Maria for "being so touchy" all the time.

1. How would you enjoy working with Maria as a client? What would be the most enjoyable and most difficult aspects of working with her?

2. What terms from family therapy might best describe Maria's family?

3. With the information you know at this point, how do you think the Hadjipavlou family would accept mental health services?

Maria and Yia have one peculiar thing in common: they're both deathly afraid of spiders. Yia tells the story that her fear of spiders began as a little girl in Cyprus, where spiders were common in the poorly built thatched houses in the country village where she was raised. Every night, she and her sisters would carefully check their blankets, which were laid out over the floor since they had no beds, for spiders. When she was eight, Yia was bitten by a spider one night while sleeping. The spider left five huge welt marks on her thigh that grew infected. Cellulitis set in, and an infection raged through Yia's body for days, causing a 104-degree fever and almost resulting in her death. Ever since that incident, Yia has been terrified of spiders.

Maria seems to have inherited her grandmother's fear of spiders despite never having been bitten by one herself. She hates being in any place where she fears a spider might lurk. She refuses to go to the insect house of the Toronto Zoo because of the spiders, even though they're safely encased behind glass. Neither Maria nor Yia will go to the pantry in the restaurant or pick flowers or vegetables in the family garden for fear of encountering a spider. Their phobia is problematic for other family members who must perform such activities in their stead. Their unwillingness to fetch needed items from the restaurant pantry is particularly inconvenient when the restaurant is packed and everyone is already working at full intensity.

When a spider somehow finds its way in the house, which happens especially in the fall, Maria will run away from it while screaming loudly. She even fainted once at the sight of a particularly large wolf spider. When Yia and Maria are together and they see a spider, even a harmless daddy-long-legs, they go berserk, screaming and pointing in tandem, rapidly scaling the kitchen stools to get to the perceived safety of the kitchen counter and then holding each other tightly. The two Marias are quite a sight—the tall young girl in her tight jeans and the tiny old woman in her flowered skirt, clinging to each other for dear life. They don't calm down for hours after the spider is killed by some family hero, and they talk about the event for hours after, embellishing details regarding the size and dangerousness of the spider. Although everyone in the family pokes fun at Yia and Maria, no one outside of the family suspects their fears.

Maria's mother, father, brother, and grandfather often are called upon to kill the spiders. Maria adores her Papou, as everyone does, because he is one of the kindest, warmest people anyone has ever met. Papou would give someone the shirt off his back. Indeed, he often actually did so when the family lived in Cyprus when he found a neighbor, or even a stranger, in need. Hospitality was a strong family value, and Papou and Yia always made others feel welcome in their home. Yia always cooked and baked "something extra" in case a hungry relative or friend happened to visit. No wonder Papou had opened a restaurant, both when he had lived in Cyprus and then again in Canada. Papou and Yia complemented each other well, with his doglike agreeableness countering her catlike skittishness.

Papou's carefree nature is a wonder given his life history. When he was a child, his family had owned a restaurant. Papou had grown up working in the restaurant and intended for it to stay in the family forever. The delectable stews and scrumptious desserts concocted by his lovely new bride, Maria (who later became known as Yia) made the old family restaurant more popular than ever. Sadly, one night when Papou was a young man, the restaurant caught fire as the family was cleaning up after a busy evening. Papou tried his best to fight the flames, covering his mouth with his wet shirt as he frantically worked to rescue his family. Despite his heroic efforts, the poorly built building burned to the ground in minutes. Helplessly, Papou watched in horror as his father, mother, and grandfather were killed by the fire. Papou's arms and legs were badly burned, and although his wounds were painful, the hurt caused by his grief for his family was even more painful.

Papou and Yia rebuilt the restaurant in a better location, and their loyal patrons made the new place as popular as the original one. They had two boys, one of whom—Andreas—would become Maria's father. The good life they had built for themselves changed in an instant in 1974, when Turkey invaded Northern Cyprus. Everyone who lived through the attack, including Andreas (who was eight at the time), remembers the frightening siege: the menacing scene of tanks rolling into their village, the roar of Turkish jets flying overhead and dropping their bombs, and the bursting of mortar shells. Thousands were killed, including many extended family members. Their small village of Karpasia was taken over by the military, and the Greek-Cypriots fled to the south. Their land was forcibly taken, and the young family lost all they owned—not only the restaurant, but also the olive fields that had belonged to their ancestors. Most tragically, they lost many family members, neighbors, and friends—and their way of life.

4. How do you think Papou was able to recover from the tragic fire?
5. Who in the family do you think was most negatively affected by the war? Explain your answer.

After a year of living as refugees in their own country, the Hadjipavlou family decided to immigrate to North America. They made their way to Canada in a sometimes harrowing journey. Despite speaking only a little French and even less English, they began life anew as immigrants in Toronto. They settled in a neighborhood among fellow Cypriots and attended the Greek Orthodox Church there. Papou and Yia took jobs cooking and cleaning, saving every dime they could. With their savings, they built the restaurant where the family now works. Any money they made from the restaurant went right back into it, except for the money they set aside to bring over Aunt Angel and other relatives and the money they saved for their children's education. The restaurant means everything to the Hadjipavlou family, and they would work their fingers to the bone to ensure its survival. The restaurant is open year-round, except for the holy days of Easter and Christmas. Once every two years, they close the restaurant for two weeks and take a trip home to Cyprus to visit remaining relatives. Barring those few exceptions, the entire Hadjipav-lou family can be found working in the restaurant, often as much as 60 or 70 hours a week. Andreas always promises that they'll work hard in the restaurant until they have "enough," but that time never seems to arrive, even as they live comfortably.

Andreas is different from both his father and mother. He works harder than anyone at the restaurant—even Papou—with a furious intensity as if to bury some hidden pain and anger. He's quick tempered but equally as quick to get over his anger, as he recognizes that he is the cause of most of his own problems. Nevertheless, he goes through life like an angry bull. Maria respects her father but is fearful of him as well. His standards for all his children are high, and Maria has witnessed his intense anger when people have disappointed him in the past. Maria learned to keep her distance from her father when possible and be quiet when she was near him. Despite his frequent anger, Andreas loves his three children and protects them with a fierce intensity, making sure no harm would ever befall them.

Maria's mother, Eria, was also a Cypriot who immigrated to Canada after the 1974 war. Eria has an ethereal nature ("like an angel fallen from heaven" according to Andreas). She's artistic and prefers the creativity of inventing a new restaurant dish to the mundane drudgery of cooking the same meal every night. Her attire is reminiscent of another country or generation, and she wears flowing dresses with long scarves, accented by multiple necklaces and chandelier earrings. She has multiple ear piercings and numerous tattoos. People often call her a gypsy or a hippie, but she is oblivious to such comments. She plays the harmonica and loves to dance the Arabiye (belly dance), although she has time to do neither. The activities that Eria manages to find time for consist of decorating and redecorating the restaurant, arranging bouquets for the tables, choosing the music to play while patrons dine, and practicing aromatherapy. Eria's restaurant creations are always a little odd, like oregano ice cream or green olive pudding, but people seem to eat them anyway, although they prefer Yia's pastries. No matter how busy the restaurant is, even as patrons line the sidewalk waiting for a table, Eria never seems to be in a hurry. The problem isn't that Eria doesn't work—it's that she always seems to be working on something that matters to no one except her. For example, she once closed herself in the restaurant office for an hour during the dinner rush, searching for the perfect sound track to set the mood for the evening.

Maria and her mother get along like oil and water. Maria resents that Eria is always off in her own little world, preoccupied with something or other, leaving Maria to shoulder the load of urgent work. Perhaps Maria is also a little jealous of Eria because her father directs his anger at everyone else in her world, but never, ever at her mother. Then again, Maria recognizes that her father is so in love with her exquisitely delicate and otherworldly mother that he is incapable of perceiving her with anything other than a sense of wonder. Eria adores Maria, her only daughter, and is quick to brag about her to anyone who will listen. She won't, however, directly tell Maria how highly she thinks of her. Perhaps as a result of these things, Maria is especially conflicted regarding her feelings for her mother. She feels irritated that she has to consider all of the possible "what if" scenarios that her mother couldn't possibly be bothered to contemplate. Eria isn't a pragmatist, so Maria worries enough for the both of them.

Maria worries obsessively, not only about her mother but about her entire family. Maria worries that a fire will consume this restaurant, just as it did Papou's old restaurant back in Cyprus. Her sleep is troubled, and she awakens regularly in a cold sweat, heart racing, in sheer panic from nightmares filled with fire. She worries that her grades will fall from their present As into Bs or even Cs and that she won't get accepted into a top-tier college. She worries that her mother drinks too much wine (although this doesn't seem to worry her mother at all). She worries that Yia and Papou will get diabetes from eating too many of Yia's delicious desserts. She worries that Papou will die from a spider bite when he's out napping in his little sleeping shed that he built in the garden. She worries about her younger brother, Sotiri, because she knows he's smoked marijuana at least once, even though she didn't tell anyone. She worries too about her big brother, Petro, for fear that some tragedy will happen that might cause him to leave school in order to tend to the restaurant or their parents.

At night, however, when Maria can't sleep, she mostly worries about herself. She lies in bed, full of anxiety as she watches the clock that sits beside what she has come to think, of as her "journal of worries"—the conduit into which she pours all her anxiety and fear—that sits on her night table.

12:01 AM.

Will I ever be able to leave my family and move out on my own? How will I ever find a boyfriend if all my time is spent at the restaurant? If I do find a boyfriend, will my father ever approve of him? What if he is not a Cypriot? What if I fall in love with a Canadian?

12:48 AM. The glow from the clock is the only light in the room. Aunt Angel sleeps soundly, quietly, peacefully on her bed.

What if I'm not as popular as I think I am among my friends? What if they realize how much energy I have to put into being so kind and friendly?

1:13 AM. The light from the clock seems to have become harsher, more intrusive.

Will my family really be ok? Who'll take my place at the restaurant if I go to college? The restaurant! Did Papou remember that we're running low on tea? I have to get to sleep or I'll be too tired tomorrow. I must stop worrying and sleep! What if I can't stay awake at school tomorrow?

1:48 AM. The intense light emanating from the clock beams painfully into Maria's eyes.

*Do my new jeans make my butt look too big? Tomorrow I won't eat so much
of Yia's baklava. Can I say no to her pastries without my family
wondering what's wrong with me? What would my father think of me if he
knew what a mess I really am? I feel another migraine headache coming on.
I need to sleep. . . .*

Maria essentially has all the concerns of a 40-year-old, although she's
only 17. She's worried her entire life, as far back as she can remember, even
as a little girl.

"Yia," she tells her grandmother the next day as she fights back tears. "I
can't sleep. And I worry too much. I think I need some help." Yia hands her
a slice of warm milk pie and hugs her, reassuring her that everything will be
just fine.

6. If you were prioritizing Maria's problems, what would be your top
three areas of concern?

7. Of all the information presented in the case study, what is the one
piece of additional information you wished you knew?

8. Draw a diagram of all of the factors that you think are contributing
to Maria's anxiety.

9. How do you think Maria should be diagnosed? Explain your answer.

CASE 6

Dylan Travers

The case of 12-year-old Dylan Travers, a Caucasian sixth grader at Sally Ride Elementary School in Los Angeles, California, reached the office of Dr. Inés Castaneda in a roundabout fashion. Laura Bonner, the mother of Dylan's best friend, Gavin, had originally contacted the school counselor with concerns about Dylan. The school counselor contacted Dylan's parents and Child Protective Services. Child Protective Services, with the agreement of Dylan's parents, had contracted with Dr. Castaneda to work with Dylan. Dylan's parents were not willing to be a part of therapy but were willing to allow Dr. Castaneda to come to their home, if necessary. Now Dr. Castaneda sat in her spacious office, trying to organize the scanned letters and emails she had received relevant to Dylan's case, to prepare for her first therapy session with him.

Where to begin with this case? Dr. Castaneda wondered aloud as she sipped her morning espresso.

> 1. What are the ethical principles of your field that Dr. Castaneda should be considering?

Dr. Castaneda first reviewed the Child Protective Service (CPS) report. The report, authored by Dylan's case worker, Mr. Bobby Harris, was brief. It noted that Mr. Harris had made an unannounced home visit to the Travers family home two weeks prior due to concerns expressed by the school counselor. In his report, Mr. Harris noted that the home of Lola and Brian Travers was messy and cluttered, but the children in the home (Dylan, aged 12, and his half-sisters Meredith, 4, and Madeline, 2) were supervised and being appropriately clothed and fed. Mr. Harris found no evidence of abuse or neglect but opened a case because he thought the family might need some "psychological intervention due to the condition of the home."

Hmm. I wonder why Bobby opened a case based on the condition of the home. Lice? Roaches? Unsafe living conditions? His report didn't indicate physical neglect, so it must be something else. . . .

Her interest piqued, she began reading a report submitted by the school counselor. According to the counselor, Laura Bonner expressed serious concerns about what she perceived as potentially unhealthy behavior she'd observed in Dylan, her son Gavin's best friend. She reported that Dylan and

Gavin had been friends for the past seven years—since kindergarten. They loved playing video games, building Lego cars, conducting science experiments, and playing with Star Wars action figures. The boys typically chose to play at the Bonners's house, because Dylan said his house was too crowded to play there. Laura always found it unusual that Gavin had never been to Dylan's house. Laura had met Mr. and Mrs. Travers once and thought it was odd that both were heavyset individuals while Dylan was quite thin. What concerned Laura presently was not Dylan's parents but Dylan himself.

Over the past year, Laura had noticed that Dylan wore a long trench coat even in the summer months, quite unusual given the southern California climate. Within the many pockets of the coat, Dylan carried numerous items that Laura viewed as "trash." Laura reported observing Dylan stashing his empty candy wrappers in his coat pockets as well as papers, toys, books, snacks, and drink bottles. She became concerned when she noticed the pockets of the coat overflowing with items and that the coat began to smell as if it had not been washed. Laura volunteered to wash his coat one day when Dylan was over at their house playing with Gavin, but Dylan refused to allow her to wash his coat or even to take it off. She asked him if he ever cleaned out his pockets and gently told him that the coat was getting a little stinky, but Dylan refused to clean out the pockets, explaining that he might need his things. Laura contacted the school counselor after an unsuccessful attempt to talk with Dylan's parents. When she had called them, they told her that they didn't see any problem with Dylan's coat. Laura wasn't sure what to do next, so she called the school counselor, figuring that she might be able to help.

Good gracious! This case is getting interesting. I wonder if the family are hoarders.
Or if they are really poor and this kid really needs his things in his coat since
he doesn't know where he will get his next meal.

> 2. Dr. Castaneda is working to conceptualize Dylan's case and try to understand his behavior. With the limited information you have, what do you think best explains what's going on with him?

The notes from the school counselor also included a report from Dylan's sixth-grade teacher, who described Dylan as disorganized and messy. His teacher noted that Dylan's folders contained every paper he'd used during the entire school year, including rough drafts of reports that could have been thrown away and flyers from events long since passed. Dylan's locker was so full of papers, books, candy and food wrappers, sweaty gym clothes, water bottles, and miscellaneous items that Dylan frequently was late to class because it was difficult for him to get the locker closed with all of the items inside. He had perfected the art of carefully bracing the belongings in his locker with one hand and then quickly slamming the locker door shut with his other hand, moving his stabilizing hand at the last second. Dylan's teacher also noted that Dylan's backpack was overflowing with papers, books, food, plastic bottles, and items brought from home such as his collection of Star Wars action figures.

This is sounding more like hoarding and less like poverty. I wonder what the Travers family home looks like if Dylan's locker looks like it does. I hope Dylan's parents are willing to participate in therapy. I'll get much further with treatment if I have them on board.

She flipped back to Dylan's CPS report, and found their names: Lola and Brian Travers.

I wonder if they work during the day and will need an evening appointment. Maybe I can do some in-home therapy, at least occasionally.

Dr. Castaneda went back to reading.

3. Is it fair for a therapist to ask self-focused questions when considering whether to take on a case (e.g., whether the family will need evening hours, whether they have insurance that reimburses at a good rate, etc.)? Is it fair to refer a family to another therapist for these reasons?
4. Do you think Dr. Castaneda is overemphasizing the importance of family involvement in this case?

Academically, Dylan has been doing well. His teacher indicated that he earns mainly Bs and Cs, except in math and science where he typically earns As. He also recently created a blue-ribbon, award-winning replication of the solar system for the annual school science fair. The teacher reported that she's concerned that Dylan's grades will fall after he leaves the elementary-school environment, where teachers help him stay organized. She reported that she's been trying to teach him better organizational skills with little success. He also has trouble making decisions and struggles to discard ideas, just like he does with his things. For example, Dylan considered hundreds of ideas for his science fair project, including ideas from geology, engineering, astronomy, biology, physics, and nutrition. From the teacher's perspective, Dylan also has difficulty with friends. Many students dislike sitting next to Dylan because they say he's messy and smelly. Dylan doesn't seem to be concerned about his lack of organization or his overall lack of friends. The teacher reported that his most consistent friend is Gavin Bonner, who always includes Dylan in his activities and insists the other kids invite Dylan to parties if they want Gavin to be there. Since Gavin's well-liked and popular, the teacher reported, it's rare for Dylan to be excluded. The teacher also reiterated that Dylan and Gavin have been best friends since kindergarten.

It's unusual that such a popular kid would befriend such an unpopular one. I wonder what Gavin is like. They've been friends for a long time, so Dylan must have at least some good social skills. I still don't understand this family at all! What are Lola and Brian like? What makes them tick?

Dr. Castaneda kept reading.

After talking with Dylan's teacher, the school counselor had contacted Dylan's mother, Lola, requesting a conference. Lola was a stay-at-home mother to Dylan and his young sisters, Meredith and Madeline. She refused to meet with the school counselor at school but was happy for the school counselor to come to their home, stating, "It would be dangerous for me to leave my house; someone might take things." The school counselor felt uncomfortable going to the home of a student and decided to interview Dylan at school instead.

OK. Hmm. Is the neighborhood safe? Or maybe Lola is a little mentally unstable. Paranoid thinking, perhaps, and afraid of others taking her things for no good reason? Or agoraphobic and afraid to leave her house? Or maybe she's a hoarder? Maybe I should call Bobby to find out more about this family.

5. What else do you want to know besides the questions that Dr. Castaneda is asking? What are the most important missing pieces of information at this point?

Dylan was described by the school counselor as tall for his age and very thin. She noted that he was wearing his trench coat when he was called from class in direct violation of school policy that no coats were to be worn during the school day. Dylan refused to remove his coat for the counselor and quickly became upset and agitated when asked to do so. She relented and let him continue to wear the coat, and she softened in her approach. "I heard you are a good collector, Dylan. Mrs. Bonner told me that you liked to collect things. Will you show me what you have in your coat pockets?"

Initially, Dylan refused to remove the items from his coat pockets, but complied after the school counselor reassured him that she wouldn't touch his things and that he'd be allowed to replace them once she'd seen them. The school counselor reported the following items: six empty chip packages, three unopened packages of candy, two partially eaten candy bars, half a package of cheese crackers, three empty plastic water bottles, three pencils, two blue pens, one red pen, one black pen, a Star Wars light saber, seven Star Wars action figures, two paperback novels, a handful of stretched out rubber bands and untwisted paper clips, 12 school-related flyers advertising events that had taken place earlier in the school year, a pocket United States Constitution, two dirty mismatched socks, a small green rain boot that wouldn't have fit Dylan, a remote control, a pair of scissors, and a large desk-sized stapler. When questioned as to why he carried all of these items, Dylan shrugged and stated, "You never know when you might need something. It's always better to be safe." The school counselor thanked Dylan for sharing and sent him back to class.

The school counselor decided to contact Child Protective Services (CPS) out of concern that Dylan's behavior was unhealthy. She felt frustrated in her attempts to deal with the situation, since Lola had refused to come to the school but agreed to give permission for Dylan to participate in therapy. Without the mother's help, the counselor believed outside intervention was needed, and she was hoping that perhaps CPS would mandate some type of therapy for Dylan.

This is a messy case, but Lola and Brian DID sign an informed consent for Dylan to receive therapy from me. I wonder whether they're still willing for me to provide therapy for Dylan? And then Dr. Castaneda found the second half of the CPS report from Bobby Harris, describing the Travers home in detail.

Child Protective Service Report, Los Angeles County
January 17, 2016
Caseworker: Bobby Harris
Family Name: Brian and Lola Travers
Child's Name: Dylan Travers

I arrived for unannounced home visit at 4 pm on Tuesday, January 17. When I arrived, Brian Travers was at work and Lola Travers was at home with Meredith (age 4) and Madeline (age 2). Dylan and his father arrived while I was talking with Lola. The Travers home is isolated, at the end of a long lane on the outskirts of town, with palm trees hiding the house from the road. Their ranch-style house has three bedrooms and was built within the last twenty years. Although the house appears to be structurally sound, it's completely filled with belongings. The small porch leading to the house itself has twenty-three pots of flowers in varying stages of decay, with even the healthiest plant drooping. The front porch also had on it a broken tricycle, a rocking chair with no seat, stacks of newspapers and magazines, and empty fast-food cups. The Travers family car in the driveway was also filled with newspapers, fast-food cups, and clothes to the extent that only the two car seats in the back and the driver's seat were useable.

When I explained that I was with CPS and the purpose of my visit, Lola Travers looked confused but welcomed me into their home. Getting inside was difficult, as the front door would not open fully due to the stacks of magazines behind it. Stacks of magazines, towering two-thirds of the way up the wall, lined the entry hall. Mrs. Travers suggested sitting in the kitchen since there was ". . . more room to relax." Getting to the kitchen involved walking through the dining room, through an obstacle course of toys, piles of clothes, and furniture. The only way through the room was to follow a narrow path that allowed for people to pass single file. The living room had three couches—two stacked on top of one another, six upholstered chairs, three straight-backed chairs, four ottomans, three coffee tables, and at least six side tables of varying shapes and sizes. Despite all of the furniture, there was no place to sit as each chair and ottoman was filled with items or other furniture. Candy dishes of every color, size, and shape sat atop the furniture, filled with a variety of candies.

The kitchen area, which Mrs. Travers said would be more comfortable, was not in any better condition. It was a relatively large eat-in kitchen with a table and chairs. The kitchen counters, the table, and all of the chairs were covered in clothes, pots and pans, sacks of groceries, newspapers and magazines, and more candy dishes. In addition to the six chairs around the table, four high chairs were pressed against the walls. After clearing off one of the kitchen chairs, Mrs. Travers invited me to sit.

Mrs. Travers was pleasant and cooperatively answered my questions. The two younger children had just finished watching a video in their bedroom while we talked, and Mrs. Travers invited me to go with her while she started another video for the girls. The bedroom floor was covered in clothes and toys to the point where the carpet was barely visible. The girls' room also contained two sets of bunk beds, three televisions mounted on the walls, three bookcases, and books stacked precariously along the walls. The girls lay together on a top bunk as they watched television, surrounded by at least 50 stuffed animals of various sizes, clothes, and books.

Mrs. Travers was surprised that CPS had been called. She noted that Dylan did well at school, was never in legal trouble, and had no other problems. When asked about the number of items in the pockets of Dylan's trench coat, Mrs. Travers smiled and said that Dylan was good about keeping track of his things. I asked Mrs. Travers if she thought his behavior might alienate him from other children and cause him problems at school. Mrs. Travers began crying and stated that she knew her family was "different" but that she felt others were " . . . just too judgmental."

Mr. Travers and Dylan arrived home at approximately the same time. Dylan reported that he had been at Gavin Bonner's house. Mr. Travers was returning from his job as a trash collector. He carried a large, bulging plastic trash bag that he set on the floor next to his wife and said, "I brought you some treasures." As I talked with Mr. Travers and Dylan, Mrs. Travers excitedly opened the bag and removed items one at a time, becoming so absorbed in looking at these items that she no longer participated in the conversation. The items included magazines, chipped candy dishes, and clothing that Mr. Travers had collected on his trash route. I asked Mr. and Mrs. Travers about the amount of things in their home and Mr. Travers sighed. He stated that he knew they were getting a little out of control with their "collecting." He reported that he loved scavenging good "stuff" that was discarded in the trash or that he found in yard sales. His wife, he reported, enjoyed his collecting but was reluctant to throw anything away as it ". . . might come in handy in the future." Mr. Travers recognized that Dylan was beginning to show the same reluctance to let go of any of his things and that his son loved collecting as well. Mr. and Mrs. Travers were willing to allow Dylan to be seen in therapy but didn't view their family's behavior as sufficiently problematic to need intervention.

Given that the house was not filthy, although extremely cluttered, and the children well cared for, I told them that I'd make a referral for therapy for Dylan to Dr. Castaneda because she specializes in this kind of work. I also told the family I would be checking back with them once a month for the next six months. I explained that the house was probably a fire hazard and that they would need to at least provide wider paths through each room, or they could be facing a CPS charge of physical neglect. They agreed to clean up the house prior to my return in six months.

—Bobby Harris, CPS Investigator

Well, now. That was a useful report. Bobby always does a thorough job in his investigations. I think I can work with Dylan, although I'm worried about the commitment to change in the family. Best practices would definitely include family involvement, but I don't see much motivation to change, from Lola and Brian. I don't have much insight into their problems, but I'll see what I can do to help. And I had better call Bobby and thank him for the referral. I'm glad he always thinks of our OCD clinic when he stumbles upon these hoarding cases.

6. What theoretical model (psychodynamic, cognitive, behavioral, family systems, client-centered) would you choose to treat this case? Explain your answer.

7. What access to Dylan's therapy progress will his parents have? What about Mrs. Bonner, his teachers, and Bobby Harris, the CPS worker?

8. Would it be appropriate for Dr. Castaneda to send Bobby a small gift to thank him for the referral? What are the ethical principles of your field regarding the relationship between providers and people who make referrals?

The initial meeting between Dylan and Dr. Castaneda occurred the following week. Dylan was tall for a 12-year-old boy (approximately 5' 8") and relatively thin. His hair was clean, as were his jeans and T-shirt. His infamous trench coat was another matter. The coat bulged from the overly-laden pockets, and Dr. Castaneda could see how the weight of it strained Dylan's back, just from the effort to stand upright. She could see just how wrinkled and dirty the coat was, and the smell of moldy food, sweat, and dirt was enough to knock even a seasoned professional like Dr. Castaneda back a step. She introduced herself, welcomed Dylan into her office, and showed him the signed informed consent form from his parents, briefly explaining what type of therapy she did and seeking his assent to participate.

Dylan willingly answered questions and admitted to being embarrassed about meeting with Dr. Castaneda. Once basic rapport had been established, which was fairly easily done since Dylan was a likeable child, Dr. Castaneda told Dylan that they might as well get to work right away.

Dr. C: Do you know why you are here, Dylan?

Dylan: Probably 'cause of my coat. It stresses everybody out.

Dr. C: You're right about that. Your coat does stress people out. Does it stress you out?

Dylan: No! Only when I can't wear it or have to take it off. I need my things and I don't want to be without them, even for a minute. They come in handy, you know. Like the other day, I was hungry and I knew exactly which pocket to look in for half of a granola bar. And then I needed some scissors to cut this plastic bracelet thing off of a fence so I could keep it. It is a beautiful bracelet, maybe worth something at a pawn shop. Maybe even part of it is made of real gold. It took me a minute, but I knew I had scissors in a pocket somewhere and I found them. So, then I could keep the plastic bracelet. Wanna see it?

Dr. C: Sure.

Dylan rummaged his pockets and found the plastic bracelet, a dime store piece of jewelry with large plastic beads, half of them missing, and a broken clasp of tarnished metal.

Dr. C: Thank you for showing me your bracelet, Dylan. So, your coat, with all of its pockets that allow you to keep track of your belongings, comes in handy sometimes. I'm wondering if you'd be willing to show me what else is important to you—what you carry in your pockets.

Dylan: You aren't going to take my things, are you?

Dr. C: No, I promise that I won't take your things. *Te lo prometo*—Oh, Dylan, I'm sorry; that means that I promise. You don't speak Spanish, do you?

Dylan: A little. The kids at school speak it sometimes so I've learned *un poco* (a little).

Dr. C: I was born in Mexico, so I learned to speak Spanish before I learned to speak English. When I speak from my head, I speak English. When I speak from my heart, I speak Spanish. So, sometimes, when I'm speaking from both my heart and my head, I speak a little bit of both languages. If I do, I'll always translate for you.

Dylan: *Si. Gracias.*

Dr. C: *Muy bien*, Dylan! Very good! Dylan, I'm a Latina woman. And you're a white boy. Do you have any worries that I won't be able to understand you because I'm a woman and I'm Mexican?

Dylan: No. My science teacher is Mexican, too, and I really like her. I think your culture is pretty cool. I wish we had siestas.

Dr. C: I think your culture is pretty cool, too. And I agree with you about the siestas!

After being assured that Dr. Castaneda would not take his belongings, Dylan emptied his pockets, revealing much of the same items listed by the school counselor. In the intervening time, an extra half-eaten chocolate bar, guitar picks, fast-food kiddy meal prizes, more school-related papers, and an unopened package of peanut-butter crackers had been added.

Dr. C: Dylan, thank you for showing me your things. Will you do me a favor? Put your things together by categories. Figure out a way to group together those that are alike, so they make sense to you.

Dylan willingly complied, placing almost each item in its own category.

Dr. C: *Gracias*, Dylan. OK. You have many categories here. I think about . . . what would you say . . . maybe 40 or 45 separate piles? Can I ask you why you put your four candy bars in four separate categories?

Dylan: This candy bar is completely chocolate, this one has nuts, this was given to me by my mom, and this one was given to me by Gavin's mom. I'd probably forget all of that if I put them in the same group.

Dr. C: I see. *Gracias*. You can put your things away now.

When replacing the items, Dr. Castaneda noticed that Dylan carefully put each item in exactly the same pocket it had been in previously—even a used piece of dental floss found its way back to the same pocket, carefully spooled.

Dr. C: You're careful about where you keep your things.

Dylan: It helps me . . . I know exactly where everything is if I always put it in the same place. I can always find things in my coat. And I can always find them in my locker. And under my bed. And in my room. I know exactly what is there. Everyone else thinks my stuff is a disorganized mess, but it's not. I always know where I leave things . . . they are with me in my mind and I just go to that place. I like to think of my things when I'm bored. Somewhere I read that a disorganized desk is the sign of an organized mind. I have a very organized mind. Nobody else thinks I'm ready for junior high school, but I am.

Dr. C: I get it. Other people don't think you're organized, but you are. I'm just wondering if any of your things have ever caused you troubles or problems.

Dylan thought for a few minutes before responding and then teared up a little when he finally spoke.

Dylan: Well, yes. Not my things, but my mom's things. Sometimes, I think she cares more about her treasures than me, especially her candy dishes. I mean, I love my mom. And I love my sisters, but . . . well . . . I don't know. Our house is just . . . different. And sometimes, well, really, all the time, it's easier to play at Gavin's house than my house since Gavin's family has space to sit down and spread out.

Dr. C: What do the kids at school think of your things?

Dylan: They think I'm weird, but I don't care.

Dr. C: I'm sure that a hundred people have told you to get rid of some of your things. What do you think when people tell you do to that?

Dylan: I hate it. I hate them. These are *my things*. I've had my Star Wars guys for years. I'm not going to just throw them away. You wouldn't throw your friends away, would you, Dr. C?

Dr. C: I wouldn't throw away a good friend. Good *amigos* are hard to come by. I'm sure sometimes people tell you to throw away candy wrappers and half-eaten snacks. Are those your friends, too?

Dylan: I'm not crazy. I'm not friends with candy wrappers and food. But some of it might still be good. I don't want to waste it if it is. Most candy and crackers have lots of preservatives so they're good for a long time. I just feel better keeping things, in case I get hungry or need them.

Dr. C: I know you're not crazy. I didn't mean to imply that you were. And I really like your honesty. I'm thinking that we can do some good work together.

9. What do you think of how Dr. Castaneda brought up the cultural differences between Dylan and herself?

10. Dr. Castaneda is a very skilled therapist. Underline the two or three comments she made that you believe would be the most impactful to Dylan. Discuss your choices with your colleagues and compare your rationales for your opinions.

11. Which comment of Dr. Castaneda's is most problematic, and why? Discuss your choice with your colleagues.

12. Dr. Castaneda chose not to follow up on Dylan's issues with his mom in this first session. Do you agree with her decision? If you were going to explore the relationship between Dylan and his mother, when in therapy would you do so? Write down a few specific things that you might say to broach the topic with Dylan.

CASE 7

Jaquishia Johnson

Jaquishia Johnson is a 16-year-old African American girl who lives in a vibrant and bustling household in a lower socioeconomic status (SES) neighborhood in Chattanooga, Tennessee, with her maternal grandmother, Ms. Naomi Washington (age 48), and maternal great-grandmother, Ms. Sheri Walker (age 66). Ms. Washington had been divorced for many years, and Ms. Walker's husband had died of a stroke at age 52.

Jaquishia calls her grandmother Granny and her great grandmother G-Granny. Ms. Washington's mother has had a series of strokes that have caused cognitive problems, so she requires ongoing care coupled with a hefty dose of patience. Jaquishia's siblings are an active and rambunctious group who require patience as well, although all four of them are good kids who attend school, play sports, and have friends.

Jaquishia's siblings are two younger half-brothers, Jadyn and Keon (ages 13 and 9, respectively), who share one room; and two younger half-sisters, Jasmine and Kiara (ages 12 and 11, respectively), who share a room with Jaquishia. Most of the children had different fathers, but Jasmine and Kiara are full sisters. With five grandchildren between the ages of 9 and 16 and her mother to care for, Ms. Washington is a busy woman. She is fair but tough on her grandchildren and is glad to have Jaquishia's help around the house as an extra set of eyes and hands. Jaquishia enjoys helping around the house and doesn't feel overwhelmed by her family responsibilities. In fact, she calls her younger siblings "my babies" and is close with all of them, especially her little sisters, Jasmine and Kiara. Jaquishia loves to braid their hair and has a knack for making tiny tight cornrows, perfect in length, with brightly colored beads at the end of each strand.

Jaquishia has been through a great deal in her 16 years of life, and sometimes she feels older than she really is. Jaquishia's mother, Tanya, was addicted to drugs throughout most of Jaquishia's life and is imprisoned for prostitution and selling drugs. She will be eligible for parole in four years when Jaquishia turns 20. Jaquishia never met her father, Charles. Tanya never really knew Charles either, and their relationship consisted of a one-night business transaction in which drugs were exchanged for sex. Tanya tried desperately to break free of her addictions, but every new street drug that became available lured her into its choking grasp with its promises of a more potent high. As a result, even when Jaquishia was living with Tanya, she wasn't really around as a mother. In fact, even as a little girl, Jaquishia called her mother "Tanya" instead of Mom, and Tanya relied on her to help care for her younger siblings. Jaquishia shuffled back and forth between Tanya's house and her grandmother's neighboring house for years, sometimes for weeks at a time and sometimes for months as Tanya tried to get her life together. But when her mom went to prison when Jaquishia was 14, her grandmother became her official legal guardian. Jaquishia was relieved the day that she came to live with her grandmother for good, because her grandmother had always been more like a mother to her than her real mother had.

Tanya didn't beat any of her five children, although she yelled at them sometimes because they were so loud and she always seemed to have a headache. Mostly, she just left them alone to fend for themselves, as she was too high to take care of them. Tanya had been a prostitute for years, and the kids knew how to "disappear" anytime their mother brought home a male client to entertain. Ms. Washington was strict with Tanya just as she was her grandchildren. She wouldn't give her money, wouldn't let Tanya live with her, and would protect her grandchildren over their mother until Tanya stopped using drugs. Ms. Washington loved Tanya and wanted her to quit using drugs, but she'd lived with drug addiction before and knew that addicts could "carve out a person's soul" with their empty promises.

The problem with Tanya not being available was that it allowed people to come and go in the house without Tanya knowing what was happening. One such person that everyone trusted to come and go whenever he pleased was their funny Uncle Marquis, or Mar, Mar-Man, or Queesy. Uncle Marquis was Tanya's older brother. Although he often stopped by to "check on the kids," as he said, he eventually started coming by just to see Jaquishia. What began for Jaquishia as a feeling of being special and being loved by someone she trusted eventually became something dirty, embarrassing, and shameful. Jaquishia was certain that she—not Uncle Mar—caused things to be wrong, because everyone loved Mar-Man.

Uncle Mar sexually abused Jaquishia from the time she was 8 up until she was 14. Typically, the abuse would occur when Tanya was sleeping, coming down from a high, or recovering from a night of being with clients. Uncle Mar would walk over from his house once or twice a week, fix dinner for everyone, and then he'd lock the younger children out of the house or upstairs so that he and Jaquishia could have a "date." He told her what to wear on their dates: her shortest skirt with no underwear underneath it, and a T-shirt without a bra. He also told her how beautiful she was, how soft she was, how although every girl wanted to be with the Mar-Man, she was the one girl lucky enough to know his "love." His love was intense—he was not a big man, but he felt big to Jaquishia when his penis was inside of her vagina or mouth. Sex itself got easier as Jaquishia got bigger and reached puberty when she was about 10. By the time she was 12, she had gained some weight and she realized that the bigger she was, the less often he came around. And that was fine with her.

At first, when she was 8 or 9, Jaquishia felt special because of Mar-Man's love. Although she knew something about their dates was wrong, sometimes it felt right, too, to be touched and loved by someone as cool as Uncle Mar. It started with back rubs and kisses on the cheek, then progressed to more intense kisses and cuddling, and eventually to cuddling when they were both naked. Things just kept going, and Jaquishia wasn't sure anymore what was right and what was wrong.

Uncle Mar would buy her special gifts, like a new tank top, lipstick, or perfume. He reminded Jaquishia to keep their love a secret because he didn't want her to get in any trouble. He made sure to mention that she was the one who wanted this, not him, and that he was only doing her a favor by recognizing and acting on the love that she felt for him. Uncle Mar's stories became real to Jaquishia, to the extent where she eventually stopped telling Tanya about Uncle Mar's visits—not so much because her mom never did anything to stop it, but because she realized that it must have all been her fault for loving him. She started to hate herself for being such a bad girl. But things began to change as she got older. When she was 13, Jaquishia started to dread Uncle Mar's visits, each week resenting him a little bit more. She also wasn't sure how she was going to get a real boyfriend, like a boy in her class she liked, as long as Uncle Mar was coming around.

Once, when Jaquishia was 14, Uncle Mar brought a girlfriend to Christmas dinner at her grandmother's house. When he and the girlfriend were passionately making out on the sofa, Jaquishia became so angry with Uncle Mar that she spat at him, called his girlfriend a whore, and left her grandmother's house, running back to Tanya's. Tanya was at home getting high. She tried to find out what was wrong with Jaquishia and encouraged her to return to her grandmother's house to open her gifts. Jaquishia refused. Instead, she told Tanya in detail about Uncle Mar being her boyfriend and how she was upset because he was cheating on her, a story that she was certain her mother could relate to because it was so similar to stories that Tanya had told Jaquishia repeatedly about Tanya's own life. To Jaquishia's surprise, her mother slapped her and yelled that Jaquishia was a big liar, "doing wishful thinking" about Tanya's brother, that she ought to be ashamed of herself for even thinking unclean thoughts about her uncle, and that "God knows the truth" that Jaquishia "was like the evil Jezebel." She then told Jaquishia, "As big and black as you are, you'd be lucky to get a man who looks half as good as Mar." That night, Jaquishia *recanted* (denied the abuse) and told her mother that she had lied about everything because she was jealous of Uncle Mar's new girlfriend.

Three weeks later, Jaquishia was still angry because of Mar's girlfriend, but then she realized she was glad for the break from their dates. She changed her mind about their relationship and was glad he had broken it off. She didn't want to have sex with him anymore and she didn't want him to ever touch her again. She was done. Even though she was sure she was going to get in serious trouble and sent away somewhere, she didn't care. She'd never wanted to tell Granny about the abuse because she didn't want Granny to think she was a bad girl, but she felt like she had no choice except to say something. She walked over to her grandmother's house and told her that Uncle Marquis was sexually abusing her, a term she'd learned in school. And Ms. Washington told her to sit down and tell her the whole story, even though Marquis was her own son.

Jaquishia didn't want to talk about it and was embarrassed to share the details, but she let her grandmother ask her a few questions:

Grandmother: Girl, you lying?

Jaquishia: No.

Grandmother: You know what sex is, right?

Jaquishia: Yeah.

Grandmother: How long this been going on?

Jaquishia: Since the summer between second and third grade.

Grandmother: Your momma know?

Jaquishia: Yeah. But she ain't doin' nothin' about it.

Grandmother: You know this serious, right?

Jaquishia: Yeah.

Her grandmother immediately called Child Protective Services (CPS) with Jaquishia still in the room. CPS said they were too busy to respond that day but would schedule an investigation in the upcoming weeks. Granny told them that wasn't acceptable and that she'd be driving Jaquishia down to the CPS office herself that afternoon. Jaquishia cried all the way down to the CPS office, begging her grandmother not to take her and not to send her away to an orphanage or facility to live. Granny looked at Jaquishia and promised her that would never happen, "so help me God."

Child Protective Services began a sexual abuse investigation and ordered no contact between Uncle Mar and Jaquishia. CPS also requested that Jaquishia and her four siblings move into her grandmother's home, which they did, and that their grandmother receive guardianship of all the children. The alternative was for all of the children to be placed in a foster home, and Granny would absolutely not accept that outcome. CPS began investigating Tanya for suspected neglect. At the same time, Tanya was charged with prostitution and selling drugs. Later that year, right after Jaquishia turned 14, Tanya was sentenced to ten years in prison. Child Protective Services shared the information about Uncle Mar with the prosecuting attorney's office so that the state-appointed lawyers could determine if there was enough evidence against him to proceed to a criminal trial.

1. Draw a genogram of Jaquishia's family.

2. Draw a timeline of Jaquishia's life. On the top half, write down normal developmental milestones for children ages 0–16. On the bottom half, write down significant events that happened to Jaquishia at various ages. How do you think these events would have affected Jaquishia's development?

3. What systemic factors influenced why Jaquishia endured abuse for so long without intervention? Think about familial, cultural, socioeconomic, and social factors as you answer this question.

4. If you could be a fairy godmother to Jaquishia and wave a magic wand to help her, what three factors associated with resilience would you give her? Put these three factors in order of importance.

* * *

Jaquishia liked living with her Granny, even though Granny was busy raising five children, caring for G-Granny, and working full time at the IHOP. Even with Granny being so busy and money being tight, she'd purchased Jaquishia and herself matching pink cell phones, and they texted throughout the day to coordinate dinner and child-care plans. Granny checked Jaquishia's homework every night and picked her up after dance team practice on the days that she had it. The two cooked together often. They also enjoyed going to their Baptist church, only a few blocks from Granny's house, where Jaquishia attended weekly youth group and also enjoyed watching the babies in the nursery during Sunday services.

Despite her life's overwhelming challenges, Jaquishia was doing well at Granny's. She'd always liked school, and her grades were historically mostly Bs with a sprinkling of As. She liked writing poetry and especially loved Maya Angelou's work, knowing exactly "why the caged bird sings." She also loved to watch Oprah and tried to read all of the books that Oprah recommended. She had a close-knit group of girlfriends at school had been friends since second grade and loved to dance together. Jaquishia had been on the school dance team for several years, even making co-captain her sophomore year. However, she quit the team this year because she had gained 30 pounds over the past year and decided she was "too fat to dance." Jaquishia had always been one of the largest girls on the dance squad but didn't consider herself heavy until this year. Being on the dance team made her popular at her high school, as the dance team not only performed with the marching band at halftime of games but also in local parades and other events. The highlight of the year was the big game with the school's cross-town rival, the other predominantly African American school in town. Jaquishia reported that she could barely bring herself to attend this game since she wasn't dancing, but she did, noting that "my girls looked good" performing their dance routines.

5. Make a running list of Jaquishia's risk and resilience factors.

6. Write down your most pressing concern about Jaquishia right now and why you are worried about this. Share your concerns your group members. Try to reach consensus on your biggest worry for Jaquishia.

7. Revisit the genogram and timeline you made earlier, adding any additional relevant information.

Jaquishia has some serious medical issues at the present time. At 5'6" and 220 pounds, she's obese, has hypothyroidism (treated by medication), high cholesterol, a low metabolism, poor nutritional habits, and recently has been diagnosed with diabetes. Heart disease and diabetes is rampant in her family, with 11 of 12 great aunts and uncles having had diabetes, and many early deaths because of heart attacks or strokes. Recently, Jaquishia was also diagnosed with Polycystic Ovarian Syndrome but says she "don't really know what that means." Jaquishia survives on a diet of McDonald's, gas-station fried chicken, chips, soda, and "Little Debbie" prepackaged cookies and cakes during the day. She eats Granny's cooking when Granny has time to cook, on Sundays after church, but school-day evening meals are often chicken nuggets, French fries, and pizza rolls.

Jaquishia's doctor has prescribed insulin pills for her diabetes and has told her to lose weight and exercise, but she's overwhelmed at managing her health problems, deciding that she'll just take the insulin pills whenever she feels tired or hungry instead of every day like she's been instructed. Jaquishia reports that she "don't like being this big" and "is tired of being stressed, hungry, tired, and grumpy all the time." Jaquishia says the only activities that she has energy for now, besides school and minding the kids, are watching reality TV shows and reading Oprah's recommended books.

Jaquishia's emotional symptoms are as numerous as her physical ones. Her main complaint is that she has trouble sleeping because of intense nightmares. In some of her dreams, she reports feeling trapped in a place that she can't escape, like a room slowly crushing her with no way out. She also has dreams in which something happens to her best friends, like a car accident or shooting, in which she watches them die but is unable to help save them or even call for help. In these dreams, Jaquishia says, "My mouth don't work. I yell and yell, but nothing comes out." Jaquishia also has what she calls "bad daydreams" in which, all of a sudden, in the middle of a school day or when watching movies with her friends, she'll get an image in her head of Uncle Mar standing over her naked that she cannot banish. One particularly painful image is a specific memory of the abuse. As Jaquishia got older, about age 13, when she first told her uncle that she did not want to "play his games," she remembers a time when Uncle Mar used to pinch her nose with his fingers so that she could not breathe unless she opened her mouth, at which time he would insert his penis. This image gets stuck in her mind, and she often gasps for breath when she thinks about it. To Jaquishia the image feels real—like her uncle is right there with her, "breathing down my neck and making my hairs stand up." She can smell his drunken breath and feel the weight of him on her, and it feels like she is reliving the abuse every time the image appears in her mind.

Jaquishia has no contact with her uncle and wants no contact with him in the future. Uncle Mar currently is under investigation for child abuse as a result of Jaquishia's allegations. The court case has been slow to make a case against Uncle Mar due to a backlog of cases in the prosecutor's office, but Jaquishia doesn't care. She doesn't want to think about or talk about Uncle Mar at all, except sometimes at night when she will talk with Granny. She "hates him" and hopes he "rots in hell." Jaquishia not only actively avoids contact with her uncle, but also with anything that reminds her of him. Although Marquis's house is only a block away from Granny's, Jaquishia will walk blocks out of her way to avoid being anywhere near it. If Granny drives by his house, Jaquishia will shut her eyes so she doesn't have to look at it. She refuses to visit her mother in jail, although allowed to do so, because her mom "reminds me of too much stuff." She hates what her uncle did to her and believes that she'll never have a boyfriend or want to have sex again. She feels that no one can understand what she's been through, and she won't tell her girlfriends about the abuse because "they'll think I'm a whore."

8. Hearing about another person's trauma can affect us as mental health experts. How did hearing details about Jaquishia's story affect you?

9. How did your age, gender, ethnicity, and life history influence your thoughts regarding Jaquishia's trauma?

10. Look up information on Jaquishia's medical conditions of obesity, hypothyroidism, diabetes, and polycystic ovarian syndrome. How do her physical problems exacerbate her emotional problems?

11. Do you think Jaquishia was trying to gain weight to be unattractive to Uncle Mar, or was her weight gain just a side effect of her health and developmental issues?

Jaquishia has just begun therapy to deal with her abuse at the request of the prosecutor assigned to the sexual abuse case against her uncle. She's repeatedly refused to talk to the prosecutor, stating, "I don't want no white woman in my business." Regarding therapy, Jaquishia says succinctly, "I don't want to do it. I don't want to talk about that stuff. Talking about it ain't changing it." The prosecutor noted that she doesn't have much of a case without Jaquishia's testimony and is hoping that therapy will help Jaquishia be a better witness for the prosecution. In fact, the prosecutor calls her therapist after every session to check on Jaquishia's progress.

Because of the ongoing court case and having to think about the abuse she faced, the last two years have been quite stressful to Jaquishia. She's struggling with her grades and has received her first D because of trouble concentrating in school and falling asleep during class. At home, she's having trouble sleeping because she's "afraid of" her dreams. In addition to gaining 30 pounds and quitting the dance team, she refuses to visit her pediatrician concerning her medical problems and doesn't take her insulin pills. Although she continues to be friends with the same group of girls, interactions are sometimes difficult for her. They regularly practice new dance moves and routines together, and Jaquishia feels left out and "different" from them now. Although she's tired of being "stressed out" all the time, she doesn't want to be in therapy. Jaquishia feels somewhat hopeless about the future and hates "everything about my life" but then adds, "except my friends, Granny, G-Granny, Jadyn, Keon, Jasmine, and Kiara."

12. If you were Jaquishia's therapist, what would you say to her in therapy when she refused to talk about the abuse because "talking about it ain't changing it"? Write several therapeutic responses to her statement.

13. Consider the inherent conflict represented by the weekly phone calls between Jaquishia's therapist and the prosecuting attorney. Explain why this dual relationship is problematic from the ethics code of your field. Also, discuss how you would navigate the conflict. Remember, the prosecutor referred Jaquishia to you.

14. Suppose that Jaquishia had waited until she was 18 to report the sexual abuse from her uncle. Would it be your ethical obligation to report the abuse to Child/Adult Protective Services?

CASE 8

Bear Hoskin

"Bear! Bear! Bear! Bear!" The last thing Bear Hoskin remembered before he passed out was everyone chanting his name as he chugged yet another beer. Bear tried to remember what had happened and to understand where he was, but his memories were only fragments: a blur of flashing lights, frantic voices, and then nothing. *"Why am I in a hospital?"* Bear wondered, staring at the bright fluorescent lights above his bed as he slowly opened his eyes. His mother, Rain, noticed his eyes opening. She jumped up and hugged him aggressively, causing Bear to let out a small whimper of pain.

His mother released him as she said, "Serves you right, scaring us like that! What were you thinking?"

Bear didn't respond, not sure of what was happening or what to say.

Despite his queasiness and pounding head, Bear's broken memory was of the best night of his life. He smiled as the night's events began to come back to him. He'd never before experienced as much fun as he did last night, as he didn't have many friends and rarely socialized. Bear's older brother, Phoenix, had practically forced him to come to his friend's party. Bear decided that whatever had landed him in the hospital was worth it.

Phoenix was 19 years old, three years older than Bear. Phoenix was the oldest son, a star point guard on the high school basketball team and straight-A student. He was the golden child. Phoenix received a full-ride scholarship to North Carolina State University and was the first person in the Hoskin family to attend college. He was nervous about leaving the reservation, but he wanted to become an attorney so that he could return home to help the Cherokee people. During his first year of college, however, Phoenix became overwhelmed with the pressure and responsibilities of living on his own. He began partying more and more. By the end of his first semester, he was placed on probation for poor grades. By the end of his freshman year he'd been kicked out of school. For the first time in his life, Phoenix had failed at something. He returned to the reservation, ashamed of his failure and uncertain of his life plans. He dealt with his shame by turning to alcohol. He had a job at the local gas station but lost it after missing several shifts. He tried working at a motel, a tourist shop, and busing tables at the stop-in diner but lost each job in succession. Phoenix, who had been so full of potential, was now full of disappointment.

Although Phoenix almost always was surrounded by a pack of friends and admirers vying for his attention, he always made time for Bear. Bear was much more introverted than Phoenix and preferred to stay home and play video games rather than go to a party full of people he didn't know. As a result, Bear spent most of his free time alone, playing video games in his room. The anonymity of multi-player games freed Bear to be himself without fear of judgment. No one could see him when he played online. Instead of the ridicule in school from his peers, he received praise from anonymous players for his speed and cunning in the Xbox Live games. Some nights, Bear would stay up until 3 AM playing Halo, getting only a few hours of sleep before being rudely awakened by his alarm at 6 AM for school. While he was playing late into the night, Bear would eat a large bag of Peanut-Butter M&M's, two or three small bags of Sour Gummy Worms, and a family-size bag of Cool Ranch Doritos, which gave him just the right amount of grease on his fingers to speedily press the controller buttons. Bear's favorite food group, however, was soda, specifically Mountain Dew. He easily could finish a two-liter Mountain Dew during one of his late-night gaming sessions. The caffeine fueled his excitement for the game, and he could feel his heart pumping energetically as he guzzled more soda, with the result that he became even more energized. Bear noticed that when he drank more soda than usual, he got particularly restless. He struggled to slow his body down enough to sleep on those nights. Ironically, he also didn't do well playing games when he had too much soda because his hands started twitching, which he guessed was from consuming too much caffeine. Or perhaps too much sugar—he wasn't exactly sure which.

Bear had always been a large boy, ever since he was a baby. Currently, Bear is 6'3" and weighs 330 pounds, placing his *BMI* (Body Mass Index, a ratio of weight to height) in the morbidly obese range. Bear always eats more than his peers, but gaming seems to cause him to eat even more than usual. During gaming sessions Bear feels as though he can't stop eating. On really intense game nights, which happen several nights a week since Bear downloaded a new super-addictive Xbox Live game, he will often eat a second bag of Doritos and down a second 2-liter Mountain Dew. Once he's consumed this much, Bear keeps eating, figuring that he's already blown his self-imposed goal of stopping after the first bag of chips and soda. Once this happens, breaking his second goal to stop playing video games by 3 AM tends to follow suit. On these nights, he plays until 4 or 5 AM. During the summer, he wakes the next day around lunchtime, hungry but still exhausted, hating himself for eating so much and vowing to do something different the next night. During the school year he tries to rouse himself after an hour or two of sleep, but he struggles to stay awake in classes the following day.

Although sleep came easily to Bear at one point in his life, he can't remember the last time he got a good night's sleep. He rarely goes to sleep before midnight, even on school nights, due to losing track of time playing video games, feeling wired from the amount of caffeine he drinks during the day, and the excitement of gaming. He never sleeps well when he eventually falls asleep anyway. Bear knows he snores, and not just because all his family members tell him so. His snoring is so loud that it sometimes wakes him in the night. He tosses and turns and wakes often, unable to catch his breath and thinking that he is drowning because he can't breathe. Sometimes he rolls over and is able to fall back to sleep when this happens. Other times, Bear just wakes and resumes playing video games until it's time for school.

Bear never thought much about his weight until middle school, when all of a sudden how people looked seemed to matter. Bear feels judged by his classmates' comments about his weight, although most of them are kind enough to at least disguise their taunts as jokes. Although he's 16, Bear has never been on a date. He's too self-conscious about his appearance to even talk to any of the girls in his class. He hates the way he looks and desperately wants to be more in shape like Phoenix, who seems to effortlessly remain lean and toned. Bear has tried more diets than he cares to count. Every diet seems to end with him eating large amounts of junk food and gaining more weight back than he lost in the first place.

Two years ago, Bear was diagnosed with Type II Diabetes. His doctor told him that his body didn't produce the insulin needed to function properly. Bear's doctor worked with him on modifying his diet. When this was unsuccessful because Bear didn't follow through on the medical advice, his doctor prescribed a pill to help Bear manage his blood sugar levels. Bear didn't believe the pill was that important, so he only took it on some days. His doctor then told Bear that he'd need to have an insulin pump in order to provide his body with the necessary insulin for healthy blood sugar levels. However, Bear didn't pay much attention to his doctor when he was learning how to use the pump. He didn't think his diabetes was a big deal, and his parents never seemed particularly concerned with it either. Sometimes Bear would lose track of how much he ate, and he wouldn't know how much insulin to use. So, he would just guess. Guessing wrong made Bear feel sick, but he always managed to recover without many aftereffects.

Bear's first thought about why he might be in the hospital was that he'd gravely mistaken how much insulin to use. As he tried to get comfortable in the starchy sheets of the propped-up hospital bed, details of the party slowly returned to Bear. He remembered that Phoenix came into Bear's bedroom and asked him for what seemed like the thousandth time to come hang out with his friends.

Phoenix begged Bear, "C'mon, Bear! Come to this party with me. You never stop playing video games. Just give the games a break and come out with me. It'll be fun, I promise! Would I lie to you, little bro?"

Bear liked it when his brother called him "little bro." Something about the way Phoenix said it made him feel loved, and it was one of the few times in his life he truly felt smaller than anyone else. Whenever Phoenix called him "little bro," Bear always had a hard time saying no to whatever Phoenix asked. Despite the fact that Bear always felt awkward at parties, he agreed to go, but just for an hour.

Phoenix responded, "Sweet, man. Good. Let's go. Just an hour."

Bear spent the first hour of the party sitting in a corner, trying but failing to look small and invisible, wondering why anyone would want to talk with him. He normally would worry that popular kids like the ones at the party would pick on him, but his concerns dissipated since the uber-popular Phoenix was with him. Every once in a while, Phoenix would stop by to talk and offer him a drink, but Bear refused the drink, at least at first. Bear had only tasted alcohol a few times in his life, and he'd never drunk more than one beer in a sitting. He didn't really like alcohol's bitter taste, and he couldn't understand why people would drink such a disgusting beverage, especially when Mountain Dew tasted so sweet and smooth.

Phoenix was polite but persistent. "Just have one beer, little bro. Seriously. It'll help you relax."

Bear nodded in agreement and Phoenix opened a can of beer for him. It took Bear a while to drink that first beer. Afterwards, he felt a little buzzed and, as Phoenix had predicted, more relaxed.

Phoenix then went up to Bear and begged him to play in a beer pong tournament with him. Bear had never heard of the game, which requires throwing a ping-pong ball across a table with the goal of landing the ball in a cup of beer. Phoenix briefly explained the game to Bear and then added, "I need you, man. You'll like this game and it'll be fun."

At first, Bear declined, but he was drinking his second beer by then and felt more confident, so he agreed to join Phoenix in the game.

Bear enjoyed games, and as Phoenix carried them to several wins, Bear quickly consumed more beer than he had ever drunk. With each can of beer, Bear felt himself enjoying the party more and more. It helped that Phoenix and Bear were winning game after game of beer pong. They won so many rounds that they reached the championship-match level. Several people had gathered around the table to watch the game and cheer the duo on. The partygoers consisted primarily of current and former high school athletes, mostly basketball players, along with their entourages of girls and less popular kids who were still more popular than Bear. No wonder Bear felt out of place at the party when he first arrived. He had never scored a game-winning shot or run for a touchdown. In fact, he had never scored a single point in any athletic game in his life. Who knew that he'd be so good at beer pong?

Initially, the people at the party were cheering for Phoenix. Bear was used to people rooting for his brother. Eventually, though, they began to cheer for him. Bear wasn't used to being the center of attention in a positive way; typically, he was only the target of cruel jokes. At first, he didn't really know how to respond to all the positive comments. He especially was thrown whenever one of the girls would cheer for him. He usually just smiled and looked the other way as quickly as possible. One girl noticed his humble nature and said out loud, "Oh! He has the sweetest smile! And look at those dimples!" Bear blushed and said nothing, but he felt more motivated to do well in the game. Although Phoenix hit the first nine cups of the championship match, Bear sank the tenth and final cup to win the game. Phoenix erupted with a "BOOM!" and immediately went over to high-five his brother. He yelled, "That's my little bro!" Bear felt a rush of euphoria and quickly grabbed another beer as the onlookers congratulated and hugged them.

After about six beers, Bear found that he didn't really mind the taste of beer that much. In fact, the more he drank, the more he was starting to enjoy both the beer and the party. The normally laconic Bear started talking. For the first time in his life, he stopped worrying that other people were judging him because of his size. A lifetime of being on the receiving end of negative comments—some well-intended and some downright mean—had made Bear ultrasensitive to others' opinions of his weight. Bear reasoned that if a few beers could make him feel this good, then he should keep drinking. With each drink, his shyness lessened. He gently went over to the girl who said he had a sweet smile and asked her, in slurred and uneven speech, if she wanted to dance with him. To his surprise, she said yes, and Bear staggered onto the dance floor with her, barely able to walk without stumbling. He wasn't exactly dancing, but Bear slowly swayed to the beat of the music without toppling. Phoenix was surprised to see his brother become the life of the party, and he encouraged Bear to keep drinking. As Bear and his new friend danced to their third song in a row, Bear couldn't believe his luck. He'd never felt so happy in his life; he was on top of the world. Then, without any warning, he collapsed to the floor.

At first, Phoenix thought that his brother had just passed out from drinking too much. Phoenix quickly realized that something was seriously wrong with Bear. He wasn't breathing normally, and he was beginning to turn blue around his mouth. Phoenix also noticed that his brother's fingernails were turning blue. He worriedly called 911. While waiting for the ambulance, Phoenix was glad that the party was on the busy side of town near the hospital, not out in the woods where they lived. The EMTs rushed to the fallen Bear and began attending to him, fearful that he'd slip into a coma. Bear didn't remember any of this, however. His memory of the party stopped somewhere between the first and second dance with the girl.

Bear was lost in the daydream of his fun evening when a doctor entered his hospital room. A white man who introduced himself as Dr. Huber explained to Bear that he had Acute Alcohol Poisoning, or Alcohol Intoxication, because of his consumption of a large amount of alcohol the previous night. Bear understood only pieces of the doctor's ramble about obesity, an obstructed airway, insulin, blood sugar levels, and Type II Diabetes.

Only when the doctor recommended Bear see a therapist did Bear say quietly, "I don't have an alcohol problem."

Dr. Huber answered brusquely, "I understand that you don't right now, but I've treated your father in here on more than one occasion and both his father and mother before him. Your family has a strong history of alcoholism. Since you don't seem to care how drinking affects you, I'm recommending therapy before you accidentally kill yourself. You're not going to drink yourself to death on my watch. In fact, you have a number of significant health problems, Bear. I'm going to refer you to the Cherokee Health Integration Clinic (CHIC) to help you manage your diabetes and sleep problems as well."

Bear helplessly and angrily looked at the doctor, not sure of what to say. His mother spoke up and promised the doctor that Bear would get an appointment at CHIC as soon as possible.

1. What are your opinions about the doctor's referral and rationale? Is therapy for alcohol problems justified for Bear?
2. What mental health diagnoses do you think are most likely for Bear?
3. Write down your single most pressing concern about Bear. Share your concerns with your classmates and discuss them until you reach consensus.

Bear's mother drove him home from the hospital, a tense quiet 45-minute drive, even for people used to silence. On the way home they passed Bear's school, the casino, and all of the town's restaurants and businesses. One side of the Cherokee reservation had all of the businesses. The opposite side, where the Hoskin family lived, consisted of cheaply made houses, sleepy streets, and boarded-up buildings. As they drove farther and farther away from the busy side of town, Bear felt his brief social life fading with each mile. He thought to himself, *"Those new friends I made will never drive clear over to our house just to see me."*

Living on the Cherokee reservation, deep in the foothills and forests of North Carolina, had its ups and downs. Bear always felt isolated from the rest of the world. Most white people who visited came to gamble at the casino, spend a free night or two at the accompanying hotel, and then return to their lives off the reservation. Bear thought that most white people were OK, as long as they respected the Cherokee people and culture, and most did. Bear was immensely proud of his Native American heritage, and white people who looked down on his culture—or sometimes worse, romanticized it—annoyed him. Bear always thought it was nonsensical how anyone could pity or admire an entire group of people. Things were never what they seemed anyway, and nothing fit easily into the boxes people created. Even the reservation had its contradictions. Most of it was modernized, but the chief and the counsel still followed traditional Cherokee ways in overseeing and running the reservation. Families still subscribed to some traditional Cherokee values, but they adopted white culture and dress as well. Most people on the reservation worked at the casino, its hotel, or the restaurants, so contact with white people often was made by serving them, which was strange as well.

4. Look up the Cherokee Indian Reservation on a North Carolina map. How might the geography of the land affect the people who live there?
5. What do you think of Bear's impressions of white people? How does your cultural background influence your perceptions?

Bear and Rain arrived home. They sat in their old car in the driveway for a moment and then wordlessly walked into their family house. They sat down together at the dining room table. Waya, Bear's father, joined them. Phoenix wasn't around, and Bear thought it was better not to ask where he was.

Rain got Bear a glass of water and finally broke the silence as she said sadly, "Alcohol flows through the reservation like blood through veins."

Waya added, "We see it every day, and unfortunately you've had to see it firsthand. Alcohol changes people. We expected this from Phoenix. But not you."

Bear sat at the well-worn, wobbly kitchen table as his parents looked at him in disappointment. He said nothing but thought to himself, *Nothing I say will change how they see me.*

Bear's father felt like a hypocrite as he lectured Bear about his drinking. Waya was embarrassed by his own history of drinking problems, so he avoided the topic of alcohol whenever he could. Waya winced as he remembered how much he'd hurt his family, especially Rain, when he was drinking. When the boys were little, Waya drank all the time. After tolerating his drinking for years, Rain began taking the children and leaving Waya for a few days while he sobered up. Waya always knew that Rain went to her sister's house, so he wasn't worried about her. However, he was filled with grief and self-recrimination over his behavior, hated to come home to an empty house, and was deeply afraid that someday Rain would take the children and leave for good. As his drinking got worse, Waya regularly yelled at Rain in an anger that seemed uncontrollable. He threatened her if she stood up for herself, accused her of infidelity, and called her names. Waya sometimes yelled at Phoenix and Bear as well. To protect them, Rain would intentionally anger her husband so that Waya would yell at her instead of them. After his angry outbursts, Waya's guilt was unbearable. He would apologize profusely and promise sincerely that it would never happen again. He'd shower Rain with flowers and bribe the boys with candy, hoping to buy back their love. He meant every apology and promise, but alcohol was in charge of his life. He spent more time in bars than at home and missed years of Phoenix's and Bear's early childhood. He lost one job after the next, and Rain's meager paycheck from the casino was their only steady source of income.

Waya hated himself for his past. Standing in the kitchen and lecturing Bear about using alcohol felt horrible. Struggling to find his composure, Waya ended his lecture by saying, "Bear, we thought you were smarter than this."

But you weren't, Dad, Bear wanted to say, remembering all the times his father was filled with alcoholic rage when Bear was young. Instead, Bear said nothing.

Waya sat down next to Bear, his anger subsiding. Replacing the anger was fear for the future he imagined for his youngest son. He admitted softly, "Bear, I made a lot of mistakes, and I had to learn from them the hard way. By hurting the people who I love the most—you, your brother, and your mom. I don't want to see you make the same mistakes I made."

Waya's decision to admit his past mistakes brought everyone's buried pain to the forefront. Bear remembered the shame he felt about his father when people in town would comment about his drinking—the same shame he felt when people taunted him about his eating. He remembered his mother's stoic endurance of Waya's verbal abuse and her willingness to protect both his brother and him. Bear always regretted that neither he nor Phoenix had ever stood up for his mom. Bear ruefully wished that he'd coped with his father's alcoholism by having the courage to come out of his room instead of just hiding in it, eating and playing video games. He wished that Phoenix had the courage to stay home instead of sneaking out of his window, walking for miles to play ball at the public basketball courts, and then staying with friends for days on end. *Everyone disappears in his own way,* thought Bear. He said nothing, however.

Waya was lost in his own thoughts as well, not just about his own alcoholism, but also about his parents' alcoholism. Waya had been terrified of his father, Mohe, a violent alcoholic who regularly would beat Waya, his mother, or his brothers and sisters. Waya vowed never to hit like his father had done, and he'd kept his promise. When he was first drinking, Waya constantly compared himself to his father and rationalized that he was a much better husband and father than Mohe had ever been because he didn't hit. Eventually, he realized that his anger was just as destructive to his own family as Mohe's had been. Mohe died of liver cancer when Bear was 9 and Phoenix was 12. Waya watched him die, a bitter man who faced a painful death. Waya decided that he wouldn't follow the same path as Mohe and stopped drinking the day after he buried his father. Sitting in the kitchen with Bear and Rain, it felt as if the ghost of his father was in the room with them.

Rain, too, was full of deep hurt. She sat at the small kitchen table, uncertain of what to say to her husband and son. Bear eyed her expectantly, waiting for her to speak. He knew by the way that she instinctively stiffened that she was fighting back tears. Rain stood and turned her back on both of them to wash some dishes, not wanting either of them to see her tears. She thought to herself, *Bear could always read me. He's so much more like me than Waya or Phoenix.* As Rain stood over the sink filled with dirty dishes, she sighed deeply. She'd put up with Waya's tirades for years, shielding her sons from as many of his drunken rages as she could. He'd never laid a hand on her, but the damage was done, just the same. She had long since forgiven Waya, but now she feared that his destructive alcoholism had somehow been passed on to Bear. She could forgive him if Phoenix became an alcoholic—Phoenix, who had always been more like his father—but never if Bear became one. She physically tried to shake off the memory of seeing her baby boy lying unconscious in the hospital earlier that day.

Bear knew his parents were right, but he liked the way that alcohol changed him. He enjoyed being the center of attention for being funny instead of being heavy. Sitting in the cramped kitchen, Bear could only think, *The problem isn't that I drank once. The problem is that I hated myself my whole life except the one night that I drank.*

6. Draw a genogram of the Hoskin family. Which family members do you feel are most significantly missing from the story thus far? Whose story would help you best understand Bear?

7. How do you think Waya's and Rain's experiences have affected them as parents?

8. How do you think Bear's weight problems connect with his family history? Why do you think he started to overeat?

Everyone, even the doctor at the hospital, was concerned about Bear's drinking problem. Bear wasn't at all worried about his decision to drink alcohol one night, and he couldn't understand why everyone thought he had a drinking problem. He was, however, worried about his weight. Bear had been worried about his weight for most of his life. Maybe, he thought, everyone is worried about my drinking alcohol because of how many calories alcohol has. Or maybe people with diabetes are not supposed to drink alcohol at all, even one time.

Bear was a big baby when he was born. Rain had gestational diabetes, a type of diabetes that can affect pregnant women. Even though he was born two weeks early, he weighed 15 pounds and 1 ounce. When he was a baby, everyone loved his triple chins and sumo-wrestler physique. By the time he was a toddler, his legs rubbed together from their chunkiness despite his bow-leggedness. When the other kids his age were in kindergarten and energetically running around the playground, Bear needed to take breaks on park benches after just a few moments of playing tag because he was winded. By age seven, he topped one hundred pounds. By age ten, he outweighed his mother at two hundred pounds.

Waya and Rain are both heavy people, but they are dwarfed by Bear's size. They never worried about Bear's weight, and assumed he'd always be "just a little on the heavy side" as well. However, when Bear entered middle school, he began gaining weight even more rapidly. Between the ages of 12 and 14, Bear gained more than one hundred pounds. At age 14, he was diagnosed with Type II Diabetes. Bear's parents took the diagnosis in stride and weren't particularly concerned about it. Diabetes was common on the reservation, and many of their friends and neighbors lived with its many side effects without much complaint.

Bear was a good kid, his parents reasoned, so they didn't have to worry too much about him. His grades were decent enough to have the majority of his college tuition covered by being on the Rolls, essentially a list that documented Native American ancestry and provided access to governmental services, casino revenue, and other resources, including college scholarship. Granted, Bear's grades weren't as strong as Phoenix's, but they were decent. Also, Bear was better behaved than the charismatic and social Phoenix. Bear was quiet at school. He constantly worried about others judging him for his weight as well as his skin color. Though Bear was full Cherokee, his skin tone was significantly lighter than that of his classmates as well as his brother. Some kids joked that Bear was white and didn't belong on the reservation. Bear hated being taunted about his skin color almost as much as he did being teased about his weight, because he took pride in being a Native American.

By the time he was 14, Bear had gained even more weight. He also became infatuated with food and loved thinking about what he was going to eat. As Bear ate more and more food, he also grew pickier about what he was eating and stopped eating some foods altogether. Most days he ate the exact same foods. For breakfast, he ate two donuts and a cup of coffee. For lunch, he had two pieces of pizza, a double order of fries, a Mountain Dew, and some chocolate chip cookies or a candy bar. He had an afternoon snack of chips and soda. For dinner, he ate three servings of whatever his mom had cooked, along with a large bowl of ice cream for dessert. Then, it was on to his evening snack of chips, candy, and soda. Bear not only ate too much during the day, he also didn't eat very many healthy foods. The Hoskin family had never been able to afford fruits and vegetables, so he never developed a taste for them.

Bear's will-power to stop eating fell apart when he began his late night video game sessions. He tried not to eat so many chips and drink so much soda, but he just couldn't stop. Bear knew that two or three family-size bags of chips and some candy was too much for one person, but the chips just seemed to call his name. Even when Bear was full, and knew he was full, it was hard for him not to open that second bag of chips or drink another soda. Bear often ate so much that he thought he was going to be sick, and sometimes he would even run to the bathroom toilet, hoping to throw up so as to relieve some of the pressure he felt in his stomach. He never did vomit. He thought about making himself vomit by sticking his finger down his throat, but he couldn't stand the disgusting thought of seeing everything he'd just eaten in the toilet.

Bear hated himself for eating so much, but he didn't know how to stop. He even wished sometimes that he was an alcoholic instead of an eat-oholic, as he privately called himself. With alcohol, he thought, it would be easier as he could just stop drinking altogether. How was he supposed to stop eating altogether? Every day seemed to mark the breaking of another self-imposed rule. Because he couldn't stop eating, he tried to hide his eating from others. Whenever he could, he tried to eat alone. He had a standing order with his big brother, whenever Phoenix drove by the McDonald's in town, for two super-sized extra value meals—each of which contained a Big Mac, large fries, and a large drink—which Bear would eat at home alone in his bedroom.

Bear gets most of his clothes from second-hand stores because his family can't afford the prices at the Men's Big and Tall store. Fortunately for Bear, obesity is common throughout the reservation, so he has plenty of choices in men's clothes. Nevertheless, Bear is embarrassed by his clothes because he can't keep up with new fashion trends. Bear doesn't like anything about his appearance except for his hair. His long black hair has always been a source of pride to him, and he maintains it religiously. Bear imagines himself thinner and wishes he could get to a healthier weight. Despite his good intentions, every diet he tries results in failure, including his efforts to switch to diet soda and low-fat chips. Bear hates the scale but has forced himself to weigh in once a month because he knows he shouldn't get any bigger. Lately, though, he feels so frustrated and anxious by the numbers on the scale that he's stopped weighing. If he happens to catch a glimpse of himself in a mirror, he looks at himself critically, disgusted by his lack of self-control.

Everything in his life feels like a failure. When Bear fails, his only recourse is to retreat to his room and his video games, isolating himself from the people who hurt him and surrounding himself with the food that makes him feel good. Bear wonders if maybe he should give up and just get used to being fat for the rest of his life.

9. How do you think Bear's relationship with Phoenix affects him?
10. Do you think that people of color can exhibit racist behavior? Why or why not?

Tyler Dawson Rudolph

Tyler Dawson Rudolph loves football. Posters of the Dallas Cowboys and the University of Texas Longhorns adorn his bedroom walls. His wardrobe consists of Cowboys and Longhorns T-shirts and sweat suits. His weekday afternoons are spent practicing football for his middle-school team, where he is quarterback. His weekends are filled with playing in school football games, watching college and pro football games, and organizing pick-up football games with his friends. When he isn't playing or watching football, he's studying Internet highlights of his favorite players or memorizing their statistics. As an 11-year-old boy living in a small town in the hill country of rural Texas, Tyler knows more about football than any of his friends—which is impressive since his friends are equally obsessed. Tyler used to play basketball and baseball, but this year he was selected to participate on an all-star football team that requires him to attend a summertime training camp at a regional university. Because of this, Tyler and his parents decided that he would give up basketball and baseball and focus solely on football.

1. What are your initial impressions of Tyler thus far? Do you think he's a "normal" kid? Are you worried about his obsession with football?
2. Draw a picture of Tyler in your mind. What does he look like? How tall is he? What is the color of his skin?
3. How does your culture and gender affect your opinion of Tyler?

As the third-born son to Roger (named after Staubach) and Maria Medina Rudolph, it was a given that Tyler would love football. Roger and Maria even chose the name Tyler Dawson so it could be shortened to "TD" for Touchdown, and TD indeed has become his nickname. Roger Rudolph is a local sports hero in the family's hometown because he played football for the Texas Longhorns, starting three years as a wide receiver. Roger is now a manager at a large home repair store, and a huge photo of his victorious team after the legendary Cotton Bowl game takes up an entire wall of his small office. In fact, some people stop by the hardware store for the sole purpose of "catching up with Rog." Roger takes it all in stride, happy to be recognized and semi-famous. Despite his night-time work schedule, which leaves him free to coach Tyler's middle-school football team during the day, at least three or four people stop by each evening just to visit with Rog, who still signs autographs even 20 years after "the game."

Maria, Tyler's mother, has also become a football fanatic over the years. Maria is three-quarters Latina and one-quarter Caucasian. She grew up in the United States but didn't love football until she met Roger in college. Maria is employed as the administrative assistant at the local school district's main office, a job that allows her flexibility to leave early every afternoon for her three sons' practices and games. Maria is lovingly called "Football Mom" by her sons' teams. She brings snacks to games, champions discouraged players, nurses injuries, and attends every game, no matter the weather. Maria is bilingual and switches between English and Spanish, often in the same sentence, to talk to players in their native language, a useful skill since many Latino boys play on the team. Tyler has two older brothers, Brett (named after Favre) and Peyton (named after Manning), who also play football. Brett plays on the high school varsity team despite being only 15, and Peyton plays on the freshman squad as a 14-year-old. Although his brothers are solid players with Division II college scholarship potential, everyone in town agrees that Tyler has the most athletic potential in the family because, as the Rudolphs' neighbor gloats, "TD runs just like his dad—quick and fast. And those hands—that boy must have Superglue instead of skin." The Rudolph family is squarely middle class and Southern Baptist, although Maria was raised Catholic and still is registered as a member of a parish. The family attends mass only on Easter and Christmas. In addition to football, they also love to travel in their RV, fish, and hunt.

> 4. What is your impression of the Rudolph family? Would you like to be raised in their home? What does your answer suggest about your values?
>
> 5. Because this book focuses on child psychopathology, you are aware that Tyler will present with a mental health problem as you read further. Without reading ahead, what problem do you think he might have?

Tyler doesn't excel just in football. He's a good student whose grades are As and Bs. His teachers report that he's "delightful" and "a real leader" in class. He has excellent behavior and manners, calling teachers "Ma'am" and "Sir." He's also extremely popular among his sixth-grade classmates. He has a core group of five or six friends who have been his classmates and teammates since first grade. Tyler is also well-liked by the other boys in his class and has an inner circle of friends, a medium circle of friends, and an outer circle of friends, but no enemies. His female classmates think he's "really cute." Several of them have crushes on him and are envious of the girl who calls herself his girlfriend. Everyone in town knows that Tyler is a nice kid and a smart kid, but it's his athletic potential, even as a young middle schooler, that has the town abuzz.

Tyler, though, has a secret that he goes to great lengths to hide. He still urinates in his bed—or "wets" his bed, as Roger and Maria say, although the technical term for this problem is *Enuresis*. Tyler has urinated in his bed almost every night since he was a little boy. Whereas other kids outgrew bed-wetting at approximately age three or four as they were toilet trained, Tyler never really got the hang of it. His family wasn't too concerned about his bed-wetting at first. Their oldest son, Brett, had also been a bed wetter, but he had spontaneously stopped bed-wetting at around age eight, so Roger and Maria had just assumed that Tyler would do the same. Tyler also has not wet his pants during the day for years, although he had done so regularly back in kin-dergarten and first grade, when he'd had to frequently and surreptitiously change into "loaner" pants from the school office. Furthermore, Tyler had experienced some lengthy stretches when he did not wet the bed. Occasion-ally, he would be dry for a few days—sometimes as many as five or six—but then he would wet again for the next three or four nights. He even had a few extended periods of 10 to 12 consecutive days when he was dry. The first time or two that this occurred, the family celebrated, thinking that he was over it. Unfortunately, the wetting would start again and Tyler would wake up in the middle of the night soaking wet, smelling like urine, embarrassed, frustrated, and asking for his mom's help to get dry sheets. Tyler was glad to have his own room and often sheepishly stripped his bed sheets in the morning before anyone woke up and could tease him for peeing the bed. Tyler has never spent the night at a friend's house, despite being asked many times. Nor has he ever had a friend spend the night, although many friends literally have begged him to allow them to sleep over, as they all like Tyler's "cool" broth-ers and "awesome" parents almost as much as they liked him.

Tyler isn't the only one frustrated with his bed wetting. His parents report that they're at their wits' end. Roger and Maria have tried "everything under the hot Texas sun" to get him to stop. They've tried restricting liquids after dinner and ensuring that he didn't drink any caffeinated drinks, because they'd heard that it causes kids to wet the bed. They'd tried punishment, which consisted of Tyler having to strip his sheets in the middle of the night and then sleep on a thin mattress on the floor with no blankets. Although Roger felt this tactic was working, Maria felt bad for Tyler and always brought him blankets, saying she couldn't bear to think of him lying there, cold and miserable. Tyler often wet a second time during those nights, soak-ing the floor mattress, and ended up sleeping on an old couch in the base-ment. They had tried "natural consequences," which consisted of allowing Peyton to make fun of Tyler for wetting the bed, provided he kept the taunt-ing "in the family" and didn't tell anyone at school about it. For years, they bought pull-ups, basically "big kid diapers," until he graduated to adult dia-pers, which were quite expensive. They'd tried a reward chart, in which Tyler could earn football-themed toys and clothes for dry nights. Their pediatrician had prescribed Desmopressin (DDAVP) for Tyler, which seemed like it might be working but was discontinued because of uncomfortable side effects like dry mouth and dry eyes. Roger and Maria heard about something called a "urine alarm" and ordered one for Tyler. He used it for a few weeks, but they stopped using it when it didn't really seem to help—he was still bed-wetting. Sometimes he even wet the bed a second time during the night after having gotten up to urinate once when the urine alarm woke him. Their present solution was for Maria to make sure Tyler woke up to use the bathroom twice a night—once at midnight before she went to bed, and then setting the alarm for 4 AM to wake him up a second time. This plan worked sometimes but not always, and Maria was exhausted. Because Roger worked nights during the week, dealing with the problem fell mainly on her shoulders, it was Maria who made the phone call to a psychologist to seek help. She said, "We don't know what else to try. Everything seems like it sort of works, but not every night and not for very long. It just keeps going back to the same thing and he's wet again."

6. Bed-wetting is a common problem, and parents often try many solutions before seeking help from an expert. Use your knowledge of psychological principles to explain why the solutions the Rudolphs have tried were (or were not) good ideas.

7. Many families tease each other. Do you think that teasing made the problem worse, better, or had no effect on Tyler?

8. What role do Tyler's gender and culture play in his level of shame about his Enuresis? Think of culture on both broad and specific levels when answering this question. How would it be different if Tyler weren't a star football player focused on his talent? How would it be different if he lived in a culture which de-emphasized sports?

9. Why do you think the urine alarm wasn't successful in treating Tyler's Enuresis in the past?

10. Do you think that Tyler's bed-wetting suggests that he has other, more serious problems, and the bed-wetting is a symptom of deeper pathology?

11. What do you think causes bed-wetting?

Maria and Roger talk almost daily with their parents for advice, and they've heard plenty of suggestions from all four grandparents, including making sure Tyler was warm when he slept, making sure he got enough sleep, sending him to bed by 8 PM, eliminating sugared drinks and sports drinks from his diet, and having him eat an extra slice of bread or roll with dinner since "carbs absorb liquid." Tyler's maternal grandmother was certain that he'd been sexually abused because she'd read somewhere that kids who wet the bed have often been sexually abused by someone. Tyler denied being abused, but his grandma continued to suspect sexual abuse despite no evidence to suggest it.

At this point, the family was desperate for help. Tyler's honor of making the all-star quarterback team would mean overnight stays at a college dorm for summer camp. At camp, the kids slept four boys to a room. Their goal was to stay up as late as they could, watch football, eat pizza, and dare each other to fall asleep as they could then playfully torment the early birds. Tyler was petrified that if he ever wet the bed and the other kids knew about it, they'd tease him mercilessly and he'd never be popular again.

Please discuss the following two ethical questions:

12. Tyler's grandmother learns that an ex-neighbor of the Rudolph family is a convicted sex offender. She insists that Tyler must have been sexually abused, despite his denial of such abuse and the parents' insistence that, although Tyler saw the neighbor from a distance while he was outside playing football, he never spent any time with the neighbor alone. How would you proceed in this situation, and do you have an obligation to call Child Protective Services?

13. When meeting with the family, you become convinced that utilizing a urine alarm is the best way to treat Enuresis. A company that produces urine alarms wants to use you as a paid spokesperson for their product. They will pay $20,000 to have a testimonial from you on their website, endorsing and recommending their urine alarm as a professional. Is this ethical? Under what conditions would it be or not be?

CASE 10

Arush Patel

Marriage was the beginning of the Patels' adventures together. Priti and Sunil Patel were chosen by their parents to marry each other in an arranged marriage. Their parents approved the match, as they were both from the Vaisyas caste (artisans) and spoke the same family and state language. The Vedic horoscopes, which assessed compatibility based on their birthdays, predicted their marriage would be an auspicious match. In short, the alignment of the stars predicted that Priti and Sunil would have a wonderful life together. Priti smiled behind her wedding veil as she followed the tradition of walking in circles in the "seven rounds" of the Hindu marriage ceremony that would join her hand in marriage to Sunil.

At 25, Sunil had completed his MBBS (Bachelor of Medicine & Bachelor of Surgery), had graduated with top marks in his class, and was keen on moving to the United States. Sunil was the first physician in his family, as his mother worked in textiles and his father in construction. From the time he was a child he had been praised for his intellect, and his parents strongly encouraged him to pursue a graduate degree. Sunil's parents gave him a choice of two professions upon graduating from high school. He could either become an engineer or a physician. Sunil did not question his destiny or his narrow range of choices about his marriage or career. Instead, he understood that it is how things are and always should be. He was a studious young boy, constantly reading and rereading medical textbooks rather than going out with his friends, so medicine was an obvious career choice. Because of his high grades he gained entrance to a prestigious Indian medical college with his tuition entirely covered through scholarships. Sunil was proud of his accomplishments, but especially proud of his beautiful wife, Priti. Future-oriented and ambitious, Sunil wanted the best for his young family, and he worked hard to earn the fees to apply for a visa to the United States. The task of securing a visa was arduous, but Sunil knew that it would be worth the effort.

Priti was also ambitious. At 22, she had completed her undergraduate studies in engineering. She believed that she could achieve her professional goals and be successful, just as her older brothers had before her. Her family was supportive of her educational goals, although her grandmother Lakshmi often asked her how many grandchildren she would live to see. Priti chose Sunil from among the choices of suitors her parents had provided for her because of his warm smile, good educational background, and goal-oriented nature. Priti knew that Sunil would not only reach his goals but would also support her in reaching her own. Priti's parents were secretly glad that their daughter had chosen Sunil, because they knew that he intended to become a doctor. As Sunil and Priti were working their way through the long process of being granted a visa, their son Akshay was born—to the delight of Sunil, Priti, and their families. Priti's grandmother was especially pleased.

1. Political issues, such as immigration laws, can affect mental health. Give some examples of how this can be the case.
2. How do your political views affect your clinical work?

After a year of paperwork, fees, and interviews, Sunil, Priti, and Akshay were finally accepted as immigrants to the United States. The move was difficult for Priti. She didn't think that she'd miss her family and homeland as much as she did, but she trusted her parents' and Sunil's judgement. She wanted to please her parents and make them proud of her. After the young family arrived in Atlanta, Priti bowed to Lakshmi, the goddess of good fortune, and prayed for the safety of her new family in the United States. Lakshmi had always been a special goddess for Priti, as Lakshmi was the name of her beloved maternal grandmother. Almost immediately after settling into their new home in suburban Atlanta, Sunil and Priti began setting aside funds for the purpose of visits to their families back home in India, and for their families to visit them in Atlanta. They also regularly sent money and goods home to their families and extended families in India. The Patels worked to secure dual citizenship for all their family members so that they could travel freely between India and the United States. Sunil and Priti were both thrilled when Priti became pregnant again. The stars once again seemed to align, as they had been hoping to have two children. Arush was born two years after his brother.

With two very young children and Sunil working long hours to complete his last year of residency as a surgeon, the Patels decided that Priti would stay home and be a full-time mother. Priti was fine with this arrangement. Although Sunil was very busy at work, he enjoyed his time with Priti and his sons. He also enjoyed watching cricket matches on TV and looking for future employment opportunities on career-focused websites. Priti adored the children but was worried that Akshay and Arush would not want to learn about Indian culture as they grew older and eventually would attend school. However, both boys seemed eager to learn the customs and language of their native land. Priti taught the boys Hindi and often spoke it at home, so that the boys grew up bilingual and would be able to speak to their older relatives back in India. She taught the boys how to bow down to the goddess Lakshmi and thank her for their good fortune.

3. If you do not know much about a culture of a client you are treating, what is the most ethical way to learn this information?

From the time he was young, it was clear that Akshay, the older son, was a miniature version of his father. At 12 and in middle school, Akshay already had plans to become an emergency room doctor. He was studious, motivated to learn, and goal oriented, even as a little child. In elementary school he always earned top grades, especially in math and science. He had won the Science Olympiad this year, making his parents extremely proud of him. From an early age, he seemed tailor-made for long hours of difficult schoolwork. Akshay was enjoying the more challenging work of middle school.

At age 10, Arush was quite different from his older brother but was still a likable boy. He was tall, lanky, and incredibly uncoordinated, even for a gangly 10-year-old. In spite of his awkwardness, Arush was high spirited—he enjoyed being silly and often made jokes, sometimes to the point of exhausting others. Priti and Sunil adored him, although they sometimes became overwhelmed by his adventurous spirit. Arush did not particularly excel at school or in sports. Nevertheless, he somehow made people forget his weaknesses because he was so endearing and just plain goofy. His grades were decent enough. Most parents would be pleased with the As and Bs he earned, but Arush always had to work hard for his grades in direct contrast to Akshay, who seemed to effortlessly receive the highest grades in every class. Teachers often were surprised to learn that the two of them were brothers because they were so different.

Arush was always willing to try new things and signed up for the Science Club, Chess Club, baseball, and choir. Whatever invitation to join a team or club was sent home from school, Arush was excited to join, at least for a while. He played baseball for a year, then quit and tried cross-country, which lasted only a year as well. He was hoping to try tennis next year. His favorite things to do were attending Indian parties, playing video games with his friends Vishu and Eddie, and reading comic books. One commitment that Arush had been able to keep was Boy Scouts. He had been a Boy Scout for three years now and never once asked to quit. He recently had his crossing-over ceremony from Cub Scout to Boy Scout and was proud of doing something that Akshay had never done. Arush's friends, Vishu and Eddie, were also in Scouts, and they enjoyed working together to earn badges. Arush was not as focused on earning badges as his friends, but he did like BMX bike riding and camping.

Overall, Arush was immature in many ways. He never quite knew the correct thing to say or when to say it. As an infant and toddler, Arush was always a little late in meeting his developmental milestones, but not quite late enough to seriously worry his parents. Akshay had been early in meeting every milestone, so the Patels tried to remind themselves that every child was different and that Arush would find his own way in time. Arush just seemed to operate on his own schedule, which was set a little slower than everyone else's was.

4. To what extent does birth order affect personality? Find some credible research that supports your view.

5. How would you describe the Patels' parenting? What can you infer about their home environment from the case study thus far?

One problem that plagued Arush from the time he was quite young was sleep troubles. Arush would go to bed without incident as a toddler; in fact, even at the age of 18 months he would toddle off in his footed pajamas and put himself to bed when he was tired. He would sleep well for a few hours and then, suddenly, waken everyone in the house with an anguished scream. The first time this happened, when Arush was almost two, Sunil and Priti were in an absolute panic. Why was their baby screaming so loudly? What was wrong with Arush? They tried to wake him, but to no avail. Sunil felt for a pulse and knew that his son's heart was racing. Arush's eyes were dilated and he stared straight ahead, yet he still seemed to be asleep. He was breathing rapidly, as if he had been running, yet he had been asleep in his bed. His breathing was so ragged that he was almost gasping for breath. Sunil and Priti were certain that Arush had just had a terrible dream, but they worried because they had never seen anyone wake from even the worst of dreams as terrified as Arush seemed to be. They were also concerned about how difficult it was to awaken Arush from these dreams.

From the time Arush was two years old until he was three, his frightening nocturnal awakenings continued about once or twice a month. Arush's parents always reacted the same way when they heard his blood-curdling screams in the middle of the night. They quickly rushed to their son and tried to wake him from his terrible dreams. However, it seemed that the harder they tried to wake him, the worse his screaming would become. On the rare night when they could finally wake him, Arush was absolutely inconsolable. During the day, however, Arush was a typical toddler. In fact, although it was difficult for him to comprehend the question, "How did you sleep?" he showed no signs of daytime sleepiness or problematic behavior. He never complained of having bad dreams and he seemed to not remember his traumatic nocturnal episodes.

Sunil and Priti discussed the possibility of getting medical intervention for his problem, but they were hoping that Arush would outgrow it. Their hopes were realized when Arush was three. Near his third birthday, just as suddenly as they began, Arush's problems with screaming in the middle of the night stopped. Sunil and Priti slept lightly every night, waiting for his next nighttime screaming fit to happen. Weeks went by, then months, and Arush slept through every night without incident. Sunil and Priti were relieved and began to sleep better.

From the time he was three to the approach of his sixth birthday, Arush seemed to sleep well every night. He had no further difficulties with his terrible dreams, or whatever it was that had caused him to awaken screaming in the night.

Then, when Arush was 5½, a new problem began. A few months before he was to begin kindergarten, he began sleepwalking. Sunil and Priti had vivid memories of the first night this happened. Priti had gone to bed while Sunil stayed up late to research a rare medical condition of a patient he had seen that day. Sunil couldn't shake the feeling that someone was watching him, yet he turned around several times in the dark den and saw nothing. Nevertheless, he kept thinking he heard a sound—some rustling or breathing. Sunil grabbed a stapler, which was the closest heavy item he could find at hand, and turned to search through the house for an intruder. The Patels had no pets, so he knew that a cat or dog could not have been making the noises he was hearing. Sunil walked into the kitchen and flipped on the overhead light, stapler in hand and heart racing. There, standing in front of the refrigerator was not a burglar, but his youngest son. Sunil screamed from surprise and fear. Priti awoke when she heard Sunil scream and ran downstairs to make sure he was OK. When she arrived in the kitchen, she saw her panicked husband holding a stapler and her son standing at the refrigerator in an aimless daze. Sunil and Priti told Arush to go back to bed, but it was as if he couldn't hear them. He stood there at the refrigerator with its door closed as if he were stuck, or on pause. Sunil and Priti realized that he was sleepwalking, and they each took one of his arms and guided him back to bed.

Initially, Arush's sleepwalking only happened once every couple of months. Priti recognized that his sleepwalking tended to happen especially on nights when he stayed up unusually late. The Patels were not too worried about Arush's sleepwalking for several reasons. First, it didn't happen that often. Second, he never tried to go outside or do anything dangerous during his sleepwalking episodes. Third, they knew such sleepwalking behavior was normal in young children. To help manage the problem, Sunil and Priti made sure to check the house every evening so that Arush would not accidentally trip over a stray shoe or toy. Keeping the house clean was not difficult for the Patels as their home was always impeccably clean, even with two young boys. The Patels also made sure that the exterior door to the house was locked. They hid the key each night just to be certain Arush could not get outside. They also put a child's safety gate atop the basement stairs to be sure he did not accidentally tumble down the stairs.

Several months later, when kindergarten was in full swing, Arush's sleepwalking became more frequent. He started sleepwalking between three and five times a week. His sleepwalking did not bother Sunil and Priti near as much as his screaming in the middle of the night, and often Priti slept right through his sleepwalking. Sunil usually woke when he heard his son rustling about the house, but he was typically able to return to sleep quickly, likely because he was so exhausted from his long hours at the hospital. When Arush was sleepwalking, one of his parents, usually Sunil, would just guide him back to his bedroom and help him gently lie down in his bed. His sleepwalking wasn't particularly a problem for his parents, who had gotten used to sleeping lightly and listening for him to ensure he was fine.

* * *

Arush was now 10. He had been sleepwalking several times a week without incident for nearly five years. His sleepwalking followed a predictable pattern of occurring less often in the summer and more often during the school year. Arush had just begun fifth grade, and his parents were gearing up for more frequent bouts of sleepwalking again. Instead, however, Arush once again began screaming in the middle of the night about once or twice a month. Sunil and Priti woke in a panic whenever they heard his blood-curdling screams. As they had done before, they would hurry into Arush's room and try to wake him, believing that he was having a terrible nightmare. At these times, his face was as white as a ghost and his features were anguished, as if he were in horrific pain. Every time Arush had his screaming fits in the middle of the night, Sunil always quickly felt for his pulse, which was almost always rapid. Arush's heart also was typically beating wildly and he was flushed and covered in sweat. His breathing was rapid and shallow. Sunil tried everything to wake his son, even splashing water on his face, and he once even gently slapped him. Nothing seemed to wake Arush, and his screaming often continued for as long as five or ten minutes. Then, as suddenly as it began, Arush would "give up the ghost" and fall back in bed exhausted, immediately appearing to be in a deep slumber.

The odd thing was that when Sunil and Priti asked Arush how he had slept the next morning after a screaming episode, he would always answer "just fine." When they asked him if he remembered any bad dreams or nightmares, he always told them no. When they asked him if he remembered screaming in the middle of the night at the top of his lungs, he laughed and thought his parents must be joking. Arush didn't remember his parents shaking him, splashing water on him, or even the one time his father slapped him in an attempt to wake him. He remembered absolutely nothing.

6. If you were a therapist working with this family and Sunil reported that he had once slapped his son in the context described above, would you be obligated to call Child Protective Services to report abuse? Why or why not?

Arush's terrible nighttime screaming continued at least one night a month for several months. Sunil and Priti wondered again if Arush were having nightmares—perhaps about school, because his sleep problems seemed to be so much worse during the school year. However, Arush said he really liked school and never reported any nightmares. He continued to remember nothing that had happened during his nocturnal screaming episodes. It took his parents a while to convince him that he actually was waking up screaming in the middle of the night. He finally believed it only because his father videotaped it on his cell phone. As he watched the video, Arush broke into tears. Once he realized his parents were telling the truth, Arush was ashamed and embarrassed. He also was worried that he would have a screaming episode at a friend's house, so he disappointedly quit going to his friends' overnight birthday parties.

> 7. Do you think that Arush's parents should have shown him the video of himself screaming? Why or why not?
>
> 8. What do you think is the most probable explanation of Arush's problem? Why do you think it is occurring?

As a medical doctor, Sunil was not sure why this could be happening. His first thoughts were of medical explanations. Perhaps Arush had an undetected heart arrhythmia. Perhaps he had a heart defect leading to *tachycardia* (a fast heart beat). Perhaps he had a breathing disorder. Or perhaps his youngest son was mentally ill and going crazy. Or maybe he was feigning the screams in the middle of the night to get attention. He wondered about the possibility of Arush being abused or mistreated at school and having nightmares as a result of his bad experiences, although Arush attended a good school, seemed to be well adjusted there, and had many friends. Uncertain of how to proceed, Sunil made plans to consult with an expert in the field of psychiatry as soon as possible.

As luck would have it, Sunil and Priti were invited to a formal dinner party honoring a family friend's graduation from medical school. The guest list was comprised primarily of members of the Indian community in their neighborhood, including many well-known doctors. Priti was looking forward to the chance to do her hair, nails, and makeup and wear one of the beautiful saris in her closet that she never had the occasion to wear as a stay-at-home mom. She also looked forward to having a date with her busy husband. Sunil was looking forward to the party as well, for these reasons and others. He had done his homework and knew that Dr. Rem Kapoor, a prominent local psychiatrist, would be attending the party. He had never met Dr. Kapoor, but Sunil knew that they would likely share a common acquaintance in the small Indian medical community in Atlanta who could introduce them to one another. Sunil was hoping to get Dr. Kapoor's expert advice on Arush's problems.

At the party, Priti and Sunil enjoyed a lovely dinner. After dessert, Priti began speaking with some of her friends, and Sunil seized the opportunity to meet and informally consult with the well-known Dr. Kapoor. After being introduced by a mutual friend, the two made small talk about the many commonalities between them: they were both Indian, of course; they lived in nearby suburbs; they attended the same Hindu temple; they both were medical doctors and fathers. Dr. Kapoor, or Rem as he quickly told Sunil to call him, had three children. The two struck up an easy conversation, and Sunil trusted Rem immediately.

"Rem," Sunil began. "I heard you are a psychiatrist."

"Sometimes," Rem answered.

"Well, would now be one of those times? I don't want to put you on the spot, but I wondered if I might have five minutes of your time to tap your expertise," Sunil asked.

9. How would you answer the question if you were Dr. Kapoor? Was Sunil's request reasonable or inappropriate?

"Maybe. I'll be honest with you in answering your question the best I can, but it depends. If your question is outside my area of expertise or requires more than a simple consultation, I'll encourage you to make an appointment, either with me or another colleague, depending on the nature of the problem," Rem explained.

Sunil wasn't certain if this meant that he should or shouldn't share his son's problem, so he sat quietly for a minute.

"Go ahead," Rem encouraged.

"Well, I have a question about my son. His name's Arush, and he's 10 years old. For years, he's had trouble sleeping. He sleepwalks. I know this is common so I'm not really worried about it. But he does something else, too. He often screams in the middle of the night, and we have no idea why. We try to wake him—my wife Priti and I—she is the beautiful woman in the jade green sari in the kitchen," Sunil said as he pointed to his wife and waved, "but without success. He screams in agony as if he were in terrible pain. We splash his face with water, call his name loudly, and shake him, but he will not wake up. Do you think he's having some kind of horrible nightmares?"

Rem answered, "Sunil, I don't think your son is having nightmares. I think he has a sleep arousal disorder. But I can't be certain of this, based only on a few minutes of conversation. Nor do I want to diagnose him after I've had a few cocktails."

Sunil agreed with Rem's decision.

Rem thought hard about what to say next. He considered having a conversation with Sunil about dual relationships and the ethical problems of trying to be his son's psychiatrist as well as a family friend. He considered how awkward it would be if he were treating the family if his children ended up in the same Balyihar classes at the temple as Sunil's boys. Rem shared none of his thoughts, but instead suggested that Sunil take his son to see a colleague who he recommended.

10. Did Dr. Kapoor act ethically? Why or why not? Informal consultations, such as occurred in this case, are common in Indian culture. Should culture be taken into consideration, or should ethical principles transcend cultural values?

Sunil said, "That sounds like a good plan. What's the fellow's name?"
Rem answered, "Not a fellow. A woman. Dr. Norah Coleman."

"Dr. Norah Coleman," Sunil repeated. He got out his phone and entered the name so he would remember it.

"Will it be a problem for you that she's a woman?" Rem asked.

"No, not at all."

"She's black as well."

"Is she good at what she does?" Sunil asked in return.

"Not just good. She's the best." Rem assured him.

---

11. Should Dr. Kapoor have described Dr. Coleman's gender and race? Why or why not?

"Dr. Norah Coleman is who we want then. Rem, could you tell me again what you think is going on with my son?" Sunil asked.

"Sure, but this is just an unofficial opinion, not a diagnosis. I think it's Non-Rapid Eye Movement Sleep Arousal Disorder, a parasomnia. Specifically, I think your son has sleepwalking and sleep terrors. You're going to go home and Google it, aren't you, Sunil?"

"You know I am," Sunil replied as he entered the information into his phone. "Wouldn't you do the same for one of your children?"

"Yes, you bet I would. We're doctors—we want to learn everything and know everything," Rem answered.

"Rem, I greatly appreciate all your help. I know nothing you said was official, but at least it gives me something to go on," Sunil said appreciatively.

"Sunil, give Dr. Coleman a call. She's terrific. And one more thing I should tell you—this is a very treatable problem," Rem said as he smiled.

"Thank you again, Rem. And thanks for the hopeful words," Sunil finished.

---

12. Have your opinions regarding Dr. Kapoor changed at all regarding how ethically he behaved?

CASE 11

Demond Jackson

Annamarie Castro was only three days into her first job as a juvenile probation officer when she was assigned the case of Demond Jackson. She knew she wanted to make a difference in the lives of Cincinnati's most troubled youth, so she took a job right after college working with boys aged 12–18 at the Cincinnati Juvenile Detention Center (CJDC). Demond's file was two inches thick, and Annamarie opened the file like a textbook, beginning to read at page one, unsure about what was important or what she needed to know. Her supervisor told her that Demond had to go to court this week, and Annamarie knew she would need to read his file, meet with him, and make decisions about placement for him at that time. She stumbled across an intake form from a previous psychiatric hospital, finding it helpful:

Demographic Information:
Name: Demond Anthony Jackson
Date of intake: 7/7/13
DOB: 09/08/1998
Age/race/sex: 14-year-old African American/Black Male

He's not quite fifteen years old, the same age as my youngest brother.

Date of Placement/Legal Charges:
Demond Anthony Jackson was placed at CJDC on July 7, 2013, for charges of Breaking and Entering, Theft, Possession of Stolen Goods, Aggravated Assault, Marijuana Possession, Public Intoxication, and Evading and Fleeing Police.

Arrest Report from Cincinnati Police:
On July 6, 2013, at 1:46 AM, Demond, along with two other juveniles (ages 16 and 17), broke into a neighbor's house and, when apprehended, had in their possession the neighbor's prescription medication, cell phone, and $420 cash. The neighbor, Robert A. Smith, woke and confronted the boys, and Demond brandished a gun and threatened to shoot him. Mr. Smith attempted to get the gun from Demond, who fired at him three times, shooting him in the arm and shoulder. A neighbor called 911 and Demond attempted to flee. He was arrested several blocks away. Demond had been using marijuana, was intoxicated at the time of arrest, and was in possession of 14 ounces of marijuana.

97

Annamarie stopped reading. *"What kind of messed up kid would do this?"* she wondered.

1. Briefly discuss how you would answer Annamarie's question.
2. On a scale of 1 to 10, write down a number representing how much you see Demond at fault for his situation and how much you see the system at fault. "1" indicates that Demond's situation is totally his own responsibility, and his current predicament is due to his own choices. "10" indicates that he has no responsibility, and that environmental or contextual factors explain his situation. Share your views with your colleagues and discuss them.

Previous placements:
Biological parents (Darren and Ladonna Jackson), 1998–2003
Cincinnati Children's Emergency Shelter 03/04/03 to 03/05/03
Cincinnati Children's Emergency Shelter 07/13/03 to 07/15/03
Cincinnati Children's Emergency Shelter 11/13/03 to 11/14/03
Therapeutic Foster Home (Collins family) 11/14/03 to 11/27/03
McCollock Psychiatric Hospital 11/27/03 to 12/03/03
Gloria Harris (Maternal Grandmother) 12/03/03 to 2/8/04
Jayla and Aaron Carter (maternal aunt and uncle) 2/08/04 to 04/02/06
  (AWOL twice)
Cincinnati Children's Emergency Shelter 04/02/06 to 04/14/06
Fairhaven Residential Facility 04/14/06 to 06/07/07 (AWOL twice)
Therapeutic Foster Home (unknown name) 06/07/07 to (date unknown)
Note: Often spent time at maternal grandmother's Home (Gloria Harris)

Geez. What happened to him from 2007 until now?

Annamarie noted additional placements in the margin as she found them later on in his file, but it took a great deal of detective work and hours of reading to make a logical chronology of Demond's life after 2007. After much effort, she penciled in the following information:

Placid Place Psychiatric Hospital (dates unknown, 2008)
Placid Place Psychiatric Hospital (dates unknown, 2010)
Cincinnati Juvenile Detention Center 07/15/11-08/22/11
Karen's Place (Residential Facility) 08/22/11 to 12/19/12
Therapeutic Foster Home (Mateo and Sofia Soto family) 12/19/12 to
  04/04/13 (Dates?)
Cincinnati Juvenile Detention Center 04/04/13 to 04/22/13
Therapeutic Foster Home (Soto family) 04/22-13-07/07/13 (Dates?)

Annamarie stared at the list, noting Demond's ages by the various dates, trying to figure out how old he was each time he moved from one place to the next.

This is crazy. Why did he move so much?
How come he just didn't stay in one place or with one family?

3. What are the reasons that Demond may have moved so much?

4. Consider that Demond was approximately four or five when he was first removed from his biological parents. What do you know about childhood development from birth to age five? How might being removed from his parents and sent to an emergency shelter have affected Demond?

Previous legal history: In addition to his current charges, Demond has a history of Aggravated Assault, Truancy, Criminal Mischief, Trespassing, Property Destruction, Terroristic Threatening, Theft, Fighting (x4), and Public Intoxication. Demond reports that he's a member of Cincinnati's Hillside Gang.

This kid's a train wreck. He's going to kill himself or someone else.

Psychiatric history: Demond has been diagnosed with Attention Deficit Hyperactivity Disorder, Oppositional Defiant Disorder, Conduct Disorder, Reactive Attachment Disorder, Mood Disorder NOS, Post-traumatic Stress Disorder, Intermittent Explosive Disorder, Bipolar Disorder, and Substance Abuse/Dependence. He's received therapy over the years at various residential treatment and outpatient mental health centers. He received one year of treatment for substance abuse problems at Karen's Place.

*Are there any diagnoses this kid **didn't** get?*
Isn't that basically the whole book of diagnoses?

Annamarie tried to remember her psychology classes from college and recall if there were any diagnoses that weren't on the long list.

Surely he can't be having all those problems at the same time.
Some of those diagnoses must be wrong, or outdated.

5. Discuss whether you think a person can have multiple diagnoses or whether these records just indicate sloppy work on the part of clinicians. Can diagnoses change as a person develops?

6. What are your hypotheses for the most likely diagnoses for Demond?

Substance abuse history: The following information was gathered from an intake summary at Karen's Place Residential Facility, which specializes in treatment of children with substance-abuse problems.

Demond reported that he first drank alcohol at age 9. He smoked his first cigarette at age 10. Demond noted that he drinks alcohol "whenever he can get it" and that he plans to keep using because it "relaxes" him. He notes that he now requires higher levels of alcohol to feel its effects and currently drinks a "12 pack without getting much of a buzz."

In addition to alcohol use, Demond reported that he began using marijuana at age 12. He noted that the amount of marijuana he needs to take to get "high" has steadily increased since age 12. Demond has also stolen goods to purchase marijuana, has sold marijuana, has used marijuana despite negative effects on his family and legal situation, and has skipped school on numerous occasions to get "high." Demond noted that he "loves to be high" and would be intoxicated "all the time if I could."

In addition, Demond noted that he's tried cocaine two times, K2, and spice (synthetic marijuana) four or five times, PCP one time ("That stuff is weird. I don't like being out of control."), and sniffed a mixture of glue, paint, and fingernail polish remover ("one time. I passed out and this guy stole all my money.")

You've got to be kidding. He started drinking when he was nine? When I was nine, I was still playing with dolls. He drinks a 12-pack of beer without getting drunk? What is K2? What is spice? Where does he get the money to buy these drugs? Can you really sniff fingernail polish remover, glue, and paint? What happens to you when you do?

Medical history: Demond weighed 5 lbs. 1 oz. at birth. He was born four weeks early, and the cord was wrapped around his neck at birth. He had to be revived at birth because he was a "blue baby." He's broken his right arm twice. No other medical problems are noted.

At least that is something good about him. He's healthy. But why was he born so early? How long did he go without oxygen when he was born? And how did he break his arm twice?

Developmental history: Unknown

Why don't we know his developmental history? And why is his placement history so long?

School history: Demond attended George Washington Carver Elementary School from kindergarten to third grade. School records reported numerous absences, poor parent involvement, and a history of poor academic progress and behavioral problems. Demond was suspended from school in first grade for bringing a knife to school.

In third grade, he came to school intoxicated from alcohol, which caused a Child Protective Service (CPS) investigation that eventually led to his removal from the Carter family home because of substantiated child abuse charges. Demond's current academics are approximately two to three years behind his expected grade level.

*He brought a knife to school in first grade? He was only six years old! Where did he even get a knife at such a young age? And he was drunk in third grade? Where does a nine-year-old kid get alcohol? And how could his mother let her son go to school drunk? Or even **get** drunk? Where was she?*

Abuse history:
Substantiated abuse charges include:
Child Neglect (Physical neglect x4)
Child Neglect (Emotional neglect x3)
Child Neglect (Medical neglect x2)
Child Neglect (Educational neglect x2)
Child Abuse (Physical abuse x4)
Child Abuse (Emotional abuse x2)

What in the world happened to this boy?

Brief family history: Demond's parents are Darren and Ladonna Jackson. Demond has two younger full siblings: Darius and Deondre (twins—a boy and girl, age 12). He has a younger half-sister, Jahzara, age 10. Darren and Ladonna were never married but lived together as husband and wife. CPS was involved on multiple occasions because of neglect and abuse charges. Abuse was substantiated multiple times over a series of years. Apparently, the children were disciplined by being whipped with extension cords, hit in the face, pushed down stairs, or locked in their rooms. They were left alone without supervision for days at a time, and Demond was expected to watch his younger brother and sisters. The home had almost no food or furnishings in it as Ladonna apparently sold any household belongings to purchase drugs. Darren and Ladonna were reportedly "crack heads" per maternal grandmother's (Gloria Harris) report. Ms. Harris regularly watched all of the children, often for weeks at a time, when Demond's biological parents were unable to do so. Darren and Ladonna were minimally compliant with CPS services and recommendations, typically doing the least amount required so that their children would not be removed.

Demond was a witness to domestic violence in the home, including a forcible rape that the children were made to watch. This occurred between Demond's biological parents, Darren and Ladonna, when Demond was approximately four years old. Darren and Ladonna separated in late February of 2003. Ladonna was pregnant by another man at the time. When she was eight months pregnant, Darren drove to her house and shot her seven times while they were standing in the driveway. Ladonna died from these injuries on March 7, 2003. Jahzara, the child with whom she was pregnant, survived but has numerous medical complications along with intellectual and developmental delays. Darren was found guilty of murder and attempted homicide (because of the baby) and currently is serving concurrent life sentences at the Ohio State Penitentiary. Darren's parental rights were terminated in 2003. The children were removed permanently at this point.

Demond, Darius, and Deondre (the twins) were sent to live with their maternal grandmother, Gloria Harris. This arrangement lasted only a few months. A school teacher filed a CPS report alleging that Demond told her that Ms. Harris had slapped him across the face when he talked back to her. CPS investigated Ms. Harris. She admitted that she slapped Demond and stated that she would not stop. She considered slapping a child for talking back to be good discipline, not abuse. The children were removed from Ms. Harris's home and placed with the Carters. Ms. Harris was granted supervised visits. She visited only sporadically after this point.

Demond and his twin siblings were adopted by his maternal aunt and uncle, Jayla and Aaron Carter. However, while under their care, numerous child abuse and neglect complaints were investigated and substantiated from 2003 to 2006. Abuse to the children included being hit, kicked, spit at, and called names. Demond had his arm broken by Mr. Carter when Demond made too much noise brushing his teeth. The children were removed permanently in 2006. Jayla's and Aaron's parental rights were terminated at that time. All of the children were sent to the Cincinnati Children's Emergency Center.

Darius is currently in a residential treatment center near Dayton, Ohio. Deondre is in a therapeutic foster home near Columbus. Jahzara lives in a facility for individuals with developmental delays in Columbus. Demond hasn't seen his siblings since they were removed from the Carter residence.

Current long-term plans for Demond are unknown. His current foster family, Mateo and Sofia Soto, are not interested in his returning to their care and don't want to be involved in treatment.

7. Revisit the scale you wrote earlier regarding responsibility. Has your number changed regarding who is at fault for his situation?

8. Explain to your group why your number regarding responsibility stayed the same or moved. What are the clinical implications of your beliefs regarding responsibility?

9. Do you believe your own cultural background/religion/ethnicity/gender affect your views of Demond's level of being responsible for his problems?

10. Do you consider Demond's grandmother slapping him to be physical abuse?

Annamarie stopped reading and got up to get a diet soda.

What a terrible history. Did anything ever go right for this kid? Who claims him?
Where do I even begin to make sense out of what should happen to Demond Jackson?
How do I pronounce his name: DaMond? DeeMond? How am I supposed to
know where to place this kid and what he needs? When I get home, I'm calling
my mom and dad to tell them that they're amazing. How did I get so lucky to
have them as parents? And how did Demond get so unlucky?

Annamarie read what seemed to be an afterthought in Demond's file:

Strengths and social history: Demond likes football, basketball, hip hop and rap music, and the Cincinnati Bearcats. He says he has lots of friends and girlfriends. He reports that he's heterosexual. He reports his religion as Christian. No denomination was specified.

OK. When do I meet this kid? And what should I say to him when I do?

11. Some children show extremely limited pro-social emotions, demonstrated by a lack of remorse and a lack of empathy to others. These children also show emotional shallowness or insincerity and can turn their emotions "on" and "off" to benefit themselves (APA, 2013). When these pro-social behaviors are particularly absent, we consider the child to demonstrate *psychopathy*—longstanding personality traits in which a person has absolutely no regard for others' feelings or rights. Do you think Demond exhibits psychopathy? Why or why not?

12. Some clinicians think that conduct problems in a child are so closely intertwined with poor parenting that it's unfair to diagnose the child with such a pejorative diagnosis as Conduct Disorder when the parents contributed to the development of the problems. What do you think? Should the parents of a child with conduct problems shoulder some diagnostic responsibility? Or is this blaming the parents for a child's choices?

Annamarie suddenly looked up at the clock and realized that she needed to leave for her appointment to meet Demond. Annamarie's mind was a jumbled tangle of thoughts as she walked the short block from the Juvenile Justice building over to CJDC. She tried to remember lessons that might be helpful from school: evidence-based social work, multicultural sensitivity, the correlation of lower socioeconomic status and conduct problems, and the racial inequity in the justice system. None of these thoughts seemed even remotely helpful to her at this moment, as she tried to figure out what to say to Demond and where to recommend placing him.

Annamarie arrived at CJDC. The CJDC security officer checked her purse and her ID, introduced himself to her, and pointed to the waiting area where she would meet Demond. She sat and waited, reflexively smoothing her clothes as if she were waiting for a job interview.

What am I going to say to him?

13. Put yourself in Annamarie's place. You are going to meet Demond
    in a moment. Remembering what you have learned about clinical
    interventions and interviewing clients, write down three or four
    good opening lines you might use to begin building a relationship
    with Demond.
14. What are your main goals for your meeting with him?
15. What do you expect Demond to be like when you meet him?
16. How would your race, ethnicity, and gender affect how Demond
    might perceive you?

Soon, an attractive, slightly built African American boy wearing a fluorescent orange jumpsuit marked CJDC sauntered over to her, smiled in an
almost flirtatious manner, and asked: "Hey, babe. Wassup? Nobody told me
my new P.O. was hot."

Although Annamarie tried not to be flattered, she was. And whatever
plans she had to speak were thwarted until she finally stammered: "Hello . . .
Demond. I'm Annamarie Castro. I've been assigned to your case." As an
afterthought, she began to add: "And please don't call me babe. . . ."

Demond interrupted. "So . . . how quick can you get me outta this place?"

"Demond, you have court coming up this week. And the charges against
you, well, they're very serious. I don't know if I *can* get you out of this place,"
Annamarie countered.

Demond grinned at Annamarie and playfully retorted, "Sure you can.
Just tell the judge that you think I'm a good kid who needs a second chance
and is misunderstood and all that shit."

"I'm sure you are misunderstood. But that doesn't mean you can go
shooting at people and committing burglary," Annamarie felt like she had her
bearings now.

Demond's face changed in a moment, his joviality replaced by sudden
rage. "Don't start that crap with me!" he shouted. "I don't have to listen to it!"

"Look, Demond. My job is to recommend to the judge what should happen to you next. So, I'm asking you. What should happen to you next?"
Annamarie asked plaintively.

Demond paused a moment and then replied, "Send me back to Mateo
and Sophia's place. They all right."

"You mean the Sotos' foster home? I don't think that's an option,"
responded Annamarie.

"You can make it be an option! Just get me outta here—I don't care
where you send me. This place sucks. I only get outta my room for an hour a
day, and they watch you shower. I got no privacy. And the kids in here is
messed up, trying to make goo-goo eyes at me and then turn around and

threaten me and shit." Demond was visibly angry, and his voice skipped an octave as he told Annamarie about his experiences at the facility.

Annamarie was unfazed by his anger. "Demond. You need to listen to me. Give me one good reason why I should convince the judge not to send you away until you're eighteen."

"Because I don't want to go," Demond said frustratedly.

"I said a *good* reason. I need something better than that," Annamarie said as she leaned in closely.

Demond's face changed again, this time registering something that Annamarie thought looked like despair. "Because I got nothing. I got nobody. I got no reason for anything," he said matter-of-factly. Annamarie was leveled—not by his stare, but by the tears that welled up in his dark brown eyes but refused to fall. With that statement, Demond shrugged his shoulders, stared another moment at Annamarie, and asked to be taken back to his room by a detention officer.

Annamarie watched him walk out of the room, wondering if he'd any idea how powerful the words he'd just spoken were. She wasn't sure whether to cry, shake him, hug him, or walk away. She also had no idea what her recommendation to the judge would be. In short, she was more confounded than she was before she met Demond. She wished for a moment that she'd listened to her mother and become an interior decorator. She looked at the detention officer, who just stared blankly at her. Annamarie got up to leave and walked slowly back to her office.

17. If you were Annamarie and Demond called you a "babe," how would you have responded?

18. Review what Demond said in the previous passage. Overall, how would you assess Demond's motivation to change?

19. If you were Annamarie, what would you recommend for Demond, and why? What factors most influenced your decision?

20. Annamarie's ethnicity is unspecified. However, because her last name is Castro, you might assume she is Hispanic. What do you think her racial, ethnic and socioeconomic status background is? Why? How do you think her race will affect Demond's treatment? How would treatment unfold if she were a different race?

21. Does Demond's last statement make you think he might be suicidal? If you were Annamarie, what would your next statement be to Demond? If you felt he were suicidal, what would your ethical obligations be?

22. Sometimes we have a strong reaction to our clients based on our own values and beliefs. Given your values, would it be hard for you to work with a child such as Demond? What aspects of his behavior would be most challenging for you?

CASE 12

Lacy Davis-Woodrow

The binder thudded as it flopped onto Camila's desk. It looked thick, maybe between 50 and 100 pages of typed notes. "Sorry about the notes, but it's the only thing we could think to do to keep things straight. We needed to keep a handle on all of Lacy's insanity, especially after her second hospitalization for suicidal behavior," Kayla Davis-Woodrow said. Kayla was Lacy's mother, a real estate agent at a local company. She was an elegant, tall, Caucasian woman, approximately 40 years of age. She wore a long black and blue dress with a beautiful, expensive-looking beaded turquoise necklace. She clearly cared about her appearance, evidenced by her impeccable makeup, hair, and nails.

Camila curiously flipped through the first couple of pages of the binder. The pages were sorted by date, with color-coded tabs for each new month. The binder also had a second set of tabs, color-coded and labeled with problem areas: "Anger," "Marijuana," "Sadness," and "Suicide." Camila had been working exclusively with teenagers at a community mental health center in New York City for almost 15 years, but she'd never been handed a detailed binder like this one. She was flustered by the enormity of the notes presented to her.

On the cover of the binder "Lacy Davis-Woodrow" was typed in 36-point font. *So much for confidentiality*, thought Camila.

* * *

Camila Rodrigues grew up in Queens to second-generation Puerto Rican parents. Both her maternal and paternal grandparents had immigrated to the United States after World War II as young adults. Camila's father was a construction worker and her mother was a hotel maid. Both stressed the importance of education to their four daughters. They believed wholeheartedly in the American Dream of working hard to gain new opportunities.

Camila took these views to heart. Not only did she earn her bachelor's degree, she also became the first person in her family to earn a master's degree. She graduated with her MS degree in clinical psychology, the only person of Puerto Rican descent in her class. Camila had entered the field when psychology was just beginning to become more receptive toward women and people of color. She knew well how people sized up her petite frame and underestimated what she was capable of doing, looking at her like a flower in danger of wilting without their protection. When she chose to do her master's-level clinical internship in a men's prison in Georgia, one of her professors was particularly dismissive and argued that the prisoners would "eat a pretty little girl like you alive." Camila enjoyed a challenge and liked to prove people wrong, but her patience for misogyny and racism had grown thin over the years. Her grittiness had served her well, as she'd spent the last 15 years specializing in substance-abusing teenagers with co-morbid personality disorders. Her favorite clients were the ones whom other therapists either referred out or dreaded seeing.

1. How should Camila have responded to the comment by her professor?
2. How do you think Camila's professional development was influenced by being the only woman and the only Puerto Rican in her master's program? How might her experiences of racism and misogyny affect her?
3. What are your hypotheses about the Davis-Woodrow family given the extensive file that they created?

"Everything spiraled out of control this last school year. We had to have a way to keep it all straight," Kayla continued. Mark Davis-Woodrow, Kayla's husband, nodded emphatically. He was an equally tall black man of about 45, muscular, and as well-groomed as his wife. He wore a suit with a colorful red tie that matched his belt and socks. He was a night manager at a hotel and typically worked long hours every week in a high-pressure environment. "Kayla's right. We were having trouble keeping things straight. Lacy's just out of control!" Mark added, waving his hands in exasperation.

Kayla shot her husband a withering look and put her hands over his waving arms. "Settle down, Mark. Don't make a scene," Kayla commanded. Mark rolled his eyes, unnoticed by Camila but not by his wife, who furrowed her brow and stared at him.

Camila nodded in their direction, thumbing over some of the notes. She noticed a longer one titled "CPS Report, July 6." It read as follows:

> I (Kayla) received a phone call at work today. I spoke with Eden Barker, another Child Protective Services worker. She stated she needed to talk to me regarding abuse allegations made by Lacy. We arranged to meet the following day. I kept the kids home from camp and stayed home from work to meet with Ms. Barker. The first thing she said when she walked in the door was, "I see this isn't the first time we've come to your house." I was terrified. Ms. Barker spoke to all of us in turn. First me, then Mark, then Lacy. The whole "investigation" took about an hour. Ms. Barker was just as snotty to me as the last worker was, as if she had already decided I was a child beater.
>
> Apparently, Lacy had some bruises on her arms from some rope activity at camp. A camp counselor noticed the bruises the next day and took her aside to talk about them. Lacy began to cry and stated that her par-

ents were hitting her. The camp counselor spoke to the director, who called CPS. I told Eden that we don't beat our daughter and that I had no idea what Lacy was talking about. Eden took some notes, but it was clear she did not believe a word that I said.

However, Eden changed her mind after she spoke with Lacy. Lacy recanted her confession and admitted that she'd made up the whole story. Mark was extremely angry. I had to calm him down while the CPS worker was there, or else we may have been in some trouble. Lacy came out of her room crying. I told Mark to take a walk and held Lacy as she cried. Eden closed her notebook and told us that she saw no evidence of abuse. I thanked her for her time. Lacy remained listless the whole evening, refusing to eat dinner or say a word to either me or Mark.

The following day, I followed up with Safe Harbor Health. They scheduled an intake appointment with Camila Rodrigues, MA, for July 26 at 3:00 PM.

Beside the note was scribbled, "Bring Mark and Lacy, Safe Harbor paperwork from online, and check for payment."

"Why don't you stop telling me what to do, Kayla?" Mark asked his wife, snapping Camila back into the immediacy of the session.

"Sorry for my husband's rude behavior, Dr. Rodrigues. I don't know what's come over him," Kayla responded, pinching her husband lightly on the leg.

"It's OK. One thing I need to let you know is that I'm not a doctor. I have my Master's degree, however, and more than thirty years of experience in the field. You can call me Camila," she said warmly.

Camila noticed how much she felt pulled to be in the middle of the family dynamics, even though they were only ten minutes into the initial intake interview. She decided to redirect the conversation entirely.

"Can you tell me more about what's bringing you here? I noticed you've also seen Dr. Carmackle, a clinical psychologist, and Mrs. Shoefer, an LCSW. How did things work out with them?" Camila asked.

Kayla snapped, "Well, they didn't seem to think anything was wrong. Yet we got notes from school almost the whole year about Lacy's emotional outbursts. One day, she loves her friends; the next day, she cusses them out. Last week, she asked our permission to get her new best friend's name, Angel, tattooed on her arm. This week she said that she and Angel were no longer speaking because Angel was trying to steal Darryl, her boyfriend. If Darryl threatens to break up, she's devastated and says she's going to kill herself. That happens at least once a month. She gets angry for no reason and the other kids think she's crazy. She hangs out with all of the wrong kids—the kids who get suspended and have a reputation as troublemakers. These kids drive crazy fast! Lacy rode with a guy—not Darryl—on his motorcycle and convinced him to go 90 miles per hour, and they weren't even wearing helmets! We know she drinks and smokes marijuana, and we even caught her using a few times in her bathroom before school. I think she's been using it more and more." Kayla scarcely paused between each sentence as she spoke.

"I don't know where or how she's even getting the pot." Mark interrupted.

Kayla ignored him, looked back to Camila, and continued. "The problem is that the last two therapists didn't believe anything was wrong. They saw her as a perfect little angel. Both Dr. Carmackle and Mrs. Shoefer made Mark and me out to be the problem. Apparently, Lacy complained to both therapists that we fought all the time, lied to her, and were physically abusive. She cuts herself, nothing serious because she uses earring backs and paper clips, but her thighs and arms are just covered with marks. Then she'll blame her cuts on me, saying that I scratch her. She lies all the time. But it's like everyone refuses to believe that she does anything wrong."

Mark added, "Kayla's right. We're really worried about Lacy, but no one else seems to be. I know we're not a perfect couple, but we're OK parents. What I worry the most about Lacy is that she doesn't seem to know who she is at all. I mean, I know she's only 17, but she's clueless as to what's important to her—what she believes in or wants in her life. Her moods are so changeable. She gets so angry that she'll even yell at the dog, whose only mistake seems to be lying on the floor in her way, and then suddenly she'll be so sad, saying that life is all a big joke and she's just a floating piece of nothingness. She actually said that to me the other day."

Camila listened to what Mark and Kayla were saying as she watched the interaction between the two. Something wasn't quite right with Lacy for certain; her substance use, cutting behavior, lying, and manipulation of others were serious red flags. However, something wasn't quite right between her parents as well.

That's odd, thought Camila.

She noticed that Mark and Kayla were holding hands. In fact, Mark had taken his wife's hand and was gently caressing it.

*Two minutes ago, his wife was pinching him. Five minutes ago, she stared
at him with such anger that I thought she might get up and hit him.
And now they're holding hands?*

"Tell me more about Lacy using pot," requested Camila.

Kayla answered, "Her pot smoking has gotten worse. She'll claim she's never smoked pot, but we've caught her red-handed twice. I found a bong, a small bag of weed, and five joints sitting in her bedside table last week. You just don't have those things if you're not using them."

Mark added, "The drug dogs found pot in her locker at school in April. She got sent to alternative school for five days. I know she's using this summer, too. She's hard to catch, but you can smell it on her clothes after she comes home from hanging out with her friends."

Kayla sighed. "It's all in the binder. Just read it. I know it seems obsessive to keep a binder on our daughter, but we had to do it. We were being told so many different stories from so many different people. Lacy would tell us one thing, her teacher another, the counselor another, and her friends' parents another. It's been awful. We had no idea what to do other than write it down. She plays us against each other constantly—telling us lies about what the other person said."

At this comment, Mark and Kayla stopped holding hands.

Camila nodded. "You've told me a little about how she is at school. Could you share a bit more?"

Mark jumped in, "At school, it's the strangest thing. Some of her teachers think she's perfect. She gets excellent grades in some classes, like trigonometry. Lacy loves trig, but she couldn't care less about other classes. If she doesn't care about them, she fails them. She makes a snap decision about the teacher at the beginning of the year. If she likes her teacher, she gets an A. If she doesn't, she fails. Really, her grades have been slipping this whole year. She never had any trouble at all up until the tenth grade. But since about two years ago, everything has been a disaster." At this point, Mark stood up and waved his hands wildly as if to punctuate his statements and continued.

"We've been shocked with her behavior at school this past year. She was suspended once for using drugs and three times for fighting. And she fights with people who are supposed to be her friends. She got in a fist fight with a girl who she was laughing and cuddling with the day before! Lacy punched her in the face at school. She said her friend 'stole some green,' whatever that means."

Kayla again chastised Mark for being too excited. "Mark, slow down. Camila can only write so fast." She rolled her eyes and added sarcastically, "Really!" as she sighed exasperatedly.

Camila thanked them for their candor. She asked them one more question to close the intake interview: "What does Lacy do well? What are her strengths?"

Kayla answered, "Well, she's smart. And beautiful. And funny, in a sarcastic way. But it's hard to see any of that anymore. In fact, it's hard to see anything except the constant train wrecks she leaves in her wake."

4. Lacy has some serious behavioral, emotional and family problems. What would most concern you if you were Camila? What diagnosis or diagnoses would best match your concerns?

5. Think about the family dynamics present. What might cause such dynamics? How do you think they might play out at home?

6. Camila chose not to comment on the marital interactions between Mark and Kayla. Do you agree with her decision? Why or why not? What would you have said if you had chosen to comment?

Camila thought for a moment. *It's a good thing that I like tough cases. This one is going to be a humdinger.*

She then said, "Let's bring Lacy in. I'd like to hear a bit about what she's experiencing."

Kayla nodded and went out into the waiting room, returning moments later with Lacy. Lacy was a very pretty, biracial girl with fairly dark skin color. She looked several years older than her 16 years of age. She had very attractive features, was tall like her parents, and was curvaceous but chunky. She was wearing very short white shorts and a hoodie with a giant 'X' on it. Camila silently reflected on how Lacy's overdone makeup detracted from her natural beauty. She recognized the hoodie from a local all-boys high school. Lacy sat down nervously between her parents.

"Hey Lacy! I'm Ms. Rodrigues. How are you?" Camila inquired kindly but firmly.

"I'm fine," Lacy answered succinctly. She looked nervous.

"Tell me what's up, Lacy. What's your story?" Camila asked nonchalantly.

Lacy hesitated, looking back and forth between her parents. "I'm afraid," she said simply.

"Of?" Camila asked inquisitively.

Lacy hesitated, looking sullen, her eyes staring daggers into the floor. "I don't know."

Camila waited.

"I feel too much. You probably don't know what I mean," Lacy continued dramatically after several moments of silence.

Camila looked at her calmly and said gently, "Perhaps not. But right now, I'm asking what you've been feeling recently. It sounds like it's been pretty rough."

Lacy relaxed a little in her chair. "Yeah, it has been. CPS keeps coming over." She shot a mischievous look at her parents.

Before they could respond, Camila said, "I heard. Your parents were kind enough to take notes. Now, you said you're afraid. Can you tell me more?"

Lacy hesitated again. "Of lots of things, I guess. What if everyone dies on the planet and it's just me left, like happened to Will Smith in *I Am Legend*? Or what if the world is just a big giant drama set and all a sham? What if everything is actually nothing? Mostly, I'm afraid that I'm nothing. That I'm completely empty and nobody can ever make me feel whole. I'm afraid my parents will abandon me, too. Just take off for Mexico or something."

She paused for a moment and looked to her parents. They looked shocked but didn't speak.

Lacy continued, growing suddenly irritable. "They fight all the time, you know. Mostly about money. We don't have any, you know. All the fancy clothes and jewelry—it's a front. The Jeep—well, it's on a lease we can't get out of. And we're upside-down on the house as well. It's all a front. At home, Dad yells and Mom just stands there. They always put me in the middle." The tone in her voice was harsher than before. Camila glanced at Mark, who looked furious.

Mark responded in quick anger, "We fight all the time? We do all of this for you because we love you, and you lie behind our backs and complain that *we* fight all the time?"

Lacy looked mortified and began to cry. In response to her tears, Kayla began to console her and pleaded with Mark, "Can you not yell at her in here? Not now. Look at what you're doing to her." Her voice was controlled as much as it was controlling. Mark continued to look furious, crossing his arms and furrowing his brow.

Lacy looked at Camila. "You see? This happens all the time."

"You got that right," Mark interjected.

Lacy cried in her mother's arms. "I love you, Mom. Why does Dad do this to me? Tell him I'm mad at him."

Camila immediately thought:

> *The wider the gap between a couple, the more space a child has in which to manipulate. This child has a big gap indeed. No wonder she's become so good at manipulation. I need to switch gears in this interview. Dealing with the triangulation and splitting in this family is too volatile right now.*

"Lacy, can you tell me about some of your friends?" Camila asked.

Lacy looked up and immediately brightened, stopping the tears instantly. "I have dope friends. They know how to keep it real. Like John. He's so nice. He gave me his hoodie to wear last night because I got cold."

"John? I thought it was Darryl?" Kayla exclaimed.

"You thought WHAT was Darryl, Mom? Honestly, you're so out of it!" Lacy lashed out at her mom.

Kayla responded with her own anger, "Lacy! I meant that I thought you were dating Darryl."

"I am dating Darryl. I'm just wearing John's hoodie," Lacy responded sarcastically. She continued, "You just don't like Darryl because he isn't black."

Kayla countered, "Lacy, it's hard to like someone when the first time you meet them they smell like they just smoked a joint."

Lacy was up for the argument, "Not for me, mom. I find it sexy."

Mr. Davis-Woodrow stepped in, "Lacy. Kayla. Stop this, please."

Kayla wanted to get in the last word. "Lacy, all I'm saying is that the first date you went on with Darryl, you came back from the movies higher than a kite. And you thought the whole thing was a joke!"

Lacy began crying again. "Mom! It was just one joint! I wasn't high! It takes a lot more than one joint for me to get high! Why do you say such mean things about me? I'm your daughter! Don't you love me?"

Camila gently turned the boiling conversation back down to a simmer as she said, "Lacy, I'm glad that you brought up Darryl not being black. If I could ask, what race is he?"

Lacy answered, "Just white, I guess. I don't know. I never really asked him."

Kayla stepped in again, sounding as if she were looking for a fight: "What do you mean, you don't know? You've been dating this jerk for like six or seven months and you don't even know his race?"

Camila slowed the conversation down again by saying, "It occurs to me that we have four different races in the room. Kayla. You're white, correct? And Mark, you're black, correct?"

Both parents nodded in assent.

"Lacy, you're biracial, right? Is that a term you like to describe your race, or do you prefer another?"

"No, biracial's cool. That's fine," responded Lacy.

"I'm Puerto Rican. So, we have one black person, one white person, one biracial person, and one Puerto Rican person. We also have three women and one man. These differences are good, but they also mean that we have plenty of chances to miscommunicate when we talk. We need to be thoughtful in our words, to make sure that they're heard as we intended them to be heard."

Lacy chimed in, "Dr. . . . I mean, Ms. Rodrigues? I think it's cool that you talk about race so matter-of-factly. You just say it like it is."

"I think it's time we headed home," Kayla said curtly, looking at Mark with a knowing stare. Camila stood up, surprised by the abrupt decision of the family to leave her office and tried quickly to regain control over the situation.

"I'd like to see you again, Lacy. Please call our administrative assistant to find an open time sometime in the next week," Camila said as the family left her office.

---

7. If you were Camila, what would be your emotional reaction to this family? What would be your clinical conceptualization?

8. Google the terms *triangulation* and *splitting*. What examples did you see of triangulation in the initial intake? What about splitting?

9. Given Lacy's age of 17, what are your responsibilities regarding the disclosure of sensitive information with her parents?

10. Review the transcript of the intake session again. Which person do you think is contributing most to the difficult family dynamics, and why? Underline some key statements or behaviors to support your perspective.

Camila was glad that her next scheduled client had canceled, as it gave her some time to reflect on the dynamics of Lacy's family. She had noticed how Lacy was able to manipulate her parents, even during this initial intake interview.

> *Control is a big issue in this family. The family members are so reactive to each other as well. They seem to struggle with keeping their emotions in check, which makes for a pretty combustible situation.*

Camila flipped though Lacy's file. She found several newspaper clippings tucked in the front of the file. One of the newspaper articles described a fatal car accident of a man named Charles Dewilt, a prominent black sociologist who died about 11 years ago.

Why is this article in Lacy's file?

Stapled to the newspaper article was an obituary. It mentioned the surviving relatives of Charles Dewilt, including his wife Kayla Davis and their daughter Lacy, age 6.

So Mark is Lacy's stepfather and Kayla's second husband.

Camila thought for a moment about the accident because the name sounded so familiar. Then she remembered the car wreck because it had been replayed on the news for days, given the professional accomplishments of Mr. Dewilt and the horrific nature of the accident. A semi-truck driver had fallen asleep, crossing the highway median into oncoming traffic. The truck hit Charles's convertible sports car at a high speed, and the car was completely crushed under the semi-truck. Charles was essentially beheaded.

I wonder how this tragedy affected Kayla and Lacy. I'm surprised it didn't come up in our intake interview today. I wonder, too, when Kayla remarried. I wonder if she deliberately tried to marry two black men in a row, or if it just happened.

11. How does the death of Mr. Dewilt affect your understanding of Lacy? Of Kayla? Of Mark?

12. Parents sometimes parent children differently if they're not their biological children. How do you think being a stepparent is affecting Mark's parenting?

13. How does Camila's background influence her work with the Davis-Woodrow family?

14. What diagnosis would you give Lacy, and why?

SECTION 2

Diagnosis and Conceptualization

CASE 1

Enrique Dominguez

Enrique's case is extraordinarily complex as he is a kindergartener with Autism who's also a Mexican immigrant to the United States. Immigrant status is associated with significant health-care challenges, including securing health insurance, accessing culturally competent care, and a lack of understanding of the cultural views of health problems such as autism.

ICD-10/DSM-5 Diagnosis:

F84.0 (299.00) Autism Spectrum Disorder, requiring substantial support in social communication, requiring substantial support in restricted, repetitive behaviors, with accompanying intellectual impairment, with accompanying language impairment

Diagnostic Discussion

The Dominguez family agreed to psychological testing for Enrique. Sarah was concerned about referring the family for testing because she understood that they didn't have insurance, nor could they pay out of pocket for such testing. Sarah also didn't know of a local Spanish-speaking child psychologist. Sarah called a friend of a friend and essentially convinced the psychologist to do the testing for Enrique *pro bono* (for free). Psychologists, as is true for many mental health providers, are expected to give to our communities by providing some reduced rate or free services to individuals in need. The psychologist interviewed Francisco and Rosa María, observed Enrique, and completed a full assessment battery. A month later, the psychologist forwarded the report to Sarah, with permission from Enrique's parents. The comprehensive testing completed by the psychologist showed a high degree of consistency across raters, including Enrique's parents and teacher, Mrs. Miller. The psychologist also completed intellectual testing with Enrique. The overall results showed that Enrique had numerous deficits in his intellectual, adaptive, communication, and behavioral skills.

Enrique meets the criteria for Autism Spectrum Disorder, requiring substantial support in social communication, requiring substantial support in restricted, repetitive behaviors, with accompanying intellectual impairment, with accompanying language impairment. This long-winded diagnosis will be explained in the following diagnostic discussion section. For simplicity, this disorder will be referred to as Autism Spectrum Disorder, or ASD.

ASD consists of five general criteria (APA, 2013, pp. 50-51):

- The person shows persistent deficits in social interaction in multiple settings. This criterion is demonstrated by behaviors such as abnormal nonverbal and verbal communication, failure to initiate social interaction, poor eye contact, problems initiating and maintaining relationships, and/or difficulties playing with peers.

- Restricted, repetitive patterns of behavior, such as stereotyped movements or speech, insistence on sameness, abnormally restricted interests, and/or hypo- or hyper- sensitivity. People with ASD may show *hyposensitivity,* or lack of a reaction to sensory input such as pain or temperature changes. Other people with ASD show *hypersensitivity* to sensory input and even the smallest, softest T-shirt tag causes a tantrum.

- Symptoms must be present during early development. No specific age cut off is noted, but the symptoms may not become fully apparent until the demands of the environment exceed the person's skills. In other words, autism may be more easily noticed in a two-year-old than in a two-month-old.

- Symptoms cause clinically significant impairment in social, occupational, or educational functioning, thus causing significant problems in day-to-day life.

- Disturbances are not better explained by intellectual disability or global developmental delay. A person with moderate or severe intellectual deficits can have ASD, but ASD is not the same disorder as intellectual disabilities. Differentially diagnosing between these overlapping disorders takes careful diagnostic skill.

Enrique meets these criteria, as demonstrated through his behavior in the case study, but also as determined in the psychological evaluation results, which included parent and teacher reports, behavioral observations, intellectual testing, and adaptive functioning assessment.

Enrique demonstrates the first criterion of impairment in social communication and interaction. He rarely initiates social interactions, and when he does, he intends to gain something, such as a crayon or toy train. When his mother took the toy train he wanted, Enrique began to yell and hit until she returned it to him. Additionally, Enrique doesn't engage in reciprocal behaviors or communication. For example, he fails to respond to his name or share with others. Enrique also exhibits nonverbal communication deficits, such as a lack of eye contact and limited understanding of facial expressions. When his mother was crying, Enrique was oblivious and continued to play and laugh. Enrique appears to have an overall limited understanding of relationships.

Enrique engages in repetitive motor movements as evidenced by the repeated flapping of his hands, rocking, and bouncing, thus meeting the second criterion of ASD. This repetitive, purposeless bodily movement is often referred to as *self-stimulatory behavior.* People diagnosed with ASD might engage in self-stimulatory behavior when they experience feelings of discomfort, such as anxiety or sadness, or alternatively, when they're happy. Enrique particularly demonstrates self-stimulatory behavior in noisy or crowded situations that make him anxious. Enrique also uses objects in a repetitive manner, as evidenced by lining up blue crayons and cars and in repeatedly throwing trains during the family meeting with Sarah.

Additionally, Enrique engages in *echolalia*, or parrot-like speech, defined as seemingly involuntary repetition of words or phrases (Arora, 2012). Enrique often repeats the sentence, "Thomas is a useful engine!" at random times and to communicate that he's content. Enrique also displays an insistence on sameness. His inflexibility with routines is best noted on the first day of school, but also when he gets upset because of changes in classroom seating or decorations. Additionally, he became frustrated when his mother interrupted his repetitive train play in Sarah's office. Further, Enrique has highly restricted, fixated interests that are abnormal in intensity, such as his fascination with *Thomas the Tank Engine*, trains in general, and the color blue. Enrique doesn't appear to have hyper- or hypo-reactivity to sensory input, but this symptom isn't necessary for an ASD diagnosis. In fact, no one symptom in and of itself is critical for the diagnosis of ASD. Instead, people diagnosed with ASD demonstrate some of the behaviors from this "illustrative, not exhaustive list" (APA, 2013, p. 50).

Enrique's symptoms began early in his development. One complicating factor is the family's stressful immigration trip from Mexico to the United States when Enrique was a baby. Enrique's parents were worried that he might not survive the trip, so the impact of trauma would need to be carefully considered as the reason for Enrique's delays in meeting his developmental milestones. Even if the trip was traumatic, Enrique is still markedly slower in meeting his developmental milestones than would be expected. For example, he didn't begin speaking until he was four years old. Children usually say their first word by their first birthday (Berk & Meyers, 2016). Enrique didn't engage in the give-and-take, reciprocal, babbling communication and social interaction that is common by age 12 to 18 months. By age two or three, children typically use simple phrases, such as "more train" (Wankoff, 2011). Enrique met none of these important social and communicative milestones. The fact that he was so globally and significantly slow at meeting developmental milestones suggests more problems than trauma.

Enrique's symptoms are clearly causing clinically significant impairment in his social, educational, and familial life. This criterion is a universal concept in psychopathology, because symptoms must be severe enough to cause significant distress in order to be considered psychopathological. Enrique is having difficulties at home, as his mother, siblings, and grandmother help him complete daily living tasks, such as brushing his teeth and getting dressed. Thus, Enrique's difficulties are impacting others. He's also struggling at school both in terms of his academic and social progress.

Lastly, Enrique's symptoms are not better explained by an intellectual disability or global developmental delay. ASD best describes Enrique's encompassing deficits in his social, intellectual, communicative, and adaptive behavior. A diagnosis of ASD involves determining the level of support required regarding social communication and behavior, as well as whether the client has an accompanying intellectual or language impairment. In Enrique's case, he requires substantial support for social communication because he fails to initiate and respond to social interactions. He also needs substantial support to manage his restricted and repetitive behaviors. Finally, Enrique shows accompanying intellectual and language impairments.

1. How do you think that a perilous immigration journey might have affected Enrique as a one-year-old? How did it likely affect his other family members?
2. How do you think Enrique's parents should be told of his diagnosis? Role play some possible dialogue from this discussion.

Case Conceptualization

Many myths have been debunked regarding the etiology of ASD, including bogus explanations that the disorder is caused by the measles/mumps/rubella vaccine, by so-called "refrigerator" moms or cold parenting, or by the presence of gluten or other dietary factors. Although these beliefs have taken root in the public's imagination, none of them are based on any scientific fact (Wilson, Mills, Ross, McGowan, & Jadad, 2003). The research-based truth is that ASD is caused by a complex interplay of genetic, neurological, and environmental factors. Each of these etiological factors are briefly discussed in the section below.

In terms of gender differences, autistic males outnumber autistic females by a ratio of about 4–5:1. In other words, for every four or five boys diagnosed with ASD, only one girl is diagnosed with the same disorder (CDC, 2014; Christensen et al., 2016). Enrique is a boy, so his gender puts him at greater risk for ASD.

Genetics also play a role in the development of ASD. Twin and sibling studies show a greater risk to individuals with family members diagnosed with the disorder (Ozonoff et al., 2011). As is often the case with psychological disorders, the genetic component of ASD cannot be isolated to a single "autism gene." Instead, multiple genetic pathways involving a myriad of genes contribute to the development of the disorder. In fact, current research suggests that up to 1,000 genes may contribute to ASD (Chapman et al., 2011).

Environmental risk factors also contribute to ASD, including maternal infections during pregnancy, maternal diabetes, and maternal drug use (Gardener, Spiegelman, & Buka, 2011). Complications at the time of birth, including fetal distress, a lack of oxygen, and other birth problems indicted by low

Apgar scores are also correlated with ASD (Gardener et al., 2011). Recent research has suggested that maternal use of some medications, including selective serotonin reuptake inhibitors, or SSRIs, also increase the risk of ASD (Boukhris, Sheehy, Mottron, & Berard, 2016). Pesticides and pollutants may also play a role (Eskenazi et al., 2007), possibly through disrupting important thyroid hormones. Finally, advanced paternal age may play a role, with men over age 50 twice as likely to father a child with autism than men younger than age 50 (Hultman, Sandin, Levine, Lichtenstein, & Reichenberg, 2011).

People diagnosed with ASD also show differences in their neuroanatomy compared to people not diagnosed with ASD, including brains that are enlarged in some areas and reduced in others (Koenig, Tsatsanis, & Volkmar, 2001). This seemingly contradictory finding is best explained by abnormal cell growth during the prenatal period as well as the months immediately after birth. The normal processes of neuronal growth and pruning goes awry in people diagnosed with ASD, resulting in brains that have too many neurons in one area and not enough in another area (Minshew, 1996).

You may be wondering what all of these findings have to do with Enrique. The truth is that given Enrique's sparse medical history, we may never know the cause of his ASD. The information in the case study allows us to rule out some factors discussed above, but Enrique's case also leaves open the possibility of many common correlated factors. As a word of caution you've previously heard many times, *correlation is not causation*. In other words, we know that a host of factors are associated with a diagnosis of ASD, but no single factor, or even combination of factors, can definitely answer what caused the disorder.

> 3. How would you challenge some of the common misperceptions about ASD in everyday conversations with friends and families?

What about Enrique's harrowing journey to the United States as a one-year-old? Could trauma from this journey have negatively affected his developing brain to the extent that it caused ASD? Although that's a good question to ask as it suggests you are critically thinking about Enrique's history, the answer is no. Currently, no research suggests that early trauma is associated with the later development of ASD, although early trauma is associated with many other problems.

Although cultural factors, such as being Mexican, are not relevant in the etiology of the disorder, they are relevant in Enrique's treatment. Let's explore a few important concepts to consider when working with Latino families. Our clinical cultural competence is increased when we understand the values of our clients (Masuda, 2014). Latino values that Masuda notes as particularly important include:

- *Personalismo* (personalism) and *amabilidad* (amiability): In Mexican culture, people are raised within a web of close interpersonal relationships; thus Mexican individuals are often more comfortable than whites in seeking interpersonal help to reach goals. Relevant to this, a personal relationship with a therapist, including higher levels of self-disclosure by the therapist, is important.

- *Familismo* (familism): Latino families tend to utilize family-centered decision making instead of the individualistic approach favored by whites. A family's needs take a high priority in treatment, and the interventions must work collectively for the whole family, not just the individual diagnosed with the problem.

- *Formalismo* (formality) and *respecto* (respect): Professionals should use courteous behavior and conversation, including formal Spanish words, such as *usted* as opposed to *tu* (formal vs. informal use of the Spanish equivalent of *you*). Clients are more likely to share if a professional is approachable, understanding, and nonjudgmental.

- *Machismo*: Mexicans tend to share a patriarchal view of gender roles with a hierarchical view in which men are considered the ultimate decision makers in their families. This view is evolving, however, towards a more nuanced and shared decision-making model (McGoldrick, Giordano, & Garcia-Preto, 2005). Although women tend to initiate contact with a mental health provider, a culturally competent therapist will work to involve a male head of household in treatment and work to understand family structure and dynamics from the family's perspective.

4. To what extent did Sarah demonstrate respect for these traditional Latino values when she met with the Dominguez family?

5. How do you think the value of machismo is demonstrated in the Dominguez family?

A major barrier to treatment in Enrique's case that must be considered is access to health care. The Dominguez family members are undocumented immigrants. Immigrant status presents a cascade of challenges. Acquiring health insurance is incredibly difficult, if not impossible (Becerra, Androff, Messing, Castillo, & Cimino, 2015; De Jesus & Xiao, 2013; Perreira & Ornelas, 2011; Ziol-Guest & Kalil, 2012). Health insurance isn't granted to people of immigrant status. Rather, immigrants must become naturalized citizens of the United States before they can apply for health insurance. The problem is that citizenship often takes years to achieve, thus many families live without health insurance simply because they're not eligible to apply. This situation is especially problematic for young children, as good health is so critical for proper development. Children who immigrate to the United States are even more in need of health care than native-born individuals because immigrant children are exposed to more environmental risks, communicable diseases, and infections (Clark, 2002).

In 2009, President Obama worked to pass the Immigrant Children's Health Improvement Act, allowing states to provide Medicaid and other health insurance to immigrant children, as well as prenatal care to immigrant mothers, without requiring the previously enforced five-year waiting period (Javier et al., 2010). However, states aren't required to comply with this act (Perreira & Ornelas, 2011). In fact, only 29 states have expanded access to Medicaid and other health insurance for immigrant children (Kaiser Family Foundation, 2016). Oklahoma is not one of these states. Additionally, the Immigrant Children's Health Improvement Act doesn't expand access to undocumented immigrants such as the Dominguez family.

According to the 2000 U.S. Census (United States Census Bureau, 2013), one in every five children in the United States is a member of an immigrant family. In other words, every child you meet has a one-in-five chance of having limited access to health care—including mental health care. In your professional work, you'll likely come across many children who not only have limited health care but also experience other substantial barriers to treatment. These barriers include lacking co-pay money and adequate transportation to attend appointments (Hamilton, Hummer, You, & Padilla, 2006; Pati & Danagoulian, 2008). Immigrant families also struggle to receive adequate health care even if they have insurance (Becerra et al., 2015; De Jesus & Xiao, 2013; Huang, Yu, & Ledsky, 2006). One of the greatest impediments to care is the language barrier, as most U.S. medical and mental health-care providers are monolingual and are not fluent in languages other than English. Training more bilingual mental health providers is of critical importance as our culture becomes more diverse.

Other reasons that immigrant families don't seek services include a lack of understanding—of paperwork, procedures, medication, and treatment (Becerra et al., 2015; Huang, Yu, & Ledsky, 2006). Value differences between Latino and white culture also come into play. Many Mexican immigrants believe U.S. physicians lack *personalismo*, or a "friendly, kind, interpersonally warm, and social approach to care" (Clark, 2002, p. 170). In fact, this lack of *personalismo*, in conjunction with language barriers, causes many Mexican immigrants and even U.S. citizens who emigrated from Mexico to travel to Mexico for medical care (De Jesus & Xiao, 2013).

As a mental health professional, you should strive to be culturally competent. This doesn't mean possessing an encyclopedic knowledge of history, culture, and language (although that may be helpful to you should you ever appear on *Jeopardy*). Instead, being multiculturally sensitive means that you reflect on your own cultural values and thoughtfully consider how they impact your interaction with the client, who has different cultural values. Research suggests that client satisfaction has more to do with multicultural sensitivity than a shared racial/ethnic/cultural background (Rogers-Sirin, Melendez, Refano, & Zegarra, 2015). Increasing your own multicultural competency means not only reflecting on your values but practicing cultural sensitivity in your interactions with others from various cultures. Sharing relevant aspects of your culture with your client is also important. Above all, listening is key, as clients want to feel understood and accepted (Rogers-Sirin et al., 2015). Becoming multi-culturally competent is a continuous, lifelong process. Don't be afraid to admit to your own lack of understanding about cultural issues, as this shows cultural humility. Let the client take the lead if you don't understand a value that's important to them. Being a culturally sensitive professional doesn't mean you have all the answers; rather, it means that you're willing and able to learn from and with your clients.

6. Even if Enrique's parents had health insurance, do you think they would seek out health care for themselves or their children? Why or why not?

7. What are some of your cultural values that differ from those of the Dominguez family? What cultural values of yours are similar to theirs?

8. Do mental health professionals have an ethical obligation to advocate for societal change for those who are marginalized by our society? Why or why not?

9. Some people are concerned about US "tax dollars" being spent on immigrants' needs. What are your opinions about this topic? How might your opinion influence your decisions as a therapist?

Evidenced-Based Treatment

One important consideration in treating ASD is that the disorder is chronic. It can't be "cured," but it can be managed to result in a higher level of functioning by an individual (Reichenberg & Seligman, 2016). In fact, depending on the time, availability, intensity, and consistency of interventions, people diagnosed with ASD might be able to achieve an independent or semi-independent level of functioning. If this occurs, these individuals would require less intensive levels of support in the long run.

10. Everyone in the Dominguez family is an undocumented immigrant. Would a mental health provider have an obligation to report them for being in the country illegally? Why or why not?

After a month of worried concern, Rosa María received a phone call from Sarah to schedule a meeting to review Enrique's testing results. Otilia, Enrique's maternal grandmother, watched Enrique during the meeting. Despite Francisco's hopeful insistence that nothing was wrong with his son, he tightly held Rosa María's hand as they sat in the waiting area of Sarah's office. Rosa María reminded herself that no matter what the test results were, Enrique was still her sweet little boy. Sarah greeted Francisco and Rosa María with a kind smile and led them to her office. She could tell they were nervous and tried to ease their tension by asking about Enrique. Rosa María explained that Enrique was glued to his *Thomas the Tank Engine* DVD.

Sarah knew that it would be hard for the Dominguez family to hear that Enrique's problems would be classified as ASD. She also knew that sharing his diagnosis was a crucial first step toward Enrique receiving appropriate treatment. ASD is not a commonly diagnosed problem in Mexico. In fact, 2016 marks the date of the first study to collect data on the epidemiology of ASD in Mexico, with a reported prevalence rate of 0.87% (Fombonne et al., 2016). Sarah began the discussion by talking about Enrique's strengths, mentioning his sweetness and vibrant smile as well as his agreeableness when he has access to trains or crayons. Then, Sarah took a deep breath and began to discuss areas of concern, speaking in Spanish as she'd always done.

> 11. Working with children means having tough talks with parents. At some point in your professional career, you'll have to be the bearer of bad news. What might you do to prepare for difficult meetings?

"You both know how Enrique often plays with trains or crayons, and how most of the time he likes to do the same activity over and over again? When you try to change something, he often becomes upset," Sarah began. "He also has some trouble with language. He can't always get his words out right and sometime has trouble understanding you. And he likes to repeat the same phrases."

Rosa María nodded, with a look of worry in her eyes as she held her husband's hand tightly. Francisco stared, listening intently as he tried to hold back his emotions.

Sarah continued gently, "What I just described about Enrique is what is called Autism, or Autism Spectrum Disorder. Have you heard of this before?"

Rosa María shook her head as Francisco dropped his eyes. "What does it mean? What does it mean for my boy?" he asked.

"Autism is a neurodevelopmental disorder. That's a big, fancy word that just means that Enrique's brain formed differently than the brains of other kids, so he's developing differently. Trouble communicating is common with Autism. Talking is hard and listening is sometimes even harder. Even if Enrique hears you, he might not know what you mean because of the way his brain developed. Liking routine is also common with Autism, just like Enrique likes to repeat things, like dropping trains off the table." Sarah paused to let the family consider the information that she shared.

Rosa María's grip on her husband's hand tightened. "But what does this mean for Kiké?" she asked.

Sarah answered honestly, "It means that Enrique will probably not grow like other children. He'll likely struggle throughout his life. He'll need lots of help, even when he's an adult."

Rosa María burst into tears. Sarah had expected, and dreaded, this reaction. From her own culture, she knew how important work was to Mexican families, especially physical labor guided by a strong work ethic. Disabilities often interfere with such work and can feel like a burden on the family.

"I know this is tough to hear. There are ways to help Enrique be more successful," Sarah continued, handing Rosa María a tissue. Francisco sat stoic but hung on every word that Sarah used, listening to nuances of verbs— if, for example, she said that Enrique *might* struggle or *would* struggle.

"What can we do to help our boy?" Francisco replied flatly.

Sarah dreaded that question. She knew that she could describe a menu of evidence-based options for Enrique to help develop his relationship, communication, play, and eventual independent living skills. She also knew that describing the myriad options would be cruel to a family who wouldn't be able to access even the smallest crumbs of treatment. The first section below will describe what Sarah knew about the treatment of autism. The second section will describe what she actually said to the Dominguez family.

Evidence-based treatment for ASD should begin as soon as possible post-diagnosis (Borden, 2011). Ideally, this *early intervention* approach will occur when a child is still a toddler or preschooler, such as ages 2–6. ASD is best treated with a team approach involving speech-language pathologists, occupational therapists, physical therapists, psychiatrists, and, most importantly, behaviorists. Because of the numerous professionals involved in the life of a family with a child who has ASD, a case manager to coordinate services is also helpful.

The most research-supported intervention for children with ASD is behaviorism (Axelrod, 2012; Borden, 2011). Behaviorists use applied behavioral analysis (ABA) to track and measure problem behaviors. Then, using behavioral principles and interventions, they work to decrease these problem behaviors and increase socially appropriate behaviors. Each child diagnosed with ASD has differing strengths and weaknesses, and no two children are alike (Borden, 2011). ASD thus requires flexible and individualized treatment. This, however, should not be confused with an "anything goes" approach to treatment. Many interventions, including chelation therapy (or detoxing), hyperbaric oxygen treatment, and probiotic and diet-related interventions are not research supported (Preidt, 2014).

An important key to success is ensuring that treatment is consistent across a child's school and home setting. Likewise, regular communication between all caregivers is paramount to success (Borden, 2011; Dillenburger, Keenan, Doherty, Byrne, & Gallagher, 2012). Behaviorists often work in homes with families, at schools with teachers, and in therapy sessions with speech, occupational, and/or physical therapists to reinforce behavioral strategies outlined in the child's behavior plan. The best-case scenario involves everyone in the child's life being on the same page. If such coordination of treatment doesn't occur, children diagnosed with ASD often progress slowly, if at all (Kovshoff, Hastings, & Remington, 2011).

Sarah knew that these behavioral interventions, based on a strong history of research, likely would help Enrique make great strides in his life. Sadly, she also knew that he wouldn't qualify for any of these interventions, nor could his family afford them.

Sarah thus shared none of this information with the Dominguez family.

Sarah had been thinking for weeks about what to say to Francisco and Rosa María. She had considered her family's own experiences with ASD, including the lack of services received by her brother. She reflected on the exhaustion of her aging parents as they cared for her brother even now. She realized that the same difficult and dismal future would likely happen to the Dominguez family. A generation had passed with no improvement in resources for families such as the Dominguez family and her own family. Sarah had been angry, upset, and frustrated by this situation and worked to separate her feelings from Enrique's case. Sarah wanted to give a message of hope, not despair, to Francisco and Rosa María. However, she also didn't want to lie and tell them that everything was going to be OK, when in all likelihood it wasn't.

Sarah said, "Francisco. Rosa María. I have something to tell you. My younger brother, Fernando, is 32. He's like Enrique in many ways, but in some ways, he's different. He has ASD."

Both Rosa María and Francisco gasped, not expecting mental illness to touch the life of a professional.

Sarah continued, "Fernando is still my brother, and I'll always love him. Nothing can take that love away. He doesn't talk very much and can't live on his own because he needs help with almost everything. My parents take care of him, and when they grow too old to do so my sister and I will care for him. It hasn't been easy caring for him. My parents and my sister and I have done what we needed to do because we love him."

Rosa María began crying as Sarah kept speaking, "When you first came into my office, I saw the same love in your eyes for your son as I see in the eyes of my mother and father for Fernando. That love is stronger than the worst problems of ASD. Caring for Enrique as he gets older won't be easy. It won't be all rainbows and butterflies. But you'll make it work somehow. You have each other. You have Otilia. You have your other three children who can help. Mrs. Miller is a good teacher who will help. You have your faith and your church."

Rosa María and Francisco nodded, glad to be reminded of all that was good in their lives.

Sarah concluded, "And I promise that I'll be here for you. I can't be everything that Enrique needs. He needs a team of people helping him and I'm just one person. But I know a little, and I can share what I know with you to help things go better for him. We can meet regularly, and I'll help your family put some interventions in place."

Rosa María and Francisco graciously accepted her help. Immediately, though, Francisco worried, "We have no insurance. We have only enough money for what we need. How will we pay you?"

Sarah smiled and reassured him, "You'll never owe me any money. I'll do this for free because I care about your family."

Rosa María couldn't stop her tears. Sarah was also teary-eyed but tried to keep her professional composure. Francisco blew his nose loudly and wiped his nose with his sleeve. Rosa María got up and hugged Sarah, and thanked her for all that she had done. Rosa María said blessings on Sarah, her brother, her sister, and her parents. Francisco nodded as Rosa María spoke of her gratitude to Sarah. Then Rosa María and Francisco walked out of Sarah's office, holding hands, both crying, and went home to Enrique.

12. Should Sarah have encouraged Enrique to be tested in the first place given the challenges to his accessing services? Would the family be better off if psychological testing didn't occur and they didn't learn Enrique's diagnosis?

13. How do you think Enrique's life will unfold?

14. Research services for children diagnosed with ASD in your community. Are these services available to those without insurance?

15. What is your reaction to Sarah's interaction with Francisco and Rosa María? Do you think it was professional? Was it ethical? Was it culturally sensitive? Why or why not?

References

American Psychiatric Association. (2013). *Diagnostic and statistical manual of mental disorders* (5th ed.). Arlington, VA: American Psychiatric Publishing.

Arora, T. (2012). Understanding the perseveration displayed by students with autism spectrum disorder. *Education, 132*(4), 799–808.

Axelrod, S. (2012). Applied behavioral analysis: Autism and beyond. *Behavioral Interventions, 27*(1), 1–15.

Becerra, D., Androff, D., Messing, J. T., Castillo, J., & Cimino, A. (2015). Linguistic acculturation and perceptions of quality, access, and discrimination in healthcare among Latinos in the United States. *Social Work in Health Care, 54*, 134–157.

Berk, L. E., & Meyers, A. B. (2016). *Infants, children, and adolescents* (8th ed.). Boston: Pearson.

Borden, M. (2011). Treating individuals who have autism: DSM-V, ABA, and beyond. *Brown University Child & Adolescent Behavior Letter, 27*(8), 1–6.

Boukhris, T., Sheehy, O., Mottron, L. & Berard, A. (2016). Anti-depressant use during pregnancy and the risk of autism spectrum disorder. *JAMA Pediatrics*, E1–E8. doi:10.1001/jamapediatrics.2015.3356

Center for Disease Control and Prevention (CDC). (2014). Prevalence of autism spectrum disorder—Autism and Developmental Disabilities Monitoring Network, 11 sites, United States, 2010, *Morbidity and Mortality Weekly Report, 63*(SS-2), 1–21.

Chapman, N. H., Estes, A., Munson, J., Bernier, R., Webb, S. J., Rothstein, J. H., …& Wijsman, E.M. (2011). Genome-scan for IQ discrepancy in autism: Evidence for loci on chromosomes 10 and 16. *Human Genetics, 129*, 59–70.

Christensen, D. L., Baio, J., Van Naarden Braun, K., Charles, J., Constantino, J. N., Daniels, J., … & Yeargin-Allsopp, M. (2016). Prevalence and characteristics of autism spectrum disorder among children aged 8 years—autism and developmental disabilities monitoring network, 11 sites, United States, 2012. *MMWR Surveillance Summaries, 65*(3), 1–23.

Clark, L. (2002). Mexican-origin mothers' experiences using children's health care services. *Western Journal of Nursing, 24*(2), 159–179.

De Jesus, M., & Xiao, C. (2013). Cross-border healthcare utilization among the Hispanic population in the United States: Implications for closing the health care access gap. *Ethnicity & Health, 18*(3), 297–314.

Dillenburger, K., Keenan, M., Doherty, A., Byrne, T., & Gallagher, S. (2012). ABA-based programs for children diagnosed with autism spectrum disorder: Parental and professional experiences at school and at home. *Child & Family Behavior Therapy, 34*(2), 111–129. doi:10.1080/07317107.2012.684645

Eskenazi, B., Marks, A. R., Bradman, A., Harley, K., Barr, D. B., Johnson, C., et al. (2007). Organophosphate pesticide exposure and neurodevelopment in young Mexican-American children. *Environmental Health Perspectives, 115*, 792–798.

Fombonne, E., Marcin, C., Manero, A. C., Bruno, R., Diaz, C., Villalobos, M., ... & Nealy, B. (2016). Prevalence of autism spectrum disorders in Guanajuato, Mexico: The Leon survey. *Journal of Autism and Developmental Disorders, 46*(5), 1669–1685.

Gardener, H., Spiegelman, D., & Buka, S. L. (2011). Perinatal and neonatal risk factors for autism: A comprehensive meta-analysis. *Pediatrics, 128*, 344–355.

Hamilton, E. R., Hummer, R. A., You, X. H., Padilla, Y. C. (2006). Health insurance and health-care utilization of U.S.-born Mexican-American children. *Social Science Quarterly, 87*(5), 1280–1294.

Huang, Z. J., Yu, S. M., & Ledsky, R. (2006). Health status and health service access and use among children in U.S. immigrant families. *American Journal of Public Health, 96*(4), 634–640.

Hultman, C. M., Sandin, S., Levine, S. Z., Lichtenstein, P., & Reichenberg, A. (2011). Advancing paternal age and risk of autism: New evidence from a population-based study and a meta-analysis of epidemiological studies. *Molecular Psychiatry, 16*, 1203–1212.

Javier, J. R., Huffman, L. C., Mendoza, F. S., & Wise, P. H. (2010). Children with special health care needs: How immigrant status is related to health care access, health care utilization, and health status. *Maternal and Child Health Journal, 14*, 567–579.

Kaiser Family Foundation (2016). *Medicaid/CHIP coverage of lawfully-residing immigrant children and pregnant women.* Retrieved from http://kff.org/health-reform/state-indicator/medicaid-chip-coverage-of-lawfully-residing-immigrant-children-and-pregnant-women/?currentTimeframe=0&sortModel=%7B%22colId%22:%22Location%22,%22sort%22:%22asc%22%7D

Koenig, K., Tsatsanis, K. D., & Volkmar, F. R. (2001). Neurobiology and genetics of autism: A developmental perspective. In J. A. Burack, T. Charman, N. Yirmiya, & P.R. Zelazo (Eds.), *The development of autism: Perspectives from theory and research* (pp. 81–101). Mahwah, NJ: Erlbaum.

Kovshoff, H., Hastings, R. P., & Remington, B. (2011). Two-year outcomes for children with autism after the cessation of early intensive behavioral intervention. *Behavior Modification, 35*(5), 427–450. doi:10.1177/0145445511405513

Masuda, A. (Ed.). (2014). *Mindfulness and acceptance in multicultural competency: A contextual approach to sociocultural diversity in theory and practice.* Oakland, CA: New Harbinger Publications.

Minshew, N. J. (1996). Brief report: Brain mechanism in autism: Functional and structural abnormalities. *Journal of Autism and Developmental Disorders, 26*, 205–209.

Ozonoff, S., Young, G. S., Carter, A., Messinger, D., Yirmiya, N., Zwaigenbaum, L., …& Stone, W. L. (2011). Recurrence risk for autism spectrum disorders: A Baby Siblings Research Consortium study. *Pediatrics, 128*, e488–e495.

Pati, S., & Danagoulian, S. (2008). Immigrant children's reliance on public health insurance in the wake of immigration reform. *American Journal of Public Health, 98*(11), 2004–2010.

Perreira, K. M., & Ornelas, I. J. (2011). The physical and psychological well-being of immigrant children. *The Future of Children, 21*(1), 195–218.

Preidt, R. (2014, April 25). FDA Warns against Bogus Autism Treatments. Retrieved from http://www.webmd.com/brain/autism/news/20140425/fda-warns-against-bogus-autism-treatments

Reichenberg, L. W., & Seligman, L. (2016). *Selecting effective treatments: A comprehensive, systemic guide to treating mental disorders.* Hoboken, NJ: Wiley.

Rogers-Sirin, L. Melendez, F., Refano, C., & Zegarra, Y. (2015). Immigrant perceptions of therapists' cultural competence: A qualitative investigation. *Professional Psychology: Research and Practice, 46*(4), 258–269.

United States Census Bureau (2013). *Census 2000 Gateway.* Retrieved from http://www.census.gov/main/www/cen2000.html

Wankoff, L. S. (2011). Warning signs in the development of speech, language, and communication: When to refer to a speech-language pathologist. *Journal of Child & Adolescent Psychiatric Nursing, 24*(3), 175–184. doi:10.1111/j.1744-6171.2011.00292.x

Wilson, K., Mills, E., Ross, C., McGowan, J., & Jadad, A. (2003). Association of autistic spectrum disorder and the measles, mumps, and rubella vaccine: A systematic review of current epidemiological evidence. *Archives of Pediatric and Adolescent Medicine, 157*, 628–634.

Ziol-Guest, K. M., & Kalil, A. (2012). Health and medical care among the children of immigrants. *Child Development, 83*(5), 1494–1500.

CASE 2

Benjie Savat

Benjie is an 11-year-old Filipino boy with numerous resources. He has educated and professional parents and attends a top-notch private school. However, these resources may not be enough to help him manage his symptoms of Attention Deficit Hyperactive Disorder–Primarily Inattentive Subtype (or ADHD-PI). How will Mr. Dub, the mental health counselor at Benjie's school, navigate his parents' reluctance to allow Benjie to participate in psychological testing? Benjie's case provides an evidence-based treatment menu for children with ADHD-PI and showcases the systemic problems in implementing such a plan.

ICD-10/DSM-5 Diagnosis:
F90.0 (314.00) Attention-Deficit/Hyperactivity Disorder, Predominantly inattentive presentation, Moderate

Diagnosis Discussion

Benjie meets criteria for Attention Deficit/Hyperactivity Disorder (ADHD), Predominately Inattentive presentation (APA, 2013). Benjie's disorder is considered to be at a moderate level. ADHD is diagnosed on a continuum, suggesting that a person's impairments can be mild, moderate, or severe, depending on the number of symptoms shown. ADHD has two different subtypes. One subtype involves problems with hyperactivity and impulsivity. The second subtype, the kind that Benjie has been diagnosed with, involves problems with inattention.

The first criterion necessary for a diagnosis of ADHD–inattentive presentation is that symptoms must be present before the child reaches the age of 12 and must last longer than two months (APA, 2013). Second, a person must show a persistent pattern of inattention that interferes with their occupational, educational, or social functioning. Third, at least six of the following symptoms must be present in two or more settings. Finally, no other psychological or medical diagnosis can better explain the symptoms.

1. Fails to give close attention to details or makes careless mistakes in schoolwork, at work, or during other activities. *Benjie's teachers report that he makes numerous careless mistakes and skips important details or steps.*

2. Often has difficulty sustaining attention in tasks or play activities. *Benjie best meets this criterion in the story that his mother told about the firefly,*

but he also has difficulty sustaining attention in classes, as James observed and Benjie's teachers reported. He also gets "bored" even when watching a movie.

3. Often does not seem to listen when spoken to directly. *Benjie's teachers and his mother report this problem.*

4. Does not follow through on instructions and fails to finish schoolwork, chores, or duties in the workplace. *This criterion is not clearly met at this point, although it is a possibility. Perhaps Benjie's grandfather completing his work for him is a misguided effort to manage this problem.*

5. Often has difficulty organizing tasks and activities (difficulty with keeping materials and belongings in order; produces messy, disorganized work; has poor time management; fails to meet deadlines). *Benjie struggles with organization, evidenced by his messy desk and messy work.*

6. Often avoids, dislikes, or is reluctant to engage in tasks that require sustained mental effort (such as schoolwork or homework). *Benjie likes to draw and read comic books, and those activities take some degree of mental effort, but he doesn't seem to enjoy more challenging school-related tasks.*

7. Often loses things necessary for tasks or activities (school materials, pencils, books, tools, or wallet). *Benjie meets this criterion by losing or forgetting important classroom material, evidenced by his current and past teachers' comments.*

8. Is often easily distracted by extraneous stimuli. *Further evaluation would be needed to determine if Benjie meets this criterion, although his mother's story suggests that this is likely.*

9. Is often forgetful in daily activities (doing chores, running errands). *Benjie's forgetfulness is best demonstrated by his mother's report that he forgets to do his chores. He also sometimes becomes distracted while playing. For example, he will be participating in one recreational activity and then leave this activity, even though he is enjoying himself, to go do something else.*

1. Utilize the above list of symptoms to prioritize Benjie's problems. What symptoms are causing him the most day-to-day difficulties and thus are the symptoms you would target in a treatment plan?

The gold-standard method of assessing ADHD is multipronged and systemic (Mash & Barkley, 2014). It involves reviewing a person's school or work history, such as James did by reviewing Benjie's educational file. It also involves interviewing a client directly about his symptoms, which James did to some extent. Best practices also involve interviewing a child's caregivers and teachers. James interviewed Benjie's mother and teachers, but it might also be helpful to interview his father and grandfather. Structured behavioral rating forms, such as the Behavioral Assessment Scale for Children (Reynolds & Kamphaus, 2015) are also recommended. James sent home structured rating scales with Aurora. These rating scales will be critical in assuring that

Benjie meets the criteria for ADHD. Rating scales can help answer the perplexing question of "How often is often?" because they are a *norm-referenced* assessment measure and thus allow us to compare a child to his agemates. In Benjie's case, the completed rating forms suggest that Benjie indeed meets the criteria for ADHD. While a complete psychological evaluation would have been helpful in making a diagnosis for Benjie, the Savats were unwilling to consent to such testing. Diagnosing an individual without completing a psychological evaluation is ethical and is a common practice in our field.

> 2. What other diagnoses do you think James considered besides ADHD-PI?

Case Conceptualization

ADHD is a diagnosis that has resulted in considerable controversy over the last twenty years. Practitioner surveys by the Center for Disease Control and Prevention indicate a rising prevalence of ADHD in the United States (Boyle et al., 2011). However, the rising rates of ADHD may reflect either an actual increase in the occurrence of the disorder or changes in how clinicians are diagnosing it. Which of these two options is occurring is not certain. According to the DSM-5, population studies have shown that ADHD occurs in 5% of children across various cultures (APA, 2013). However, in one national study in the United States, the one-year prevalence for children and adolescents was 8.5% (Muthén & Muthén, 2000). This high prevalence rate has caused some concern about the possibility of overdiagnosis of the disorder in the United States (Boyle et al.).

ADHD is considered "complex" because its etiology is multifactorial and probabilistic (Nigg & Barkley, 2014). *Multifactorial* means that many factors contribute to the cause of the disorder. *Probabilistic* means that even if we knew all of the factors contributing to the disorder, chance events may make the disorder more or less likely to occur.

Neurology plays a role in the development of ADHD. One part of the brain that seems to function differently in people with ADHD is the prefrontal cortex (Barkley, 1997; Casey, Nigg, & Durston, 2007). The *prefrontal cortex* is located in the frontal lobe of our brain and is responsible for executive functioning. *Executive functioning* refers to our higher-order cognitive processes, including our ability to pay attention, remember information, think abstractly, plan, make decisions, problem solve, and manage our impulses. Needless to say, we need our prefrontal lobes functioning at their best.

One possible reason why the brain of a person diagnosed with ADHD may be underfunctioning is dysregulation of *neurotransmitters,* the chemical messengers of the brain and nervous system that transmit important messages between our *neurons,* or nerve cells. Researchers have found more than a hundred different kinds of neurotransmitters, but the ones most indicted in ADHD include dopamine and noradrenalin (Arnsten, 2001; Connor, 2006; Tripp &

Wickens, 2008). Neurotransmitters play a role in almost every aspect of human functioning, including coordinating movement, feeling emotions, having energy, thinking clearly, and in general everyday functioning. Given that people with ADHD show abnormalities in their executive functioning and neurotransmitter levels, the extent of their problems in daily life makes sense.

Like many other disorders discussed in this book, genetics plays a role in the etiology of ADHD as well. A baby born to a family in which a first-degree relative (such as a parent or sibling) has ADHD is two to four times more likely to be diagnosed with the disorder himself (Mick & Faraone, 2009). In fact, the overall *heritability index* is .70. Heritability indexes can be hard to understand. The heritability index takes into account both the environment and the variation that occurs in physical and behavioral traits (phenotypic traits). A .70 heritability index suggests that, within a population, the differences between individuals in relation to ADHD symptoms is 70% due to genetics. Since genes interact with our environment, leading to different phenotypes, teasing out how much of a disorder is "true genetics" is difficult. In any case, we know that genetics plays an important role in the development of ADHD (Nigg & Barkley, 2014; Stawicki, Nigg & von Eye, 2006).

However, genetics is not sufficient to explain ADHD. Because the etiology of ADHD is multifactorial, environmental factors play a role in the development of the disorder as well. Low birth weights are associated with an increased risk of ADHD (Willcutt, 2012). Unfortunately, having a baby with a low birth weight is also associated with several other risk factors for ADHD. These risk factors include poor maternal health and nutrition, maternal smoking, maternal alcohol use, low socioeconomic status, and high levels of stress during pregnancy (Huo et al., 1992; Nigg & Barkley, 2014; Sagiv et al., 2010). This long list of *correlated*, or interrelated, risk factors makes it difficult to determine which factors are most important. The lengthy list of correlated factors also highlights why the etiology of this disorder is probabilistic.

3. Summarize the research-supported etiology of ADHD.

4. The general public holds numerous beliefs about ADHD, including that it's not a "real" disorder, that eating a gluten-free diet can lessen its symptoms, and that the disorder is caused by poor parenting. Look up three misconceptions about ADHD and challenge them with the best research articles you can find.

A very interesting conversation is currently occurring in the mental health field, spurring a flurry of related research articles (Nigg & Barkley, 2014). The hotly contested debate is whether the three different subtypes of ADHD actually represent two entirely different disorders instead of subtypes of the same disorder. Benjie has one subtype, called ADHD Predominately Inattentive Presentation, or ADHD-PI. The other subtype of ADHD is ADHD-Predominately Hyperactive-Impulsive presentation, or ADHD-H. A third subtype is a mixed category of the two subtypes in which a person shows inattentive, impulsive, and hyperactive symptoms.

Some researchers suggest that ADHD-PI should be called something entirely different than ADHD, because it confuses people to have the word "hyperactive" in a diagnostic label when the child is actually not hyperactive, which is the case with ADHD-PI children. The term Slow Cognitive Tempo has been suggested as an alternative diagnosis (Barkley, 2016; Barkley, 2013; Bauermeister, Barkley, Martinez, & McBurnett, 2012). The key proposed symptoms of this disorder include daydreaming, staring into space, drowsiness, confusion, and slow processing of information (Barkley, 2013; Bauermeister, Barkley, Martinez, & McBurnett, 2012). Thus, a child diagnosed with Slow Cognitive Tempo might appear lost in thought, be slow moving and sluggish, withdraw from others, act spacey and confused, underachieve in school, struggle to process questions, and lack persistence when completing difficult tasks (Saxbe & Barkley, 2014). Researchers suggest that this new diagnosis would be more likely to co-occur with depression and anxiety and less likely to co-occur with acting out and conduct problems (Bauermeister et al., 2012). The discussion regarding this topic is interesting, so stay tuned to see how it develops.

5. Do you think that ADHD-PI is a subtype of ADHD or a different disorder all together? Support your hypothesis with research information.

Let's stitch together this information to understand Benjie. He is very inattentive, but we don't know what's causing his inattention. Perhaps he has a low energy level, is sleepy, or has a poor working memory. Or perhaps he has deficits in his *self-regulation,* or ability to manage his behavior, emotions, and thoughts. We can imagine that genetic reasons may underlie his inattentiveness, but we don't know if this is the case. Certainly, his parents don't seem to demonstrate any inattentive problems, as people who are kicked out of libraries at closing time generally are not people with attention problems! We might also suspect that Benjie has neurological or neurotransmitter abnormalities that contribute to his inattention. However, these hypotheses are just conjectures. We cannot explain with certainty why Benjie demonstrates the symptoms of ADHD-PI.

One consideration that we should explore is how Benjie's Filipino culture affects his case. A challenge to working with individuals like Benjie is that a clinician may not know many individuals of Filipino descent. In cases where we are unfamiliar with the culture of a client, we have an obligation to learn more about that culture, so we can be sure to consider the context of a client when diagnosing and treating. Some information about Filipino culture is provided below so that you can form a *culturally competent case conceptualization* of Benjie, or a thoughtful, culturally rooted understanding of Benjie's symptoms, strengths, family, context, and treatment needs. When considering such information, we must always remind ourselves that research applies to groups of individuals, not necessarily one individual. Just because a person fits within a particular group—in this instance, being of Filipino descent—doesn't mean he shares the same characteristics as others of Filipino descent. Assuming an individual will match the characteristics of a group is a form of prejudice. Our recommendation is to be informed about cultural differences and then discover for yourself what's true of an individual client.

As a whole, consideration of racial differences in the United States has classically concentrated on the division between Caucasians and African Americans. The tendency to forget about other racial groups is seen throughout American history, where racial groups that differed from "Black" or "White" were placed in the "Other" category (Gibson & Jung, 2002). The Asian population in the United States has become one of the fastest-growing minority populations, with a 45.6% increase between 2000 and 2010, a remarkable explosion (Jones, 2012). Filipinos have migrated to the United States in fewer numbers than those of Chinese and Japanese ancestry, but Filipino people are the third largest category after these two ethnic groups (Corrigan, 2004).

Someone born in the Philippines who immigrated to the United States during childhood, adolescence, or adulthood is called a *first-generation Filipino American* (Nadal, 2011). Benjie's parents would be considered first-generation immigrants. Those whose parents were born abroad, like Benjie, are considered *second-generation immigrants* (Nadal, 2011). Each generation has varying experiences, beliefs, and values.

A common belief among first-generation Filipinos is that they see themselves as sojourners. They believe their stay in the United States is only temporary until they get an education or save up enough money so that they can return to their homeland (Pido, 1997). Because they see their stay in the United States as temporary, they often tolerate discrimination and insults, and consequently they remain quiet on economic, social, or political problems confronting minorities (Pido, 1997). This view is changing, however, as more Filipino immigrants are choosing to stay in the United States (Corrigan, 2004). Second-generation immigrants often don't share this mentality with their parents and are more likely to assert their rights as "true Americans" instead of behaving like guests in their adopted culture (Pido, 1997).

Due to their work opportunities, Benjie's parents settled in Pittsburgh, which has a small Filipino population. Thus, Benjie may be beginning to realize how his family differs from others not only in their appearance, but in their values as well. It may be that Benjie's private school represents a homogeneous Caucasian student population; it may be that his school is multiracial. We don't know this information from the case study.

6. How would the racial composition of Benjie's school affect his development and symptom presentation? How do you think Benjie would react to overt discriminatory behavior and *microaggressions* (subtle but offensive comments or behavior that reinforce stereotypes)?

Two particular Filipino values may be relevant in Benjie's case. First is the idea of *Utang ng loob*, which translates into debt of reciprocity, meaning that when someone is generous to another, the person is expected to return the generosity (Nadal, 2011). This value often plays out between parents and children. Filipino parents expect their children to be respectful and grateful toward them. Children of Filipino parents are expected to honor their parents' needs before their own. A second value related to understanding Benjie is the idea of *hiya*, or shame, as a major motivator in behavior. Hiya encompasses the importance of representing oneself in an honorable way (Nadal, 2011). A Filipino American would want to avoid anything that could make himself look shameful in front of family, friends, or the community.

7. How do the concepts of *Utang ng loob* and *hiya*, as well as other information presented about Filipino families, influence your conceptualization of Benjie?

Evidence-Based Treatment

James's request to complete a full assessment battery for Benjie was denied by Benjie's parents. James was hopeful that testing would provide an overall snapshot of Benjie's intellectual, achievement, and behavioral level of current functioning. James was especially interested to see if Benjie demonstrated slow *processing speed*, a measure of the speed of one's thinking and doing that's a component of intellectual functioning (Dodonova & Dodonova, 2012; Weiss, Saklofske, Holdnack, & Prifitera, 2016).

James was disappointed that Benjie's parents denied his request for assessment and wondered why they had made this decision. His questions were answered when Mr. Magnus again stopped by his office. (Fortunately, he was able to find it this time.) Mr. Magnus told James that he had advised the Savat family against testing because he thought that a diagnosis of "some sort of learning disability" would hurt Benjie's chances of getting into an advanced track in middle school. Mr. Magnus told James that no follow-up meetings with the family were to be scheduled, because he "knows the family very well and Benjie's problems have nothing to do with them." However, Mr. Magnus also emphasized that he was expecting James to do "top notch work with a VIF—Very Important Family."

Mr. Magnus left James's office before James could even respond. James thought to himself that Mr. Magnus was an idiot and then subjected himself to an exceptionally strenuous workout that afternoon at the gym. While James was in the gym, imagining Mr. Magnus as the punching bag he was attacking, he tried to figure out how to proceed with Benjie's case when he could neither do an assessment nor work with the family, two critical steps to successful intervention.

8. In his role as a school principal, did Mr. Magnus behave unethically? How would you proceed if you were James, given the situation? Did James behave unethically?

James remembered something that one of his favorite supervisors from his master's degree program had always told him: "When in doubt, ask." The supervisor's explanation of this statement was that difficult cases often require consultation from an expert. James knew that he had a limited multicultural background that didn't go far beyond having taken Spanish in college—which he did because a foreign language was required in order to get a degree—and having once traveled to Puerto Rico. James was wise enough to realize that he knew very little about Filipino culture. He wasn't even sure where "Filipines" was on a map and was frustrated when his efforts to find it turned up empty. He decided to call his buddy Glenn for some help.

9. What are the risks and benefits of consulting with someone outside our field?

James had met Glenn in college, and they'd stayed in touch over the years. Glenn's mother was from the Philippines, and his father was in the U.S. Army. Glenn himself was currently in the military, serving in Hawaii. James remembered Glenn telling stories about his life as a child and how different Glenn's experiences were from his own, growing up in Iowa's cornfields. Getting a release of information to talk to Glenn wasn't necessary, as James wasn't going to share confidential information, instead just seeking Glenn's expertise on Filipino culture.

When Glenn and James made contact, Glenn's first comment was to rib his old friend about looking up a place called "Filipines" on a map. "Try looking up the Philippines, instead, buddy. Starts with a P-H. Not an F. Duh, dude," Glenn said sarcastically.

James did as his friend advised and looked up the Philippines, although he felt dumb for not recognizing his error. As Glenn talked at length with James about Filipino values, James grew motivated to learn about the Philippines and spent a few days studying the culture. He also cracked open one of his long-forgotten but favorite books from his master's program, *Ethnicity and Family Therapy* (McGoldrick, Giordano, & Garcia-Preto, 2005). This book provided useful information about how cultural values can affect therapy.

Although this information helped, James realized his knowledge was incomplete. He called his previous supervisor, who had suggested that James consult her when "stuck," for information about how to proceed in a case like this—when he could neither work with the family nor do a formal assessment. His ex-supervisor was a school psychologist with 30 years of experience in the field. She gave James some useful advice and suggested that he focus on changing the system he could change (Benjie's school environment) and not on the system he couldn't change (Benjie's family environment). She specifically suggested that James investigate evidence-based intervention for ADHD-PI. After he had generated a list of evidence-based interventions, she advised him to carefully review it and consider what interventions made sense given Benjie's particular array of symptoms, developmental level, gender, Filipino family background and values, and strengths. She also encouraged James to consider his school organizational context, and the particular aptitudes and goals of the teachers with whom he worked, since the teachers at Merseyside would do the heavy lifting in implementing the plan.

10. Sometimes we don't get the luxury of working with a child's family. In these cases, is there a better way to proceed than what James's previous supervisor advised?

James took his previous supervisor's advice and did his homework. In preparation for meeting with Benjie's teachers, James interviewed each at length, asking them to share what they had tried with Benjie and what had worked. Then James created a summary of possible interventions in a graph form, reprinted on the following page.

James went to the meeting with Benjie's teachers and was careful to both lead and listen as the team discussed the pros and cons of each intervention. The team selected a few interventions to implement with Benjie and also determined how they would collect data to measure the efficacy of the different approaches they wanted to try. They agreed to meet monthly to discuss Benjie's progress. Benjie's parents were sent a copy of the intended interventions, and they signed their consent for the school to work with Benjie as proposed. Surprisingly, they agreed for Benjie to participate in individual therapy with James. James encouraged the Savats to consider the possibility of medication for Benjie, but they were unwilling to do so.

11. What interventions do you think the teachers selected? Do you think they were successful? What do you think the long-term prognosis is for Benjie?

12. Make a case that Benjie should or should not be involved in therapy, using both research about evidence-based treatment for ADHD and information from the case study itself.

13. Should James have invited Mr. Magnus to the meeting with the teachers? Why or why not?

Fortunately for Benjie, Merseyside had a strong group of committed teachers who were willing to implement an array of educational interventions to help Benjie succeed. In fact, his teachers selected most everything from the list of possibilities that James generated. One intervention that was particu-

Possible Intervention	Why it might work	Concerns	For more information
Behaviorally-Focused Social Skills Training	Could happen during school hours with parental consent. Other children could benefit from this group (MC, JB, KW)	Benjie would likely be shy at first. Will need a small group.	Pfiffner & McBurnett, (1997) Weisz & Kazdin (2010)
Medication	Recommended in conjunction with parent management and classroom behavioral interventions. Medication can help with academic achievement.	Uncertain if the Savats will allow it. Also, all medication has side effects.	AAP (2011) Fisher & O'Donohue (2006) Pelham et al. (2014) Visser et al. (2015)
Teacher-Administered Behavior Therapy: • Reward attentiveness • Token economy with a point system • Homework in class to assure mastery • Daily report cards • Ongoing data collection to show what is working • Connecting classroom learning objectives with Benjie's interests	One of the best research-supported ideas. Plus, we have awesome teachers here at Merseyside!	Hard to implement individualized interventions when teachers have a classroom full of students.	Anastopoulos, Shelton, & Barkley (2005) DuPaul & Eckert (1998) Weisz & Kazdin (2010)
Teaching meta-cognitive skills, including time management and task perseverance	These deficits are exactly why Benjie struggles.	Will these skills generalize from one setting to another? (If Benjie learns them in my office, can he do them in the classroom?	Reichenberg & Seligman, (2016)
Individual Therapy	Benjie might enjoy the one-on-one positive attention of therapy.	Individual therapy isn't research supported, but I'll work with Benjie if his parents give permission	Weisz & Kazdin (2010)

larly successful was incorporating more active learning approaches in classrooms, such as small-group discussions, laboratory experiments, and problem-based learning activities. During these active classroom experiences, Benjie found it more difficult to zone out and retreat to his superhero world. Benjie's teachers also began a token economy that allowed Benjie to earn a comic book every week by accruing "paying attention points." Another successful intervention was changing most of Benjie's homework to become in-class work. His teachers continued to worry that Benjie's grandfather was completing his homework for him and thought that Benjie would master more concepts if he did his independent work in school.

Other interventions were less successful. Helping Benjie to learn metacognitive skills, such as time management and task perseverance, failed because Benjie had trouble with generalizability. *Generalizability* refers to a person's ability to implement new skills across settings or over time. Although Benjie did learn new metacognitive skills, he struggled to use them at the right place and time when they would be effective.

This same generalizability problem affected Benjie's individual therapy with James, an intervention that the teachers supported despite the lack of research support for it being an effective intervention for children with ADHD. Although James was an excellent therapist and made a good connection with Benjie over the Fighter Warriors, Benjie didn't demonstrate any better social skills because of it. Likewise, Benjie participated in a behaviorally focused social skills group. These groups can be helpful in breaking down complex skills, such as asking for help, into small steps and then practicing the steps until mastery is reached. Benjie learned the social skills and could demonstrate them perfectly in the group. However, outside the group therapy setting, Benjie was still the same introverted child that he'd always been. Overall, Benjie made no measurable gains in his social skills despite individual and group therapy.

At home Benjie also continued to struggle, although this was expected since nothing in his home environment had changed. Children with ADHD aren't likely to change their behavior unless their environment changes to help them be more successful (Fisher & O'Donohue, 2006). Benjie's parents loved him and wanted him to be successful. However, they weren't willing to change their parenting style to better meet his needs. They thought that if they did so they would be lowering their standards, and that prospect was unacceptable to them. The Savats were unwilling to consider medication for Benjie, which also might have made a difference for him. Thus, when at home Benjie remained the same highly distractible child he'd always been.

Despite the overall lack of substantial improvements for Benjie, Mr. Magnus recommended the accelerated track for him as he began middle school. James and Benjie's teachers were outraged and disappointed at Mr. Magnus's recommendation. They felt that Mr. Magnus had placed the needs of the school (i.e., receiving donations from the Savat family) ahead of Benjie's needs as a student. They drafted and co-signed a letter to formally state their disagreement with Mr. Magnus's recommendation. Mr. Magnus didn't respond to the letter, nor did he alter his recommendation. The teachers were frustrated with Mr. Magnus but knew that the battle was too big for them to fight. James felt differently. He went to Mr. Magnus's office and complained about the decision. The tense meeting ended in a stalemate. After the meeting, James hit the gym again—with a vengeance. He began preparations to start his own private practice, a professional opportunity that he realized he should have pursued many years ago.

What will happen to Benjie as an adult? The research is clear that people don't grow out of ADHD (Mash & Barkley, 2014). Although overall ADHD symptoms lessen as they age, children with ADHD tend to be outliers regarding inattentive and distractible behavior when compared to their peers. Thus, although Benjie's behavior will likely improve, he'll still look markedly different than children his age, whether he's 16, 18, 21, or 25. The difficulties in changing the behavior of children with ADHD provide support for the strong genetic and neurological etiology of the disorder. The key to effective intervention is changing the environment rather than expecting the child to change (Reichenberg & Seligman, 2016).

Because of the importance of the child's environment in promoting success, niche picking will be vital to Benjie as he ages. *Niche picking* refers to the idea that people function at their best when they choose environments that complement their genetics. For example, Benjie would do best in a middle school that relies on active learning approaches, such as small-group work and collaborative problem solving, rather than in a school that utilizes passive learning approaches like large-group instruction and rote memorization. As an adult, Benjie would make a great illustrator for Marvel Comics but a poor long-distance truck driver. The more that Benjie can learn to niche pick, the happier and more productive he'll become.

14. Design the ideal school day for Benjie. Do you think that children without ADHD would also do better in this utopian environment than in our current educational system?

15. Many parents believe, as Rafael and Aurora do, that children become spoiled if parents reward them for good behavior or that they're compromising their parenting values if they expect different behavior out of children with disabilities. How would you challenge this common parenting belief?

References

American Academy of Pediatrics (2011). Clinical practice guidelines for the diagnosis, evaluation, and treatment of attention-deficit hyperactivity disorder in children and adolescents. *Pediatrics, 128,* 1007–1022. Retrieved from www.aapolicy.aapulciations.org.

American Psychiatric Association. (2013). *Diagnostic and statistical manual of mental disorders* (5th ed.). Washington, DC: Author.

Anastopoulos, A. D., Shelton, T. L., & Barkley, R. A. (2005). Family-based psychoso-cial treatments for children and adolescents with attention-deficit/hyperactivity disorder. In E. D. Hibbs & P. S. Jensen (Eds.), *Psychosocial treatments for child and adolescent disorders: Empirically based strategies for clinical practice* (pp. 327–350). Washington, DC: American Psychological Association.

Arnsten, A. F. T. (Ed.). (2001). *Dopaminergic and noradrenergic influences on cognitive functions mediated by prefrontal cortex.* New York: Oxford University Press.

Barkley, R. A. (1997). Behavioral inhibition, sustained attention, and executive func-tions: Constructing a unifying theory of ADHD. *Psychological Bulletin, 121*(1), 65–94. doi:10.1037/0033-2909.121.1.65

Barkley, R. A. (2013). Distinguishing sluggish cognitive tempo from ADHD in chil-dren and adolescents: Executive functioning, impairment, and comorbidity. *Jour-nal of Clinical Child and Adolescent Psychiatry, 30,* 752–761.

Bauermeister, J. J., Barkley, R. A., Martinez, J. V., & McBurnett, K. (2012). Validity of the sluggish cognitive tempo, inattention, and hyperactivity symptoms dimen-sions: Neuropsychological and psychosocial correlates. *Journal of Abnormal Child Psychology, 40,* 683–697.

Barkley, R. A. (2016). Sluggish cognitive tempo: A (misnamed) second attention dis-order? *Journal of the American Academy of Child and Adolescent Psychiatry, 55*(3), 157–158. doi:10.1016/j.jaac.2015.12.007

Boyle, C. A., Boulet, S., Schieve, L. A., Cohen, R. A., Blumberg, S. J., Yeargin-Allsopp, M., ... & Kogan, M. D. (2011). Trends in the prevalence of developmental disabilities in US children, 1997–2008. *Pediatrics, 127*(6), 1034–1042. doi:10.1542/peds.2010-2989

Casey, B. J., Nigg, J. T., & Durston, S. (2007). New potential leads in the biology and treatment of attention deficit-hyperactivity disorder. *Current Opinion in Neurology, 20*(2), 119–124. doi:10.1097/WCO.0b013e3280a02f78

Connor, D. F. (2006). Other medications in the treatment of child and adolescent ADHD. In R. A. Barkley (Ed.), *Attention-deficit hyperactivity disorder: A handbook for diagnosis and treatment* (3rd ed., pp. 564–581). New York: Guilford.

Corrigan, J. (2004). *Filipino immigration.* Broomall, PA: Mason Crest.

Dodonova, Y. A., & Dodonova, Y. S. (2012). Processing speed and intelligence as predic-tors of school achievement: Mediation or unique contribution? *Intelligence, 40*(20), 163–171. http://dx.doi.org.proxyse.uits.iu.edu/10.1016/j.intell.2012.01.003

DuPaul, G. J., & Eckert, T. L. (1998). Academic interventions for students with atten-tion-deficit/hyperactivity disorder: A review of the literature. *Reading and Writing Quarterly, 14,* 59-83.

Fisher, J. E., & O'Donohue, W. T. (2006). *Practitioner's guide to evidence-based practice.* New York: Springer.

Gibson, C., & Jung, K. (2002). Historical census statistics on population totals by race, 1790–1990, and by Hispanic origin, 1970–1990, for the United States, regions, divisions, and states. U.S. Census Population Division. Retrieved from http://www.census.gov/population/www/documentation/twps0056/twps0056.html

Huo, M. H., Salvati, E. A., Browne, M. G., Pellicci, P. M., Sculco, T. P., & Johanson, N. A. (1992). Primary total hip arthroplasty in systemic lupus erythematosus. *Journal of Arthroplasty, 7*(1), 51–56.

Jones, N. A. (2012). The Asian population in the United States: Results from the 2010 Census. Retrieved from http://www.ssa.gov/aapi/2010census-data.pdf

Mash, E. J., & Barkley, R., A. (2014). *Child Psychopathology* (3rd ed.). New York: Guilford.

McGoldrick, M., Giordano, J., & Garcia-Preto, N. (2005). *Ethnicity and family therapy* (3rd ed.). New York: Guilford.

Mick, E., & Faraone, S. V. (2009). Genetics of attention deficit disorder. *Child and Adolescent Psychiatric Clinics of North America, 17,* 261–284.

Muthén, B., & Muthén, L. K. (2000). Integrating person-centered and variable-centered analyses: Growth mixture modeling with latent trajectory classes. *Alcoholism: Clinical and Experimental Research, 24*(6), 882–891. doi:10.1111/j.1530-0277.2000.tb02070.x

Nadal, K. L. (2011). *Filipino American psychology: A handbook of theory, research, and clinical practice.* Hoboken, NJ: John Wiley & Sons.

Nigg, J. T., & Barkley, R. A. (2014). Attention-Deficit/Hyperactivity Disorder. In E. Mash & R. Barkley (Eds.), *Child Psychopathology* (3rd ed., pp. 75–144). New York: Guilford.

Pelham, W. E., Burrows-MacLean, L., Gnagy, E. M., Fabiano, G. A., Coles, E. K., Wymbs, B. T., & Waschbusch, D. A. (2014). A dose-ranging study of behavioral and pharmacological treatment for children with ADHD. *Journal of Abnormal Child Psychology, 42*(6), 1019–1031. http://doi.org/10.1007/s10802-013-9843-8

Pido, A. J. A. (1997). Macro/micro dimensions of Filipino immigration to the United States. In M. Root (Ed.), *Filipino Americans: Transformation and identity.* Thousand Oaks, CA: Sage.

Pfiffner L. J., & McBurnett, K. (1997). Social skills training with parent generalization: Treatment effects for children with ADD/ADHD. *Journal of Consulting and Clinical Psychology, 65,* 749–757.

Reichenberg, L. W, & Seligman, L. (2016). *Selecting effective treatments: A comprehensive, systematic guide to treating mental disorders.* Hoboken, NJ: Wiley.

Reynolds, C. R., & Kamphaus, R. W. (2015). *Behavioral Assessment System for Children, Third Edition (BASC-3).* London: Pearson.

Sagiv, S., Thurston, S., Bellinger, D., Tolbert, P., Altshul, L., & Korrick, S. (2010). Prenatal organochlorine exposure and behaviors associated with attention deficit hyperactivity disorder in school-aged children. *American Journal of Epidemiology, 171*(5), 593–601. doi:10.1093/aje/kwp427

Saxbe, C., & Barkley, R. A. (2014). The second attention disorder? Sluggish Cognitive Tempo vs. Attention-Deficit/Hyperactivity Disorder: Update for clinicians. *Journal of Psychiatric Practice, 20*(1), 38–49. doi:10.1097/01.pra.0000442718.82527.cd

Stawicki, J. A., Nigg, J. T., & von Eye, A. (2006). Family psychiatric history evidence on the nosological relations of DSM-IV ADHD combined and inattentive subtypes: New data and meta-analysis. *Journal of Child Psychology & Psychiatry, 47*(9), 935–945. doi:10.1111/j.1469-7610.2006.01628.x

Tripp, G., & Wickens, J. R. (2008). Dopamine transfer deficit: A neurobiological theory of altered reinforcement mechanisms in ADHD. *Journal of Child Psychology and Psychiatry, 49*(7), 691–704. doi:10.1111/j.1469-7610.2007.01851.x

Visser, S. N., Bitsko, R. H., Danielson, M. L., Ghandour, R. M., Blumberg, S. J., Schieve, L.A., … Cuffe, S. P. (2015). Treatment of attention deficit/hyperactivity disorder among children with special health care needs. *Journal of Pediatrics, 166,* 1423–1430.

Weiss, L. G., Saklofske, D. H., Holdnack, J. A., & Prifitera, A. (2016). *WISC V assessment and interpretation: Scientist-practitioner perspectives.* San Diego, CA: Academic Press.

Weisz, J. R., & Kazdin, A. E. (2010). *Evidence-based psychotherapies for children and adolescents* (2nd ed.). New York: Guilford.

Willcutt, E. G. (2012). The prevalence of DSM-IV attention-deficit/hyperactivity disorder: A meta-analytic review. *Neurotherapeutics, 9*(3), 490–499. doi:10.1007/s13311-012-0135-8

CASE 3

Zynthia Miller

Schizophrenia is a devastating diagnosis for anyone, regardless of age. Zynthia is a 15-year-old Caucasian girl with a family that has significant mental health challenges of their own. In cases like Zynthia's, is it better to return a child to her biological family after hospitalization or to consider residential treatment programming?

 ICD-10/DSM-5 Diagnosis:
R/O F20.9 (295.80) Schizophrenia, first episode, currently in acute episode
Z62.820 (V61.20) Parent-Child Relational Problem

Diagnostic Discussion

Zynthia's working diagnosis is Schizophrenia, although we'd certainly want to meet with Zynthia several more times and gather additional collateral information to ensure that this serious diagnosis was accurate. Misdiagnosing a person can have a significant negative impact on her life, so we have a tremendous responsibility to diagnose carefully in all cases, but especially in the case of someone with a chronic and serious psychological disorder such as Schizophrenia.

Nevertheless, Zynthia's behavior warrants a Rule-Out diagnosis of Schizophrenia, suggesting that we think Zynthia has this diagnosis but cannot meet criteria at the present time. A brief summary of the diagnostic criteria for Schizophrenia (APA, 2013) is:

- Two or more of the following symptoms during a one-month period, which must include at least one of these first three symptoms listed below:
  — Delusions
  — Hallucinations
  — Disorganized speech
  — Grossly disorganized or catatonic behavior
  — Negative symptoms
- A significantly below expected level of functioning in work, relationships, self-care or other important areas. Adolescents demonstrate a failure to achieve expected developmental milestones.
- Continuous signs of the disturbance must persist for at least six months. If the person is successfully treated during that time period, the symptoms may be more residual and less active.

- Other related mental disorders have been ruled out.
- The disorder is not due to a medical condition, medication, or drug use.
- The disorder is not due to an autism spectrum disorder.

Let's define some of these terms and apply them to Zynthia. The first criterion is often challenging for students to understand because it introduces some terms that are commonly used, but not commonly understood, in everyday language. *Delusions* are defined as "fixed false beliefs that are unrealistic in the context of one's life experience and culture" (Mash & Barkley, 2014, p. 574). For example, a person believing that she is being poisoned, has special powers, or is being followed by the CIA are examples of delusions unless these events are actually true. Zynthia has a delusion—that is, an organized, ongoing belief about "the troops" preparing to kidnap her, take her to their camp, and replace her brain with a washing machine motor. Although this belief may sound comical to you, delusions feel real to people with Schizophrenia and are anything but comical. From the perspective of someone who has a delusion, what they believe is real, serious, and often frightening to them.

Hallucinations are false sensory experiences (Mash & Barkley, 2014). Hallucinations may involve any one of a person's five senses. A person may see things that are not really present (*visual hallucination*) or hear voices or sounds that are not real (*auditory hallucinations*). Less common are when people touch (tactile hallucinations), smell (*olfactory hallucinations*) or taste (*gustatory hallucinations*) things that are not real. Zynthia demonstrates an auditory hallucination when she discusses how she talks to God and specifically, that God told her that the clinician would understand her. Zynthia also believes that God told her that her math teacher and principal had been infiltrated by the troops and were thus enemies. We have to be particularly careful when diagnosing hallucinations that are religious in nature. Plenty of non-mentally ill individuals with a rich spiritual life report having conversations with God in which God actually talks back to them. However, Zynthia's report of what God says to her is quite different than what a normal person with a close relationship with God would report. Zynthia's experiences with God are also out of the range of normal cultural expectations (Iyassu et al., 2014).

Disorganized speech refers to speech that is tangential, unusual, or incoherent (Mash & Barkley, 2014). Sometimes individuals with disorganized speech appear to be responding to their hallucinations or private thoughts, and thus they may change topics or have conversations that aren't connected to their present environment. Language requires complex mental processes, and thus Schizophrenia can disrupt speech in many ways. For example, people with Schizophrenia may demonstrate *neologisms* (speech that is filled with made-up words), *loosening of associations* (rapid shifts from topic to topic), *perseveration* (repetition of the same words), or *clanging* (a meaningless use of rhyming words). Consider this quote from Zynthia that I tried so hard to record verbatim:

Bearings, bearing down, bare. Big bears. Little bears. Berries and berries. Blueberries and strawberries. Bears eating berries. The berries are gone! The berries are gone. The bearings are broken, broken down, bare.

This quote is important because it demonstrates elements of clanging and perseveration. Zynthia also demonstrates some unusual speech when she refers to a "lollipop/pop" as being the way that she disappears at night. Disorganized speech is problematic because it makes it difficult for others to understand what the person speaking is trying to communicate. I was lost when Zynthia talked about the bears and berries and bearings. Although I was trying to make logical sense of what Zynthia was saying, it was too incoherent. These communication difficulties can be extremely frustrating to a person with Schizophrenia.

Grossly disorganized or catatonic behavior is a term used to describe behavior that is bizarre and out of context for a person's environment (Mash & Barkley, 2014). For example, a person may engage in a behavior that serves no purpose and/or reflects a serious lack of impulse control, such as picking her nose and eating "boogers" or engaging in sexually provocative behavior with strangers. *Catatonic behavior* essentially means that a person does not respond to her environment but instead seems to be in a stupor, is mute, or shows highly unusual physical posture (Mash & Barkley, 2014). Zynthia doesn't show signs of grossly disorganized behavior. Her hiding from the troops under her sheets is consistent with her delusional thinking and her fear that she's in danger, so this behavior wouldn't be considered disorganized.

Negative symptoms can be contrasted with *positive symptoms* of Schizophrenia. *Positive symptoms*, described above, are the broad category of atypical and bizarre symptoms present in a person with Schizophrenia. *Negative symptoms* of Schizophrenia reflect an absence of healthy behavior that should be present in a person, such as a *flat affect* (or a lack of emotional expression), a lack of enthusiasm or interest in the world, and a lack of self-care or hygiene. These symptoms can lead to withdrawal from others (APA, 2013). Negative symptoms are only briefly described for Zynthia, and it's hard to gather from the case study the extent to which she exhibits these behaviors. She may indeed withdraw from her classmates into her art, have poor hygiene, and have a flat affect, but we don't have sufficient information to know this for certain.

Thus, Zynthia exhibits three of the symptoms noted in the first criterion as necessary for a diagnosis of Schizophrenia. She has delusions, hallucinations, and disorganized speech. She also meets the second criterion in that she's failing to meet important developmental milestones. Consider that at age 15, the highest functioning teenagers are doing well in school, are active in recreational activities, have a rich friendship life, are learning to drive, and, perhaps, are dating. They may also be involved in part-time work or volunteer activities. Zynthia hasn't achieved any of these important developmental milestones.

The third criterion involves the length of time that a person must show symptoms of Schizophrenia. Based on the information we have available, we can't be sure that Zynthia meets the prescribed timeline of six months for continuous symptoms. Symptoms of Schizophrenia may wax and wane. In other words, they may remit somewhat (*residual phase*) or worsen (*prodromal phase*). Zynthia demonstrates the *prodromal phase* as she is increasingly withdrawing from social contact, including her best friend and her family. However, because I'd only been working with Zynthia for one month, I could only list Schizophrenia on a Rule-Out basis for her, suggesting that it is likely a correct diagnosis but she is not meeting all the criteria for the disorder. There's some indication that Zynthia's symptoms have been occurring for much longer that six months. Her mother reported that Zynthia's symptoms worsened approximately one year prior to her hospitalization and she quit interacting with her friend, Sarah, at about that time. Although this is suggestive, the information from the family isn't detailed enough to meet this criterion.

Finally, Zynthia's current symptoms aren't due to a medical problem, medication, or drug use. Revisiting Zynthia after my first visit with her was important to ensure that her unusual behavior was not just a one-time fluke. Interviewing her family provided additional information regarding Zynthia's problematic developmental history. Consulting with the psychiatric nurses and medical doctors was also essential to ensure that medical problems or drugs were not responsible for her behavior. Finally, carefully reviewing Zynthia's chart provided additional useful information about her past and present course of illness and previous treatment notes.

1. The diagnostic discussion section introduced you to many new terms. Write down all the italicized terms and define them in your own words.
2. Do you think that the clinician was overly cautious in making Zynthia's diagnosis a Rule Out? What problems do you see with that approach?

Case Conceptualization

Some background information about Schizophrenia will likely be helpful to you. You should know that although Schizophrenia is often portrayed by the media as being the prototypical mental illness endured by people, it's actually far less common than depression, anxiety, and trauma-related diagnoses. The lifetime prevalence rate of Schizophrenia is 0.3% to 0.7%, which means that less than 1 in 100 people, on average, will develop Schizophrenia (APA, 2013). Compare that with rates closer to 10% for anxiety, depression, and PTSD, which means that these affect about 1 in 10 people each (APA, 2013). Although Schizophrenia is uncommon, its prevalence rates vary across cultures, ethnicities, gender, and immigration status (APA, 2013). The risk for females is slightly lower than males, and females tend to have a later age of onset than males (APA, 2013). African Americans are almost twice as likely as Caucasians to be diagnosed with schizophrenia (Keval, 2015). New immigrants in the United States, especially those with darker skin color, are also at increased risk of being diagnosed with schizophrenia (Dealberto, 2010). Prevalence rates across ethnicities are misleading, however, because they reflect societal biases in diagnosis and treatment—in which people of color and people who live in poverty tend to receive more serious diagnoses than people who are white or who have financial resources (Keval). Although we would like to believe that all mental health providers are immune from societal prejudice and discrimination, this unfortunately isn't the case.

Schizophrenia in children and adolescents is rare and is much less common than in adults (APA, 2013). Most symptoms usually emerge during late adolescence or in the early 20s (APA, 2013). Nevertheless, schizophrenia can and does show up in children. Seminal research from the field in the early 1970s showed that the same diagnostic criteria can be used with both children and adults (Kolvin, 1971; Rutter, 1972). However, diagnosing children and adolescents with schizophrenia is fraught with challenges due to developmental differences. Children are more likely than adults to show immature language and thinking (McClellan, 2011) which can result in misdiagnosis. Common childhood traits, such as wild imaginations, disruptive behaviors, unusual speech, and magical thinking shouldn't lead a clinician to diagnose schizophrenia (McClellan et al., 2013). The immature but developmentally appropriate responses of young children can be hard to distinguish from the pathological responses of a person with schizophrenia. A five-year-old child with an active imagination or an imaginary playmate, or who believes that lightning bugs are magical fairies, should not be diagnosed as having hallucinations and delusions. Similarly, an adolescent who shows moodiness and social withdrawal is probably not a person with Schizophrenia. Clinicians always need to take care to consider development, intelligence, environmental stress, and culture when diagnosing any disorder. One important recommendation to consider is that the negative symptoms of Schizophrenia typically appear in children before the positive ones (McClellan et al., 2013). In other words, Zynthia probably showed a flat affect, disinterest in the world, poor hygiene, and a withdrawal from others long before she began talking about "the troops."

With those considerations in mind, your next question might be, "But why does schizophrenia develop?" That's an excellent question, and the answer is complicated but worth understanding.

Schizophrenia is a disorder best understood as having a *diathesis-stress* etiology. This means that two conditions are necessary for a diagnosis to occur. The word *diathesis* just means a genetic vulnerability or a susceptibility towards a certain disorder. You certainly know what the word *stress* means, since you are a student!

The first component of a *diathesis-stress* model is genetics (Rapoport, Giedd, & Gogtay, 2012). An individual must have inherited a genetic tendency to develop schizophrenia. Schizophrenia tends to run in families, with between 5 and 20 times a greater risk in individuals with a strong family history of the disorder (APA, 2013). Schizophrenia thus has a *high heritability index.* That is, given equal environments, genetics plays a large role in determining the differences we see in schizophrenic symptoms between people.

Studies of genetics rely frequently on *monozygotic* (identical) and *dizygotic* (fraternal) twins. Monozygotic twins share 100% of their genes. Dizygotic twins are no more alike genetically than any other pair of siblings. The unique genetic pattern of monozygotic twins allows for rich research that helps answer questions about how strong a genetic influence is for a particular disorder. If a disorder has a strong genetic base, then monozygotic twins would have a higher rate of both twins having the disorder than would be the case in dizygotic twins. When both twins do have a particular trait or disorder, it is called a *concordance rate.* Concordance rates of schizophrenia in monozygotic twins are higher than in dizygotic twins (Cardno & Gottesman, 2000). This suggests that schizophrenia is influenced by genetics. The genetic story of schizophrenia is quite complex, most likely involving multiple genes.

The second part of the *diathesis-stress* model is environment. The person must grow up in the right environment for the disorder to appear. In the case of schizophrenia, a stressful, difficult, non-supportive environment makes the disorder more likely (Mash & Barkley, 2014). Families who exhibit high levels of criticism, emotional over-involvement, and hostility are associated with the diagnosis and severity of schizophrenia (Wearden, Tarrier, Barrowclough, Zastowny, & Rahill, 2000). This triad of factors—high level of criticism, emotional over-involvement, and hostility—is collectively called *high levels of expressed emotion.* Other factors that make schizophrenia more likely to develop include childhood neglect and abuse (van Os, Kenis, & Rutten, 2010). This does not mean that families are to blame when a family member develops schizophrenia. It just means that psychological disorders are complicated and have multiple factors in regards to their etiology.

> 3. Use the term *diathesis-stress model* to explain a behavior or trait that you exhibit.

A person's environment matters because it affects how the brain develops. Early neglect and trauma impact the stress pathways of the brain, leading to problems in how neurons respond and communicate with one another. These neurological changes can especially affect the *frontal lobe,* the part of the brain most responsible for abstract thinking, communication, and planning. Such impairments can lead to changes in brain connectivity (Bear, Connors, & Paradiso, 2015) and changes in various neurotransmitters, such as dopamine. A *neurotransmitter* is a chemical messenger that carries information to nerve cells, or *neurons* (Bear, Connors, & Paradiso) Dopamine is one neurotransmitter that seems to be particularly important in the development of schizophrenia. Madras (2013) has described the historical foundation of the development of the so-called "dopamine hypothesis," explaining how the discovery of what was called the antipsychotic receptor in the brain would lead to an excess of dopamine, which can contribute to delusions and hallucinations. This hypothesis has received a great deal of research support over the years. Recently, however, the dopamine hypothesis has been criticized due to a lack of evidence (Moncrieff, 2009).

Consider these research findings in regards to Zynthia. First, let's think about the genetic component of the diathesis-stress model. Zynthia likely inherited a genetic tendency towards schizophrenia; we know her maternal grandmother was hospitalized in a state psychiatric institution for many years. Although we don't know her grandmother's diagnosis, most individuals who are hospitalized for a long time and receive electroconvulsive therapy likely have some form of depression, schizophrenia, or *schizoaffective disorder*, which is a disorder in which an individual has both symptoms of schizophrenia and a mood disorder. We also don't know the diagnosis of Zynthia's mother or father, but we can certainly agree that her father, and perhaps her mother as well, exhibits unusual behavior.

Zynthia's early developmental history also provides clues that she may be *genetically predisposed* (or genetically more vulnerable) to developing schizophrenia. Rabeckah reported that Zynthia was delayed in meeting major developmental milestones. From a young age, Zynthia demonstrated a lack of coordination, an inability to connect with others, and odd behaviors. This pattern of early development suggests genetic factors at play.

However, Zynthia appears to be the only family member with diagnosable schizophrenia. Why not Rabeckah? Why not Seraphina? Why not Nixon? The second part of the diathesis-stress model helps us answer this question. In Zynthia's case, it seems from the interview with her family that she has a long history of not being supported by her family. Her family is critical of her and actually struggles to find anything positive to say about her. The example that I remember the most of this negativity is when Rabeckah turned my positive comment about Zynthia's name into a focus on her own unique name, which seemed to indicate that she's unable to hear anything positive about her oldest daughter. Zynthia's family is also openly hostile and rejecting towards her. For example, Beau will not allow any family members to visit Zynthia in the hospital. Seraphina is clearly disparaging of her older sister and repeatedly made mean comments about Zynthia's friends, art skills, academic skills, and possibly her sexual orientation. The Miller family is also emotionally involved with one another, although Zynthia is not necessarily a part of those connections. Although we have no clear-cut indications of childhood sexual abuse between family members, I was most certainly concerned about the inappropriate relationship between Beau and Seraphina—especially given the flirty behavior between father and daughter and the lack of physical boundaries, as well as the elevation of Seraphina almost to the level of a third adult in the family.

Together, the combination of high levels of criticism, emotional overinvolvement, and hostility are considered to be *high levels of expressed emotion*. High levels of expressed emotion in families predict future relapse in people diagnosed with schizophrenia and are associated with worse outcomes for these people (Wearden et al., 2000).

The Miller family also has some additional unique dynamics that likely made it difficult for Zynthia as she was growing up. Although a single family interview is not sufficient to understand all of the Miller family dynamics, their interactions suggest a long-standing pattern of pathology. Neither of Zynthia's parents was supportive of her or tried to understand her difficulties. Zynthia appears to have been mostly alienated in the family, as Beau and Seraphina formed one alliance while Rabeckah and Nixon formed another.

Finally, the interactions of the Millers and their responses to my questions made me concerned about what it meant to grow up in this family. Beau's beliefs about the government, although shared by a subset of the population, created a siege mentality of "us against the world." Rabeckah's seeming passivity and willing dismissal of Zynthia's needs likely contributed to a non-validating and non-protective environment. The hostility and criticism toward Zynthia, displayed by all members of the family except Nixon, would be extremely difficult for anyone to cope with on a daily basis, much less an individual prone to developing schizophrenia. No wonder Zynthia felt under siege by "the troops."

4. The Miller family is worrisome for many reasons. Prioritize the top three issues that you think are most problematic and explain your rationale.

5. Do you think that Nixon will develop an overly close or inappropriate relationship with Rabeckah? Explain your answer.

6. Given what you know at this point regarding the Miller family, would you call Child Protective Services to report potential abuse or neglect? Why or why not? If you answered yes, what specifically would you report?

Evidence-Based Treatment

The treatment of schizophrenia is better conceptualized as helping patients manage their symptoms instead of curing them. Although about 14% of patients recover significantly after a first episode of psychotic symptoms, the remaining, roughly 86% of patients show poor to moderate improvement in their symptoms (Moore et al., 2007). As described in the case conceptualization section, schizophrenia is a lifelong, chronic disorder that has a complex etiology and affects a person's neurological functioning. Managing the most problematic symptoms of the disorder is a more realistic plan of treatment than attempting to cure it.

The treatment of schizophrenia requires a multi-pronged intervention, including medication management, individual/group therapy, and family therapy (Reichenberg & Seligman, 2016). Family therapy seems particularly crucial. In fact, although dated, one study found a relapse rate of 83% among children who received medication only compared to a relapse rate of 17% among children who received medication and family therapy (Bellack & Mueser, 1993). Zynthia and her family received all three components of this multi-prong approach. To organize this section, we will first discuss Zynthia's medication management, then her individual/group therapy, and finally, the family therapy for the Millers.

Medication Management

While at the hospital in her first month of treatment, Zynthia was referred to a psychiatrist for prescription and monitoring of antipsychotic medication. Antipsychotic medication is critical in the treatment of schizophrenia (Tandon, 2011). One significant challenge to prescribing this type of medication is the paucity of research on the long-term effects of such medication in children as compared to adults (Masi & Laboni, 2011). Another significant problem is the significant side effects of both older and newer antipsychotic medications. It was hoped that the newer types of medication would reduce the number of side effects, but this hasn't been shown to be the case (Tandon, 2011). Side effects can include *cognitive dulling,* or a reduced ability to concentrate and focus, leading to problems with short-term memory. People on antipsychotics often report feeling sedated or drowsy when taking the medication (Masi & Laboni, 2011). Additionally, some patients report gastrointestinal and cardiac problems (Tandon, 2011). Finally, and most significantly, a small group of patients show *extrapyramidal side effect*s, a group of symptoms that includes tremors, muscular rigidity, slurred speech, inability to sit or stand still, involuntary muscle contractions, and slowed thoughts or movements (Masi & Laboni, 2011).

Despite these significant and worrisome side effects, people diagnosed with schizophrenia generally need antipsychotic medication. Without proper medication, 65% to 75% of patients will relapse within a year (Harkavy-Friedman, 2006). Thus, an important part of treatment for schizophrenia is helping patients understand why their antipsychotic medication is important and encouraging them to take it as prescribed, despite the serious list of side effects.

Zynthia was a highly motivated and willing patient when it came to taking her antipsychotic medication. After her psychiatrist explained to her why the medication was important and how it would help her, Zynthia never refused her medication. The psychiatrist at the hospital prescribed risperidone (Risperdal). Zynthia had several of the side effects listed above, including feeling sleepy and drowsy when on her medication, but she reported that she'd rather feel sleepy than under attack from the troops. She also complained of having a dry mouth, but sucking on a piece of hard candy seemed to help this problem. Zynthia gained about five pounds on the medication over the first two months she was on it, and another five pounds over the second two months. She was happy that her jeans actually fit a little better since she gained the weight. Her sister Seraphina noted that Zynthia was "getting fat" and teased Zynthia about her weight gain.

Despite the side effects, the antipsychotic medication made a tremendous difference for Zynthia within a few weeks of taking it. She reported that she was much less worried about the troops and no longer thought that other people, such as her teacher, had been brainwashed by them. After two months on the medication, she was demonstrating fewer hallucinations. Regarding her delusions, Zynthia reported that she still talked to God and didn't want to stop talking with Him. However, her conversations with God were much less odd than they once were and no longer focused on special messages that she received from Him. Zynthia also exhibited less suicidal behavior on the medication, including less *suicidal ideation*, or thoughts about killing herself. The difference in Zynthia since she began taking antipsychotic medication was truly remarkable. She was still an unusual girl with awkward social skills and atypical beliefs, but she was markedly less psychotic than she had been when I first met her in the hospital.

Individual and Group Therapy

Because I was on my doctoral-level internship, I was still working under supervision. Fortunately, I had a clinical supervisor whom I trusted immensely and who had a great deal of experience working with children and teenagers diagnosed with serious psychological disorders. My supervisor and I talked at length about treatment options for Zynthia. We both agreed that Zynthia should be referred to another clinician for individual therapy. Initially, this was difficult for me to accept. I thought that my supervisor was questioning my competence, and I had to deal with my own self-doubts—feeling like I was an imposter. However, under my supervisor's patient tutelage, I grew to understand that we should always put the clients first. Clinical decisions should not be made on what was best for me, but instead what was best for my clients. I swallowed my pride and learned some lifelong lessons from this supervisor that have served me well.

> 7. What would you think, and how would you feel, if Zynthia's case were referred to someone else?

Zynthia was referred for individual therapy to Dr. Nancy Rialto, a seasoned psychologist who specialized in adolescents. Dr. Rialto provided inpatient and outpatient therapy at the hospital and also offered individual and group therapy. Because Zynthia trusted me at least a little bit, I introduced Dr. Rialto to Zynthia while she was still an inpatient at the hospital. I explained that Dr. Rialto was an expert in helping teenagers with the same type of problems that Zynthia had. Zynthia was shocked to learn that other teenagers had similar experiences. Zynthia was slow to warm to Dr. Rialto and asked that I be present for the first several meetings with her, so we conducted joint therapy sessions for two weeks. After this, Zynthia began to trust Dr. Rialto and was willing to meet with her by herself.

In individual therapy with Zynthia, Dr. Rialto took a cognitive behavioral treatment approach. Dr. Rialto worked with Zynthia to help her manage her delusions and hallucinations through mindfulness. Specifically, she worked with Zynthia to accept her hallucinations without judging herself for having them, fearing she was going crazy, or being filled with anxiety that the situation would become worse. Instead, Zynthia was encouraged to allow herself to experience positive emotions while she was coping with her hallucinations and delusions. This mindfulness approach has received good empirical support (Shawyer et al., 2012). Zynthia made excellent progress in individual therapy and enjoyed her one-on-one conversations with Dr. Rialto. Cognitive behavioral approaches have been reported to be effective in reducing both the positive and negative symptoms of schizophrenia (Klingberg et al., 2010; Wykes, Steel, Everitt, & Tarrier, 2008).

Dr. Rialto also provided *psychoeducation* for Zynthia, teaching her about her diagnosis of schizophrenia, its etiology, prognosis, and treatment. Dr. Rialto even explained the diathesis-stress model to Zynthia. At first, Zynthia was upset about the genetic factors of schizophrenia, stating that it was unfair that she'd been born with "bad genes." Zynthia was also upset that her genetics were out of her control but yet could influence her entire life. She also struggled with learning that schizophrenia doesn't usually just go away, as she was hoping that therapy would "fix her." Dr. Rialto patiently worked through Zynthia's concerns with her. She allowed Zynthia to grieve about the life that she had hoped she might have while looking for silver linings in the life that she'd be more likely to have. Dr. Rialto worked with Zynthia to recognize "danger points" for Zynthia—stressful events which caused her to isolate herself from others. The main danger point that Zynthia identified was family arguments. Another danger point was holidays and weekends. She did much better when she had a daily routine that she followed, and she actually did better when school was in session than when it was out of session. As Zynthia realized what her danger points were, she and Dr. Rialto crafted an individual crisis plan to manage these stressful situations without becoming overwhelmed and retreating to a world where "the troops" took charge.

Zynthia also participated in the daily inpatient social skills group at the hospital, which Dr. Rialto led. These groups were vital for Zynthia's progress since her social skills were so poor at the onset of therapy. Social skills training involves education, *modeling* (demonstration of appropriate behaviors), *behavioral rehearsal* (practicing skills in lifelike situations), corrective feedback, and homework. Social skills groups focused on teaching the most important tools for being successful in every day relationships, beginning with practicing making eye contact and saying hello. Zynthia likely would have benefitted from an all-girls group, as homogeneity can be helpful in forming group cohesion (Muno, 2014). As it was, Zynthia was in a group of 10–12 adolescent boys and girls who had been admitted to the psychiatric wing of the hospital for a variety of reasons and ranging in diagnoses. One problem for Zynthia was that the composition of the group was constantly changing based on the admissions and discharges of patients to the hospital. Zynthia would just start to get more comfortable with one group of teenagers and feel confident enough to do a role play but then would retreat back into her quiet shell when new patients were admitted, particularly if they were loud or confrontational. Dr. Rialto recognized Zynthia's uneven progress in developing her social skills in a group format. In individual therapy with Zynthia, Dr. Rialto made certain to review and practice with Zynthia the social skills that she'd learned that week in group therapy. Another potential challenge to the social skills group was that it was modular-based and followed a set curriculum that repeated on a predictable schedule. Because Zynthia was at the hospital longer than most other children during her inpatient stay of 28 days, she heard the same material on multiple occasions. While this repetition would have offended and bored other adolescents, Zynthia wasn't offended. Indeed, she likely benefitted from it.

Dr. Rialto, my clinical supervisor, the psychiatrist, the psychiatric nurses and the *psychiatric technicians* (the front-line staff at the hospital responsible for the day-to-day supervision of the adolescent patients), and myself worked as a team to manage Zynthia's case. We met at weekly treatment team meetings to review her medication, progress, and challenges, and determine an appropriate discharge plan for her. We also discussed the Miller family's progress in family therapy (discussed in the following section). As a fledgling clinical psychologist, I greatly appreciated the treatment team meetings. I learned a tremendous amount from my more experienced colleagues in other disciplines. I also began to understand the complexities of long-standing turf wars between various disciplines. I sometimes marveled at how people I enjoyed so much as individuals could be so difficult as professionals in a team setting. On one hand, I learned what my supervisor meant when she said, "It's one thing to enjoy eating a good hot dog but another thing entirely to walk inside the hot dog factory and see exactly how hot dogs are made." On the other hand, I learned that patients frequently get better despite the infighting and disagreements of the various professionals treating them. Relevant to this wisdom, I learned that *iatrogenic effects,* or unintended negative side effects of treatment, can be brought about by systems as well as medication.

Family Therapy

When my supervisor told me that I wouldn't be working with Zynthia in individual therapy, I was disappointed because I felt that Zynthia and I had already formed a connection. I was also eager to work with someone who demonstrated such severe psychopathology and, as I mentioned earlier, I feared that Zynthia's referral to another professional was a vote of no-confidence in my skills. I was just working through my feelings regarding this referral when my supervisor hit me with another bombshell. She wanted me to provide family therapy for the Miller family.

Honestly, I couldn't believe what I'd just heard. My first thought was, *"Is she nuts? I can't work with this family! They are beyond . . . anything I've ever seen!"*

8. Do you believe that the clinician has the clinical skills necessary to work with the Miller family? Why or why not?

My supervisor explained that she felt I was competent to do the difficult work of family therapy with the Millers under her expert guidance. She'd even be providing me with live supervision of the family at least once a month, using "bug-in-the-ear" technology where she could make suggestions to me as she watched our therapy sessions from another room. My first thought when I heard this was, *Beau is not going to like being watched by someone in another room. There's no way he'll consent to this. It's not going to happen.* My focus on Beau allowed me to ignore just how nervous I'd be if I were leading a family therapy session in front of a supervisor who was a nationally known expert in family therapy.

My supervisor also explained her feeling that, in Zynthia's case, we needed to have two therapists working with the family: an individual therapist with Zynthia and a different family therapist with the Millers. Although sometimes the same clinician can provide both family and individual therapy, my supervisor didn't think this was the right choice for this family. She explained that given the strong alliances in the Miller family, she felt that I'd not be able to align with the family and make a connection with them if I were aligned with Zynthia. The Miller family had expertly scapegoated Zynthia. The danger was that any person who advocated for Zynthia and understood her perspective on the world would be immediately marginalized and alienated by the family. My supervisor explained that in family therapy, I'd need to form good relationships with Beau, Rabeckah, Seraphina, and Nixon. I was pretty confident that I could connect with Nixon as a gun-loving four-year-old, but I was doubtful about my ability to build meaningful relationships with any of the other three. When I shared this concern with my supervisor, she encouraged me to "work slowly and listen loudly" to understand each family member's goals and fears. With trepidation, I accepted the task of working with the Miller family in therapy.

9. Who in the Miller family would be most difficult for you to work with, and why?

10. How do you think the Miller family would have related to the clinician if she had been black instead of white? Or gay instead of straight? Could they have worked through these demographic differences?

My supervisor suggested family psychoeducational (FE) therapy to address the high levels of expressed emotion in the Miller family, including their intense criticism, emotional over-involvement, and hostility. FE has been shown to be effective in reducing relapse and re-hospitalizations by as much as 40%. FE also improves medication adherence, social functioning, and patient–family relationships (Shean, 2009). The components of FE therapy were designed to counteract the problems associated with high levels of family expressed emotion. In FE therapy, the entire family is provided information about a family member's disorder and its treatment. The family is also provided with access to crisis intervention, emotional support, and strategies for coping with the family member's symptoms and related problems. Sessions might include problem solving, coping and communication skills development, and crisis management.

As my supervisor and I discussed the benefits of FE, I realized that this type of therapy was exactly what the family needed and that it could greatly benefit Zynthia. However, in addition to the high level of expressed emotion in the family, I had other concerns about the family that I shared with my supervisor. These concerns included the alignment of Beau and Seraphina on one hand and Rabeckah and Nixon on the other. I was also concerned about the potentially inappropriate and overly close relationship between Seraphina and her father, particularly the way they interacted more as girlfriend and boyfriend than as father and daughter. Finally, I was concerned about Rabeckah's choice to continue to breast feed Nixon at age four. I knew that breast feeding is natural and healthy, and I could quote verbatim the advice of the American Academy of Pediatrics (2012) that breast feeding was advised until babies are at least one year old—and after that, as long as the baby and the mother desire to continue breast feeding. My supervisor and I looked up another statistic: less than 12% of children in the United States continue to breast feed after age the age of six months (CDC, 2007). While Rabeckah breast feeding Nixon was certainly unusual, I was uncertain as to whether it was unhealthy and indicated problematic family boundaries. I also remembered something odd that Zynthia had said in our first interview—that the school was more private than her home. Ordinarily, such a comment would prompt little concern, but given the dynamics of the family, this statement seemed salient.

I called the Miller family to begin family therapy. Unfortunately, I immediately hit a substantial barrier. The family was unwilling to return to the hospital for any reason except to pick up Zynthia when she was discharged. They refused to visit Zynthia or to attend any family therapy sessions, citing distance and cost as their barriers. After Zynthia was discharged, they were also unwilling to transport her to the hospital for outpatient therapy. My supervisor and I worked out an arrangement in which I'd travel weekly to a small satellite clinic in their hometown to provide family therapy. I was secretly relieved that my supervisor would not be able to provide live supervision under this arrangement, for I continued to doubt my competence as a family therapist in this case.

Seraphina kicked off the first family therapy session with a bang, complaining that Zynthia was the problem and that the rest of the family was "perfectly okay." I was expecting Beau and Rabeckah to echo Seraphina's belief, but I was shocked when Beau disagreed and said that the family needed to be in therapy because they could all improve in some areas. I was even more shocked by Beau's total reversal of his resistance towards mental health services, and, in particular, towards me as a therapist. Beau was downright charming to me, almost seductively so. I spoke with my supervisor about this behavior, and we were both confused as to why it had changed so substantially. My supervisor's advice was to continue to build rapport with him and, not to assume that his charming behavior meant that any meaningful alliance had been formed. She also told me to be careful to maintain good boundaries with him and not to be flattered by his overtures. Rabeckah was silent and withdrawn these first few weeks of therapy, so I made an extra effort to connect with her, to understand what she wanted for her family, and to demonstrate how I could help her reach these goals.

Around the fourth week of family therapy, a month after she was discharged from the hospital, Zynthia began to show marked decreases in hallucinations, delusions, and illogical thinking. Zynthia began to move out of the role of being the family scapegoat or *identified patient*, the family member in a dysfunctional family system who essentially represents the family's struggles. I was interested to see how the family would adapt to the change in Zynthia's behavior. The pioneers of family therapy, including Murray Bowen and Salvador Minuchin, have discussed how families have a set *homeostasis* (Nichols, 2013). Homeostasis refers to the equilibrium of the family. Imagine a family as a mobile. If one side of the mobile is greatly altered, the other side of the mobile must change as well to stay in balance. As a practical example, consider a mother in a family who always bakes a birthday cake, buys a birthday gift, and writes a card for every family member's birthday. If the mother were to stop buying the gifts and baking the cake, her change in behavior would disturb the equilibrium of the family. To maintain homeostasis, either the mother would be pressured to resume her role or another family member would step in to maintain this balance.

> 11. Who do you think might change the most in response to Zynthia's changes? Explain your answer.

In response to Zynthia's improved behavior, it was Seraphina who changed the most dramatically. As her complaints about her sister decreased, she increased her complaints about Nixon, Rabeckah, and, eventually, Beau. Seraphina's changed behavior most affected Beau. He quickly dropped his charade of being motivated to get help for his family. He returned to being hostile and controlling, as he was in my first interview with him. Rabeckah retreated as Beau grew more outspoken.

At the fifth family session, the Miller family imploded. Seraphina began the session by announcing that she wanted me to "fix a few things." First, she stated that she wanted her mother to stop sleeping in the same bed as Nixon. When I asked Seraphina why her mother's sleeping habits were of concern to her, she answered that as long as her mother slept with Nixon, it meant that her father would sleep with her (Seraphina). Seraphina also complained that she was tired of her father coming into the bathroom when she was showering and then waiting in the bathroom while she showered so he could dry her with the towel. She angrily continued that she was no longer going to let her father touch her breasts.

As Seraphina finished talking, Beau's face grew crimson red. He rose to his feet and began shouting, clenching his fists and pointing alternatively at Seraphina and then me, for causing so many problems in his family. He yelled, "I'm sick of this crap. I'm going to South America with the militia where I'll get the respect I deserve instead of being treated like a dog by the rest of you."

I tried to get Beau to sit down, but he stormed out of the therapy room, slamming the door behind him. I never saw him again.

After Beau had left, Seraphina remained defiant, stating that none of her friends had to endure their fathers touching their breasts or watching them shower. I asked Rabeckah what she thought of the situation. With no emotion whatsoever, Rabeckah flatly stated that as long as her husband left her alone, she really didn't mind what he did to anyone else. Rabeckah reported that she hadn't slept in the same bed as her husband since Nixon was born and that she had no intentions of ever allowing him back into her bed. I asked Rabeckah what she thought about Seraphina's allegations against Beau. She answered wearily, "I don't know." Throughout this session, Zynthia sat in her chair without saying a word. Nixon, seemingly carefree, played with his toy army men, unconcerned even when his father left the room.

I told Rabeckah that I was a mandated reporter of child abuse due to my professional role as a psychologist. I would have to call Child Protective Services (CPS) and report all that Seraphina had said. Rabeckah seemed unconcerned about this development. This struck me as odd because Rabeckah could be found guilty of not protecting her daughter if she did indeed know that the abuse was happening. Seraphina was extremely concerned about my calling CPS, not because she worried about telling the authorities about the abuse, but because she was worried that if Beau left, their family would not have sufficient money to survive.

After the therapy session, I called my supervisor to talk over what had happened and how to proceed with the new information. I called CPS to report the allegations from Seraphina.

12. Would it be difficult for you to continue working with this family due to the concerns of abuse? When we're working with CPS on an open case that is currently being investigated, what are some of our ethical and legal obligations as mental health workers?

Three days later, I received a call from CPS regarding their investigation of the allegations of sexual abuse. CPS reported that they wouldn't be able to do much with the allegations, since both Seraphina and Rabeckah had denied any misbehavior on Beau's part. CPS closed the Millers' case with a notation that the child abuse was unsubstantiated. The day of the next scheduled family session, Rabeckah called and canceled, indicating that Beau was out of the country and they were unsure when he would be returning. Rabeckah reported that Beau had refused to return for therapy, insisting that "the girls got the wrong ideas from all of that attention."

Zynthia, fortunately, was allowed to continue with Dr. Rialto and her psychiatrist. I continued to be a part of the treatment team for Zynthia despite no longer providing family therapy. After a month in South America, Beau was informed by Rabeckah that the abuse charges were unsubstantiated and he returned home. Six months after Zynthia was initially hospitalized, she was hospitalized again for suicidal ideation and a return of her delusions. During this hospitalization, the treatment team discussed the pros and cons of Zynthia returning to the Miller household. We collectively agreed that returning home wouldn't be in Zynthia's best interest due to ongoing concerns about Beau's behavior and Rabeckah's unwillingness to protect the children from possible abuse.

The treatment team decided to recommend residential treatment for Zynthia after her discharge from the hospital. Dr. Rialto worked with Child Protective Services to declare Zynthia a *child in need of services* (CHINS). A CHINS designation meant that Zynthia would become a ward of the state instead of her parents. CHINS status is reserved for children under the age of 18 whose parents either can't or won't provide the child with needed services. I was expected to inform Rabeckah and Beau, whom I expected to be outraged, that Zynthia was declared a CHINS and would be going to a residential treatment facility. Instead, Rabeckah responded that she was fine with that decision because Zynthia was causing "too much trouble in the family."

The decision to recommend residential treatment was taken seriously by the team. *Residential treatment* is an umbrella term used to describe an array of living situations in which children live away from their parents for an extended time. Typically, residential treatment refers to a child living at an institution or facility, such as a group home with shift workers, on a designated campus. Another option for Zynthia would have been therapeutic foster care, where she would have lived with a family in the community.

Research on residential treatment programs is mixed. These programs often decrease behavioral problems when a child is in place, but these gains may disappear when they return home. However, about one of every two children maintain the gains they make in residential treatment after they're discharged (Kapp, Rand, & Damman, 2015). A disadvantage of residential treatment is that it is expensive and resource intensive. In addition, residential treatment centers provide services to a heterogeneous population, so Zynthia might be placed in a unit for female adolescents with conduct problems and trauma histories (Hagaman, Trout, Chmelka, Thompson, & Reid, 2010). Staff turnover is high in residential treatment facilities (Connor et al., 2003) and the centers themselves vary greatly in quality. Nevertheless, residential treatments provide a valuable service for children who are unable to live safely in a less restrictive environment.

A therapeutic foster home would have been a viable option for Zynthia, as it has received more favorable research support (Chamberlain et al., 2008), especially if the foster families receive intensive support, training, respite help, education, therapy, and special education and case management services (Chamberlain et al., 2008). However, many therapeutic foster parents do not receive that level of support (Ellermann, 2007). An additional challenge is that there are not enough foster parents for all of the children who might benefit from living in a foster home. Children who are older, children who aren't white, and children who show severe behavioral problems are often difficult to place in foster homes (Orme, Cherry, & Krcek, 2013).

Zynthia did reasonably well in the residential treatment facility in which she was placed. When she moved to the facility, she had to change therapists from Dr. Rialto and her psychiatrist to a mental health team at the facility. I checked in with the residential facility after Zynthia had been a resident for six months. She was taking her antipsychotic medication as prescribed and continued to show few problems with hallucinations, delusions, or illogical thinking. However, she struggled in getting along with the other girls and tended to isolate herself. She did say she enjoyed taking an art class. Because Zynthia was almost 17 years old, the treatment team at the residential facility was struggling to find the intense and ongoing services that Zynthia would need as an adult. The residential treatment facility could only serve children up until age 18, so concerns were mounting about Zynthia's future. She stated that she didn't wish to go home but would do so if that were her only option.

Zynthia's family initiated no contact with her after she was placed in the group home. They had not visited her once in the six months that she was placed there, nor had they called or written letters. I called the Millers to follow up, but their telephone number was disconnected. Letters sent to them were returned from the post office stamped with "address unknown."

13. Why do you think Seraphina and Rabeckah denied any type of abuse when the family was being investigated by CPS?
14. Do I have an ethical obligation to report the Millers to CPS for abandoning their daughter?
15. What do you think will happen to Zynthia in the long term? What will she be like when she's 25 years old? What services are available in your local community that you think would be most beneficial to Zynthia?

References

American Academy of Pediatrics. (2012). Breastfeeding and the use of human milk. *Pediatrics, 129*(3), e827–e841. doi:10.1542/peds.2011-3552

American Psychiatric Association (2013*). Diagnostic and Statistical Manual of Mental Disorders* (5th ed.) Washington, DC: Author.

Bear, M. F., Connors, B. W., & Paradiso, M. A. (2015). *Neuroscience: Exploring the brain* (4th ed.). Hagerstown, MD: Wolters Kluwer.

Bellack, A., & Mueser, K. T. (1993). Psychosocial treatment for schizophrenia. *Schizophrenia Bulletin, 19,* 317–336.

Cardno, A. G., & Gottesman, I. I. (2000). Twin studies of schizophrenia: From bow-and-arrow concordances to Star Wars Mx and functional genomics. *American Journal of Medical Genetics, 97,* 12–17.

CDC. (2007). Breastfeeding trends and updated national health objectives for exclusive breast feeding—United States, birth years 2000–2004. *Mortality and Morbidity Weekly Report, 56*(30), 760–763.

Chamberlain, P., Price, J., Leve, L. D., Laurent, H., Landsverk, J. A., & Reid, J. B. (2008). Prevention of behavior problems for children in foster care: Outcomes and mediation effects. *Prevention* Science, *9,* 17–27.

Connor, D. F., McIntyre, E. K., Miller, K., Brown, C., Bluestone, H., Daunais, D., … & LeBeau, S. (2003). Staff retention and turnover in a residential treatment center. *Residential Treatment for Children & Youth, 20*(3), 43–53.

Dealberto, M. J. (2010). Ethnic origin and increased risk for schizophrenia in immigrants to countries of recent and longstanding immigration. *Acta Psychiatrica Scandinavica, 121*(5), 325–339. doi:10.1111/j.1600-0447.2009.01535.x

Ellermann, C. R. (2007). Influences on the mental health of children placed in foster care. *Family and Community Health, 30,* 23–32.

Hagaman, J. L., Trout, A. L., Chmelka, M. B., Thompson, R. W., & Reid, R. (2010). Risk profiles of children entering residential care: A cluster analysis. *Journal of Child and Family Studies, 19*(4), 525–535.

Harkavy-Friedman, J. M. (2006). Can early detection of schizophrenia reduce suicidal behavior? *American Journal of Psychiatry, 163,* 768–770.

Iyassu, R., Jolley, S., Bebbington, P., Dunn, G., Emsley, R., Freeman, D., … & Garety, P. (2014). Psychological characteristics of religious delusions. *Social Psychiatry and Psychiatric Epidemiology, 49*(7), 1051–1061. http://dx.doi.org/10.1007/s00127-013-0811-y

Kapp, S., Rand, A., & Damman, J. L. (2015). Clinical gains for youth in psychiatric residential treatment facilities: Results from a state-wide performance information system. *Residential Treatment for Children & Youth, 32*(10), 37–57. doi:10.1080/0886571X.2015.1004287

Keval, H. (2015). Schizophrenia and psychosis: The magical and troubling disappearance of race from the debate. *Diversity and Equality in Health and Care, 12*(1), 6–8.

Klingberg, S., Wittorf, A., Fischer, A., Jakob-Deters, K., Buchkremer, G., & Wiedemann, G. (2010). Evaluation of a cognitive behaviourally oriented service for relapse prevention in schizophrenia. *Acta Psychiatrica Scandianica, 121*(5), 340–350. doi:10.1111/j.1600-0447.2009.01479.x

Kolvin, I. (1971). Studies in childhood psychoses. I. Diagnostic criteria and classification. *British Journal of Psychiatry, 118,* 381–384.

Madras, B. K. (2013). History of the discovery of the antipsychotic dopamine D2 Receptor: A basis for the dopamine hypothesis of schizophrenia. *Journal of the History of the Neurosciences, 22*(1), 62–78. doi:10.1080/0964704X.2012.678199

Mash, E. J., & Barkley, R. (2014). *Child psychopathology* (3rd ed.). New York: Guilford.

Masi, G., & Laboni, F. (2011). Management of schizophrenia in children and adolescents. *Drugs, 71*(2), 179–208. http://dx.doi.org/10.2165/11585350-000000000-00000

McClellan, J. (2011). Clinically relevant phenomenology: The nature of psychosis. *Journal of the American Academy of Child and Adolescent Psychiatry, 50,* 642–644.

McClellan, J., Stock, S., & AACAP Committee on Quality Issues (2013). Practice parameter for the assessment and treatment of children and adolescents with schizophrenia. *Journal of the American Academy of Child and Adolescent Psychiatry, 52,* 976–990.

Moncrieff, J. (2009). A critique of the dopamine hypothesis of schizophrenia and psychosis. *Harvard Review of Psychiatry, 17*(3), 214–225. doi:10.1080/10673220902979896

Moore, T. H. M., Zammit, S., Lingford-Hughes, A., Barnes, T. R. E., Jones, P. B., Burke, M., ... & Lewis, G. (2007). Cannabis use and risk of psychotic or affective mental health outcomes: A systematic review. *Lancet, 370(9584),* 319–328. http://dx.doi.org/10.1016/S0140-6736(07)61162-3

Muno, A. (2014). And girl justice for all: Blending girl-specific and youth development practices. *Afterschool Matters, 19,* 28–35.

Nichols, M. (2013). *Family therapy: Concepts and methods.* Boston: Pearson.

Orme, J. G., Cherry, D. J., & Krcek, T. E. (2013). Who is willing to foster children with disabilities? *Journal of Public Child Welfare, 7*(5), 566–585. doi:10.1080/15548732.2013.843494

Rapoport, J. L., Giedd, J. N., & Gogtay, N. (2012). Neurodevelopmental model of schizophrenia: Update 2012. *Molecular Psychiatry, 17,* 1228–1238.

Reichenberg, L. W., & Seligman, L. (2016). *Selecting effective treatment: A comprehensive, systematic guide to treating mental disorders.* Hoboken, NJ: Wiley.

Rutter, M. (1972). Childhood schizophrenia reconsidered. *Journal of Autism and Childhood Schizophrenia, 2,* 315–337.

Shean, G. D. (2009). Evidence-based psychosocial practices and recovery from schizophrenia. *Psychiatry: Interpersonal & Biological Processes, 72*(4), 307–320. doi:10.1521/psyc.2009.72.4.307

Shawyer, F., Farhall, J., Mackinnon, A., Trauer, T., Sims, E., Ratcliff, K., ... & Copolov, D. (2012). A randomized controlled trial of acceptance-based cognitive behavioural therapy for command hallucinations in psychotic disorders. *Behaviour Research and Therapy, 50* (2), 110–121. doi:10.1016/j.brat.2011.11.007

Tandon, R. (2011). Antipsychotics in the treatment of schizophrenia: An overview. *Journal of Clinical Psychiatry, 72* (Suppl.), 4-8.

van Os, J., Kenis, G., & Rutten, B. P. (2010). The environment and schizophrenia. *Nature, 468*(7321), 203-212. doi:10.1038/nature09563

Wearden, A. J., Tarrier, N., Barrowclough, C., Zastowny, T., R., & Rahill, A. A. (2000). A review of expressed emotion research in health care. *Clinical Psychology Review, 20,* 633–666.

Wykes, T., Steel, C., Everitt, B., & Tarrier, N. (2008). Cognitive behavior therapy for schizophrenia: Effect sizes, clinical models, and methodological rigor. *Schizophrenia Bulletin, 34,* 523–537.

CASE 4

Carly Prochaski
Shandiin Begay

Carly's story is a heavy one, from the moment this 15-year-old Native American girl was adopted by her white parents until the end of her case, when she receives no treatment for her depression and suicidal behavior. Carly's case examines cross-racial adoption, the etiology of depression, and factors that contribute to suicide.

ICD 10/DSM-5 Diagnosis:
F32.0 (296.21) Major Depressive Disorder, Mild, Single Episode

Diagnostic Discussion

Based on the intake interview with Carly, the CAMS Suicide Status Form, the meeting with Carly's teacher, and the interview with Carly's parents, Ms. Hammett gave Carly a diagnosis of Major Depressive Disorder, Mild, Single Episode. To receive this diagnosis, a person must demonstrate at least five of the following symptoms during the same two-week period (APA, 2013). The criteria listed below are followed by Ms. Hammett's clinical judgment about how Carly demonstrates the symptoms.

- Depressed mood most every day, evidenced by feeling sad, empty or hopeless, or by appearing to others as tearful. In children, depressed mood often masks as irritability. *Carly doesn't admit to being sad, empty, or hopeless, nor do others see her as tearful or upset. She was also pleasant in our interview and wasn't irritable.*

- Markedly diminished interest in activities most every day. *Carly definitely meets this criterion. She's not only quit the soccer team, but her school grades have plummeted. She also doesn't seem interested in school or learning anymore, calling it boring and wondering what the point of it was. She's not hanging out with her friend Diane as much, nor does she talk to her friends at school between classes. She kept saying that she was bored with things and that life seemed kind of blah, so she definitely sounds less interested in activities and events than she once was.*

- Significant weight gain or loss when not dieting; change in appetite. *We can't be certain that Carly has lost a significant amount of weight. Although she's thin now, it sounds like this has always been the case. She does show a change in her appetite, as she noted that food doesn't taste as good as it used to taste and that she isn't eating as much since she quit playing soccer.*

165

- Insomnia or *hypersomnia* (sleeping more than would be expected). *Carly seems to have no problems sleeping, so she doesn't meet this criterion.*

- Psychomotor agitation or retardation nearly every day. *I don't think Carly meets this criterion. She was agitated in my office and restless to leave, but most teenagers aren't too enthused about meeting with a mental health counselor.*

- Fatigue or loss of energy nearly every day. *Carly noted several times that she didn't have as much energy as she used to have. This criterion is tricky, however, because engaging in exercise actually makes people feel more energetic. I'm wondering how much of her loss of energy is a side effect of not exercising as much and not eating as much. Nevertheless, I think Carly shows evidence of this problem.*

- Feelings of worthlessness or excessive guilt nearly every day. *I don't think Carly meets this criterion. She was critical of herself regarding how she did both in the classroom and on the soccer field, but she didn't show excessive guilt or feelings of worthlessness. Instead, she seemed mostly OK with herself. It seemed like what she showed in the interview was fairly normal adolescent self-doubt, not a feeling of extreme worthlessness.*

- Lessened ability to think or concentrate, or indecisiveness, nearly every day. *Carly certainly shows this symptom. She's struggling to concentrate in school and said that learning takes more energy than it used to take. She's failing her classes and she used to earn straight As. Her teacher said that she walks through the halls in a daze, which is a change of behavior for her.*

- Recurrent thoughts of death, suicidal *ideation* (thinking about suicide) or a suicide attempt or plan. *Although Carly denied any suicidal ideation in my office, it was clear that she'd been thinking about suicide at least to some extent. She did try to kill herself before, too, by taking aspirin. I'm worried about this girl. I didn't think she was a danger to herself and I thought the risk of self-harm was fairly low overall, but I was wrong.*

Two modifiers were given to Carly's base diagnosis. Despite her suicide attempt, her diagnosis of Major Depressive Disorder is considered Mild because she only meets the minimum five criteria required for her to be diagnosed with this disorder. If Carly demonstrated more symptoms, her diagnosis of Major Depressive Disorder might be considered Moderate or Severe (APA, 2013). Carly's diagnosis is also considered to be a Single Episode in that this is the first time she has shown depressive symptoms. Thus, her depression is not recurrent.

1. Do you think that Ms. Hammett "missed" the seriousness of Carly's suicidal behavior? If you were the mental health provider in this case, do you think you would have predicted Carly's suicide attempt? Relatedly, do you think that Ms. Hammett "put the idea in Carly's head" to kill herself and that Carly wasn't thinking about suicide before the interview?

2. In the DSM system, all symptoms are weighted equally. In other words, although Carly tried to kill herself, that serious behavior "counts" for only one of the five symptoms necessary to receive a Major Depressive Disorder diagnosis. Therefore, despite her suicide attempt, Carly's depression is considered to be in the mild range. Do you agree that all symptoms should be equally weighted in a diagnostic system? Why or why not?

Case Conceptualization

Why did Carly develop such a serious depression so quickly? Or had she been depressed for a longer time than just the past few months? Did her parents, teachers, friends, and coach miss any warning signs she might have been giving in the past that she was going to try to kill herself? Did her adoption and search for her Native American ancestry somehow play into her depressed feelings? How did the loss of her identity as an athlete affect her depression when she realized that she would not be able to use soccer to further her education? Did that loss somehow affect her search for her ancestry, perhaps to find a new identity? What made Carly so desperate that she took that bottle of aspirin? These are difficult questions to answer. The following section will consider three relevant areas of research to help us understand Carly: adolescent depression, adoption, and suicidality. Before discussing these issues, we want to make clear that children who are adopted aren't generally at greater risk of killing themselves than non-adopted children. In Carly's case, however, the situation surrounding her adoption likely played a role in the development of her depression.

First, let's consider the etiology of depression. It runs in families, especially in the case of depression that first appears in adolescents, as was true of Carly's adolescent-onset depression (Rice, 2010). Interestingly, depression that begins in childhood doesn't seem to be particularly heritable (Rice, 2010). We don't know the mental health history of Carly's biological parents, so we have no way of knowing if Carly was genetically predisposed to experience depression. In general, just being an adolescent is a risk factor for depression. Teenagers in general, not just depressed ones, show increased levels of the stress hormone *cortisol* in their bodies. They also show greater reactivity to stress after they hit puberty (Gunnar, Wewerka, Frenn, Long, & Griggs, 2009). Thus, even if Carly doesn't have a genetic risk for depression, being an adolescent is a risk factor for her.

People with certain temperaments are also more likely to develop depression. In particular, children with high levels of negative emotionality, or a tendency to experience frequent and intense periods of being down, are more likely to be depressed (Hyde, Mezulis, & Abramson, 2008). People prone to depression also show low levels of positive emotionality, or a reduced ability to experience joy and pleasure. Finally, people with depression often have poor effortful control, or struggle to manage their impulses (Hyde, Mezulis, & Abramson, 2008). Despite consistent research about the role of temperament in the development of depression, Carly's history provides no clues that she was a temperamentally difficult child. By all indications, she seemed to be well-adjusted as both a child and a teenager until the last month. She had friends, made excellent grades, behaved well, and played sports, all evidence suggesting that she had good self-regulation and an easygoing temperament.

Another possible reason that depression develops is that some people show a cognitive vulnerability to become depressed (Beck, 1987). Beck's model of depression is explained in more detail in another case study (see Bear in Case 8). The key elements are that an individual possesses core dysfunctional attitudes which lead them to process information differently than non-depressed people. Thus, people who are depressed are more likely to have a "negative cognitive triad" (Beck, 1987) and have negative views of themselves as worthless, the world as unfair, and their future as hopeless. Mental health experts sometimes refer to this worldview as *stinkin' thinkin'*. These individuals tend to ruminate and brood on their problems instead of solving them.

Does Carly show this depressive style? No, not particularly. She may be critical of herself and have high expectations for what she can accomplish, such as her expectations for herself regarding soccer, but she seems to have an overall decently balanced view of herself. She demonstrates no evidence of devastatingly low self-esteem. Likewise, we've no evidence from Ms. Hammett's interview with Carly that she views the world as unfair. Finally, she doesn't seem to view the future as hopeless. Instead, she seems optimistic that things might get better, including that Diane will again spend time with her after soccer season. Carly also states at the end of the session with Ms. Hammett that she was just in a funk "right now" and that things will get better because they always do. Thus, Beck's cognitive model, one of the most enduring and research-supported models of depression, is not particularly helpful when understanding why Carly is depressed.

Another model that might explain Carly's depression focuses on depression being correlated with adverse life experiences. This research suggests that difficult life circumstances can predispose people to depression (Goodman & Brand, 2009). These life experiences can include parental depression, or their own history of abuse, trauma, or loss. In Carly's case, she would be too young to remember being adopted, so her adoption and any loss of attachment with her biological parents would not be considered a trauma. At three days old, children are too young to show a strong attachment to their caregivers. Carly had experienced no major traumas throughout her life and was not abused. Perhaps not making the travel soccer team was an adverse life experience which overwhelmed her coping skills. Teenagers often have difficulty coping with stressful life circumstances (Wenzel & Beck, 2008), because they've had limited opportunities to build up their responses to them. Was the loss of her dreams as a soccer player stressful enough to overtax her coping skills? This is unlikely. The impact of one negative event such as this doesn't seem to equate to the impact of a lifetime of early trauma and loss. Thus, the early adversity model doesn't seem to shed much light on Carly's depression.

One final etiological model that might help us understand Carly's depression is the interpersonal model (Coyne, 1976; Joiner & Timmons, 2009). This model of depression suggests that depression is fundamentally an interpersonal disorder. According to this model, depressed individuals both react and contribute to interpersonal difficulties. Individuals prone to depression tend to experience more interpersonal stress (Carter & Garber, 2011). In particular, children with stressful home lives, such as high levels of parent–child conflict, parental hostility, and low levels of parental warmth, are more likely to be depressed (Schwartz et al., 2011).

Does this interpersonal model explain Carly's depression? Perhaps, but not exactly. Carly lost some important interpersonal relationships when she quit the soccer team, and this might be a factor in her depression. Additionally, Carly's relationship with her parents is stressful. Carly's parents have their problematic behaviors, such as not being supportive of Carly's Native American ethnicity and her search to find her roots, and this may have contributed to Carly's depression. This lack of support in helping Carly find her ethnic identity is likely to be particularly salient for Carly because she attends school with few other Native Americans. Adolescence is a critical time in life for searching for one's values, beliefs, and self-definition. In this way, the Prochaskis have likely contributed to Carly's not feeling understood by her parents. Not to diminish the importance of this cultural component, but the balance of their parenting seems to be decent. They support Carly in school and sports. They seem to provide her with supervision as well as parenting warmth, evidenced by their Sunday-night Scrabble ritual. Their lack of knowledge about Carly's current problems is alarming, and Carly also seems pretty good at pretending that she's doing OK. Another consideration is that her problems have developed suddenly. The Prochaskis seem to have been caught off guard by how serious her mental health problems are.

3. Of all of the theoretical models of depression discussed, which one do you think best explains Carly's depression? Why?

4. In your opinion, are the authors of this book too lenient or too harsh when explaining the role of Carly's parents regarding her depression? Why?

Let's consider a secondary factor that might relate to Carly's developing depression, the fact that she's adopted in a cross-racial adoption. In general, children who are adopted tend to have more learning and emotional difficulties than other children (Levy-Shiff, 2001). These problems are more likely to occur if children are adopted later in life. Many reasons might explain why adoptees tend to struggle more as a group than children raised by their birth parents.

First, the reasons that parents give children up for adoption, such as mental health issues, lower cognitive functioning, and substance abuse, tend to have a genetic component. Second, children adopted later in life likely have lived in poverty or in conflict-ridden homes during their first few years of life. These older children also may experience a disruption in attachment to their primary caregivers, which can be extremely difficult for children. Finally, adopted children are more likely to be temperamentally, intellectually, and behaviorally different from their adoptive parents as compared to biological children. These differences mean more chances for parent–child conflicts (Levy-Shiff, 2001).

Despite these challenges, most children who are adopted fare well (Johnson, 2002). One common finding with adopted children is that they often express curiosity about their birth families during adolescence, as they begin searching for their own identities, or during young adulthood, as they pursue marriage and childbirth (Schaffer & Kral, 1988). What about cross-racially adopted children, like Carly? As long as trans-racially adopted children are supported in learning about their heritage, they generally form a bicultural identity that represents their both their birth and adopted heritages (Brooks & Barth, 1999). This merged identity is a healthy outcome for children adopted trans-racially.

Carly wasn't supported by her adoptive parents in exploring her ethnic roots. Instead, her parents inadvertently gave Carly messages that it was necessary to rescue her from a Native American upbringing. They were reluctant to let Carly explore her Native American roots when she began asking questions about her ethnic background as an adolescent. For example, they refused to let her visit the reservation where she was born or use her given Navajo name. Their misguided messages may have led Carly to believe that she should be ashamed of her Native American ancestry instead of celebrating it.

Finally, let us take a brief look at the literature about suicidal behavior. What are some of the risk factors of suicide? Suicidal ideation, self-injurious behavior, and suicide attempts all increase in adolescence as compared to childhood (Nock et al., 2013). In fact, more than 20% of community-based adolescents aged 12 through 19 have engaged in suicidal gestures (Nock et al., 2013). These numbers are staggering, because the data are based on normal children who haven't been referred for mental health services. Being female is also a risk factor for suicide: girls are twice as likely as boys to engage in suicidal behavior (Nixon, Cloutier, & Jansson, 2008). However, although girls are more likely than boys to attempt suicide, boys are more likely than girls to die by suicide. This is because boys typically choose more reliably lethal ways to kill themselves than girls do (Berman, Jobes, & Silverman, 2007), including firearms. Having a mental health diagnosis such as Major Depression also makes suicide attempts more likely (Nock et al., 2013). Carly exhibits all of these demographic risk factors, as she is an adolescent girl with a mental health diagnosis.

Why do youth try to kill themselves? We don't know all of the answers to this important question. Hopelessness is one key factor, in that youth who are hopeless tend to focus on suicide as being the only choice to escape from their present situation (Wenzel & Beck, 2008). Carly denies feeling hopeless, but her behavior might suggest that she's more hopeless than she is willing to express, so this may be a factor in her suicide attempt. Another reason that may contribute to a teenager's suicidal behavior is that the teenager perceives herself to be a burden to others (Joiner et al., 2009). Carly doesn't seem to worry about being a burden, so this factor doesn't seem to figure prominently in her decision to try to kill herself. A final reason that teenagers engage in suicidal behavior is a lack of *belongingness* (Joiner et al., 2006). This lack of connection with other people is worrisome in Carly. She doesn't feel that her parents understand her. She lost her connection with Diane and her other soccer teammates when she quit the soccer team. She also lost her connection with her coach. Her recent apathy towards school has likely affected her relationships with her teachers and classmates, who would be less connected to a student who was failing all her classes. In fact, Carly names her cats as the only individuals to whom she feels a sense of connection.

When considering the many reasons that Carly is depressed enough to try to kill herself, you might be frustrated, as no easy answers emerge to explain her behavior. This lack of airtight explanations is common in the mental health profession. People are complicated beings with unique histories and an endless array of behavioral and lifestyle choices. Finding the answer to why we do what we do is never easy, despite our most educated guesses. In cases like Carly's, the research takes us only so far in explaining her behavior. After the research is applied, we're still left with tremendous shortcomings in understanding why people do what they do. As frustrating and difficult as this situation is from a mental health provider's perspective, it is even more challenging from the perspective of a person with a mental illness, or as a family member of a person with mental illness.

5. Do you have a family member or someone close to you who struggles with mental illness? If so, how will these experiences affect you as a professional? If the converse is true and you do not know any people with a mental illness except as clients, how will this affect you?

Evidence-Based Treatment

The night that Carly had taken the bottle of aspirin, she was admitted to the local hospital. She was placed in the psychiatric wing of the hospital, for patients experiencing serious mental health problems whose behavior was a danger to themselves or others, thus justifying inpatient care. Carly was released from the hospital after 48 hours. While at the hospital, she worked closely with mental health providers. She promised not to try to kill herself again and explained that she didn't actually want to die when she took the bottle of aspirin. Instead, she was just trying to let other people know how much she was struggling and how alone she felt in the world right now. Carly was discharged to her parents with a follow-up appointment at an outpatient mental health counselor scheduled three days after her release. Carly was prescribed an SSRI, Prozac (fluoxetine), and was also scheduled to see a psychiatrist two weeks after her discharge. The Prochaskis called Ms. Hammett to update her on Carly's hospitalization and discharge plan. Ms. Hammett was relieved to hear that Carly was under expert mental health care. She made an appointment with Carly to check in with her at school the next day to see how things were going for her.

Carly seemed to be in better spirits after she was released from the hospital. The night she came home, she played Scrabble with her parents and laughed with them. She texted her friend Diane just to say hello and ask her what was up with her.

Carly never made it to any scheduled appointment, however. Two days after she was released from the hospital, she couldn't sleep one night. She petted both of her cats and told them that she loved them. Then she quietly left her home in the middle of the night. Her parents neither heard nor saw her leave. Carly walked for several miles to the center of town, to a bridge that spans a major river. She deliberated what she should do for several minutes, as cars sped quickly by her. Then, suddenly, Carly jumped off the bridge into the river. She didn't survive the fall. The police found her body the following morning, contacting her parents who made a positive identification.

When Helen heard the news, she immediately went into Carly's bedroom, shut the door, saw Carly's cats snuggled together in her unmade bed, and fell to her knees in overwhelming grief. Glen shut himself in his bedroom closet, trying hard to contain his emotions but unable to do so. He tried to scream "Why? Why, Carly, why?" but no words would come to his lips. Helen found a note in Carly's room that she had written the night that she'd killed herself. The note simply said,

> I am going to find light instead of living in rain.
> Let me go on my journey without calling my name.
> Signed,
> Shandiin Begay

The Prochaskis were in shock as they tried to understand what had happened with Carly. They tried to do what they were expected to do as a loved one dies—make funeral arrangements, write an obituary, contact extended family and friends. They found themselves going through the required motions without any real understanding of what was actually happening in their lives. They couldn't believe that this was real. They couldn't believe that Carly, their daughter, had killed herself. In the moments they could believe it, they were overwhelmed with grief and sadness. They wondered what they'd done wrong. They blamed themselves; they blamed each other. They wished they could have one more conversation with Carly—one more soccer or Scrabble game, one more family dinner, one more time to see their daughter smile or give her a hug. They felt that a giant chasm had opened up—between them, within each of them—that was so large it threatened to swallow their entire lives.

In their distraught state, they hadn't thought to contact Ms. Hammett to let her know that Carly had killed herself. Ms. Hammett went to school the following morning and learned of Carly's death from the school principal. Ms. Hammett went to her office, closed the door, and cried.

Cases like Carly's are heartbreaking for everyone involved. They leave everyone wondering what they could have done differently to prevent some-one's death, but it's important to realize that ultimately, each person is in con-trol of his or her destiny. If someone is intent on killing herself, she'll find a way to do so. Nevertheless, as mental health providers, we question, struggle, mourn, and grieve, although not to the extent of the families of suicide victims.

The Prochaskis declined mental health counseling to deal with their grief. Instead, they decided to try to get through the ordeal as best they could on their own.

6. If you were Ms. Hammett, what would you do to survive your busy day at work, full of scheduled clients? How would you engage in self-care, both during and after work?

7. If you were Ms. Hammett, would you contact the Prochaskis after Carly's death? What would you say or do?

The mental health services that Carly should have received are numer-ous. The services that she did receive are fairly typical. Psychiatric hospital-ization, a mainstay in interventions with suicidal individuals, has actually been shown to have limited effectiveness in preventing suicide (Hankammer, Snyder, & Hankammer, 2006). As therapists, we often refer clients for hospi-talization because of our own discomfort and fear in working with people who are suicidal. Other treatment options besides involuntary hospitalization include voluntary hospitalization, partial-hospitalization programs, intensive outpatient therapy, medication, and ensuring that the client isn't left alone (Reichenberg & Seligman, 2016).

Evidence-based practice doesn't involve the use of so-called no-suicide contracts, in which clients agree in writing not to kill themselves. Many clini-cians continue to use these tools despite their lack of effectiveness (Bartlett, 2006). No-suicide contracts tend to sever connections between the client and the therapist. Practitioners' continued use of them has been suggested as a reflection of our own discomfort with the possibility of client suicide rather than actual concern for the patient (Reichenberg & Seligman, 2016). Unlike no-suicide contracts, safety plans are recommended as a suicide prevention tool. Safety plans are collaborative and focus on active prevention and coping skills. In a safety plan, a client and therapist discuss and record what the client will do if she feels like killing herself, including who she might contact and how she might manage her suicidal feelings (Reichenberg & Seligman, 2016).

One important caveat to assessing suicidality is to understand that all suicidal behavior is serious. Suicidal ideation, suicidal gestures, and self-injurious behavior such as cutting all must be given careful clinical consideration. No behavior should be discounted by concluding that "She's just seeking attention; she doesn't really want to die." Actually, most people who attempt suicide don't want to die. They just want to end the pain that they currently feel, and suicide seems like the only way to do so. Remembering this ambivalence, and trying to find it in the client, is crucial. Trivializing self-injurious behavior as merely attention-seeking isn't helpful (Reichenberg & Seligman, 2016).

The key to a therapist's conducting a good suicide assessment is to ask open-ended questions while carefully assessing key areas. Areas that must be assessed include coping skills, protective factors, and lethality, such as asking if the client has a plan to kill herself and the means to carry out the plan (Reichenberg & Seligman, 2016). These factors help clinicians to determine whether the overall risk of a client killing herself is low, moderate, or high. While assessing these areas, current research supports that our best tool in dealing with suicidal clients is demonstrating genuine concern, respect, and empathy for the suicidal person (Clark, 2010). Conveying a sense of hope is also crucial. Balancing our compassion for the client with our own fears is challenging, especially in an outpatient or private-practice setting where we don't have the resources of an institution or organization supporting us.

Ms. Hammett demonstrated many therapist characteristics associated with successful treatment of suicidal individuals, including carefully assessing suicidality while still building a meaningful therapeutic alliance. She utilized an emerging model of suicide prevention in her work with Carly. This model is called the collaborative assessment and management of suicidality model, or CAMS (Jobes & Linehan, 2016). The CAMS model has received some good preliminary support as a tool to help prevent suicide among both adults and adolescents (Jobes & Linehan, 2016). However, CAMS is only a tool, as Michael Jobes, the creator of the instrument, is clear to acknowledge. The real power of therapy is the compassionate relationship between two people.

8. Do you think Ms. Hammett and Carly had a good rapport in their only therapy session? Underline key sentences from the dialogue to support or refute this position.

9. Did Ms. Hammett sufficiently consider culturally relevant factors in Carly's case?

Carly also received, or was about to receive, two additional services that have been helpful in the treatment of Major Depression. Carly was prescribed fluoxetine (Prozac), an SSRI (selective serotonin reuptake inhibitor), at the hospital. Such medication often is helpful in individuals with severe depression (Nemeroff & Schatzberg, 2007). Antidepressant medication has a dangerous side effect, however. Sometimes, clients who begin an antidepressant gain some energy and clarity after beginning the medication. While this would seem a promising sign, clients sometimes utilize their newfound energy to follow up on a dormant plan to kill themselves (Christophersen & Vanscoyoc, 2013). Perhaps this explains part of Carly's calmness in the days before she killed herself, as she played board games with her parents and texted her friend Diane.

In addition to medication, Carly was going to receive intensive outpatient therapy, which likely would have involved either cognitive behavioral therapy (CBT) or interpersonal therapy (IPT). Both CBT and IPT have been shown to be effective treatments for adolescents like Carly who have depressive disorders (Reichenberg & Seligman, 2016). Given Carly's intelligence, excellent past level of adjustment, good coping skills, and supportive family, she would have been a good candidate for either type of therapy and likely would have made tremendous gains in therapy. Sadly, we will never know how therapy might have helped Carly.

10. What do you think would have been the most important factors that would have made a difference for Carly? What might have changed the outcome of her case?

11. If this case negatively affected you due to its potential stressful and traumatic content, how would you ethically deal with your own feelings?

References

American Psychiatric Association. (2013). *Diagnostic and statistical manual of mental disorders* (5th ed.). Washington, DC: Author.

Bartlett, M. L. (2006). The efficacy of a no-suicide contract with clients in counseling on an outpatient basis. Dissertation Abstracts International, 67, 3438, 06B UMI No. 3225247.

Beck, A. T. (1987). Cognitive models of depression. *Journal of Cognitive Psychotherapy, 1*(1), 5–37.

Berman, A. L., Jobes, D. A., & Silverman, M. M. (2007) Adolescent suicide: Assessment and intervention. Washington, DC: American Psychological Association.

Brooks, D., & Barth, R. P. (1999). Adult transracial and inracial adoptees: Effects of race, gender, adoptive family structure, and placement history on adjustment outcomes. *American Journal of Orthopsychiatry, 69*(1), 87–99. http://dx.doi.org/10.1037/h0080384

Carter, J. S., & Garber, J. (2011). Predictors of the first onset of a major depressive episode and changes in depressive symptoms across adolescence: Stress and negative cognitions. *Journal of Abnormal Psychology, 120*(4), 779–796. doi:10.1037/a0025441

Christophersen, E. R., & Vanscoyoc, S. M., (2013). *Treatments that work with children: Empirically supported strategies for managing childhood problems* (2nd ed.). Washington, DC: American Psychological Association.

Clark, A. J. (2010). Empathy: An integrated model in the counseling process. *Journal of Counseling and Development, 88*(3), 348–356.

Coyne, J. C. (1976). Depression and the response of others. *Journal of Abnormal Psychology, 85*(2), 186–193.

Goodman, S. H., & Brand, S. R. (2009). Depression and early adverse experiences. In I. H. Gotlib & C. Hammen (Eds.), *Handbook of depression* (2nd ed., pp.249–274). New York: Guilford.

Gunnar, M. R., Wewerka, S., Frenn, K., Long, J. D., & Griggs, C. (2009). Developmental changes in hypothalamus pituitary-adrenal activity over the transition to adolescence: Normative changes and associated with puberty. *Development and Psychopathology, 21*(1), 69–85. doi:10.1017/S0954579409000054

Hankammer, W., Snyder, B., & Hankammer, C. C. (2006). Empathy as the primary means in suicide assessment. *Journal for the Professional Counselor, 21*, 5–19.

Hyde, J. S., Mezulis, A., & Abramson, L. Y. (2008). The ABCs of depression: Integrating affective, biological, and cognitive models to explain the emergence of gender differences in depression. *Psychological Review, 115*(2), 291–313. doi:10.1037/0033-295X.115.2.291

Jobes, D. A., & Linehan. M. M. (2016). *Managing suicidal risk: A collaborative approach.* New York: Guilford.

Johnson, D. E. (2002). Adoption and the effect on children's development. *Early Human Development, 68*(1), 39–54. http://dx.doi.org/10.1016/S0378-3782(02)00017-8

Joiner, T. E., & Timmons, K. E. (2009). Depression and its interpersonal context. In I. H. Gotlib & C. Hammen (Eds.), *Handbook of depression* (2nd ed., pp. 322–339). New York: Guilford.

Joiner, T. E., Van Oden, K. A., Witte, T. K., Selby, E. A., Ribeiro, J. D., Lewis, R., & Rudd, M. D. (2009). Main predictions of the interpersonal-psychological theory of suicidal behavior: Empirical tests in two samples of young adults. *Journal of Abnormal Psychology, 118*(3), 634–646. doi:10.1037/a0016500

Levy-Shiff, R. (2001). Psychological adjustment of adoptees in adulthood: Family environment and adoption-related correlates. *International Journal of Behavioral Development, 25*(2), 97–104. doi:10.1080/01650250042000131

Nemeroff, C. B., & Schatzberg, A. F. (2007). Pharmacological treatments for unipolar depression. In P. E. Nathan & J. M. Gorman (Eds.), *A guide to treatments that work* (3rd ed., pp. 271–288). New York: Oxford University Press.

Nixon, M. K., Cloutier, P., & Jansson, S. M. (2008). Nonsuicidal self-harm in youth: A population-based survey. *Canadian Medical Association Journal, 178*(3), 306–312. doi:10.1503/cmaj.061693

Nock, M. K., Green, J. G., Hwang, I., McLaughlin, K. A., Sampson, N. A., Zaslavsky, A. M., & Kessler, R. C. (2013). Prevalence, correlates and treatment of lifetime suicidal behavior among adolescence: Results from the National Comorbidity Survey Replication—Adolescent Supplement (NCS-A). *JAMA Psychiatry, 70*(3), 300–310. doi:10.1001/2013.jamapsychiatry.55

Reichenberg, L. W., & Seligman, L. (2016). *Selecting effective treatments: A comprehensive, systematic guide to treating mental disorders.* Hoboken, NJ: Wiley.

Rice, F. (2010). Genetics of childhood and adolescent depression: Insights into etiological heterogeneity and challenges for future genomic research. *Genome Medicine, 2*, 68–73.

Schaffer, J., & Kral, R. (1988). Adoptive families. In C. S. Chilman, E. W. Nunnally, & F. M. Cox (Eds.), *Variant family forms* (pp. 165–184). Newbury Park, PA: Sage.

Schwartz, O. S., Dudgeon, P., Sheeber, L.B., Yap, M. B. H., Simmons, J. G., & Allen, N. B. (2011). Developing constructs for psychopathology research: Research domain criteria. *Journal of Abnormal Psychology, 119*, 631–639.

Wenzel, A., & Beck, A. T. (2008). A cognitive model of suicidal behavior: Theory and treatment. *Applied and Preventive Psychology, 76*, 39–44.

CASE 5

Maria Hadjipavlou

Canada and the United States have historically welcomed immigrants to strengthen our diverse culture. However, children of immigrants face unique cultural and family pressures, as is demonstrated in the case of this 17-year-old Cypriot girl with high anxiety. Maria's case illustrates the co-morbid nature of anxiety disorders. Her case also elucidates how the stigma of mental health problems can impact treatment. The topics discussed below include the literature on behaviorally inhibited temperament, the Tripartite Model of Emotion, and the Coping Cat program for treating anxiety disorders.

ICD 10/DSM-5 Diagnosis:
F41.1 (300.02) Generalized Anxiety Disorder
F40.218 (300.29) Specific Phobia, Animal

Diagnostic Discussion

Maria's diagnosis is straightforward compared with others in this book. She qualifies for two related diagnoses: Generalized Anxiety Disorder and Specific Phobia, Animals. These two disorders are often co-morbid and are both fueled by anxiety.

To be diagnosed with Generalized Anxiety Disorder, a person must show evidence of the following symptoms (APA, 2013).

1. The person experiences excessive anxiety and worry, for more days than not, spanning a period of at least six months, about a number of events or activities.

2. The person finds it difficult to control the worries.

3. The anxiety and worry are associated with at least three of the following six symptoms: (a) being restless; (b) becoming easily fatigued; (c) having difficulty concentrating; (d) being irritable; (e) having muscle tension; and (f) experiencing sleep problems. (Important note: Children need to show only one of these symptoms.)

4. The anxiety, worry or physical symptoms cause distress at work, school, or in relationships.

5. The anxiety isn't better explained by the effects of a substance.

6. The anxiety isn't better explained by another mental disorder.

In Maria's case, she meets the first criterion by worrying more days than not. She's also been worried for more than six months. In fact, she has worried since she was a little girl. We have ample evidence that Maria chronically worries about a variety of things, including her grades, her romantic life, her family, the restaurant, a fire, and being accepted at school. She is also apprehensive about her future. Although most of Maria's worries are developmentally typical for a 17-year-old, her worries are more severe than those of most adolescents. They impact her day-to-day functioning as well as her ability to sleep at night. This level of impairment is what makes anxiety diagnosable instead of just a normal teenage problem.

Maria meets the second criterion of finding it difficult to control her worries, as illustrated by the numerous examples in the case study. Her worries dominate her entire life on a daily basis—at school, at the restaurant, with Yia, and at night. In the case study, no successful strategies that Maria might use to cope with her anxiety are ever mentioned. Even her journal is a journal of worries. Once her concerns begin spiraling into a vortex in Maria's mind, she can't stop the spring from coiling tighter and tighter.

Because she's technically still a child, she needs only one of these symptoms for diagnosis. However, taking a developmental perspective is useful when considering symptoms. Next year, Maria will be 18 and technically an adult. At that point, she'd need three symptoms from the list to warrant a Generalized Anxiety Disorder diagnosis. Given that she's so near adulthood, we'd expect her to exhibit closer to three symptoms than just one.

The third criterion focuses on the physiological and behavioral manifestations of anxiety. Maria shows many of these symptoms. She's described as restless, including her demonstrating such nervous behavior as jiggling her foot. Although the case study doesn't mention her as being easily fatigued, we've seen that Maria stays awake at night, worrying about being too exhausted to function the next day if she doesn't get some sleep—and given the family tendency to keep things to themselves, Maria would likely attempt to hide her exhausted state as well. Maria does not have particular difficulties concentrating despite her restless nights. In fact, she is amused at Yia's attempts to "check" her work, given Maria's straight As and Yia's inability to read much English. Maria also concentrates fairly well at school—at least up until the present time—since she has excellent grades. Maria also demonstrates irritability, mostly with her mother but also with her brother and father. Sotiri describes her as touchy and her relationship with her father is certainly tense. Maria also shows evidence of muscle tension, best seen as Yia tries unsuccessfully to get Maria to relax in their afternoon homework sessions. Finally, Maria has significant sleep problems.

The fourth criterion is that the anxiety affects the person to the point where it causes distress in her job, schooling, or relationships. Maria's anxiety definitely affects her life. She's doing well in school and at her job, but her anxiety makes it hard for her to feel like herself and to let her friends get to know her. One important lesson in Maria's case is to realize that her psychological problem is not particularly noticeable to others, even those who know her well. In fact, Maria goes to great lengths to hide her mental health problems, and she is mortified that someone might discover the demons that she so carefully hides. She's struggling internally, but she's also functioning well. She's earning excellent grades, is popular in school, has friends, works hard in the restaurant, and has no behavioral problems. Everyone would consider her a nice, well-adjusted teenager. Sometimes, though, a person can be functioning well in society but still be struggling with a serious problem. A psychological disorder is different than physical illness because there are usually no visible external symptoms—no lesions, bleeding, wounds, or fevers—to let others know a person is hurting.

The fifth and sixth criteria are basically that a person's anxiety is not caused by something else, such as substance use, medical problems, or another mental disorder. These criteria are called *exclusionary criteria*, and they basically ensure that another, more obvious cause of the displayed symptoms isn't available. In other words, we want to make sure we don't overlook an obvious explanation for a person's behavior instead of diagnosing her with something inappropriate. In Maria's case, no such alternative explanation is available. Maria has a separate but related disorder called Specific Phobia discussed directly below. However, the symptoms of Specific Phobia can't be explained by Generalized Anxiety Disorder. Therefore, Maria needs two diagnoses.

The hallmark symptom of Maria's second disorder, Specific Phobia, is an irrational fear of something—dogs, snakes, insects, heights, storms, water, blood, tunnels, bridges, enclosed places, flying, or many other discrete objects or situations. In Maria's case, her fear is of spiders. Although she's not the focus of this case study, Maria's grandmother Yia likely could be diagnosed with Specific Phobia, subtype Animal, as well.

To be diagnosed with a Specific Phobia, an individual must meet seven criteria (APA, 2013):

1. Marked and persistent fear about an object or situation. In children, this fear can manifest itself through crying, temper tantrums, freezing, or clinging.

2. The phobic object almost always provokes immediate fear or anxiety.

3. The phobic object is actively avoided or is endured with intense fear or anxiety.

4. The fear or anxiety is out of proportion to the actual danger presented by the phobic object.

5. The fear, anxiety, or avoidance persists longer than six months.

6. The fear, anxiety, or avoidance causes clinically significant distress or impairment.

7. The disturbance is not better explained by another mental disorder.

Let's apply these criteria to Maria. First, she must have a marked and persistent fear of an object or situation. This fits, as she's terrified of spiders and shows extreme fear around them on every occasion in which she's exposed to them. She meets the second criterion of immediate fear and anxiety around spiders, evidenced by the story of how Maria and Yia immediately scaled the kitchen stools to reach the safety of the counter upon seeing a spider. The third criterion is evident as Maria actively avoids spiders by refusing to view them at the zoo. She also refuses to go places, such as the restaurant pantry or the family garden, where she might see spiders. The fourth criterion is that an individual's fear is out of proportion to the actual danger of the feared object. Although spider bites can be dangerous and even deadly, such outcomes are exceedingly rare. Maria's fearful behavior when she sees a daddy-long-legs, a nonthreatening species of spider, is out of proportion to any actual danger. Her fainting at the sight of a wolf spider is debatable in terms of meeting this criterion. Wolf spiders are a little unnerving, even to those of us who don't have a fear of spiders! However, fainting at the sight of a spider is an atypical response.

Maria meets the fifth criterion, which is a time specifier stating that the fear must have been present for at least six months. Maria has been afraid of spiders for a long time, although the case study does not specify exactly how long. We can safely assume that her fear has persisted more than six months. The sixth criterion is that the person must experience significant distress or impairment. This criterion is actually a little challenging for Maria to meet. We don't know the extent to which Maria is bothered by her fear of spiders. Spiders cause her distress, but is she bothered by her stressful reaction to them? We aren't certain at this point. We know that her fear of spiders burdens other family members, since they must make trips to the pantry or garden in her place. Thus, this sixth criterion is met by Maria's "impairment" but not necessarily her "distress," as only one of these symptoms is required to meet this criterion. Finally, no other mental disorder can explain her fear of spiders, not even Generalized Anxiety Disorder. Although Maria is fearful and worries about many things, spiders seem to be in a class of worry all by themselves, and she's more afraid of them than anything else.

What other diagnoses were considered for Maria? A decision-tree process would start on a big-picture level. When you were reading the case study, you likely realized fairly quickly that Maria has a disorder somehow connected to anxiety. But the DSM-5 (APA, 2013) has many anxiety-related diagnoses. Social Anxiety Disorder doesn't fit Maria as a diagnosis because she fears many things, not just social situations in which she'll be evaluated. Panic Disorder isn't a possibility because Maria doesn't demonstrate the discrete and intense panic attacks that are central to this disorder. Agoraphobia was ruled out because she isn't particularly fearful about being in places from which she can't escape, like elevators, crowded malls, or planes.

One of the eating disorder diagnoses, such as Unspecified Feeding or Eating Disorder, was also considered. However, Maria's hinted-at concerns about her weight and eating seem in line with cultural and gender expectations of a 17-year-old girl living in North America.

The other diagnosis that was considered was Insomnia, a sleep disorder in which an individual has problems initiating and maintaining sleep. However, Insomnia wasn't given for two reasons. First, Maria's sleep problems seem directly related to, and in fact caused by, her anxiety. Second, in order to diagnose Insomnia a person's "predominant" complaint must be sleep problems. Although poor sleep is a part of Maria's problems, her anxiety is her main concern at this point. If Maria's sleep problems persist after she learns to better manage her anxiety, then Insomnia Disorder might be warranted. However, it shouldn't be diagnosed at this point.

1. Do you agree with the diagnoses given to Maria? Why or why not? Should she have received the Specific Phobia diagnosis? What about Insomnia, which was not diagnosed?
2. Look up insomnia on a reputable website. If you were to treat Maria's insomnia, what would you recommend for her?

Case Conceptualization

The challenging part in understanding a person is not what, but *why*. In other words, we ask *why* people do what they do. Let's consider why Maria might be such an anxious person. First, let's think through genetic and temperamental factors.

Maria's gender puts her at risk to develop anxiety disorders. Females are twice as likely as males to experience Generalized Anxiety Disorder (APA, 2013). Of people with Specific Phobias, girls outnumber boys at approximately the same rate, or 2:1 (APA, 2013). Numerous studies have indicated that girls tend to report more anxiety than boys, even in community samples of children who are not referred for treatment (Okamura et al., 2016). Interestingly, research also suggests that gender role orientation, or how closely children identify with being female or male, is more closely related to anxiety than actual biological sex (Muris, Meesters, & Knoops, 2005).

3. Apply the research on gender role orientation and anxiety to Maria's case. Why do you think that gender role orientation may be more closely related to anxiety than a person's actual gender?

Anxiety also tends to run in families, and anxiety disorders are more common in first-degree relatives (Bartels et al., 2007). Bartels and colleagues found that genetic factors are especially useful in explaining why younger children are anxious. What children actually inherit is not "anxious genes." Instead, children who become anxious are likely to be temperamentally *behaviorally inhibited* (Smoller et al., 2005). Behaviorally inhibited is a term that describes people who are shy, fearful, quiet, and tend to withdraw from new or noisy things. People who are behaviorally inhibited are not thrill seekers and prefer the comfort of their daily routine, relationships, and home life. They have to push themselves to get out of their comfort zone by taking a trip, signing up for a class, or going on a big life adventure. Behavioral inhibition appears to be biologically based and is present early in life, evidenced by a tendency to withdraw from novel situations and to show more distress in these situations, including higher cortisol levels, heart rate, and muscle tension (Smoller et al., 2005).

> 4. In question 8 in Part 1 of Maria's case, you drew a diagram of the factors you thought might influence Maria's anxiety. Refer to your diagram again and add relevant etiological factors that you may have forgotten or overlooked.

In addition to genes contributing to children's behaviorally inhibited temperament, genetics also affect a child's emotional style. The model that has received the most research support in understanding anxiety in both children and adults is the *tripartite model of emotion* (Mineka, Watson, & Clark, 1998). Tripartite is an intimidating word, but all it means is that something has three parts. The tripartite model of emotion just means that three important emotional factors contribute to the development of anxiety. These three factors are *positive affectivity, negative affectivity, and physiological hyperarousal.*

Positive affectivity refers to a person's overall pleasant feelings. These feelings include interest, enthusiasm, delight, and excitement. As you would expect, overall positive affectivity is low in people who are depressed. However, positive affectivity isn't particularly low in people who are anxious. Think about Maria for a moment as she nicely exemplifies this finding. Throughout the case study we see numerous examples of Maria's active interest in things, she likes school, and she enjoys being popular among her social circle and spending time with Yia. She's interested in dating, and boys in general.

The second factor is negative affectivity, which refers to a person's overall adverse feelings. These feelings can include anger, contempt, disgust, fear, and nervousness. Also, as you would expect, negative affectivity is high in people who are anxious as well as people who are depressed. Again, consider Maria. She's irritable, fearful, and certainly nervous. She doesn't feel contempt or disgust, but she certainly has high levels of anxious feelings.

The third factor, physiological hyperarousal, is the wildcard factor which makes things really interesting. Physiological hyperarousal describes a person's bodily responses to environmental stressors or events. People with high levels of physiological hyperarousal show an intense reaction to such events, including a pounding heart, quick and shallow breathing, trembling, lightheadedness, and experiencing dry mouth and dizziness. What do you think the research will show about the role of physiological hyperarousal? You would be right if you answer that only anxious people are high in physiological hyperarousal, especially anxious people with panic symptoms. Depressed people are low in physiological hyperarousal.

In summary, the tripartite model of emotion helps us understand Maria. She was likely born with a genetic tendency to have normal levels of positive affectivity, high levels of negative affectivity, and high levels of physiological hyperarousal. That combination of emotional factors makes it more likely that she'll be anxious than depressed.

> 5. Explain the tripartite model of emotion without using any jargon.
> 6. Draw three thermometers to apply the tripartite model of emotion to Maria.
> 7. Utilize the tripartite model of emotion to explain Papou, Yia, Andreas, and Eria. Whose emotional thermometer is most similar to Maria's? Whose is most different?

As you've learned, however, psychological disorders are caused by an interesting mix of nature and nurture, swirled together like Eria's oregano ice cream. Let's consider some factors from Maria's environment and development, including her family and culture, that may have contributed to her anxiety. Papou is not an anxious person, despite an abundance of tragic life circumstances that might have made him so. Yia sounds quite high strung and temperamentally similar to Maria. She would likely have high levels of physiological hyperarousal, if we utilize the tripartite model of emotion to understand her. Andreas is an interesting person who's described as being full of negative emotions, including a great deal of anger. Eria is difficult to categorize. We really don't know to what extent, if at all, she experiences anxiety or depression.

Anxious children don't just inherit their family's genetics. They also "inherit," if you will, their family's environment. Parents or grandparents who behave anxiously model such anxious behavior for their children. Thus, children learn from watching their parents engage in anxious behavior and are likely to imitate this behavior (Rapee, 2012). Children with anxiety disorders are more likely to have mothers who show anxiety and are overinvolved (Hudson, Dodd, & Bovopoulos, 2011). However, Maria's mother doesn't seem anxious and hasn't been overly involved in her life. Andreas may model negative affect for Maria, as he comes across like a blustery storm that can blow in and change the family climate at any moment. Maria also spends a great deal of time with Yia, who definitely models anxiety. Although this is certainly true in the case of Yia's fear of spiders, it may also be true of Yia in general, who's described as a fairly high-strung, birdlike individual.

When attempting to understand how families can model behavior for others, think of a child's environment as something akin to cultural DNA. Cultural values and historical events provide an important backdrop for Maria's anxiety. Consider Papou's family's restaurant fire. Maria has heard many stories about this fire but didn't experience it directly. Nevertheless, it has seeped into her nightmares. The family's experience in the War of 1974 is important to understand as well. In the 1970s the people of Cyprus endured a great deal of poverty, which led to widespread famine. In July of 1974 the Turkish troops invaded the northern part of Cyprus, forcing many Cypriots to flee south. Many human rights violations occurred, including threats, shootings and other massacres, and many instances of people who went missing and were presumed dead. Cyprus is a small enough country that everyone knew someone who was killed, witnessed horrific events, or was forced to relocate. The Turkish occupation and forced relocation meant losing connections—not only with the land, but also with one's family, history, and livelihood.

Think how witnessing this time in history affected Andreas as a young boy. Perhaps some of his present-day anger is related to the trauma of what he saw and the grief for what he lost. Andreas's intense focus on the restaurant reflects its importance to his own security and his way of providing for his family. Immigration to the other side of the world comes with its own set of stressors and leaves its mark on a person as well. Maria's parents and grandparents were forced to leave behind their family and friends. They had to learn a new language and understand new systems of government, money, and education. They also were exposed to cultural values that often clashed with their own. Western societies tend to emphasize the individual over the family. They have more relaxed rules regarding dating and sex, and they also have differing gender role expectations and different parent-child relationships (Killian & Agathangelou, 2005). Thus, the members of the Hadjipavlou family now cling to everything they hold dear that had been threatened and lost: land, food, and family.

Maria was born in Canada and didn't experience the fire, the war, or immigration, yet she is still affected by these events. Key family values affect Maria as well. Maria's family maintains close ties to the Greek Orthodox Church, which is often at the core of expatriate Greek and Cypriot culture. When Maria attends family weddings on the weekends, the ceremonies may last for days and include rituals such as children being bounced on the marrying couple's mattress and open circle dances (Killian & Agathangelou, 2005). Maria remembers being bounced on a mattress once as child. She spent the whole time crying for fear she'd fall off the mattress, even though the other children were giggling.

Cypriot women are expected to maintain strong cultural ties by teaching their values to their children as well as taking care of their elders. Greek families also define themselves by their relationships to others in their family rather than by who they are as individuals. In Maria's case, she is defined by whose daughter she is. Families are strongly *patriarchal*, in that the male in the family typically has ultimate power in the family structure. Additionally, in Cypriot culture parents are very proud of their children's accomplishments, but generational separations are sharp, as children are expected to obey their parents.

8. Hypothesize how the cultural difference between Cypriot and Canadian culture might impact Maria's family on a day-to-day basis.

9. Would it be ethical for you to treat Maria if you know little about Cypriot culture? Why or why not?

10. Maria is struggling to integrate what it means to be a Cypriot and a Canadian. Would you address these factors in therapy, or would you just focus on her anxiety? How would you address these issues if you think it's important to do so?

11. How would you handle this case if your personal or professional values are strongly different than the Hadjipavlou family's values? For example, how would it affect therapy if you strongly valued independence or feminism?

Applying all this general information to Maria allows us to utilize a *cultural case conceptualization*, or an understanding of a client within a cultural context. Maria is struggling to find her own identity and is frustrated because most people view her as Andreas's daughter. Maria feels pressure to marry a fellow Cypriot. She also fears that she'll fall in love with someone who's not Cypriot and thus might be rejected by her family. From her parents' perspective, such a union would be the best way to ensure the continuity of the culture. Cultural survival is especially important, especially in cases like this one when so many fundamental pieces of culture were lost as the family immigrated. Maria is frustrated because she wants to go on dates and to movies with her friends, but her weekends are filled with family celebrations. These rituals are vital from her parents' perspective but annoying from Maria's perspective because they aren't typical for her non-Cypriot friends. The role of women and men is quite different between Cypriot and Canadian cultures, affecting what Maria and her parents think is appropriate: dating rules, clothing styles, music, and relationships. Maria is more *acculturated* than her parents, as often happens among second-generation immigrants, when children more willingly adopt the values of their new country than their parents do. Cypriot families' concern about what others think comes into play here, as well, for both Maria and her parents. Andreas and Eria want Maria to act in line with their expectations of how a 17-year-old girl should behave—to make them proud and honor their family name. Maria feels the tremendous pressure of her parents, especially from Andreas, to be perfect. This pressure is exponentially increased by her believing that she must hide her flaws from her parents for fear they will discover that she is not the daughter she strives to be. Of course, Maria is concerned about what others (besides her parents) think as well. She wants other people to like her and so is friendly to everyone, but being so perpetually kind and friendly doesn't allow anyone to get to know her true identity behind this polite front. Everyone has their bad days, but Maria doesn't feel like she can have hers. Maria feels the pressure to make her parents proud, but trying to understand how she can do this and still be who she wants to be is not easy. From a cultural case conceptualization perspective, then, Maria's anxiety makes sense.

In summary, it's no wonder that Maria has so many worries. Like she insightfully asks in her journal, how can she figure out who she is when everyone is telling her who she is supposed to be?

12. Who would you want to participate in therapy, and why? Would you include Maria's brother? Parents? Grandparents? Or just Maria?

13. If Papou and Yia decided to participate in therapy, how would you handle the problem posed by the fact that they speak only limited English? What are the ethical concerns with your chosen approach?

Evidence-Based Treatment

"Yia, I can't sleep. And I worry too much. I think I need some help."

Let's get back to Maria. What happens next in her life? Yia tried to reassure Maria that everything was fine by offering her a slice of pie, but Yia was intuitive enough to know that perhaps pie wouldn't solve the problems of her granddaughter. She talked to Eria about Maria, bypassing her son Andreas in fear that he wouldn't understand the worries of a 17-year-old girl. Eria agrees that Maria might need some help, but she isn't sure what to do. Eria is also worried about letting anyone know that their daughter is having mental health problems. What would others think?

Without telling Andreas anything, Eria decides to contact one of her old friends, a Greek woman who lives on the other side of the city and isn't part of their daily social fabric. The old friend is a counselor, and although she doesn't specialize in adolescents, she recommends someone who does. The therapist she recommends is Gabrielle LeBlanc. Eria hesitantly set up a first appointment for Maria. The earliest available intake appointment with the therapist was in three weeks. Eria and Maria waited nervously for the appointment, not knowing what to expect since they'd never before participated in any type of therapy or mental health services. They swore Yia to secrecy in not telling Papou or Andreas their plan of action.

At the first appointment, Gabrielle decided to conduct some brief assessment measures to determine Maria's level of anxiety. Maria and Eria both completed a global behavioral rating form as well as a specific form related to anxiety. Gabrielle also interviewed both Maria and Eria. The assessment results strongly made the case that Maria was struggling with managing her anxiety. The therapist asked if Andreas could attend a therapy session and complete a behavioral rating form, but Eria explained that he couldn't leave the restaurant in the afternoon. Anyway, Eria noted that both she and Andreas were perfectly on the same page with how they perceived Maria and how important it was for her to get treatment, so Eria saw no reason for Andreas to attend a therapy session.

Gabrielle informed Eria that Andreas was a custodial parent of Maria and that he'd need to give his signed consent for Maria to participate in therapy. Additionally, Gabrielle explained that she'd like to meet Andreas so that she could understand the family a little better. Eria and Maria groaned in unison. They'd hoped to keep the therapy a secret by taking Maria out of school early one afternoon a week. They figured that Andreas would never need to know about therapy because they were fairly certain he'd react with anger and skepticism. Their plan thwarted, they agreed to take Andreas the informed consent and health protection privacy information and tried to plan the next session around his schedule.

Regarding the format of therapy, Gabrielle considered multiple options. She considered referring Maria to a psychiatrist for medication, specifically a class of anti-anxiety medications called selective serotonin reuptake inhibitors (SSRIs), which have been used successfully with adults with depressive and anxious symptoms (Stein, 2006). She considered involving Maria and her family in a cognitive-behavioral family intervention, but this plan was thwarted by Eria, who felt that Maria was the one with the problem and that she alone should be in therapy. Eria also explained that it would be difficult for Maria, Andreas, and herself to be absent from the restaurant at the same time. Maria agreed with her mother and said that she'd prefer to be in therapy without her parents. Gabrielle also considered the possibility of Maria participating in group therapy with other anxious teenagers. The only problem with this option was that, despite Gabrielle's best efforts, no such group existed because there weren't enough group members to sustain it. She determined that individual therapy with Maria would be the best route to take for treatment.

Gabrielle negotiated a deal with Maria and the Hadjipavlou family that at least one parent would come to two therapy sessions over the next three months. She also asked Eria to be certain to explain to Andreas how important his participation in therapy would be and to make sure to get his consent for Maria to participate. Gabrielle knew that anxious children and teenagers whose parents are involved in therapy show a greater reduction of anxious symptoms and more active coping strategies than children whose parents aren't involved (Christophersen & Mortweet, 2001).

For the evidence-based treatment for Maria, Gabrielle selected a teenage version of the widely disseminated Coping Cat program (Kendall, Furr, & Podell, 2010) The C.A.T. Project, as this teenage version is called, has received promising support in randomized controlled clinical trials. For example, children who receive the treatment show significant positive changes in their anxiety compared to wait-list control children, as measured by self-report and parent report. These changes in anxiety are long lasting and are typically maintained three years after treatment ends (Kendall, Furr, & Podell). The program utilizes a 16-session format to help children understand and cope with the physiological, cognitive, and behavioral components of anxiety. The first half of treatment focuses on skill training to deal with the anxiety. The second half of treatment focuses on skill practice to manage anxiety in "real life" settings.

Eria was able to get an early afternoon session with Gabrielle each week. Eria told Maria's school that Maria would be seeing the allergist every Thursday afternoon, so she would miss the last period of school. Maria was relieved that her mother lied to the school about why she'd be absent once a week, as she didn't want anyone to know about her troubles.

Maria was nervous about the first session, so Eria drove her to therapy. Maria was hoping Yia could take her to therapy instead, but Yia didn't like driving across town in Toronto traffic. Eria brought all of the necessary paperwork, including signed permission from Andreas for Maria to participate in therapy. Maria was certain that her mother had signed the forms for her father without discussing the matter with him, but she didn't mention this probability to Gabrielle. Instead, Maria just handed over all of the paperwork to Gabrielle and hoped that her new therapist wouldn't ask any questions.

14. What are the rules for parental consent to treat adolescents in the state in which you hope to practice?

15. How do you think Eria's deception about Andreas would affect the therapeutic relationship between Gabrielle and Maria? How would it affect the relationship between Maria and her mother?

16. What is your prognosis for Maria in therapy? What evidence supports your opinion?

Despite being nervous about therapy and anxious in general, Maria connected easily with Gabrielle, a French Canadian woman in her late 30s. Gabrielle was pleasantly plump, dressed almost exclusively in vintage clothes, and was especially partial to patterned fabrics, and the color purple. This greatly impressed Maria, who was always very careful to dress exactly like everyone else. She was immediately drawn to this no-nonsense woman who seemed to be so at ease in her own skin. Rapport was built quickly and the two women got immediately to work. Gabrielle explained the C.A.T. Project to Maria and shared the research behind it. Maria appreciated how Gabrielle treated her like an adult, trusting her to understand the research and the rationale behind the program. Teenagers often appreciate this direct approach to therapy (Edgette, 2006).

Gabrielle also openly discussed Maria's diagnoses. She leafed through the DSM-5 (APA, 2013) with her and explained how she thought Maria met criteria for the two disorders of Generalized Anxiety Disorder and Specific Phobia. She invited Maria to challenge her thinking if Maria disagreed with her. Gabrielle practiced therapy from a feminist perspective (Israeli & Santor, 2000) and was as egalitarian as possible in her approach to therapy. When the two were openly discussing goals for treatment, Gabrielle asked Maria what she wanted to focus on in therapy. Maria agreed that her worrying was problematic and wanted to learn some ways to manage her anxiety. She had no interest in working through her fear of spiders and didn't care if she ever tackled that particular problem. Gabrielle followed her lead and agreed that therapy would focus on Maria's overall anxiety.

The first part of therapy focused on psychoeducation, namely, teaching Maria the FEAR steps of anxiety. The F step involves asking the client to assess if they are Feeling frightened or anxious. This first step also asks the client to identify somatic, or physical, responses to anxiety and create a hierarchy of fear-related situations. Maria was motivated to complete this task. She listed her most fearful situations as:

- Imagining talking to my dad about asking permission to go on a date,
- Studying hard for a French test but still not feeling prepared as teacher passes out the test,
- Forgetting to reorder an important staple at the restaurant, and
- Other kids at school seeing me be mean or rude.

Gabrielle also worked with Maria to identify her *somatic responses* to stress, or how stress feels in her body. She talked about feeling jumpy and restless and how her foot wouldn't stop jiggling, even when she was exhausted late at night. Gabrielle and Maria also discussed Maria's trouble falling asleep and how her shoulders and neck feel tense and knotted. Maria made a spontaneous comment that she tended to eat more of Yia's pastries when something stressful had happened with her friends at school, such as learning that a boy she liked actually liked someone else. Gabrielle helped Maria realize that she converted anxiety to somatic symptoms in many ways, including migraine headaches and sleep problems.

The next step of treatment was a meeting with Maria's parents to keep them abreast of what was going on in therapy. Eria and Maria came to therapy without Andreas. Eria quickly reassured Gabrielle that Andreas wanted to attend the session, but he was absolutely swamped at the restaurant. She airily promised Gabrielle that she'd fill him in on what they discussed.

Eria was a big contributor to the parent information session. She was helpful in identifying situations that Maria found stressful. However, she mostly listened as Maria talked about how overwhelming her anxiety was. Eria was stunned. She'd had no idea that things were so bad for Maria.

Eria repeatedly said, "But Maria! You're such a good girl! You're so smart! You have so many friends! You don't need to be worried about such things!"

Gabrielle was able to step in at this time and provide a "both/and" perspective to the family. "Yes, these things are true," Gabrielle said to Eria. "Maria's smart, popular, and hard-working. And she's also worried about things. Very worried about many things."

Eria started to see how both perspectives might be true. She truly had no idea that Maria was such a "worrywart."

Maria explained, "I know this is my issue, Mom. But sometimes I have to worry because you don't."

Eria sat silently, not sure of how to respond.

After the parent meeting was over, Gabrielle and Maria went back to their individual therapy work. Gabrielle asked Maria about her relationship with her mother and what she'd meant by the comment about needing to worry for both of them. Maria tried to explain about her mother's personality but found herself at a loss for words. Gabrielle wasn't overly worried about the relationship between Eria and Maria. Instead, she concentrated on Maria's response to her mother.

Gabrielle said, "Maria, I know you and your mom aren't always on the same page. And I understand that this is hard for you. But therapy—all of the stuff we're working on in here—and your anxiety—aren't about your mom. You have the power to manage it, regardless of anything your mom says, does, or thinks. It's under your control. Not hers."

Maria sat silently after Gabrielle's comment. She'd never before considered that her anxiety was not endlessly intertwined with her mom's issues, whatever they were. Maria felt energized by the fact that her reactions were completely under her control, even if her family environment was not.

The next step in the individual therapy sessions was relaxation training. Maria enjoyed this part of treatment more than the first part. She loved Gabrielle's slow and soothing voice during relaxation, the darkness and stillness of the small office as the late afternoon winter sun went down, and the honest and sweet smell of the vanilla candle that burned. Maria would always begin to relax by staring at the intricate floral or paisley patterns on Gabrielle's skirts until she focused so singularly on a tiny printed curve that she couldn't help but relax. Then Maria would close her eyes and practice, imagining that she could let all of the thoughts that entered her head float in one ear and out the other. She imagined each worry tied to a balloon and drifting effortlessly out of her mind. Maria practiced deep breathing and muscle relaxation. She learned square breathing, practicing breathing in and out for slow, four-second counts. All of the worries that seemed so important fell to the ground like crumpled pieces of paper that were then blown away by the breeze of her exhale.

As Maria learned to relax, she began to understand how to differentiate between how her body felt when it was tense and how it felt when relaxed. She realized that with her busy days and long to-do lists, she'd never actually relaxed until now. After one day of relaxation, she told Gabrielle a story about her father. Maria had never seen him relax either, except "home" in Cyprus once, laughing with his cousins over cognac after a backgammon game and a long discussion about politics one night around 2 AM. Her father was laughing so hard that it had awakened Maria. How strange it was to hear a sound that she'd never before heard! As she held the fragmented image of her father in her mind, she realized that many of her family members were so busy all the time that they didn't know how to relax, even her beloved Papou.

Maria went home that evening after therapy and confessed to Andreas that she was in therapy for anxiety. He was shocked, but not angry. She told him about the memory of him laughing in Cyprus, and how she wished he'd laugh more often. She also told him that she understood the restaurant meant everything to him, but that sometimes it felt that he cared more about the restaurant than he did her. Maria wasn't sure what to expect in response from her father. She knew he wouldn't break down in tears or change his blustery ways. She stood for a minute, waiting for him to say something. He said nothing, choking on whatever he was trying to say. Maria went up to him, gave him a big hug, and told him that she loved him. Her father quietly said, "Maria, I love you more than the restaurant. I love you more than you'll ever know."

Maria went back to therapy for the next phase of C.A.T. Project, the **E** step: **E**xpecting bad things to happen. In this stage, Gabrielle taught Maria to identify the self-talk that accompanies anxious situations. Maria recognized that her catastrophic thinking errors made everyday problems into worst-case scenarios. She also recognized that she tended to worry about situations that she couldn't control, such as what would happen to her family after she went to college and the substance use of her brother. She realized that she engaged in all-or-nothing thinking and assumed that everything would either be perfect or catastrophic. She further realized that she engaged in all-or-none behavior, too. For example, she believed that she always had to be friendly and positive at school, even to kids who were kind-of jerks. Gabrielle worked with Maria to review her anxious self-talk and to replace it with coping self-talk.

Learning coping skills was a critical component in the **A** step of therapy. Gabrielle helped Maria identify **A**ttitudes and **A**ctions that might help instead of engaging in anxious thinking. They explored coping strategies that might be useful, including keeping a journal of gratitude instead of a journal of worries. Maria's favorite, newly learned thinking-based coping skill was to ask herself, "Is this my problem or someone else's?" She realized that many of her worries actually belonged to her parents or brothers. When she found herself replaying family arguments in her head, she instead began to repeat a phrase that she'd often heard Yia say: "Live today. Forget tomorrow. Forget yesterday." She began drinking a cup of chamomile tea instead of eating extra pastries before bedtime and also began doing relaxation exercises every night. Andreas agreed to let her leave the restaurant at 9 PM every night, even if they were busy with customers, providing her an extra hour to unwind and write in her "gratitude journal." She found that it was much easier to fall asleep when she came home by herself, had a cup of tea, took a shower, and went to bed. She was long asleep when her family arrived home every night around 11 PM, when they drank coffee and animatedly talked about politics for hours. She began sleeping much better. She learned to pay attention to her feelings and to recognize, on a moment-by moment basis, when she was anxious. She realized that she was more anxious in bigger crowds than with smaller groups of friends. Once she realized this, when she attended big weddings and christenings she began sneaking off to find quiet corners to talk with one or two relatives.

Maria and Gabrielle were both happy with Maria's excellent progress in therapy. They moved to the **R** step of the C.A.T. Project, which focused on **R**esults and **R**ewards. At this stage of therapy, Maria contrasted what happened to her mind and body when she used her coping skills instead of letting her anxiety run away with her. To remember all she was learning, Maria made a FEAR poster for her bedroom and decorated it with purple butterflies and flowers. She also made a small FEAR card for her purse so she could stay focused on how to manage her anxiety and on how much better she felt when she did. As she took these coping steps, Maria's anxiety became less uncontrollable, overwhelming, and painful for her.

Therapy at this point called for another family visit. Maria really wanted Andreas to meet Gabrielle. Surprisingly, he agreed to take an afternoon off from the restaurant, his first afternoon off in almost a year except for Easter and Christmas. He told Eria to tell everyone that he had an appointment with the accountant so that no one would actually know where he was. When Andreas met Gabrielle, she began the conversation by telling him how highly Maria thought of him and how proud Maria was to be his daughter. After talking for a while, Andreas was surprised when Gabrielle gave him some homework. He was to take ten minutes a night and share a cup of tea with Maria without mentioning the restaurant the entire time. Maria thought her father would scoff at the idea. Instead, he agreed to at least try. Then he chuckled—not an outright laugh, but a gentle, contented sound that reminded Maria a little of the joyful laughter she had heard one time in Cyprus.

As therapy was coming to a close with the completion of the sixteen sessions, Maria wanted to continue working with Gabrielle. Maria liked talking to someone outside of the family about dating, being a Cypriot-Canadian, and figuring out who she was apart from being Andreas's daughter. Eria and Andreas, who had noticed big changes in Maria, agreed that Maria could continue in therapy every other week. Andreas realized a few things during their late evening tea ritual. He came to see that perhaps Maria was right in thinking that work was taking up too much of his life. He decided that the restaurant would be closed every Monday and the family would take a little holiday together once a week. Eria couldn't believe it. She'd tried for years to convince Andreas not to work so hard, telling him he was going to give himself a heart attack. When Eria asked Andreas why he'd finally changed his mind about closing the restaurant once a week, he said, "I didn't change my mind. I always knew I'd do this when the time was right. And now, it's right."

17. How was Andreas able to make so much progress in therapy? If he sticks to his promise, how do you think his changes will affect his relationship with Eria?

18. Do you think Gabrielle made the right decision by sticking to a manualized treatment approach instead of adopting a more client-centered and fluid approach to therapy? Can a manualized treatment approach be consistent with a feministic therapy perspective?

References

American Psychiatric Association. (2013). *Diagnostic and statistical manual of mental disorders* (5th ed.) Washington, DC: Author.

Bartels, M., van Beijsterveldt, C. E. M., Derks, E. M., Stroet, T. M., Polderman, T. J. C., Hudziak, J. J., & Boomsma, D. I. (2007). Young Netherlands Twin Register (Y-NTR): A longitudinal multiple informant study of problem behavior. *Twin Research and Human Genetics, 10(1)*, 3–11. http://dx.doi.org/10.1375/twin.10.1.3

Christophersen, E., R., & Mortweet, S. L. (2001). *Treatments that work with children: Empirically supported strategies for managing childhood problems.* Washington, DC: American Psychological Association.

Edgette, J. S. (2006). *Adolescent therapy that really works.* New York: W.W. Norton.

Hudson, J. L., Dodd, H. F., & Bovopoulos, N. (2011). Informing early intervention: Preschool predictors of anxiety disorders in middle childhood, *PloS One, 7*(8), e42359.

Israeli, A. L., & Santor, D. A. (2000). Reviewing effective components of feminist therapy. *Counseling Psychology Quarterly, 13*(3), 233–247.

Kendall, P. C., Furr, J. M., & Podell, J. L. (2010). Child-focused treatment of anxiety. In J. Weisz, & A. Kazdin (Eds.), *Evidence-based psychotherapies for children and adolescents.* New York: Guilford.

Killian, K. D, & Agathangelou, A. M. (2005). Greek families. In M. McGoldrick, J. Giordano, & N. Garcia-Preto (Eds.), *Ethnicity and family therapy.* New York: Guilford.

Mineka, S., Watson, D., & Clark, L. A. (1998). Comorbidity of anxiety and unipolar mood disorders. *Annual Review of Psychology, 49*(1), 377–412.

Muris, P., Meesters, C., & Knoops, M. (2005). The relation between gender role orientation and fear and anxiety in nonclinician-referred children. *Journal of Clinical Child and Adolescent Psychology, 34*(2), 326–332.

Okamura, K. H., Ebesutani, C. E., Bloom, R., Higa-McMillian, C. K., Nakamura, B. J., & Chorpita, B. F. (2016). Differences in internalizing symptoms across specific ethnic minority groups: An analysis across Chinese American, Filipino American, Japanese American, native Hawaiian, and white youth. *Journal of Child and Family Studies, 25,* 3353–3356. doi:10.1007/s10826-016-0488-4

Rapee, R. M. (2012). Family factors in the development and management of anxiety disorders. *Clinical Child and Family Psychology Review, 15*(1), 69–80.

Smoller, J. W., Yamaki, L. H., Fagerness, J. A., Biederman, J., Racette, S., Laird, N. M., Kagan, J., … Sklar, P. B. (2005). The corticotropin-releasing hormone gene and behavioral inhibition in children at risk for panic disorders. *Biological Psychiatry, 57*(12), 1485–1492. doi:10.1016/j.biopsych.2005.02.018

Stein, D. J. (2006). *International Journal of Psychiatry in Clinical Practice, 10*(sup 1), 16–21. doi:10.1080/13651500600552487

CASE 6

Dylan Travers

A significant challenge in Dylan's case is that the Travers family was recommended to participate in therapy by Child Protective Services. This Los Angeles-based family struggles with hoarding, and Dylan, their 12-year-old son, exhibits symptoms of this disorder as well. Our understanding of hoarding as a disorder has greatly improved in the last ten years, and Dylan's case examines this literature. Evidence-based treatment in Dylan's case focuses on tailored cognitive behavioral therapy.

ICD 10/DSM 5 Diagnosis:
F42.3 (300.3) Hoarding Disorder, Poor Insight
T76.02XA (995.52) Child Neglect, Suspected, Initial Encounter

Diagnostic Discussion

After their first meeting together, Dr. Castaneda wrote her initial diagnostic impressions on Dylan's chart. As she thought through her diagnosis, she carefully considered how he met diagnostic criteria for Hoarding Disorder. She was well-versed in the diagnosis and treatment for this disorder, so she was able to remember all of the major criteria without even looking up any information in the DSM 5. Still, Dr. Castaneda was perpetually cautious in diagnosing.

- **Criterion A.** Persistent difficulty discarding or parting with possessions, regardless of their actual value (APA, 2013).

   Dylan certainly demonstrates this behavior, with all the nonsensical items such as candy wrappers, outdated flyers, and broken rubber bands and paper clips that he insists on keeping. That used piece of dental floss that he wrapped up so carefully to save doesn't have much value, that's for sure!

- **Criterion B.** Difficulty discarding items due to a perceived need to save them and distress with discarding them.

   Well, he certainly feels that he needs all of his belongings. And sometimes he actually does need them, which just reinforces his conviction that he should keep all of his things. He's distressed when others suggest that he throw them away. What did he say today? Hate. Odio. He hates it when people say that. In fact, he said he hates people when they say it. That's strong language.

194

- **Criterion C**. The difficulty discarding possessions results in an accumulation of things that clutter living areas so that people can't actually use the living space as it is intended.

   Well, this criterion is tricky for Dylan to meet, since he's only 12. Certainly, based on Bobby Harris's CPS report, his parents would meet this criterion. But would Dylan? I think I can safely assume this is the case—his locker and desk at school are basically unusable. And his coat—it weighs so much that it actually interferes with his posture and gait.

- **Criterion D**. Hoarding causes significant distress in social, occupational, or other important areas.

   Yes, this is certainly true. Other kids think Dylan's weird, so that affects him socially. And if I consider school to be his occupation, then certainly his teachers are distressed by his hoarding behavior. I don't think Dylan himself is stressed, and that is probably because his mother and father are hoarders so he just fits right in with them—but his behavior is certainly causing distress outside his family.

- **Criterion E**. The hoarding symptoms are not due to a general medical condition.

   Probably not, but I need to get a good developmental history on Dylan. I don't know his medical or developmental history well enough to rule this out for certain.

- **Criterion F**. The hoarding is not better explained by symptoms of another mental disorder (e.g., hoarding due to obsessions in Obsessive-Compulsive Disorder, decreased energy in Major Depressive Disorder, delusions in Schizophrenia or another Psychotic Disorder, cognitive deficits in major neurocognitive disorder, restricted interests in Autism Spectrum Disorder).

   No. No. Dylan doesn't show these other problems. He's just a hoarder—nothing else. This is so treatable, but he family's going to make it tough. How can I get them on board?

Dr. Castaneda knew the specifiers for the diagnosis equally as well as the criteria for the diagnosis itself. "Specify if hoarding behaviors are characterized by . . ."

- **With Excessive Acquisition**: If symptoms are accompanied by excessive collecting or buying or stealing of items that aren't needed or for which there's no available space.

   Hmm. His parents would meet this specifier. But Dylan? No. He can't buy items because he has no money, and he doesn't steal. And at this point, his most important treasures all fit in the pockets of his one coat, and in his locker and bedroom. He hasn't resorted to wearing two or three coats.

Specify with:

- **With good or fair insight**: The person recognizes that hoarding-related beliefs and behaviors are problematic.
- **Poor insight**: The person is mostly convinced that hoarding-related beliefs and behaviors are not problematic despite evidence to the contrary.
- **Absent insight**: The person is completely convinced that hoarding-related beliefs and behaviors are not problematic despite evidence to the contrary.

I wouldn't consider his insight totally absent, but it's certainly poor, even taking into account that his thinking skills are not totally developed at age 12.

Dr. Castaneda's second diagnosis—that of Child Neglect, Suspected, Initial Encounter—was selected to reflect the fact that Dylan's family has an open Child Protective Services (CPS) investigation pending. At this point, the family hasn't been formally charged with abuse or neglect, but Dr. Castaneda understands that hoarding cases are tricky and can lead to documented physical neglect, so she is careful to note this code on Dylan's chart.

1. Do you agree with the rationale that Dr. Castaneda provided when considering the diagnostic criteria?
2. Why do you think Dr. Castaneda is so careful in diagnosing? What are the pros and cons of being conservative when you are diagnosing a client? Can you err on the side of being too conservative?
3. Do you think Dr. Castaneda will ultimately be successful at getting the family into treatment? Why or why not?
4. How do you think the pending CPS case will play out for Dylan's family? Will they ultimately be charged with child neglect due to the condition of their home?

Case Conceptualization

Dr. Castaneda reflected on the etiology of Dylan's behavior as she drove home from work, stuck in yet another traffic jam on I-405, with traffic at a total standstill. Her inner dialogue switched between English and Spanish but will be recorded here in English.

Why is Dylan so attached to his things?

Theories explaining hoarding can be grouped into two large categories: theories suggesting physiological or biological causes and theories suggesting environmental causes.

Let me consider his biological risks.

Hoarding runs in families, with about 50% of individuals who hoard reporting that they have a relative who also hoards (APA, 2013). Dylan is clearly nested in a family of hoarders. People who compulsively hoard also show changes in their brain structures, including the cingulate cortex, ventromedial prefrontal cortex, and limbic structures (Saxena, 2008). People who get lesions in these areas through some type of accident or stroke are more likely to become hoarders (Anderson, Damasio, & Damasio, 2005). Compulsive hoarders also show a unique pattern of an abnormal resting brain state that is different from people who don't hoard (Pertusa, Fullana, Singh, et al., 2008; Saxena, 2008). Perhaps the genetic influence of hoarding is apparent in the neurological wiring of hoarders.

That all makes sense for Dylan. It seems both his mother and father are hoarders,
but his dad seems to have some better insight into his hoarding than his mom does.
Our behavior truly is evident in our brains. The longer I practice psychology,
the more I realize how important an understanding of neurology is.
Now I wish I had taken a few more neuroscience classes.

Hoarding also may be seen as a deficit in information processing (Frost & Hartl, 1996; Steketee & Frost, 2003). Specific information-processing deficits that have been found in hoarders include significantly greater problems with categorization of objects (Wincze, Steketee, & Frost, 2007; Luchian, McNally, & Hooley, 2007).

I certainly saw Dylan demonstrate this difficulty with categorization today.
He even had separate categories for each of his half-eaten candy bars!

Research suggests that people who hoard also have trouble making decisions (Coles, Frost, Heimberg, & Steketee, 2003; Samuels, Bienvenu, Pinto, et al., 2007).

Oh yes. I remember the report from his teacher. She did such a nice job describing
this problem for Dylan when she noted that he has trouble letting go of ideas,
just as he has trouble letting go of things. He must have exhausted her with all
his ideas for his science fair project. People who hoard also demonstrate attention
deficits (Hartl, Duffany, Allen, et al., 2005). *I don't see any evidence of attention*
problems in Dylan, except perhaps that his teacher reports that he is disorganized. His
grades are good, so he must be able to manage any attentional problems that he has.
Hoarders also demonstrate memory deficits (Hartl, Frost, Allen, et al., 2004).
I don't think Dylan has any memory deficits at all. He seems to have a strong
visual memory and knows exactly where he's placed each of his things.

In addition to these deficits in information processing, people who compulsively hoard show emotional attachments to their possessions, sometimes equating them with their sense of self and well-being, and occasionally giving them human characteristics (Steketee & Frost, 2003).

I think Dylan definitely has emotional attachments to his belongings, at least his Star Wars figures. Maybe he's not attached to all of his belongings, however, as he did say that he wasn't friends with his candy wrappers. I wonder about this, however. He may be more emotionally attached to his things than he realizes. Or he may realize it but may not yet totally trust me enough to let me know how he feels about his things. His mother is certainly very enamored of her candy dishes and all the other "treasures" her husband brings home for her. Because of these emotional attachments, people who hoard show false beliefs (misconceptions resulting from faulty beliefs that are not supported by reality) about their possessions. For example, they may consider that an item has feelings and would be hurt if it were discarded, or that an item has great value when it actually has none (Frost & Hartl, 1996; Steketee & Frost, 2003). These false beliefs lead to emotional distress when attempting to discard items. This is most definitely true for Dylan. He hates it when people try to convince him to get rid of his belongings. He clearly believes his Star Wars figures have feelings, equating them with friends. He also believes that bracelet he found is worth something. A bright 12-year-old should have understood that it had no real value.

So, both biological and neurological perspectives are helpful in understanding Dylan's behavior. Let me think from another perspective and consider the research on environmental reasons that might contribute to compulsive hoarding. I remember reading some research by Landau about how trauma is associated with hoarding (Landau et al., 2011).

Environmental causes implicated in the etiology of hoarding behavior include traumatic and stressful life events. Landau and her colleagues (2011) investigated the link between traumatic and stressful events, maternal deprivation, and hoarding behavior. Specifically, they found people who hoard reported a greater exposure to traumatic and stressful life events compared to people who don't hoard. Results remained unchanged after controlling for age, gender, education level, depression, and obsessive-compulsive symptoms. About half (52%) of people who hoard linked the onset of hoarding difficulties to stressful life circumstances, although this was significantly less common among those reporting early childhood onset of hoarding behavior. Interestingly, there was no link between levels of material deprivation and hoarding.

What does that Landau article mean for Dylan? Well, I don't know his history well enough to know whether he's experienced traumatic events. His teacher, parents, and Gavin's mom didn't mention any such trauma, but that doesn't mean that some trauma hasn't occurred. He is a child, so it's less likely that a stressful life event contributed to his hoarding behavior. More likely, it just came about gradually, piece by piece, from watching his mom and dad accumulate things and from living in an environment in which belongings were valued at least as much as people—if not perhaps more than them. And Dylan did tell me that he sometimes thought his mom cares more about her treasures than about him. I don't know the extent to which Dylan experiences maternal deprivation, even if the research hasn't supported this relationship to hoarding. However, exploring this will be an important component of our work together. I'm worried about his mom and her candy dishes and how she stopped talking with Bobby when the bag of "treasures" arrived at her feet.

Many adults report the onset of hoarding symptoms during childhood (Samuels, Bienvenu, & Pinto, 2007).

Ah, yes. So true with Dylan. And Samuels's research underlines why we need to intervene now, at age 12.

Especially, in the case of childhood onset of hoarding, hoarding is often present in one or both parents (Samuels, Bienvenu, & Pinto, 2007).

Also true for Dylan. I wonder about his sisters. They're also at risk to become hoarders (if they aren't hoarders already) unless we break this family cycle. And just because they're girls doesn't put them at less risk than being boys (Timpano, Exner, Glaesmer, Rief, Keshaviah, Brähler, & Wilhelm; 2011).

5. Do you think Dylan has ADHD? Why or why not?
6. What are some of Dylan's false beliefs about himself, others, and his world?
7. Would you spend time in therapy exploring whether some sort of traumatic event contributed to Dylan's hoarding? Why or why not? How would this decision be influenced by your theoretical orientation?
8. How do you think Dylan's relationship with his mother is impacting his present symptoms?

I'm glad Bobby referred Dylan to our clinic, recognizing that we specialize in more than just Obsessive Compulsive Disorder here. I know people think that hoarding and OCD are the same thing, but they're not. I'm glad that DSM-5 finally separated the two disorders as they are so different.

In DSM-IV TR, hoarding often was considered a symptom of obsessive-compulsive disorder (OCD) (APA, 2013). Specifically, when hoarding was extreme—as in the case of Dylan's family, with accumulated stacks of worthless objects presenting a fire hazard and making it difficult to walk through the house—a diagnosis of OCD was indicated. However, the majority of people who hoard present with no other symptoms of OCD (Mataix-Cols et al., 2010). Specifically, people who hoard items behave quite differently than people with OCD. Even when people with OCD hoard items, they do so differently than people with Compulsive Hoarding Disorder (Reichenberg & Seligman, 2016). People with OCD who hoard are more likely to hoard bizarre items, such as rotten food and bodily products like empty deodorant containers or shampoo bottles. They also have a ritualistic and compulsive quality to their hoarding that ties in closely with their obsessive thinking. For example, people with OCD who hoard fear catastrophic consequences if items are discarded. They are also more likely to perform compulsions related to their belongings, such as checking and mental rituals. These differences have led researchers to separate the categories of Hoarding Disorder and OCD. In addition, hoarding symptoms don't respond well to the evidence-based treatments for OCD, such as exposure plus response prevention and serotonin reuptake inhibitors (Pertusa, Frost, Fullana, et al., 2010; Steketee, Frost, Tolin, Rasmussen, & Brown, 2010).

Dylan's a good example of a child who demonstrates Hoarding Disorder but not OCD. I work with lots of OCD children at the clinic, and they're quite different than Dylan. One of my kids with OCD hoards things, but he collects only half-used deodorant containers and begins each day by putting on a swipe of deodorant from each of the containers, counting as he does, and taking care to put the deodorant on the right underarm first, then the left. If he deviates from this pattern, he has to begin all over. It takes him more than an hour to get ready for school. Dylan is nothing at all like that child, who is much more rigid in his thinking and far more socially awkward than Dylan. Dylan actually has some good social skills.

Interestingly, Tolin and Villavicencio (2011) have recently reported that hoarding behavior may be more similar to Attention Deficit Hyperactivity Disorder (ADHD) than OCD. However, people with ADHD who hoard are less likely to exhibit an emotional attachment to the objects they collect (Storch et al., 2011).

I don't think that Dylan has ADHD. He just doesn't show the core symptoms of poor self-regulation, inattentiveness, and impulsive behavior. And he's clearly emotionally attached to his belongings.

OK. I think I have a good handle on this kid and understand what's going on. I hope Dylan and I are going to be a good team and that I'll be able to help him with his hoarding problems. I hope I can get his parents involved in therapy. It seems doubtful—but at least they consented to let him participate

9. What are the ethical and clinical concerns you have about Dr. Castaneda comparing Dylan to another client with whom she's working?

10. Summarize the key reasons that Hoarding Disorder is now considered a disorder in its own right instead of just a symptom of OCD.

Evidence-Based Treatment

Evidence-based treatment begins with a good assessment of the symptoms shown by an individual. Dr. Castaneda considered multiple clinician and self-administered measures to assess Dylan's level of hoarding, including the Saving Inventory-Revised or SI-R (Frost, Steketee, & Grisham, 2004), the Hoarding Rating Scale (Tolin, Frost, & Steketee, 2010; Tolin, Frost, Steketee, Gray, & Fitch, 2008), and the UCLA Hoarding Severity Scale (Saxena, Brody, Maidment, & Baxter, 2007). She ultimately decided to utilize the Saving Inventory-Revised because of its short length of only 24 items. The questionnaire is self-administered and measures a person's attachments and beliefs about their possessions. Dylan scored in the clinically significant range on this scale, helping confirm Dr. Castaneda's clinical impression of Dylan having Hoarding Disorder. One important finding on this instrument was that Dylan's behavior appeared relatively normal in his home environment, as both of his parents also might be diagnosed with difficulties in this area. His mother, in particular, appeared to excessively acquire items and have difficulty discarding them. This finding didn't surprise Dr. Castaneda, but it helped her understand what the potential roadblocks to treatment might be.

Dylan's high score on the Saving Inventory-Revised is useful, because we can check his progress monthly and have him retake the assessment instrument later to see whether therapy is benefitting him. I always like some objective data to confirm that a child is actually making progress.

Dr. Castaneda considered two treatment options for Dylan: medication and therapy. In terms of medication, research has supported the use of selective serotonin reuptake inhibitors (SSRIs) for individuals with hoarding problems (Frost, Steketee, & Tolin, 2011). In general, therapy is considered to be more effective than medication with hoarding, but adding an SSRI may help with treatment success in severe cases (Frost, Steketee, & Tolin). Given Dylan's age, Dr. Castaneda was reluctant to recommend SSRIs for two main reasons. First, she was concerned about the possibility of *iatrogenic* side effects, a term used to describe negative side effects caused by treatment. Second, Dr. Castaneda was always conservative in her approach to utilizing medication as the front-line treatment choice with children due to the scarcity of *longitudinal* (long-term) research focused on the use of psychiatric medication with children. Dr. Castaneda kept up as much as possible with the research in her field, often reviewing journal articles in bed until her eyes drooped. The question she always asked herself regarding treatment decisions was, *What if this child were my own son or daughter or grandchild? How would I proceed then?* She gave each child on her case load this same level of considerate care.

11. Do you agree with Dr. Castaneda's conservative approach to using psychiatric medication with children? Why or why not?

12. Dr. Castaneda uses her children and grandchildren as a lens to consider what type of treatment her clients should receive. Is this an example of excellent care or poor boundaries? Why do you believe as you do?

13. Without reading ahead, how successful do you think therapy will be with Dylan? What is his prognosis?

Because she knew the research so well, Dr. Castaneda could thoughtfully consider many variables as she chose the right evidence-based treatment for

Dylan. She categorized questions in three main areas: questions about the treatment itself and research; questions about the client and his cultural and family values and preferences; and questions about herself as a clinician, including her expertise and familiarity with treatment. When analyzing Dylan's case and the research, she selected tailored cognitive behavioral therapy (TCBT) (Frost, Steketee, & Tolin, 2011). TCBT is a 20-session evidence-based intervention for hoarding, and Dr. Castaneda liked the fact that treatment could occur within a five-month format, based on weekly sessions. People who hoard often are resistant to therapy and many drop out before successfully completing therapy—they *prematurely terminate* therapy. In fact, hoarding symptoms predict premature termination, poor treatment compliance, and tepid treatment response (Frost, Steketee, & Tolin). But TCBT is successful with about half of patients, a good success rate given how tough hoarding behavior is to change.

TCBT also focused on the individual client instead of his or her family, an important consideration given Lola's and Brian's reluctance to participate in therapy. Dylan's parents were willing to have one session a month conducted at their home. Home-based therapy is often a critical component of therapy with people who hoard, given that the belongings they keep in their home are often the crux of the problem. So, the plan was for Dylan to meet with Dr. Castaneda in her office once a week for three consecutive weeks. On the fourth week of the month, Dr. Castaneda was to go to Dylan's house, or his school, to do their work.

During their first several sessions Dr. Castaneda and Dylan worked on developing an organizational plan. Dr. Castaneda was careful to let Dylan lead the sessions, so he would feel in control of treatment—that it was something being done *with* him, not *to* him. At first, Dylan didn't understand why he needed to develop categories. However, he acquiesced when Dr. Castaneda explained that he needed categories for his things because he was so fond of his belongings that he needed to be able to organize them so he could find them. Dylan got excited about organizing his things and started to draw out detailed plans of how he would organize his locker and the area under his bed. Dr. Castaneda challenged him to think about how he could sort his belongings into categories that would be easy to remember. Then Dylan was asked to think about how he would decide which items would go in which category, and where his belongings would be kept. Lola and Brian helped by purchasing several see-through plastic tubs for his Star Wars action figures and light sabers. His parents also found shoeboxes and cigar boxes to help him organize his belongings.

After Dylan bought into the idea of organizing his things, Dr. Castaneda worked with him to make decisions about how to organize his things. The first few weeks, all they did was to practice sorting items into categories that would be easy for Dylan to remember, and to determine where items would be kept. They developed index cards with a list of questions that would help Dylan decide whether he should keep something or discard it, and, if he was keeping it, where to put it (Is it usable? Is it dirty? Does it belong in my room? At school? In my coat?). Dr. Castaneda was careful not to pressure Dylan to discard his belongings. She knew that pressuring him to discard things before he was ready—even the used dental floss—would create a rift in their relationship. In short, therapy couldn't be set up as a power struggle of "Dylan keeping his things" vs. "Dr. C making him give them all away." She didn't want to undermine Dylan's feelings of being in control of his therapy, his belongings, and his life. Dr. Castaneda and Dylan called themselves the "Decluttering Dynamos" and became a good team.

Dylan made a big decision about three weeks into therapy that his trench coat was getting too heavy and that he wanted to leave some of his belongings at home, under his bed, in their new plastic bins. Dr. Castaneda approved of this decision but was careful not to excessively praise Dylan for it. Instead, she supported his decision to try something new and said that they could check in next week to see how his plan worked out for him. The following week, Dylan reported that he didn't actually miss or need the things that he had stored under his bed instead of his trench coat, including his stapler, socks, and the child's rain boot.

The following week, Dr. Castaneda and Dylan met at school right after the final bell to look at his locker and think of some ways that Dylan might organize it. Using the list of questions written on his index cards, Dylan was able to eliminate approximately 20% of the clutter from his school locker by taking it home. Dr. Castaneda asked one of Dylan's teachers why Dylan had been allowed to continue wearing his trench coat in class despite a school policy forbidding the wearing of coats in class. The teacher stated that it was easier to allow Dylan to wear the coat, as he became so upset when asked to remove it. When Dr. Castaneda shared this information with Dylan, he sheepishly agreed that his coat was becoming a "little bit of a problem." Again, Dr. Castaneda didn't expect change to occur too quickly. Instead of pressuring Dylan to remove his coat, they continued working on which items were "essential" to keep and which were "important but not essential." Dylan didn't have a category for items that were useless. To this point in therapy, he was willing only to move stuff from his coat and his locker to his bedroom. He wasn't yet willing to actually throw anything away.

The next week, an initial crisis for Dylan became a turning point in therapy. Dylan had lost Han Solo, one of his favorite Star Wars action figures, on the playground at school. He was devastated and cried openly in Dr. Castaneda's office, fearing that the action figure was irreplaceable. He'd gotten it from a yard sale and "he was from the original Star Wars movie, not the new one." Dylan ruminated out loud about what Chewbacca, another of Dylan's action figures from the movie, would do without Han Solo. "He's going to be so lonely, Dr. C. Chewy's going to be so lost without Han." Dr. Castaneda empathized with the young boy while also recognizing just how strongly attached he was to his belongings. And then, suddenly, Dylan exclaimed, "I know the solution. My Star Wars guys are just too valuable to take to school every day. They would be safer, and happier, in the plastic bin underneath my bed. And they'll still be able to see since the bin is clear."

As Dylan began reducing the number of items in his trench coat, Dr. Castaneda gently explored the possibility of leaving the trench coat in his locker during classes. Dr. Castaneda asked Dylan to pick one class during the day when he would remove his coat in class and leave it on the floor next to his desk or on the back of his desk chair. Dylan offered that he was now in a physical education class at school and was required to dress in gym shorts and a T-shirt. His teacher had been upset with him for wearing the trench coat, so he thought that would be the best class for this. Dylan agreed to remove the coat when he played basketball, leaving it on the bleachers next to the gym floor. He reported that he attempted this on a Monday but "chickened out." However, on Tuesday he successfully played basketball without his coat. He noted that the other kids didn't say anything about the coat but were excited that he made a basket. Dylan continued to leave the coat on the bleachers in his physical education class.

Over the course of the next several weeks, Dylan worked on removing his coat during other classes and placing it on the floor or on the back of his chair. He reported that his friend Gavin told him he was glad that Dylan wasn't wearing the coat anymore because it made him look like a "flasher," especially since Dylan always wore shorts to school.

By about the halfway point of therapy, approximately two and a half months after they began their work together, Dylan began leaving his coat in his locker throughout the school day. By this point his locker, while still messy, was de-cluttered enough that he could shut the locker door with the trench coat inside. Dr. Castaneda re-administered the Saving Inventory-Revised to Dylan and found that he'd moved from the clinically significant range of hoarding to the "at risk" range, a step in the right direction. This meant that he wasn't as attached to his belongings as he once was and was closer to being within the normal range of behavior.

During the last month of therapy, the therapy session at the Travers house led to several surprises. Dr. Castaneda was working with Dylan in applying his index card questions to the items in his still-cluttered room. All Star Wars action figures, light sabers, and costumes were easily organized into the clear, plastic containers that had been purchased for this purpose. Once Dylan finished organizing his Star Wars collection, he spontaneously took his extra plastic container to the kitchen where his mother was cooking and handed it to her, saying, "Here, Mom, I thought you might like to store some of your extra candy dishes in here. I could help you put your best ones in here so they don't get broken." Mrs. Travers looked hesitant and then broke down and started crying, saying that she liked all of her candy dishes and would feel bad about putting some in a bin because they might be lonely and miss the other dishes. And how would she ever decide which candy dishes to store? The ones that she didn't choose might feel rejected. She just thanked Dylan for his offer and went back to cooking. Dylan shrugged and then said, "Ok. Well, I guess I could use the extra bin for all my school papers." He went back to sorting with Dr. Castaneda.

Over the final weeks of therapy, Dr. Castaneda carefully began paying attention to Dylan's maladaptive or exaggerated beliefs about his possessions. Dylan was convinced that he might "need" an item at some point in the future or that he'd be wasting the item if he threw it away. Using a *Socratic dialogue technique*, an intervention from CBT that involves rationally exploring assumptions, Dr. Castaneda asked Dylan to consider some papers in his trench coat pockets:

> Dr. C: What about those two school announcements, Dylan? They're both way back from the first week of school, right?
>
> Dylan: They might come in useful sometime—my mom might need to know about these events.
>
> Dr. C: OK, that's a good reason to save them. What would be a reason to throw them away?
>
> Dylan: Well, this one is about a football tryout that was the first week of school. That was over months ago. This one is about cheerleading practice. I'm definitely not going to be a cheerleader!
>
> Dr. C: So, they're both about events that have already passed and that neither you nor your mom would be interested in attending?
>
> Dylan: Well, I think I could throw away the one about football, but my little sisters might decide to be cheerleaders someday and this could help my mom get them started in cheerleading.
>
> Dr. C: So, how do you feel about throwing away the football announcement?
>
> Dylan: I guess okay, but it's a real waste.
>
> Dr. C: A waste . . . ?
>
> Dylan: Yeah, this is a perfectly good piece of paper. I'm sure the back side could be used for something.
>
> Dr. C: So, how long have you been carrying that football notice?
>
> Dylan: Well, I guess about six months.
>
> Dr. C: And, in all of that time you've never needed that blank side of the paper?
>
> Dylan: That's true. (Pause.) Okay, I think I can pitch this sheet. Wait, I can put it in the recycle bin at school tomorrow! That way it won't be wasted.

After Dylan decided to put the football sheet in the recycle bin, he recognized that he needed a new category for his belongings, "Things I don't need." After the session that day, Dylan had added only one item to the category, the football flyer. But over the following weeks, he began to add papers to it. He still wasn't comfortable putting any other items besides paper in the pile, but the stack of papers he was comfortable throwing away was becoming larger each week, and it seemed that the idea of recycling might possibly lessen Dylan's concern about wasting paper. After Dylan took the papers to school one day to actually recycle them, Dr. Castaneda asked him how it felt to let go of some of his things. He answered her, "Honestly, Dr. C., it was hard. At first, I thought about diving in the recycling bin so I could save all the papers. But then I just decided I didn't want to mess with it. And when I was walking away from the big pile of papers . . . well, I just felt better. Lighter. Cleaner, somehow."

Therapy finished up a few weeks after the recycling event. Dr. Castaneda administered the Saving Inventory-Revised, and Dylan's scores were near the normal range. Dylan rarely wore his trench coat anymore and decided it wasn't worth wearing, since the pockets were mostly empty. He continued to keep snacks in his shorts pockets in case he got hungry. The removal of the trench coat was greeted with great relief by Dylan's teachers. According to them, Dylan was less ostracized by his classmates, who no longer viewed him so negatively. As his teacher reported, "Now, he's just messy, not disgusting." Dylan's backpack, locker, and desk were still cluttered, but significantly less so than they were initially.

Dylan clearly benefitted from CBT, but not as fully as Dr. Castaneda would have liked, probably due to his challenging home environment. Overall, however, everyone was pleased with his progress. As Dr. Castaneda drove home on the last day of Dylan's therapy, stuck in Los Angeles traffic again, she teared up a bit and said to herself, *Voy a extranar ese chico* (I'm going to miss that boy).

14. How might meeting at Dylan's school compromise confidentiality or affect Dylan's peer relationships? Do you think the benefits of meeting at school outweigh the drawbacks?

15. Do you think Dylan will be able to maintain the gains he made in therapy given his family's lack of progress?

16. Bobby Harris, the CPS worker, is due to return to the Travers home this month. What do you think he will find, and how will events likely unfold with regard to the ongoing CPS investigation?

17. Do you agree with Dr. Castaneda's decision not to praise Dylan too much for his decisions to declutter? How would you have responded in this situation?

18. How would you feel about discontinuing therapy when a client is making so much progress but still has ongoing symptoms, yet an external payment source, such as an insurance company, limits the number of sessions?

References

American Psychiatric Association. (2013). *Diagnostic and statistical manual of mental disorders* (DSM-5) (5th ed.). Washington, DC: Author.

Anderson, S. W., Damasio, H., & Damasio, A. R. (2005). A neural basis for collecting behaviour in humans. *Brain, 128*, 201–212.

Coles, M. E., Frost, R. O., Heimberg, R. G., & Steketee, G. (2003). Hoarding behaviors in a large college sample. *Behavior Research and Therapy, 41*, 179–194.

Frost, R. O., & Hartl, T. L. (1996). A cognitive-behavioral model of compulsive hoarding. *Behavior Research and Therapy, 34*, 341–350.

Frost, R. O., Steketee, G., & Grisham, J. (2004). Measurement of compulsive hoarding: Saving inventory-revised. *Behavior Research and Therapy, 42*, 1163–1182.

Frost, R. O., Steketee, G., & Tolin, D. (2011). Comorbidity in hoarding disorder. *Depression and Anxiety, 28*(10), 876-884. doi:10.1002/da.20861

Hartl, T. L., Duffany, S. R., Allen, G. J., et al. (2005). Relationships among compulsive hoarding, trauma, and attention-deficit/hyperactivity disorder. *Behavior Research and Therapy, 43*, 269–276.

Hartl, T. L., Frost R. O., Allen, G. J., et al. (2004). Actual and perceived memory deficits in individuals with compulsive hoarding. *Depression & Anxiety, 20*, 59–69.

Landau, D., Lervolino, A. C., Pertusa, A., Santo, S., Singh, S., & Mataix-Cols, D. (2011). Stressful life events and material deprivation in hoarding disorder. *Journal of Anxiety Disorders, 25*(2), 192–202.

Luchian, S. A., McNally, R. J., & Hooley, J. M. (2007). Cognitive aspects of nonclinical obsessive-compulsive hoarding. *Behavior Research and Therapy, 45*, 1657–1662.

Mataix-Cols, D., Frost, R. O., Pertusa, A., Clark, L. A., Saxena, S., Leckman, … & Wilhelm, S. (2010). Hoarding disorder: A new diagnosis for DSM-V? *Depression & Anxiety, 27*(6), 556–572. doi:10.1002/da.20693

Pertusa, A., Frost, R., Fullana, M. A., et al. (2010). Refining the diagnostic boundaries of compulsive hoarding: A critical review. *Clinical Psychology Review, 30*(4), 371–386. doi:10.1016/j.cpr.2010.01.007

Pertusa, A., Fullana, M. A., Singh, S., et al. (2008). Compulsive hoarding: OCD symptom, distinct clinical syndrome, or both? *American Journal of Psychiatry, 165*, 1289–1298.

Reichenberg, L. W., & Seligman, L. (2016). Selecting effective treatments: A comprehensive, systematic guide to treating mental disorders. Hoboken, NJ: John Wiley & Sons.

Samuels, J. F., Bienvenu, O. J., III, Pinto, A., et al. (2007). Hoarding in obsessive-compulsive disorder: Results from the OCD Collaborative Genetics Study. *Behavior Research and Therapy, 45*, 673–686.

Saxena, S. (2008). Neurobiology and treatment of compulsive hoarding. *CNS Spectrums, 13*, 29–36.

Saxena, S., Brody, A. L., Maidment, K. M., & Baxter, L. R., Jr. (2007). Paroxetine treatment of compulsive hoarding. *Journal of Psychiatric Research, 41*, 481–487.

Steketee, G., & Frost, R. (2003). Compulsive hoarding: Current status of the research. *Clinical Psychology Review, 23*, 905–927.

Steketee, G., Frost, R., Tolin, D., Rasmussen, J., & Brown, T. A.,. (2010). Waitlist-controlled trial of Cognitive Behavior Therapy for Hoarding Disorder. *Depression & Anxiety, 27*(5), 476–484. doi:10.1002/da.20673

Storch, E. A., Rahman, O., Park, J. M., Reid, J., Murphy, T. K., & Lewin, A. B. (2011). Compulsive hoarding in children. Journal of Clinical Psychology, 67(5), 507–516. doi:10.1002/jclp.20794

Timpano, K. R., Exner, C., Glaesmer, H., Rief, W., Keshaviah, A., Brähler, E., & Wilhelm, S. (2011). The epidemiology of the proposed DSM 5 Hoarding Disorder: Exploration of the acquisition specifier, associated features, and distress. *Journal of Clinical Psychiatry, 72*(6), 780-786.

Tolin, D., Frost, R., & Steketee, G. (2010). A brief interview for assessing compulsive hoarding: The Hoarding Rating Scale-Interview. *Psychiatry Research, 178*(1), 147–152. doi:10.1016/j.psychres.2009.05.001

Tolin, D., Frost, R., Steketee, G., Gray, K. D., & Fitch, K. E. (2011). The economic and social burden of compulsive hoarding. *Psychiatry Research, 160,* 200–211.

Tolin, D. F., & Villavicencio, A. (2011). Inattention, but not OCD, predicts the core features of Hoarding Disorder. *Behavior Research and Therapy, 49*(2), 120–125.

Wincze, J. P., Steketee, G., & Frost, R. O. (2007). Categorization in compulsive hoarding. *Behavior Research and Therapy, 45,* 63–72.

CASE 7

Jaquishia Johnson

Jaquishia's case is difficult to read because of the level of trauma, specifically sexual abuse, she has encountered. She's a 16-year-old black girl living in Chattanooga, Tennessee. Her situation is challenging because she has complicated medical issues that exacerbate her trauma symptoms. Jaquishia's case describes trauma-focused cognitive behavioral therapy in detail and discusses the importance of resiliency factors in helping children cope with abuse.

ICD 10/ DSM 5 Diagnosis:
F43.10 (309.81) Posttraumatic Stress Disorder ✓
Z91.19 (V15.81) Nonadherence to Medical Treatment (Diabetes)
T74.22XD (V61.21) Sexual Abuse of Child (995.5 Victim)
T74.02XD (V61.21) Neglect of Child (995.5 Victim)

Jaquishia also has medical diagnoses of hypothyroidism, polycystic ovarian syndrome, Type II Diabetes, and obesity.

Diagnostic Discussion

Jaquishia meets criteria for Posttraumatic Stress Disorder (PTSD). Like many other disorders discussed in this book, this disorder is difficult to diagnose in children because they often present different symptoms than adults do (Wolfe, 2006). In children, PTSD often shows itself in play. Children's play with toys, such as dolls or stuffed animals, may reflect or suggest the themes of the abuse in a repetitive, almost compulsive manner. Children may also re-enact the trauma themselves, as if they were performing a skit or play. Many may have difficulty recognizing that their flashbacks are not real. Whereas adults have the cognitive skills to understand that they're having a flashback; these images often seem "too real" to children to be understood as memories. Because Jaquishia is 16, however, her symptoms are beginning to look more adult-like. Jaquishia currently shows the following PTSD symptoms: exposure to a traumatic event (the sexual abuse by her uncle); intense fear or helplessness associated with the event (she did not feel that she could even try to say "no" to her uncle until she was about 13); re-experiencing of the trauma (recurrent, stressful memories of the trauma; dreams about it; feeling like she is reliving the abuse); avoidance of reminders of the trauma (not wanting to come anywhere near her uncle's house and refusing to visit

209

her mother in prison); and increased arousal (her trouble concentrating, diffi-culty falling asleep, and feeling stressed all the time).

When a person's abuse is a primary focus of treatment, it should be listed as a focus of clinical treatment, as has been done in Jaquishia's case. When diagnosing Jaquishia with PTSD, the clinician should remember that the abuse is not her fault. Why should she be the one diagnosed with something if it's not her fault? If we think of a diagnosis as a pejorative, negative way to label someone, this is a valid problem. On the other hand, if we think of a diagnosis as a name for a cluster of symptoms that hang together and provide a clear path towards evidence-based treatment, diagnosing a person is less of a problem. Regardless of where on this continuum you stand, one advantage of the DSM diagnostic system is that it allows us to consider contextual fac-tors and psychosocial stressors. Certainly, Jaquishia has many of these life stressors, and a good therapist should thoughtfully consider how Jaquishia's trauma impacts her thinking and behavior. We also need to remember that people are not defined by their trauma, and we're more than just the sum of our past. Jaquishia is a good example of the importance of taking a strengths-based perspective in treatment, as she has amazing resilience and numerous personal and family strengths.

1. Individuals often are diagnosed with a disorder that's "not their fault." Under these circumstances, do you consider it problematic that those individuals then carry a diagnosis? Why or why not?

2. Do you think PTSD is Jaquishia's only diagnosis? What other addi-tional diagnoses would you give her, and why?

3. From what you know about her history, would Jaquishia have met criteria for a diagnosis at age 10? How do you think her symptoms would have appeared at that time?

A tough decision in terms of diagnosis in Jaquishia's case is deciding if she has co-morbid (i.e., co-occurring) depression along with her PTSD. Co-morbid-ity, which is common among children, means that two disorders are affecting the child at the same time. Co-morbid disorders are tricky to diagnose—in Jaquishia's case, because so many symptoms of PTSD overlap with depres-sion. The therapist decided to focus on treating Jaquishia's PTSD first. If the symptoms that are common to both depression and PTSD remain problematic for her after her PTSD treatment, then diagnosing Jaquishia with depression is probably a good decision. For the present time, however, it seems that the PTSD is the most relevant diagnosis and the one that is "fueling the fire."

Case Conceptualization

Jaquishia's case reminds us of some painful truths about abuse. Statistics suggest that sexual abuse happens to roughly one in every four or five women, depending on the definition of sexual abuse used. Sexual abuse is also common in men, occurring in about one in every 10 or 15 men (Finkelhor, 1994). However, some recent research suggests that sexual abuse is equally common among boys and girls but that boys are less likely to report it (Craner, Martinson, Sigmon, & McGillicuddy, 2015). Risk factors for sexual abuse include being female, having a lower level of intelligence, being physically abused or neglected, having a disability, being socially isolated, and not having an adult as a confidant. In fact, researchers have found that when three or more risk factors are present, the likelihood of a girl being sexually abused is a staggering 50% (Bagley & Mallick, 2000). Although Jaquishia is bright, she has a number of these risk factors. She's a girl, she's been neglected, and she wasn't able to trust her mother. Her relationship with her grandmother, however, is a key protective factor. In fact, her grandmother's advocacy, support, protection, and love of Jaquishia are the most hopeful factors in her recovery.

Childhood sexual abuse is related to *internalizing* problems, which include *emotional* problems such as depression, anxiety, posttraumatic stress problems, lower self-esteem, and somatization. It's also related to *externalizing* problems, which include *behavioral* problems such as oppositional and defiant behavior, acting out, substance-use problems, and anger-management problems (Wilson, Samuelson, Staudenmeyer, & Widom, 2015; Wolfe, 2006). A good way to understand the difference between internalizing and externalizing problems is whether parents and/or teachers can easily see the child's problems, and may even get frustrated by them (externalizing behavior), or whether the child is suffering in silence and no one really knows how badly she's struggling (internalizing behavior). Jaquishia has mostly internalizing symptoms, which are more common in girls (Wolfe, 2006). Even so, most kids with problems, boys and girls alike, exhibit a complex mix of internalizing and externalizing symptoms.

What's behind the symptoms Jaquishia is exhibiting? PTSD often impacts children in four key ways (Wolfe, 2006). First, the survivor feels a sense of *learned helplessness*, which means that she believes that she can't control or improve her life situation. People who believe this often have negative feelings about their future, themselves, and the world, a perspective aptly called the *negative cognitive triad* (Wolfe, 2006). Jaquishia expresses this view eloquently whe[...] that talking about what happened "ain't changing things" and say[...] [Negative Cognitive Triad: Future, Themselves, World] [...] her life. Viewing the world with a negative [...] npty" way of seeing things and is associa[...] essness. People frequently develop this w[...] osed to catastrophic events beyond their c[...] itrol in her life given Tanya's drug use and [...] xual abuse. This feeling of learned helple[...] irrent life in that she's given up on some o[...] ike managing her health and diet. Alternatively, Jaquishia may [...] control her life by gaining weight, as Uncle Mar was less interested in her when she did so.

According to Wolfe (2006), the second key way in which PTSD develops is when children develop dysfunctional ways of coping with their environment. Jaquishia's *avoidant style of coping* with the world mainly consists of quitting or avoiding. For example, she avoids dealing with reminders of her past that are too painful to face. The saddest example of Jaquishia's coping strategies not working for her is when she tried to stop the sexual abuse—an effort that ended up with her uncle violently forcing her to engage in sexual acts. Jaquishia learned not to directly confront problems and instead to ignore and avoid them. We can also see Jaquishia's avoidant style of coping in the choices she makes regarding her health. She won't see the pediatrician about her diabetes and isn't motivated to learn about polycystic ovarian syndrome. Jaquishia's core beliefs are that she's a victim of an uncontrollable environment that no one will help her navigate. These beliefs lead to automatic thoughts of hopelessness concerning her future. For example, Jaquishia believes that she'll never have a boyfriend or enjoy sex. Because she feels overwhelmed by her environment, she shuts down and loses herself in books and reality TV shows. Jaquishia's decision to quit the dance team may reflect her avoidance of coming to terms with her heavier body (and the reason for her weight gain). However, it also may be a symptom of depression, as a loss of interest in recreational activities is common among people who are depressed. The problem is that avoiding problems doesn't make them go away. When we eventually face them, we find that they haven't dissipated and sometimes even feel worse to us, because avoiding things takes a great deal of energy and concentration. Actively ignoring things (or people) takes a great deal of work.

A third way that PTSD develops is *dissociation*, or the tendency for a person to "space out" and remove themselves to a different mental place. While this is a good coping skill to use in horrific situations like Jaquishia's sexual abuse by her uncle, it becomes problematic when people start to use it as a way to cope with life's everyday challenges. We all dissociate from time to time. Imagine, for example, "zoning out" while driving across the bleak landscape of western Kansas for hours. But, dissociation at its worst can lead to a sense of *depersonalization*, or no longer feeling like a human being. Fortunately, Jaquishia doesn't seem to be exhibiting a great deal of dissociation or depersonalization, although her "bad daydreams" that occur in the middle of the day may be an example of brief dissociative moments. The key reason that these symptoms may not be present is her strong connection with her grandmother, siblings, and friends, who help keep her present and "in the world," so to speak.

The fourth way that PTSD develops is when trauma causes a person to experience *affect dysregulation*, or trouble managing her emotions. This might mean that a person has trouble recognizing and labeling feelings, has trouble understanding the causes and consequences of these feelings, and has difficulty managing them in appropriate ways. We see affect dysregulation in Jaquishia when she reports being "stressed, hungry, tired, and grumpy" all the time. The main way we learn about our feelings (as well as the feelings of others) is through our connections with other people, especially our parents or caregivers. The deep, long-standing connection between a child and a parent/caregiver is called *attachment*, and our attachments impact how we understand ourselves and the world. Think about Jaquishia's life and the connections with the adults around her. She never knew her father. Her mother was a substance abuser and prostitute who used any income the family had to purchase drugs. She not only neglected Jaquishia and her siblings but also gave Jaquishia messages that she was "too big" and "too black" to be loved. Her uncle was sexually abusive, and her mother didn't protect her from this abuse. Tanya also invalidated Jaquishia's abuse by not believing Jaquishia when she told her about it, a painful experience that makes sexual abuse more difficult to understand. Her mother's denial of this abuse may have led Jaquishia to believe that she couldn't tell her girlfriends, prosecutors, or the court about her experiences because others wouldn't believe her or would think badly of her. She doesn't want to talk about it in therapy either, because she wants to avoid re-experiencing the trauma and doesn't want to be *invalidated*, or not believed, in therapy. Jaquishia states that "talking about it can't change it"—and in the past, that was true: talking about it didn't stop the abuse at all.

Recent research has also explored the neuropsychological impact of childhood sexual abuse (Barrera, Calderón, & Bell, 2013). Increasingly, researchers have linked the experience of childhood sexual abuse with adult hallucinations (Hammersley et al., 2003; Read, Agar, Argyle, & Aderhold, 2003; Shevlin, Dorahy, & Adamson, 2007). Such a link might suggest that childhood sexual abuse disrupts the child's ability to differentiate internally and externally generated cognitive events. That is, the child may come to believe that internal events, such as voices inside of her head, are actually external and thus real (Aleman & Larøi, 2008).

This lifetime of being abused and invalidated has understandably led Jaquishia to adopt core beliefs about the world—that adults put themselves first and cannot be depended on for food or basic needs, especially the most vital of all human needs, love. These core beliefs affect her negative views of herself, how difficult it is for her to trust others, and how little control she feels she has over her life. Perhaps her good relationship with Granny will help ameliorate some of the early negative attachments in Jaquishia's life, but remnants of her painful early childhood will likely always be with her.

4. What symptoms do you think will be most difficult to treat?

5. Imagine that Jaquishia were a boy instead of a girl. How would the presentation of Jaquishia's symptoms be different? What if she were a white girl instead of a black one? Or a wealthy girl?

6. Imagine that Jaquishia's grandmother wants her to participate in therapy, but with a counselor through the church. This counselor doesn't practice from an evidence-based perspective and isn't famil-

iar with the best treatment for trauma problems. How do you manage this situation with Jaquishia's grandmother from the point of view of the therapist currently working with her?

7. Would you address Jaquishia's weight problems and diet in therapy? If so, how and when would you do so?

8. Would you involve Jaquishia's siblings in therapy due to their own histories of neglect? If you think the answer is "it depends," then on what does it depend?

Evidence-Based Treatment

The first challenge to doing therapy with Jaquishia will be building a relationship with her. Edgette (2006) suggests that one of the best ways to build a relationship with a teenager is to "keep it real" and talk openly with her about the reasons she doesn't want to be in therapy. And Jaquishia has some good reasons not to want to be in therapy! She's been sent to therapy against her will, she doesn't trust the prosecutor who sent her to therapy, her culture may view therapy as being for "crazy" people, and talking about the abuse is horribly painful. Honestly discussing these worries will be the first step of therapy. Another critical first step will be a clear conversation about what will and will not be shared between the therapist and the prosecutor. Jaquishia has a right to know exactly what information will be kept _confidential_, or private, between her and her therapist, and what information will be shared with others involved in the legal system.

Another intervention that should happen at the beginning of therapy is a candid discussion about ethnicity and race and how they impact the therapeutic relationship. Why might Jaquishia not trust the white prosecutor, and perhaps white people in general? A long history of racism, discrimination, and slavery perpetrated by white people helps answer this question. These dynamics still operate today in the form of _institutional racism_, widespread policies that allow _differential_, or unfair, access to goods and opportunities. For example, African American people earn just 66% of the income of whites (Moore Hines & Boyd-Franklin, 2005). Others examples of institutional racism include how blacks, on average, fare worse than whites in key quality-of-life indicators, including home ownership, business ownership, physical health, professional and managerial success, and life expectancy (Moore Hines & Boyd-Franklin, 2005). In other words, Jaquishia has some valid reasons not to trust white people.

9. How would you bring up issues of ethnicity and race with Jaquishia in therapy—exactly what would you say? How does your own ethnicity affect what you would say?

10. Do you think that your ethnicity would influence therapy? If so, how? Does racial similarity in therapist and client matter?

Jaquishia's ethnicity and her therapist's ethnicity bring up a relevant question about *therapist matching.* Do clients get better in therapy when they're ethnically matched with their therapist? The short answer to this question is, "It depends"—on where a client is in her own ethnic identity journey as well as where a therapist is in his/her journey. Being an ethical practitioner means considering how both one's own and one's client's race, ethnicity, gender, sexual orientation, religion, and socioeconomic status impact treatment. In terms of where Jaquishia is in her own ethnic development, a black female therapist might be ideal for her currently. Yet, the sad reality is that we don't presently have enough people of color practicing in the mental health field (Murphy & Dillon, 2011) with only 2% of psychiatrists and psychologists and 4% of social workers identifying as African American (Black & Jackson, 2005). Cabral and Smith (2011) conducted a meta-analysis of 81 studies related to *racial/ethnic match*—that is, to determine if therapeutic success was related to the ethnicity of the therapist matching that of the client. They concluded that racial/ethnic matching was unrelated to treatment outcomes. However, clients in racial/ethnic minority groups tended to prefer therapists of the same race and ethnicity and had more positive perceptions of therapists who were of the same race and ethnicity as themselves.

Whatever the ethnicity of her therapist, a key consideration in working with Jaquishia will be to spend time gaining her trust. It is also crucial to understand—and sh_____ _____nding of and appreciation for—African American family v_____ _____es often have strong extended family kin_____ _____al adoptions and children born out of the_____ _____ructures, a heightened importance of multi_____ _____ilies, somewhat equalized gender roles o_____ _____*parentified responsibilities* (adult-like responsi_____ _____ong connection to their church and God (N_____ 5). Of course, each African American fan_____ _____aracteristics is true for some, but not all, African American families.

Once a trusting relationship has been established, the research suggests that trauma-focused cognitive behavioral therapy (TF-CBT) is an evidence-based intervention that makes good sense for Jaquishia (Cohen, Berliner, Mannarino, & Steer, 2004). This module-based program is built around the following goals, which spell the acronym PRACTICE (or technically PPRACTICE). The primary goals of the program are **P**sychoeducation, **Pa**renting skills, **R**elaxation skills, **A**ffective expression and modulation skills, **C**ognitive coping skills, **T**rauma narration and understanding of traumatic experiences, **I**n vivo mastery of reminders of the trauma, **C**onjoint parent and child sessions to discuss the trauma, and **E**nhancement of the safety and future development of the client. You'll recall that TF-CBT was an effective intervention for Annabelle in Case 14, and it would be the recommended intervention for Jaquishia as well.

11. Do you think that evidence-based therapy is a helpful tool, or that it limits therapists' creativity? Explain your answer.
12. Do you think that TF-CBT would work with Jaquishia? Why or why not? What are your concerns about this type of intervention given Jaquishia's response to therapy so far?

Let's take a look at how therapy played out with Jaquishia. As a first step to building a trusting relationship with Jaquishia, the therapist clarified what information the prosecutor could and could not access and empowered Jaquishia to make ongoing decisions about how much information would be shared with the prosecutor. While this is an important discussion to have with clients, if the legal system and courts are involved, a client's records are not truly protected. Attorneys can request copies of records and, with a judge's order, therapists have to release them. Accordingly, therapists need to be careful about making promises to clients that they cannot keep. In addition, any abuse that hasn't been previously reported must be reported to Child Protective Services. Such disclosure laws are important in Jaquishia's case because of the good probability that some of Jaquishia's sisters and brothers also may have been abused (Happel, 2016).

The therapist and Jaquishia frankly discussed race and ethnicity, and the ways in which therapy might be affected by their values and beliefs. The therapist asked Jaquishia what she wanted from therapy. Jaquishia was clear about her therapy goals: "I ain't talkin' about the bad stuff, but can you help me lose some weight?" The therapist agreed to wait on addressing Jaquishia's trauma symptoms until Jaquishia felt better able to talk about this difficult subject.

The therapist also needed to build a relationship with Jaquishia's grandmother, who was clear from the beginning that she'd prefer to be called Ms. Washington, not Naomi. She explained that her name tag at work used her first name and that she felt disrespected by the restaurant patrons calling her by her first name when they didn't even know her. Ms. Washington's first question for the therapist was, "Who are your people?" a question to ascertain the therapist's family and community roots.

Once she was satisfied with the therapist's answer, Ms. Washington agreed to give her *consent* (legal, signed permission) for therapy and the sharing of information with key service providers. After securing Jaquishia's *assent* (verbal agreement), the therapist consulted with Jaquishia's pediatrician. As a result, Jaquishia enrolled in a school-based, family-centered, anti-obesity program to help her make better food choices and learn how to manage her diabetes. Granny supported Jaquishia by having her write her own grocery list, providing more fruits and vegetables, and working together to cook healthier. Granny's agreement to cook healthier was evidenced by her saying, "Well, I could lose a few pounds myself." Jaquishia and her grandmother began taking a Zumba class at their church and also started having Wii Dance battles with each other.

Because Tanya was not involved in therapy, Ms. Washington was enlisted as the key caregiver who could make the biggest impact in Jaquishia's life. The therapist and Ms. Washington met for several sessions alone at the therapist's request, to develop a relationship and talk about how Ms. Washington could best support Jaquishia in her life. Granny's participation was vital, but accommodations were made in acknowledgement of her busy schedule. Therapy was carefully designed to not waste her time. Some sessions were conducted over the phone, where Ms. Washington could care for her mother and watch the other children while participating. When she came to the office for a therapy session, Granny enlisted the help of a neighbor to watch her grandchildren. Coming to office-based sessions was sporadic, because "time off of work means time off of pay," as she told the therapist.

13. Given our field's emphasis on limiting self-disclosure by therapists in the mental health setting, how would you have answered Ms. Washington's question, "Who are your people?"

14. Suppose that Ms. Washington shares a letter with you, the therapist, that Tanya wrote to Jaquishia apologizing for the kind of mother she was and begging Jaquishia to visit her in jail. Do you show Jaquishia the letter? Do you encourage her to visit her mother? Explain your answers. What if Ms. Washington strongly insists that Jaquishia accompany her on her next visit to see Tanya? Does Jaquishia have a right to refuse if her grandmother insists?

After about four months, Jaquishia was still overweight but had lost 20 of the 30 pounds she had gained in the past year. She made plans to try out for the dance squad at the next round of try-outs. She still resisted talking about her sexual abuse, saying, "I still ain't talkin' about that stuff." The therapist then asked what Jaquishia's next goals were, and Jaquishia stated that she wanted to find a "hot boyfriend." The therapist was unwilling to agree to this specific goal but did agree to help Jaquishia figure out what qualities make a person a good friend and a good boyfriend. As they were talking about friends and boyfriends, Jaquishia agreed to at least listen to information about trauma, although she continued to refuse to talk about her own experiences.

The therapist responded with a sensitive, careful implementation of the TF-CBT modules described above. Ms. Washington was invited back, and both she and Jaquishia were educated about different types of trauma, body awareness, and risk reduction. These conversations constituted the **P**sychoeducational component of treatment. Ms. Washington learned some of the "best things" to say to Jaquishia when she had painful memories or bad dreams of the abuse. Ms. Washington also was encouraged to set aside a little time each week for just her and Jaquishia, listening to music, dancing, or cooking with her (**P**arenting Skills). Although Ms. Washington was busy, she said she'd do what she could. The therapist encouraged Ms. Washington to give Jaquishia some breaks from household, cooking, and child care responsibilities, but neither Jaquishia nor Ms. Washington agreed with this recommendation, so they basically ignored it.

Jaquishia learned deep breathing exercises and how to relax her muscles when she was stressed and how to apply these skills, not just in therapy sessions but at school and at other times when she was tense (**R**elaxation Skills). She learned how to better manage her emotions, including how to label stress and differentiate it from hunger. She also learned to understand the source of these emotions, that they exist on a continuum, and what strategies to use when she felt overwhelmed by them. Specifically, Jaquishia began to do video game dancing when she was stressed, or before snacking when she was tempted to eat (**A**ffective expression and modulation skills). She learned how to replace some of her negative, hopeless views (e.g., "hating everything about her life") with views that were more specific and included something positive (e.g., "I hate what my uncle did to me, but I do like some things about myself") (**C**ognitive coping skills).

When it came time to create a *trauma narrative*, to tell the story of the abuse in detail, Jaquishia was still reluctant to talk. Although she didn't agree to talk about the abuse, she agreed to write a series of poems to tell her story (**T**rauma narration). At first she wouldn't share these poems with the therapist, and the therapist respected her decision while still encouraging her to share the poems and to continue writing them. After several weeks, Jaquishia decided she was ready to share her poems. At first, Jaquishia wouldn't be in the same room with the therapist as she read Jaquishia's trauma poems. The next session, Jaquishia agreed to be in the same room as the therapist read the poems silently. The following session, the therapist read them aloud with Jaquishia in the room. The therapist read these words, written by Jaquishia:

He Said
He said
"You know you want it, you little whore.
I need to score,
So lick me good
And let me lick under your hood.
If you're bad,
I'll tell your mamma
If you're sad,
That's on you.
It feels so good, baby.
Don't stop.
Get on top.
You know I'm the only one who ever loved you,
The only one who ever will love you."

Why did I cry?
Why did I lie?
Why did I stay by
him?

Why did HE lie?
Why did he try
to make me his girlfriend?
Why did I let him
Make me cry?

As the therapist read the poem, Jaquishia sobbed loudly, eventually running from the room and saying that she was done with therapy and never coming back. She missed the next five sessions, and the therapist was worried that Jaquishia wouldn't return to therapy. Then, unannounced and unscheduled, Jaquishia returned as if nothing had happened. She gave no reasons for either her absence or her return. The therapist complimented Jaquishia on her strength in returning to face her painful memories and reminded Jaquishia that she was in charge of her treatment and of her life. Jaquishia just shrugged.

Jaquishia was taught how to manage the intrusive reminders of the trauma, such as reminding herself that dreams aren't real, that she had already lived through those bad times and they were over, and that she was safe now. This is called an In vivo mastery of reminders of the trauma. Jaquishia learned to imagine her safest place in the world whenever she had bad thoughts: in her bed, piled under blankets, or in the room at her Granny's that she shared with her sisters. When Jaquishia imagined being safe and warm, her bad thoughts of Uncle Mar began to feel less powerful.

15. How would you know that Jaquishia is ready to share her trauma poems with her grandmother?

16. How would you know if her grandmother was ready to hear the poems? How would you "coach" Ms. Washington to get ready to hear the stories? Would you worry that Ms. Washington's religious values would make hearing such graphic details difficult? How do you think Ms. Washington would respond given that her son is the perpetrator of the sexual abuse? Explain how you would handle this situation.

After another month of listening to the therapist read her what she had written, Jaquishia found that she was able to read her trauma poems aloud in front of the therapist (Sharing of the Trauma Narrative). Finally, the day came when she felt strong enough to read them in front of Ms. Washington. Jaquishia was extremely worried about how her grandmother would react when hearing her story and was particularly worried that Granny would blame Jaquishia for "wanting" or "causing" the sexual abuse. The therapist had met with Ms. Washington on several occasions to prepare her for the sharing of Jaquishia's poems, and she assured Jaquishia that Granny was ready to hear her story (Conjoint parent and child session to discuss the trauma).

On the days of the reading of the poems, which actually took about six conjoint therapy sessions spread out over two months, Jaquishia dressed up in her best church clothes and read the poems so quietly that she was almost inaudible. Granny was stoic and closed her eyes as she listened intently to what her son had done to her granddaughter, saying nothing. After the sixth therapy session, Granny gave Jaquishia a giant hug and said over and over, "My dear baby. My baby. I'm so sorry." She didn't blame Jaquishia for the abuse, but instead cried, prayed, and embraced Jaquishia. Granny's words helped immeasurably, as Jaquishia began to recognize that Mar-Man was responsible for abusing her and that the abuse wasn't her fault. And with that growing recognition, Jaquishia left therapy with a new bounce in her step and sass in her voice that showed her old spirit and energy were coming back.

After Jaquishia had shared her trauma narrative, Ms. Washington called the therapist to set up an appointment for herself—an unforeseen turn of events. In this session, Ms. Washington, who was normally highly composed and businesslike in her interactions with the therapist, stunned the therapist by asking to be called Naomi instead of Ms. Washington.

Naomi shared with the therapist that "all of the talk" about Jaquishia's sexual abuse had "gotten her thinking." She now realized that her ex-husband had been sexually abusive to Tanya when Tanya was about 12 or 13, but that Naomi hadn't been able to fully comprehend that the abuse was happening. She just knew that her ex and Tanya had started to act strangely around each other. She discovered at the same time that he was having an affair with a friend of hers. Because of the affair, she kicked him out of the house, never being sure of any details regarding what had happened with Tanya.

Naomi was quiet for a few minutes and then said, "But, there's more." She took a deep breath and grew almost as quiet as Jaquishia had initially been in therapy. Naomi shared that she'd been sexually abused by her own father. Although never truly forgetting the abuse, she simply didn't focus on it as she raised her children and her grandchildren. At times, events in her own life would bring back a sharp memory, but she was so busy that she easily pushed such memories to the side. After listening to Jaquishia talk about Uncle Mar, she found she was no longer able to push aside her own memories so easily. She hadn't unlocked the door to this haunted room in her head for years, but now the memories had come flooding back. Not only did her own sexual abuse come back to her, but so did stories of abuse from so many women in her family—stories that had often been shared after too many drinks at family picnics when the men were outside pitching horseshoes. Naomi's own mother, Ms. Walker (G-Granny), had been sexually abused as well, by an uncle, Naomi thought, or someone close, although Ms. Walker couldn't remember the details of the abuse anymore. When Naomi had gone to her mother to share how she, Naomi, had been abused, Ms. Walker had believed her daughter but felt powerless to stop it. And there was more sexual abuse—a great aunt, a cousin, a great-great grandmother who had been abused by a white slave owner. Naomi didn't want therapy for herself, figuring she could make her peace with the Lord about these terrible memories on her own, but she did want the therapist's advice on whether she should share any of this information with Jaquishia.

> 17. Would you advise Naomi to share the family stories of sexual abuse, including her own sexual abuse, with Jaquishia? Why or why not? If you think that Naomi should share the stories, how would you recommend that she do so?

The therapist and Naomi worked out a plan for a joint session for the purpose of sharing the familial sexual abuse information in a structured and supportive way, but this session was cancelled repeatedly—once due to weather, once due to Keon being sick, once due to a change in Naomi's work schedule. And then a month went by, and then another. Naomi and Jaquishia never returned to therapy after this day, so the final step of role playing ways to escape from potentially abusive situations in the future never happened (Enhance the safety and future development).

Nevertheless, Jaquishia's therapy had mostly been successful. It took another two years, but ironically, so did the court case against Uncle Mar. Jaquishia's therapist had shared the success of her therapy with the prosecutor's office. With Jaquishia's testimony, the prosecuting attorney believed that the case against Uncle Mar was winnable. The therapist contacted Jaquishia, who was now 18 and pregnant with her first child. Jaquishia had no problem in agreeing to testify against Uncle Mar. The court case against him was scheduled, then postponed, then rescheduled again. Jaquishia was undeterred by the delays and felt confident that she could testify against her uncle.

In the meantime, Jaquishia was still living with Granny and was dating her baby's father, her first boyfriend, a young man she'd dated for a year. Her pregnancy was a surprise given her Polycystic Ovarian Syndrome. She thought that she'd never be able to become pregnant, so she hadn't been using any birth control. When she found out she was pregnant, she was more excited than worried. Mostly, she was happy that she was going to be having a baby of her own, although Granny didn't share her excitement. She was hoping that Granny might let her boyfriend move in when her daughter was born, although Granny wasn't convinced that this was a good idea.

Jaquishia had rejoined the dance team her last two years of school. After she graduated, she still struggled with her weight but was doing better at managing her diabetes. She also had a better understanding of her other health problems, although it was still tough for her to make good food choices. Jaquishia was hoping to get a nail technician's or beautician's license, but she also thought she might enjoy getting a child-care license.

Jaquishia was active in the church and still helped with the babies during Sunday services. Although Tanya was still in jail, Jaquishia had visited her once on her own. The visit had been difficult but had gone well enough. Conversation was awkward but civil, and Jaquishia had a better understanding of how difficult her mother's life had been. As a result, she was less angry with her mother and more forgiving of her shortcomings.

Jaquishia had her driver's license now and had a car of her own, an old Buick that was a gift from G-Granny. It helped when transporting her brothers and sisters to sports practices after school. Jaydn was now 15 years old, Keon was almost 11, and Jasmine and Kiara were 14 and 13. All were eager to help out with Jaquishia's baby girl, whom they couldn't wait to meet.

When the therapist spoke to Naomi one final time, Ms. Washington summarized all the family had been through eloquently, "Our family has been through everything you could imagine and we don't need any more bad things. The Lord has promised good to us. The bad stuff is stopping right here and right now with Jaquishia. And when Jaquishia has that little baby girl, she's gonna be safe. Nobody, I mean *nobody*, is gonna touch her."

18. Did therapy progress the way you thought it would? Why or why not?

19. How does working on the case of Jaquishia inform your clinical work?

References

Aleman, A., & Larøi, F. (2008). *Hallucinations: The science of idiosyncratic perception.* Washington, DC: American Psychological Association.

Bagley, C. C., & Mallick, K. (2000). Prediction of sexual, emotional, and physical maltreatment of mental health outcomes in a longitudinal cohort of 290 adolescent women. *Child Maltreatment, 5*, 218–226.

Barrera, M., Calderón, L., & Bell, V. (2013). Long term mental health implications of sexually abused children: The cognitive impact of sexual abuse and PTSD in children: A neuropsychological study. *Journal of Child Sexual Abuse, 22*(6), 625–638. doi:10.1080/10538712.2013.811141

Black, L., & Jackson, V. (2005). Families of African origin. In M. McGoldrick, J. Giordano, & N. Garcia-Preto (Eds.), *Ethnicity and family therapy.* New York: Guilford.

Cabral, R. R., & Smith, T. B. (2011). Racial/ethnic matching of clients and therapists in mental health services: A meta-analytic review of preferences, perceptions, and outcomes. *Journal of Counseling Psychology, 58*, 537–554.

Cohen, J. A., Berliner, L, Mannarino, A. P., & Steer, R. A. (2004). A multisite, randomized controlled trial for children with sexual abuse-related PTSD symptoms. *Journal of the American Academy of Child and Adolescent Psychiatry, 43*, 393–402.

Craner, J. R., Martinson, A. A., Sigmon, S. T., & McGillicuddy, M. L. (2015). Prevalence of sexual trauma history using behaviorally specific methods of assessment in first year college students. *Journal of Child Sexual Abuse, 24*(5), 484–505. http://dx.doi.org/10.1080/10538712.2015.1026014

Edgette, J. S. (2006). *Adolescent therapy that really works.* New York: W.W. Norton.

Finkelhor, D. (1994). Current information on the scope and nature of child sexual abuse. *The Future of Children, 4,* 31—53.

Hammersley, P., Dias, A., Todd, G., Bowen-Jones, K., Reilly, B., & Bentall, R. P. (2003). Childhood trauma and hallucinations in bipolar affective disorder: A preliminary investigation. *British Journal of Psychiatry, 182,* 543–547.

Happel, R. F. (2016). The process of disclosure for child victims. In W. T. O' Donohue & M. Fanetti (Eds.), *Forensic interviews regarding child sexual abuse: A guide to evidence-based practice.* Cham, Switzerland: Spring International.

Moore Hines, P., & Boyd-Franklin, N. (2005). African-American families. In M. McGoldrick, J. Giordano, & N. Garcia-Preto (Eds.), *Ethnicity and family therapy.* New York: Guilford.

Murphy, B. C., & Dillon, C. (2011). *Interviewing in action in a multi-cultural world.* Belmont, CA: Brooks/Cole.

Read, J., Agar, K., Argyle, N., & Aderhold, V. (2003). Sexual and physical abuse during childhood and adulthood as predictors of hallucinations, delusions and thought disorder. *Psychology and Psychotherapy, 76,* 1–22.

Shevlin, M., Dorahy, M., & Adamson, G. (2007). Childhood traumas and hallucinations: An analysis of the National Comorbidity Survey. *Journal of Psychiatric Research, 41,* 222–228.

Wilson, H. W., Samuelson, S. L., Staudenmeyer, A. H., & Widom, C. S. (2015). Trajectories of psychopathology and risky behaviors associated with childhood abuse and neglect in low-income Urban African American girls. *Child Abuse & Neglect, 45,* 108–121. http://dx.doi.org/10.1016/j.chiabu.2015.02.009

Wolfe, V. V. (2006). Child sexual abuse. In E. J. Mash, & R. A. Barkley (Eds.), *Treatment of childhood disorders.* New York: Guilford.

CASE 8

Bear Hoskin

Bear, a 16-year-old Native American, is battling obesity and eating problems. His taciturn nature challenges the skills of his therapist, Dr. McFall.

▌ **ICD-10/ DSM-5 Diagnosis:**
▌ F50.81 (307.51) Binge-Eating Disorder, Moderate
▌ F10.929 (303.00) Alcohol Intoxication
▌ F15.929 (305.90) Caffeine Intoxication
▌ R/O G47.00 (780.52) Insomnia Disorder
▌ R/O G47.33 (327.33) Obstructive Sleep Apnea Hypopnea
▌ Z60.4 (V60.4) Social Exclusion or Rejection

> 1. Do you agree with the diagnoses given to Bear? Why or why not? Why do you think that two disorders are listed on a Rule-Out basis?

Diagnostic Discussion

Bear's list of diagnoses is lengthy, but they tie together in a meaningful way, with each diagnosis impacting another. The following section will briefly explain why Bear meets criteria for the above diagnoses. The Case Conceptualization section will explain how Bear's problems interact and exacerbate each other.

Let's begin with the diagnosis that reflects the crisis the night Bear was hospitalized, Alcohol Intoxication. The diagnosis of Alcohol Intoxication requires that three criteria be met. The first criterion is a recent ingestion of alcohol. Bear consumed copious amounts of alcohol at the party that he attended with his brother Phoenix. The second criterion is significant problematic behavioral or psychological changes because of alcohol consumption. Bear meets this criterion by demonstrating impaired judgment that caused him to continue drinking all evening. He also showed mood lability, with his mood changing from emptiness to euphoria. The third criterion requires that a person shows one or more of the following six symptoms: slurred speech, lack of coordination, unsteady gait, nystagmus (rapid, involuntary movement of the eyeball), impairment in attention or memory, and stupor or coma (APA, 2013). Bear showed symptoms of slurred speech and lack of coordination as he asked a girl to dance and tried to dance with her. Mild intoxication typically occurs after about two drinks, especially for an individual like Bear who has no tolerance for alcohol. When people have more than a few drinks, they're likely to fall asleep or demonstrate *anesthesia,* a general loss of sensation (APA, 2013). Bear didn't stop drinking after just a few drinks, however. He drank to the point where his blood alcohol level was affecting his respiration and pulse, having potentially fatal consequences. Bear lost consciousness that night because of a lack of oxygen reaching his brain as a result of his slowed respiration. This lack of oxygen was evident in the blueness around his lips and nails, the symptoms that convinced his brother to call 911. A person can be diagnosed with Alcohol Intoxication without having a Substance Use Disorder, as is true for Bear. However, Bear could develop a Substance Use Disorder given the markedly positive experiences he had the first night that he drank and given his possible genetic predisposition for alcohol. Potential problems with alcohol would have to be carefully monitored, as will be discussed in the case conceptualization section.

Bear's immediate problem that night was his alcohol intake, but his chronic problem is his Binge Eating Disorder, which is at the Moderate level. The first criterion of Binge Eating Disorder is eating an amount of food that is larger than what most people would eat in the same period of time and circumstances. Bear's typical daily diet was shared in the case study. Although you might not remember the specific details or amounts, you likely remember that his diet consisted of thousands of calories worth of pizza, donuts, soda, chips, french fries, and hamburgers. Although Bear's diet is unhealthy, it wouldn't necessarily qualify him for an eating disorder. To be considered a binge-eating episode, not only must a person eat a great deal of food, but he must also feel that he lacks control over eating while he's bingeing. When he eats at night, Bear feels like he can't stop eating even though he tries to do so, and he also feels that he has no control over the food he eats.

The second criterion requires that a person show three or more of these five symptoms: eating much more rapidly than normal, eating until feeling uncomfortably full, eating when not physically hungry, eating alone due to embarrassment, and feeling disgusted or guilty after bingeing. Bear reports eating when he's not hungry and eating after he's full. He also tries to eat alone, best demonstrated by his standing take-out order at McDonald's with Phoenix. Bear definitely feels disgusted with himself because of his eating habits as well as his overall weight. Bear's disgust with himself for his binge eating is closely connected with the third criterion, that a person shows marked distress over his binge eating. Bear is clearly upset by his overeating.

The fourth criterion is that the binge eating must occur at least once a week for three months. Bear easily demonstrates binge eating at least once a week—in fact, he does so at least once a day. Binge Eating is considered to be at the moderate level of severity when an individual has four to seven binge-eating episodes a week. Bear meets this level of severity because of his late-night overeating. We would want to talk with Bear about his diet in more detail to determine if this level of severity is accurate for him. Based on the available evidence, it's a reasonable estimate. Finally, Bear meets the fifth criterion for Binge Eating Disorder, that a person can't be demonstrating another disorder such as anorexia nervosa or bulimia, which are separate eating disorders.

Bear's Binge Eating Disorder is closely tied to his caffeine use, so a disorder of Caffeine Intoxication is warranted. You might scoff at this diagnosis, as perhaps you're reading this case study late at night while downing a highly caffeinated soda or energy drink. In fact, 85% of children and adults consume caffeine regularly (APA, 2013), so you're not alone in your choices. However, when individuals consume too much caffeine (typically a high dose of more than 250 mg), they can develop physiological symptoms that impair their ability to function. Bear consumes enough caffeine to experience such problems. On any given day he consumes four or five sodas, including several two-liter servings of soda during his gaming session. His drink of choice, Mountain Dew, has 324 milligrams of caffeine per two-liter bottle. Bear's body reacts to this high level of caffeine by showing restlessness, excitement, insomnia, muscle twitching, periods of inexhaustibility, and tachycardia, or a rapidly beating heart. These symptoms are problematic for him because they disrupt his sleep-wake cycle and cause him to be sleepy the following day at school.

However, Bear's high levels of caffeine use don't explain his sleep problems. Certainly, consuming high levels of caffeine can disrupt sleep, but Bear's sleep problems are far more severe than can be explained by caffeine use alone. Bear has been diagnosed with two sleep disorders as *Rule Outs*. Remember, a Rule-Out diagnosis does not mean that we're ruling it out as a possibility. Instead, it means that we think this diagnosis is a possibility, but we'd need more information to definitively diagnose it.

Let's carefully consider why Bear has two sleep disorders listed on a Rule-Out basis. The first sleep disorder that's a possibility for Bear is Insomnia Disorder (APA, 2013). The first criterion of Insomnia Disorder requires that a person complain about the quality or quantity of his sleep. Examples of such sleep complaints can include difficulty falling asleep, difficulty staying asleep, and difficulty falling back asleep if a person wakes up too early. The second criterion is that the person's sleep difficulties must cause distress or problems. The third criterion focuses on frequency. The sleep problems must occur at least three nights a week. The fourth criterion focuses on duration. The sleep problems must be present for at least three months. The fifth criterion is that the sleep problems must not be due to a lack of opportunities to sleep. The final criterion articulates that the sleep problem can't be explained by other sleep problems, substance use, mental health problems, or medical problems.

Bear solidly demonstrates every criterion listed above, except for one important factor that's easy to overlook. Let's walk through the criteria and see if Bear should be diagnosed with Insomnia Disorder. Bear meets the first criterion as he often stays up until 3 AM playing video games and has trouble falling asleep despite the late hour. When he does fall asleep, he often wakes up feeling like he can't sleep, so he has difficulty staying asleep. His sleep problems cause him distress, because he's exhausted for school the next day. Poor quality sleep can also contribute to self-regulation problems. In fact, not getting enough quality sleep contributes to overeating (APA, 2013). Bear struggles to sleep most nights, and his sleep problems have persisted for over three months. His sleep problems aren't due to having inadequate opportunities to sleep, such as might be caused by shift work or other environmental problems.

However, let's take a close look at the final summary criterion, that the person's sleep problems can't be explained by other sleep problems, substance use, mental health problems, or *medical problems*. In Bear's case, we aren't sure if another medical problem, such as Obstructive Sleep Apnea Hypopnea, is causing his Insomnia Disorder. Therefore, before Bear's insomnia can be diagnosed or treated, he should be referred to a sleep clinic or sleep specialist to ensure that his breathing problems aren't causing his sleeping problems. Because we aren't certain of the *etiology,* or cause, of Bear's sleep problems, he receives a secondary Rule-Out diagnosis of Obstructive Sleep Apnea Hypopnea (APA, 2013). This is a medical disorder wherein a person demonstrates breathing problems while sleeping, diagnosed by polysomnography, which records a person's biological functions while sleeping, including breathing, heart activity, and limb movements. Apnea refers to a total lack of oxygen to the brain, and Hypopnea refers to a reduction of oxygen to the brain (APA, 2013). Common symptoms of this problem include breathing troubles at night, such as snoring, snorting/gasping, or breathing stoppages while sleeping.

Bear's awakening in the night and feeling like he's drowning and can't breathe is a serious symptom. It suggests that Bear may be unable to breathe while he's sleeping due to insufficient oxygen as a result of the softening of the muscles in his airway. His loud snoring is another indicator of this same possibility. Obstructive Sleep Apnea Hypopnea is a serious medical problem that requires immediate treatment; the problem is progressive and tends to worsen with age. Risk factors for this condition include being male, being obese, having a family or genetic history of sleep problems, and advancing age (APA, 2013). Bear shows the two most common risk factors for this disorder because he's male and obese.

Bear meets criteria for one other condition that may be a focus of clinical attention. These *Z Codes* (a special group of codes provided in ICD-10-CM for the reporting of factors influencing health status and contact with health services) are not formal diagnoses but help provide more insight into the problems of the client. Bear is diagnosed with Social Exclusion or Rejection due to his exclusion or rejection by others in the form of bullying, teasing, intimidation, humiliation, purposely being excluded from activities, and being targeted for verbal abuse. Sadly, individuals who struggle with obesity often experience such social rejection and taunting by others.

2. Now that you've read more, do you agree with the diagnoses given to Bear? Why or why not?

3. Where would you begin if you were a clinician working with Bear? Which diagnosis or problem would you tackle first, and why?
4. Make a list of all of the possible etiological explanations of Bear's diagnoses, including genetic, social, cultural, cognitive, and systemic.

Case Conceptualization

Consider the list of serious medical and mental health problems Bear demonstrates: insomnia, possible sleep apnea, obesity, binge eating, heavy caffeine use, diabetes, and possible alcohol problems. These disorders are difficult enough to treat separately, but when combined, they tend to exacerbate one another almost exponentially. Although the intertwined relationship between these disorders makes treatment seem hopeless, the opposite is actually true. If Bear could sleep better, he likely would binge less late at night and use less caffeine. If he could better manage his obesity and diabetes, he'd likely sleep better. Unraveling these disorders can take some effort, but ultimately, the payoffs for Bear could be substantial.

Let's begin with Bear's serious difficulties in sleeping, which makes Insomnia Disorder a possibility for him. Good-quality sleep is critical to a person's mental and physical health, so skimping on sleep—even if to stay up late studying or reading this book—doesn't usually pay off for a person. Poor or insufficient sleep puts people at risk for medical problems, including hypertension and heart disease, and psychological problems, including depression (Bonnet & Arand, 2010).

Why does Bear have trouble sleeping? First, he may have Obstructive Sleep Apnea Hypopnea. The etiology of this sleep problem is medical in that a physiological problem causes people to struggle to breathe while sleeping. This restriction of oxygen in a person's airway could be due to obesity, elevated blood pressure, or an obstructed airway (APA, 2013). We don't know why Bear is having so much difficulty sleeping, but ensuring that medical problems are not causing his insomnia is an important first step in treatment.

Bear's sleep problems may be connected with other factors as well, including just being a teenager. Teenagers tend to have problems with their *circadian rhythms,* the roughly 24-hour clock that controls a number of biological functions, including sleep. In fact, adolescents often show a delayed-sleep disturbance in their circadian rhythms (APA, 2013), which makes it difficult for them to go to bed at a reasonable hour at night and wake up at a reasonable hour in the morning. A perfectly normal teenager might prefer to go to bed at 2 AM and wake up at 11 AM, although finding a high school that begins classes at noon might be difficult!

Other risk factors contribute to Bear's sleep problems as well. Risk factors for insomnia include being male, having poor sleep habits such as irregular sleep and wake times, and having a co-morbid mental health problem (Fossum, Nordnes, Storemark, Bjorvatn, & Pallesen, 2014; Reichenberg &

Seligman, 2016). Bear has all of these risk factors. He's male, doesn't have good sleep hygiene, and has a co-morbid Binge Eating Disorder.

Thus, Bear's obesity is a factor in his sleep problems. Ironically, his sleep problems likely contribute to his obesity. Not getting sufficient sleep makes it harder to maintain a healthy weight. Poor sleep impairs a person's metabolism and also interferes with hormones. Poor sleep quality also decreases a person's energy level during the day, leading to less energy for exercise. A person who lacks sleep is also likely to struggle with self-regulation and making good choices during the day regarding overall health, including decisions about what to eat and how much to eat (National Sleep Foundation, n.d.). Sleeping and eating problems thus often go hand and hand.

Bear's obesity is connected not only to his sleep problems, but also to his Binge Eating Disorder. A few points of clarification may be helpful regarding Binge Eating Disorder, since the diagnosis is new in DSM-5 and thus still being studied (APA, 2013). Most individuals who are obese don't binge eat. However, most individuals who binge eat are obese (APA, 2013). Being obese and binge eating puts Bear at risk for several problems. First, he's likely to overemphasize the importance of his weight and body shape as a problem more so than individuals who are obese but don't binge eat (APA, 2013). We see this with Bear when he shows a high degree of dissatisfaction with his body as compared to his brother, and also when he expects others to reject him because of his body size. Binge Eating Disorder is correlated with a poor overall health prognosis, including medical problems above and beyond those caused by obesity (Bulik & Reichborn-Kjennerud, 2003). On a more hopeful note, when individuals have Binge Eating Disorder and obesity, several effective treatment options are available (APA, 2013). This stands in stark contrast to the lack of effective long-term treatments for obesity.

Why did Bear develop Binge Eating Disorder in the first place? The *cognitive model*, upon which cognitive-behavioral therapy (CBT) is based (Beck, 2011) may help explain some of Bear's struggles with eating. The key premise to the cognitive model is that a person's emotions, behaviors, and even bodily responses are influenced by how that person thinks. An often-told story epitomizes the cognitive model: If you have a flat tire, you have a problem. If you get upset because you have a flat tire, you now have two problems. For Bear, this means that how he thinks about everyday things and events in his life—including his weight, the party he attended, alcohol, food, school, friends, and family—affects how he reacts to these things and events.

The cognitive model utilizes the term *core beliefs* to describe enduring understandings of the self, others, or the world. Core beliefs are our deepest, most fundamental beliefs about the world, ourselves, and others (Beck, 2011). Ironically, we can have a core belief that isn't actually true! But we're certain that our core beliefs are accurate, and accordingly we just accept life as "the way it is." Thus, we tend to generalize our core beliefs across many settings (Beck, 2011). Bear's core beliefs about himself are likely "I'm inferior" or "I'm not good enough." This belief about his inadequacy is evident when Bear is at school, where he believes others will reject him because of his weight and appearance. It's apparent at home, where he believes he'll always be found lacking when compared to his brother Phoenix. It also shows itself in his unhealthy food choices and binge eating, because he believes that losing weight is a hopeless task that he'll never be able to accomplish.

Bear's core beliefs affect his *intermediate beliefs* (Beck, 2011), patterns of thought that aren't as deeply ingrained as our core beliefs, so they're easier for people to be aware of. Intermediate beliefs are our rules and expectations about ourselves, others, and the world. Bear's intermediate beliefs likely include such ideas as, "I always fail at losing weight," "My online friends like me better than my classmates because my online friends can't see me," "I don't belong at a party with popular kids, so I should just stay home," or "I'll never be as popular as Phoenix." Bear's tendency to withdraw and remain isolated in his room playing video games likely stems from his intermediate beliefs about not having the skills to be socially successful in the world. It's no wonder that Bear didn't want to attend the party with Phoenix. He felt certain that he'd be rejected by the popular kids and believed that he didn't belong with them.

Intermediate beliefs, in turn, give rise to *automatic thoughts* (Beck, 2011), the first quick thoughts that enter our mind in response to a specific situation or event. Automatic thoughts are spontaneous, and they represent our most superficial level of thinking. Although automatic thoughts tend to be briefly considered and then dismissed, they still influence our behavior. Some examples of Bear's automatic thoughts the night of the party might include, "I won't have fun at the party," "I'm only going to the party for one hour to get Phoenix off my case," "No one will talk to me at the party so I'm going to make myself invisible," and "Drinking is better than I thought it would be."

5. What might be some of Bear's core beliefs, intermediate beliefs, and automatic thoughts regarding Waya, Rain, and Phoenix?

6. Why do you think Bear's binge eating began in the first place?

Let's determine how the cognitive model could be specifically applied to Bear's binge eating. Bear often engages in late-night binge eating, when he eats far more than the average person would. After these episodes he feels guilty and ashamed, further exacerbating his issues of self-esteem and triggering his *core beliefs* of not being good enough. Dieting often follows binge-eating, but keeping weight off through dieting is incredibly difficult, especially in people who binge eat (APA, 2013). Bear's struggle to lose weight may bring forth an *intermediate belief* that people would like him more if he didn't weigh as much. Bear is berated by classmates about his appearance, causing him to retreat to his room and become absorbed in video games. Playing video games while exhausted puts Bear at high risk to engage in poor self-regulation and not make good choices. Bear's *automatic thoughts* become apparent in specific situations, like when he overeats at night and decides to just eat another bag of chips because he's already broken his own rules about how much he should eat.

Collectively, Bear's core beliefs, intermediate beliefs, and automatic thoughts lead to feelings of worthlessness, defeat, and self-loathing. These feelings, in turn, lead to behaviors such as isolating himself and binge eating. In fact, Zerbe (2008) found that most binges are triggered by a change in mood, especially depressive symptoms, which predict the onset of binge eating. Sadly, feelings of shame and guilt after an episode of bingeing can worsen depression. Thus, problems regarding *mood* self-regulation are tied closely with problems regarding *food* self-regulation. Bingeing behaviors also lead to physiological reactions, including increased weight, diabetes, and insomnia. Bear exhibits all of these physical problems. Binge eating also results in social role adjustment problems and impaired life satisfaction (APA, 2013). We can see numerous examples throughout the case study of Bear struggling with his social world. We also see how Bear isn't satisfied with his life overall. All these emotional, cognitive, and physiological reactions interact to cause Bear to feel worse about himself. Thus, the cycle of binge eating and self-berating continues.

Although the cognitive model is useful in understanding Bear's thoughts and behaviors, other factors impact him as well, including genetics as well as environmental and cultural factors. In terms of genetic influences, eating disorders (McElroy & Kotwal, 2006) tend to run in families, although we don't know if this is true for Bear's family. Overeating tends to begin in childhood, as happened with Bear (von Ranson & Wallace, 2014). Perhaps the food insecurity and poverty of the family was a factor in Bear's overeating. His lack of access to healthy foods, such as fruit and vegetables, because of the "food desert" on the reservation likely exacerbated the problems. Having easy access to large amounts of high-fat, sodium-laden, and heavily sweetened food, such as chips and soda, also encourage overeating.

Bear's list of struggles doesn't stop with sleep problems and eating problems. He also qualifies for a diagnosis of Caffeine Intoxication. The intertwined nature of his problems is apparent with this disorder, as high levels of caffeine can lead to poor sleep. Likewise, eating certain foods, such as salty chips, can contribute to an individual's pairing such food with a certain drink, such as a sweet soda (Nguyen-Michel, Unger, & Spruijt-Metz, 2007). As mentioned earlier, a lack of sleep interferes with a person's ability to make good choices. So, even if Bear were highly motivated to reduce his caffeine intake, it would be difficult for him to follow through on this goal in his sleep-deprived state at 2 AM.

Bear has an underlying, untreated medical problem that's also very concerning. He has diabetes and isn't keeping his blood sugar levels in check. Diabetes is a serious disease (National Institute of Diabetes and Digestive and Kidney Diseases, 2011). Having diabetes means that Bear's blood sugar levels are too high. Diabetes can be controlled through a person's diet but often has to be managed through an insulin pump or insulin shots. Uncontrolled diabetes like Bear has can lead to high blood pressure, heart attack, and stroke. It can also damage a person's blood vessels and lead to serious problems that affect a person's eyes, kidneys, toes, feet, and teeth. For Bear's long-term health, getting his diabetes in better control is absolutely critical. Uncontrolled diabetes can affect a person's sleep, eating choices, energy level, caffeine use, and alcohol use; making the treatment of Bear's diabetes critical to his success.

Finally, Bear has one important problem that hasn't yet been addressed, Alcohol Intoxication. Bear was referred to therapy as a result of Alcohol Intoxication after a party that landed him in the emergency room. As this has been his first time drinking, Bear likely doesn't have an Alcohol Use Disorder. However, Bear is at risk to develop alcohol problems without intervention. The younger a person is when he first becomes intoxicated, the more likely the person will develop an Alcohol Use Disorder in the future (APA, 2013). Bear was only 16 when he was diagnosed with Alcohol Intoxication. Furthermore, Bear has a strong family history of alcoholism on both his paternal and maternal sides. Alcoholism tends to run in families. The risk of developing alcoholism is three to four times higher in people who have close relatives who also have alcohol problems (APA, 2013). Particularly worrisome in Bear's case is his positive experiences at the party when he drank. Bear had fun, loosened up, and felt accepted by other teenagers, experiences that are atypical for him. He attributed his ability to relax and have a good time to his alcohol use. Positive expectancies about substance use predict a person's future drinking behavior (Smith, Goldman, Greenbaum, & Christiansen, 1995), which doesn't bode well for Bear.

7. How might Bear's intermediate beliefs about alcohol use have changed as a result of his experiences at the party? What intermediate beliefs do you think Phoenix has about alcohol use?

8. How do you think that Native American cultural values helped shape Bear, both in terms of risk factors and resilience factors?

9. What strengths does Bear have? How might you integrate his strengths into a treatment plan?

Evidence-Based Treatment

Before Bear was discharged from the hospital after his alcohol intoxication, he was referred to a sleep specialist for a polysomnography and sleep study. The results of the sleep study and polysomnography showed that Bear had Obstructive Sleep Apnea, the more severe version of sleep apnea/hypopnea, wherein a person experiences episodes of no airflow during sleep. Bear wasn't happy with the treatment; it was recommended that he lose weight and exercise—advice he'd heard many times before—but also that he get fitted for a Continuous Positive Airway Pressure (CPAP) machine. To use a CPAP machine, a mask is fitted over a person's nose and mouth. The mask is connected to a tube that's connected to a motor, which blows air into the tube (National Heart, Lung, and Blood Institute, 2011).

Bear got his CPAP machine about a week after his stay in the hospital, and he hated it. It was noisy, awkward to use, and Bear had a hard time turning over in bed without the mask falling off. He put the machine in his closet and decided he wasn't going to mess with it.

Two weeks after Bear's hospital stay, it was time for a series of same-day appointments at CHIC, the Cherokee Health Integrated Clinic.

Bear heard his usually quiet mother's voice ring throughout the house. "Hurry up! We can't be late to therapy on the first day!" Rain cajoled Bear.

Bear begrudgingly walked to the door, and said exasperatedly, "I don't need this."

Rain said nothing.

Bear frowned and sighed. "How many appointments do I have today?'

Rain looked over the referral sheet. "You have an appointment with a nurse practitioner who specializes in diabetes nutrition, another appointment with the sleep specialist you saw that day at the hospital, and an appointment with a psychologist."

Bear's frown grew even bigger. "Why do I have to see a psychologist?"

Rain answered, "Bear. Give it a chance. It might help."

"What's the shrink's name again?" Bear asked.

"McFall. Dr. Robert McFall," his mother answered.

"That isn't a Cherokee name. I'll bet he's a white guy," Bear reasoned.

Rain said nothing.

Bear's first two appointments at Cherokee Health Integrated Clinic went fairly well. He really liked the nurse practitioner who specialized in diabetes management. She was Cherokee, about his mother's age, and was diabetic herself. She was a straight shooter and frankly laid out her concerns about Bear's eating habits, uncontrolled diabetes, and weight in a forthright manner, but without judgment.

The first question the nurse practitioner asked Bear after introducing herself caught Bear off guard.

"So, are you here because other people made you come or because you want to change things for yourself?"

Bear wasn't sure what the right answer was. Of course, he wanted to change things, but he didn't want to be here either and certainly wouldn't have come on his own accord. The nurse practitioner listened as Bear answered and respected his right to make his own decisions about his diet and life. She didn't judge Bear, nor did she give him any unsolicited advice. Instead, when she wanted to suggest something to him that might improve his life, she said, "Well, Bear. I'd like to share some information that might be helpful. Would you rather that I not share it, or would you be OK with me telling you some facts about diabetes?"

When she asked in this manner, Bear couldn't help but want her to continue with what she was about to say. The nurse practitioner also carefully considered Bear's worries about changing his behavior. When he said that he didn't think it was possible for him to ever successfully lose weight, she didn't ignore his concerns. Instead, she said, "So you're worried that you can't lose weight. Tell me how you arrived at that conclusion."

After Bear told her his story of trying and failing at every diet, from the cabbage soup diet to veggie smoothies and the caveman diet, she gently asked, "Bear, what if dieting isn't the way to solve this problem? What if there were another way?"

The nurse practitioner followed the key components of *motivational interviewing* (Rosengren, 2009). This evidenced-based treatment intervention has been shown to be effective with a wide range of problems including changing health behavior; substance use and addictive behavior; impulse control problems; smoking; and a host of other behavioral challenges. The key components of motivational interviewing are collaboration, autonomy, and evocation (Rosengren, 2009). Collaboration is partnering together to solve a goal, such as a therapist and client working with each other instead of against each other. Autonomy recognizes that each person can choose his own goal. Therapists should have faith in their clients' abilities to do so wisely. Finally, evocation refers to the exchanges between therapist and client which serve to bring out the best in the client. Some key concepts to motivational interviewing include that the therapist not wanting change more than the client does, encouraging change talk, and rolling with resistance.

Bear didn't know anything about motivational interviewing. He only knew that he left the office of his first appointment, the one with the nurse practitioner, encouraged and hopeful. He felt like he finally heard and understood why he had to manage his diabetes and the serious consequences if he didn't manage it. Bear had been told this hundreds of times previously, but somehow, today, it clicked for him. He was also encouraged to start attending to his food choices—not to diet, but just to watch what he ate, when he ate it, and why he ate it. Bear really liked the nurse practitioner and was looking forward to seeing her on his weekly visit to CHIC. When Bear left her office, his mother asked him how the visit went.

Bear smiled and said, "Good. She reminded me of you."

Rain smiled but remained silent as they walked across the CHIC campus to Bear's next appointment.

Bear's second appointment was with the sleep specialist. This appointment didn't go as well as the first. Bear was honest about his not using the CPAP machine, and the sleep specialist was visibly upset with him for not doing so. Bear felt judged and angry, and he felt like the doctor didn't listen to his concerns at all. Nevertheless, he agreed to try the CPAP machine every night for the next week, when he'd have his next appointment.

Rain asked Bear how this appointment went. Bear shrugged and said nothing.

Bear and Rain next went over to the office of the psychologist. Dr. McFall is a 29-year-old white male psychologist who recently got his first job at the CHIC after completing his doctorate degree. Dr. McFall took some multicultural classes in school, but he had no experience working with Native Americans. Despite this, he wasn't particularly concerned with his overall level of multicultural competence, believing that he could learn what he needed to know on the job. Dr. McFall believed that therapy with Native American adolescents was probably very similar to therapy with white adolescents, and he'd worked extensively with white teenagers. One of the reasons Dr. McFall accepted a job on the reservation was to receive tuition repayment by working with an underserved population in a remote area of the country. He was also excited to go hiking with his dog at the nearby Smoky Mountains National Park.

Dr. McFall was on his first day at work, and his very first patient that day was named Bear Hoskin. The doctor reviewed the referral information for Bear, which noted that Bear was a 16-year-old referred to him for Alcohol Intoxication that resulted in a hospital visit. *No problem,* thought Dr. McFall, *I've worked with teenagers with alcohol problems before.*

Bear silently entered Dr. McFall's office, again trying to look invisible as he'd done the night of the party. Bear was quiet throughout the session with Dr. McFall and answered his questions with short one-word answers. Following some initial failed attempts at building rapport, Dr. McFall asked Bear what he hoped to get out of their time together.

Finally speaking more than one or two words at a time, Bear responded, "Nothing. I don't need therapy, and I don't have a drinking problem. You don't know me."

Dr. McFall didn't know how to respond to Bear's comment, so he just overlooked it, hoping he could help Bear break through his denial about his drinking. Bear remained quiet for the remainder of the session. After Bear left, Dr. McFall wondered if he'd gotten into the wrong profession.

After the session, Rain asked Bear how it went. Bear shrugged and said nothing.

10. What mistakes did Dr. McFall make, and how could he have conducted a better therapy session?

11. Bear insists that he doesn't have a drinking problem, but the intake referral clearly noted Alcohol Intoxication as the presenting problem. How would you decide whether Bear has a drinking problem?

12. Should Dr. McFall address the cultural differences between them? How? Should he bring up Bear's weight problem or wait for Bear to bring it up?

Because this book primarily focuses on psychological problems, Bear's next meetings with the nurse practitioner and sleep specialist won't be explained in further detail. Bear continued to work closely with the nurse practitioner and made substantial changes, becoming active in controlling his diabetes. Bear began wearing the CPAP machine, mostly because he didn't want to anger the sleep specialist. After a few weeks, he agreed that it was easier to use and he didn't "hate it as bad."

The CHIC treatment model was integrated primary care, so the entire health team met every Monday to discuss progress and challenges and to ensure that they were all following a unified treatment plan. Dr. McFall, the nurse practitioner, the sleep specialist, and a nutritionist who met with Bear monthly were all a part of this meeting. When the team initially met to discuss Bear, Dr. McFall couldn't believe that the nurse practitioner had made so much progress with Bear when he'd made so little.

Dr. McFall's second and third sessions with Bear were as unproductive as the first. At the beginning of the fourth session, Dr. McFall leaned back in his chair, not sure of what to do next. He couldn't understand why he wasn't having any success with Bear. He was following the treatment manuals for Substance Use Disorder, but he still saw no progress in Bear's attitude toward his drinking problem. Bear had even told him that he might drink alcohol again in the future, on one of the few occasions when he actually said something. Dr. McFall was thinking about referring Bear to another therapist. He wondered if he should bring up the cultural differences between them and ask about what it meant to Bear to be a Cherokee (Trimble, 2010), but he wasn't sure how to initiate the conversation, so he just avoided the topic.

During the fifth session, Dr. McFall decided that he'd make one more attempt at building rapport with Bear.

Dr. McFall said, "You know Bear, in our first session, you told me that I don't know you. You're right, and over these last four sessions, you've made sure that hasn't changed. Listen, if you feel you don't need therapy, then I'm not going to make you sit here for no reason. But I can't give your parents a clean report until I get to know you. So why don't you tell me a little about yourself, and maybe we can see if there's any way I can help you. Let's start with you telling me about school." Dr. McFall figured that he had nothing to lose by taking such a heavy-handed approach, given that therapy with Bear was off to a terrible start.

Although Bear was still wary of Dr. McFall, he figured that talking to him would be the quickest way to get out of therapy. He haltingly began telling Dr. McFall about school. He told him that he made decent grades, and that he liked computer class and was pretty good at math. Dr. McFall said that math was always his favorite subject, too, but he spent most of his time on computers playing the SIMS. Bear was surprised to hear that Dr. McFall played computer games.

"Seriously? SIMS?" Bear responded. "That's gotta be the worst game of all time."

Although he didn't approve of Dr. McFall's video game of choice, Bear relaxed a little after this exchange. Dr. McFall chuckled too, happy to at least have made a superficial connection with Bear. For the first time, he set down the treatment manual that he'd been following so precisely, putting it on the desk between the two of them, where it landed with a thud.

Dr. McFall and Bear stared awkwardly at the manual for what seemed to both of them to be an eternity.

Bear was naturally a quiet, taciturn person and not fond of small talk. Dr. McFall, despite his doctorate degree in clinical psychology, was also less than socially skilled himself. They both looked around the room in a widening silence, hoping the other would say something.

Eventually Dr. McFall spoke. "Bear, I don't think therapy is working for you. I've been following the manual for treating alcohol problems to a T, but it doesn't seem to be helping you."

Bear politely answered, "Dr. McFall, no offense, but I don't have an alcohol problem. I only drank one time in my life—on the night I went to the hospital."

"Bear, all alcoholics say they don't have a problem," countered Dr. McFall.

Bear sat in silence and looked out the small window in the therapy office.

Dr. McFall tried again, "The truth is that I really don't know. I don't know what to say to you to get therapy started. I don't know if you have an alcohol problem or not."

Bear grew even quieter than usual and said only, "I don't."

Dr. McFall argued with Bear. "But, Bear, I mean, your intake form said that you had Alcohol Intoxication and almost died. Dying is kind of a big deal."

Bear said nothing but wondered if Dr. McFall realized what a ludicrous statement he'd just made.

As Bear sat in silence, Dr. McFall realized just how stupid his statement sounded and, in the same moment, how pompous he had been. His tone softening, he said, "OK, Bear. That was a dumb thing for me to say. In fact, I feel like I've said nothing but dumb things since we started working together. I'm trying my best to follow the manual, but things just aren't working. It's like you think the manual doesn't apply to you."

Bear said nothing, figuring that he'd already told Dr. McFall that he didn't have a drinking problem several times and didn't need to say it again.

"What if we put the whole drinking thing aside for a while? What if we just start someplace else—wherever you want to start," offered Dr. McFall.

Bear shrugged.

Dr. McFall encouraged him again. "No, really, Bear. I'm trying to get to know you. I'm listening. Is there anything I can do to help you? I feel like I've been an idiot and I want to try to set things right."

> 13. In your textbooks, therapists' dialogues with their clients are often portrayed as being perfect. We thought you could learn more if we featured a therapist like Dr. McFall who made a series of mistakes. Review the previous exchanges between Dr. McFall and Bear and circle all the problematic comments made by the doctor. Then jot some notes in the margins as to comments Dr. McFall could have made that would've been more therapeutic.

Bear felt a little bad for Dr. McFall. He didn't really like him, but Bear understood what it meant to feel like a failure. Bear recognized that Dr. McFall was failing therapy instead of Bear failing therapy. Bear was kind-hearted by nature, and he didn't want to be the reason this guy failed.

"Well, people hate on me because I'm fat," Bear offered. He continued, "But how could someone regular-sized like you help me? You don't know what it's like to have people laugh at you day after day because of your size. You don't know what it's like to have to buy new clothes every couple of months because the old ones don't fit anymore. You don't know how it feels to be me."

Dr. McFall interrupted, "Oh, yes, I do. I've battled with weight my whole life. I got big, I mean really big. Kids used to pick on me all the time. It started in grade school and got worse in high school. Oh my God, I hated high school. Kids were so mean to me because I was fat. In college I got even bigger. I probably weighed close to 300 pounds. I was just so stressed with studying. It wasn't until I took a year off school after college and starting hiking that I got control of my weight, but I still see myself as a fat guy sometimes."

Bear sat quietly, listening intently, not sure of what to make of Dr. McFall's story. Bear asked only, "You were big?"

Dr. McFall nodded.

Bear said nothing but considered the doctor carefully. On one hand, this guy was awkward, inexperienced, didn't listen well, and talked too much. He was kind of full of himself and thought he knew everything about Bear, when he didn't know anything at all. On the other hand, he seemed to have his heart in the right place. At that moment, Bear decided he could trust him despite the terrible start to therapy.

14. Do you think that Dr. McFall's self-disclosure was inappropriate or appropriate? Explain your answer.

15. Is Dr. McFall acting ethically? Why or why not?

Dr. McFall went to the next integrated treatment team meeting excited to share his breakthrough with Bear with his colleagues. The team was glad that he was making some headway with Bear. The nurse practitioner asked to speak to him privately after the meeting. She gently encouraged Dr. McFall to understand that evidence-based treatment is not always as straightforward as it seems. Dr. McFall was fresh from his doctoral studies, and he felt most comfortable following a manualized protocol. He realized, with embarrassment, that he'd placed his own comfort level ahead of the client's. Dr. McFall also realized that he'd attempted to jump right into a manualized approach before he'd established a therapeutic alliance with Bear. Edgette (2006) suggests that one of the best ways to build a relationship with teenagers is to "keep it real" and talk openly with them about the reasons they don't want to be in therapy. The nurse practitioner reminded Dr. McFall that Bear had been sent to therapy against his will, and that Bear is in therapy for a problem that he doesn't believe exists. She encouraged Dr. McFall to listen to Bear instead of just jumping in and trying to solve his problems.

After talking with the nurse practitioner, Dr. McFall was in a more open and reflective state of mind. He started thinking about his self-disclosure with Bear about being overweight. He decided to do some research on self-disclosure in therapy and learned that it can be a helpful tool in building the therapeutic alliance when utilized appropriately. Dr. McFall found a particularly helpful article that explored self-disclosure by European American therapists in cross-cultural counseling (Burkard, Knox, Groen, Perez, & Hess, 2003). The key finding of the article was that when therapists share their honest reactions to clients' experiences of racism and oppression, clients often feel understood. In other words, judicious self-disclosure can have a positive effect on helping clients move toward more important issues. Dr. McFall realized that his self-disclosure had been impulsive and self-centered, but that ultimately it had worked.

Dr. McFall shared with the nurse practitioner that he'd done some reading about cross-cultural differences in therapy. She was excited to hear that he was learning and asked him to come to her office, where she shared with him her favorite article about Native American values and how they can be strengths in the therapeutic context (Sutton & Broken Nose, 2005). Dr. McFall read the article and began feeling a bit more confident, although he found that he was still quite awkward and wooden with Bear. Dr. McFall began the sixth session with a goal of discussing the cultural differences between Bear and himself.

"OK, Bear," Dr. McFall opened. "Now that we understand each other a little better, I think it's important to have a conversation about the elephant in the room."

Bear looked at him with apprehension and asked, "You mean me?"

"No, no, no! Bear, you are not an elephant! I'm sorry. I didn't mean to imply that—oh man, I'm sorry. Could we start again?" Dr. McFall's newfound confidence quickly eroded. Bear sat looking at him, hoping that Dr. McFall knew where he was going but absolutely uncertain as to where that might be.

Dr. McFall began again, "Bear, I mean, we need to talk about what it's like for you to have a white therapist when you're Native American. I can imagine that brings up some stuff for you, and you're wondering how I could possibly understand your culture." Dr. McFall recalled his required multicultural class from graduate school and thought his professor would be proud of him if he could see him now, being so willing to have this awkward conversation with Bear.

Bear stared at this man who was trying so hard to understand him but failing miserably. He let Dr. McFall talk without interrupting him as the doctor tried to summarize all the articles that he'd just read, referencing each one in rapid succession, as if he were presenting a lecture to Bear on therapist-client matching. Dr. McFall breathlessly shared how therapist-client matching depends on where clients are in their own ethnic identity journey, as well as where the therapists are in their journey. He shared that he was trying to monitor his own automatic thoughts and level of discomfort so that his mind would be freer to focus on Bear (Beck, 2011). Then, Dr. McFall said something about wishing that Bear could have a Native American therapist but that only 1.7% of practicing psychologists identify as Native American (APA, 2015), and that he'd have to do the best he could given his whiteness.

Bear was silent, not sure he comprehended where Dr. McFall was going with his mini-lecture. Bear didn't know the meaning of half of Dr. McFall's words. He wondered what an ethnic identity journey was, and what automatic thoughts were, and what it meant to have a therapist-client match. He thought it sounded like Dr. McFall didn't want to be white, but he wasn't sure how that could be true. He wasn't sure who this Beck guy was that Dr. McFall mentioned.

A full minute passed.

Finally, Bear spoke. "Look, you and I are good. I know you're white. I know you're trying. Just don't try so hard."

Dr. McFall felt dumb and relieved all at the same time. On one hand, he was glad he'd breached a difficult subject with Bear. On the other hand, he clearly had made a much bigger deal about their difference in race than Bear had. Dr. McFall again reminded himself to listen better to Bear, and to all of his clients.

16. Dr. McFall made a good choice by researching current articles relevant to his work with Bear and also by consulting with his colleagues. What else could he have done to improve his clinical work with Bear?

The nurse practitioner continued to educate Dr. McFall. She explained how she was using motivational interviewing with Bear, with great success. He'd taken charge of his diabetes and was monitoring his blood sugar level carefully. He'd learned to utilize his insulin pump and was doing so as necessary. He'd begun to keep a food journal and was willing to share it with the nurse practitioner. Dr. McFall was astonished at Bear's progress with her and how his work paled in comparison. She shared some resources with the doctor about motivational enhancement therapy (MET) to ensure that Bear, not Dr. McFall, was leading the push for change.

In the seventh session, Dr. McFall made a classic error that works against the key principles of MET: he wanted change more than the client did. Dr. McFall really wanted Bear to reduce his soda intake. Dr. McFall knew that if Bear better controlled his soda intake, he would see a positive impact on his sleeping habits and his binge eating, and he would likely improve his ability to control his weight and manage his diabetes (Fisher & O' Donahue, 2010).

Dr. McFall was hoping to put a plan in place to slowly decrease the amount of caffeine that Bear ingested daily. He'd even created a reward program that would help Bear meet his goals.

Bear wasn't concerned about his caffeine intake and told Dr. McFall so.

Dr. McFall had an epiphany. He realized that helping Bear manage his caffeine intake was *his* goal, not Bear's. Dr. McFall then did something new for him. Just as he was about to share his air-tight caffeine reduction reward plan with Bear, he stopped talking and started listening. *Bear isn't worried about caffeine right now. Let go of your stupid plan, Rob. Therapy isn't about you. It's about Bear,* Dr. McFall admonished himself.

Dr. McFall said to Bear, "Bear, I hear you. You don't want to give up gaming or drinking soda. And you aren't really worried about your sleep problems. I understand. But you're really motivated to work on not bingeing so much on chips late at night. Let's tackle that problem together."

Bear smiled.

In their eighth session, Dr. McFall tentatively began using some key ideas from MET. He shared structured feedback with Bear about his binge eating behavior as compared to other people his age and gender (Dunn, Neighbors, & Larimer, 2006). Dr. McFall recognized that Bear was truly committed to changing his binge eating behavior, although he realized how difficult it would be. Bear identified many of the barriers to changing his behavior as well, including the extent to which much late-night gaming was a cue for his late-night eating. Bear didn't want to stop playing video games, as his online friendships were the most significant relationships he had outside of his family.

With Bear on board, Dr. McFall considered cognitive-behavioral therapy (CBT) and interpersonal therapy as possible interventions to reduce the frequency of binge eating (Peat et al., 2012). The goal of both types of therapy is to reduce the frequency and intensity of binge eating episodes. Both types of therapy would also help Bear understand what causes, and maintains, his binge eating so that he could learn new coping strategies. Dr. McFall and Bear decided together to begin with *behavioral activation,* an intervention that has met with some success for treatment of eating problems (Peat, Brownley, Berkman, & Bulik, 2012). Essentially, behavioral activation involves having an individual do something fun and interesting to distract himself when he feels like engaging in the problem behavior, in this case binge eating.

Ironically, the next week in therapy both Dr. McFall and Bear showed up excited about a new idea that they'd both had independently of one another. Dr. McFall wanted to share what he'd learned, but stopped himself. Instead, he listened to Bear's ideas first.

"Dr. McFall, I think I have an idea. Have you heard about active gaming, like video games that make you walk around to get points? Those games will help me. I can't eat if I'm walking," Bear said in the longest comment that Dr. McFall had ever heard him utter.

Dr. McFall had the same idea as Bear. He was excited to share the research on how playing active video games can significantly increase a person's heart rate and step count and thus provide positive overall health benefits (Witherspoon & Manning, 2012). He also had already downloaded both games and knew they were fun and interesting. Dr. McFall was eager to share all of the facts and relevant research that he'd learned about active gaming. But he refrained, asking himself, *Wait. What does Bear need?*

Then Dr. McFall smiled and said nothing, except "Good idea, Bear."

17. Sometimes, therapists learn as much from their clients as clients learn from therapists. What did Bear learn from Dr. McFall, and what did Dr. McFall learn from Bear?

18. What is your prognosis for Bear? How will his life play out over the next few years? What about Waya, Rain, and Phoenix? Finally, what about Dr. McFall?

Bear is now 20 years old and still working with Dr. McFall as well as the specialists on the CHIC team. They've worked together steadily for almost four years. During those years Bear made excellent progress in managing his binge eating. He also began to work on improving his diet in general and taking better control of his diabetes. Bear lost a remarkable 100 pounds over the last two years of high school, although it took a loss of 30 or 40 pounds before anyone noticed. After about one year in therapy, Bear finally felt comfortable talking with Dr. McFall about his alcohol use. Bear hadn't used any alcohol in that year, but began to understand why he was at high risk to use given his past positive experiences with alcohol, expectancies around drinking, and family background of use. His main motivation not to use alcohol was not due to anything that Dr. McFall or anyone else had said. It was watching Phoenix follow the footsteps of his father and becoming an alcoholic. Once Bear grew to trust Dr. McFall, he was unwaveringly committed to working hard for him.

After high school graduation Bear floundered, unsure of what he wanted to do with his life. He was glad to have the support of his family and Dr. McFall in those unsettled times. Like Phoenix, he began working at different jobs, including at the local cinema and fast-food restaurants on the other side of town. Bear quit working in the fast-food industry, as the weight he'd lost began to return because of the free fast-food lunches available to him while working. Instead, Bear found a good job doing data entry for Smoky Mountains National Park, which is near the reservation. The position was full time and offered benefits. Bear decided that he liked computer work and is hoping to continue working at the park, perhaps as a career. Bear also decided to attend college, as his good high school grades and ethnicity as a Native American qualified him for free college tuition. Bear was hesitant to move off the reservation to attend college full time, but he began taking online classes in data management. He'll earn his Associates Degree in Computer Science next fall.

References

American Psychiatric Association. (2013). *Diagnostic and statistical manual of mental disorders* (5th ed.). Washington, DC: Author.

American Psychological Association. (July, 2015). 2005-13: Demographics of the U.S. Psychology Workforce. Retrieved from http://www.apa.org/workforce/publications/13-demographics/index.aspx.

Beck, J. S. (2011). *Cognitive behavior therapy: Basics and beyond.* New York: Guilford.

Bonnet, M. H., & Arand, D. L. (2010). Hyperarousal and insomnia: State of the science. *Sleep Medicine Reviews,* 14, 9–15.

Bulik, C. M., & Reichborn-Kjennerud, T. (2003). Medical morbidity in binge eating disorder. *International Journal of Eating Disorders, 34,* S39–S46.

Burkard, A. W., Knox, S., Groen, M., Perez, M., & Hess, S. A. (2006). European American therapist self-disclosure in cross-cultural counseling. *Journal of Counseling Psychology, 53*(1), 15–25.

Dunn, E. C., Neighbors, C., & Larimer, M. E. (2006). Motivational enhancement therapy and self-help treatment for binge eaters. *Psychology of Addictive Behaviors, 20*(1), 44–52. doi:10.1037/0893-164X.20.1.44

Edgette, J. S. (2006). *Adolescent therapy that really works.* New York: W.W. Norton.

Fisher, J. E., & O'Donohue, W. T. (2010). *Practitioner's guide to evidenced-based psychotherapy.* New York: Springer Science Business Media, LLC.

Fossum, I. N., Nordnes, L. T., Storemark, S. S., Bjorvatn, B., & Pallesen, S. (2014). The association between use of electronic media in bed before going to sleep and insomnia symptoms, daytime sleepiness, morningness, and chronotype. *Behavioral Sleep Medicine, 12*(5), 343–357. doi:10.1080/15402002.2013.819468

McElroy, S. L., & Kotwal, R. (2006). Binge eating. In E. Hollander & D. J. Stein (Eds.), *Clinical manual of impulse-control disorders* (pp. 115–148). Arlington, VA: American Psychiatric Publishing.

National Heart, Lung, and Blood Institute. (2011). What is CPAP? Retrieved from http://www.nhlbi.nih.gov/health/health-topics/topics/cpap/

National Institute of Diabetes and Digestive and Kidney Diseases. (2011). Tips for teens with diabetes: What is diabetes? Retrieved from https://www.niddk.nih.gov/health-information/health-communication-programs/ndep/living-with-diabetes/youth-teens/what-diabetes/Pages/publicationdetail.aspx)

National Sleep Foundation (n.d.). Obesity and sleep. Retrieved from https://sleepfoundation.org/sleep-topics/obesity-and-sleep/page/0/1

Nguyen-Michel, S. T., Unger, J. B., & Spruijt-Metz, D. (2007). Dietary correlations of emotional eating in adolescence. *Appetite, 49*(2), 494–499. http://dx.doi.org/10.1016/j.appet.2007.03.005

Peat, C. M., Brownley, K. A., Berkman, N. D., & Bulik, C. M. (2012, May). Binge eating disorder: Evidenced-based treatments. *Current Psychiatry, 11*(5), 32–39.

Reichenberg, L. W., & Seligman, L. (2016). *Selecting effective treatments: A comprehensive, systematic guide to treating mental disorders.* Hoboken, NJ: Wiley.

Rosengren, D. B. (2009). *Building motivational interviewing skills: A practitioner workbook.* New York: Guilford.

Smith, G. T., Goldman, M. S., Greenbaum, P. E., & Christiansen, B. A. (1995). Expectancy for social facilitation from drinking: The divergent paths of high-expectancy and low-expectancy adolescents. *Journal of Abnormal Psychology, 104,* 32–40.

Sutton, C. T., & Broken Nose, M. A. (2005). American Indian families: An overview. In M. McGoldrick, J. Giordano, & N. Garcia-Preto (Eds.), *Ethnicity and family therapy*. New York: Guilford.

Trimble, J. E. (2010). The virtues of cultural resonance, competence, and relational collaboration with Native American Indian communities: A synthesis of the counseling and psychotherapy literature. *Counseling Psychologist, 38*(2), 243–256.

von Ranson, K., & Wallace, L. M. (2014). Eating disorders. In E. J. Mash & R. A. Barkley (Eds.). *Child psychopathology* (3rd ed.). New York: Guilford Press.

Witherspoon, L., & Manning, J. P. (2012). Active gaming: The future of play? *American Journal of Play, 4*(4), 464–487.

Zerbe, K. (2008). *Integrated treatment of eating disorders: Beyond the body betrayed.* New York: Norton.

CASE 9

Tyler Dawson Rudolph

For most children, bed-wetting disappears fairly early, usually before the first grade. However, some children like Tyler, an 11-year-old white / Latino boy from Texas, continue to wet the bed throughout their childhood, leading to embarrassing social incidents. This case focuses on behavioral interventions that are the cornerstone to effective treatment for Enuresis. Key terms from classical conditioning are explained in the case.

 ICD 10/DSM 5 Diagnosis:
F98.0 (307. 6) Enuresis, Nocturnal Only

Diagnostic Discussion

Tyler's case is more straightforward than many of those presented in this book, as the sole diagnosis for which he qualifies is Nocturnal Enuresis, a term used to describe nighttime bed-wetting. The criteria for an Enuresis diagnosis are as follows: (1) repeated voiding of urine into the bed or clothes; (2) urinating the bed is *clinically significant*, meaning that it happens frequently (at least twice a week for at least three consecutive months) or causes distress in a person's academic or social functioning; (3) it occurs an age level of at least five years; and (4) it is not caused by a medical problem (APA, 2013).

Let's consider Tyler's case with respect to each of these criteria. First, Tyler repeatedly voids his urine, or wets his bed, at night. Second, the behavior is frequent, occurring far more often than the required twice a week necessary for diagnosis and for much longer than the required three-month period. Tyler essentially wets the bed every night of the week and has done so his entire life. In addition to meeting the time requirements for clinical significance, Tyler also meets the criterion for Enuresis causing him distress. Tyler's petrified of what his friends will think if they find out he wets the bed. Tyler's bed-wetting also keeps him from having friends spend the night, or from spending the night with them in their respective homes. In addition, he's ashamed of his bed-wetting, which may impact his self-esteem in other areas. The third criterion for Enuresis focuses on age, as children must be at least five to receive a diagnosis. Young children and toddlers normally wet their beds. In fact, about 40% of children wet the bed at age 3, and psychologists don't diagnose a behavior as problematic if it's part of normal development. The prevalence of Enuresis drops with age; 22% of children wet the bed at

245

age 5, 10% at age 10, and 3% at age 15 (Binderglas, 1975). At age 11 like Tyler, between 8 and 9% of kids are still wetting the bed—a significant number of kids! Boys also wet the bed more often than girls. Regarding the fourth criterion, Tyler demonstrates no medical problems that would cause his Enuresis. We can be fairly sure about this because his pediatrician tried medication to treat the disorder and would not have done so without a thorough medical check-up.

In diagnosing Enuresis, we have a *specifier* to consider. A specifier is a subtype of a disorder that allows a clinician to communicate a finer-grained analysis of a bigger diagnostic category. The main specifier in the case of Enuresis is diurnal (daytime wetting only), nocturnal (nighttime wetting only), or both. Specifiers can have treatment implications. For example, in the case of nocturnal and diurnal Enuresis, the same type of treatment would not necessarily be equally successful. Tyler likely would have been diagnosed with both types of Enuresis (Nocturnal and Diurnal) back in kindergarten and first grade, when he was wetting his pants so often at school, but he wouldn't meet the criteria for this specifier now as he no longer wets his clothes during the day.

1. Do you think Tyler's parents pushing him to excel in football and academics is affecting his Enuresis in any way? Why or why not? Do you think their involvement in his life overall is more positive or more negative? Would you address their high level of involvement in his life in therapy?

2. Imagine that you're 11 years old again and back in middle school. How would you feel if you were struggling with bed-wetting like Tyler is?

Case Conceptualization

A good conceptualization of a person's problem goes a long way towards answering one important question: "Why?" In Tyler's case, we need to better understand why he is wetting the bed, especially when he and his parents have tried so many interventions over the years. Is Enuresis due to sugar or caffeine intake? Is it due to willful, intentional, defiant behavior on a child's part, and if so, he should be punished for it? Or could his grandmother be right in that Tyler was likely sexually abused?

The key to answering these questions is to know the research. Current research soundly answers all these questions with a resounding "No!" So, why does Tyler wet the bed? First of all, most kids who have Enuresis are like Tyler in that they don't have another diagnosis or mental, emotional, or behavioral problem (APA, 2013). In other words, they're just regular, well adjusted kids who wet their beds. That said, Enuresis occurs at a higher rate among people with developmental disabilities or other co-existing mental problems. But most kids, about 85% (Houts, 2010), who have Enuresis have *only* this problem. They're not likely to have been sexually abused or to have any other family or developmental problems. The big factor that's implicated in the etiology of Enuresis is genetics. Approximately 75% of children who wet the bed have a first-degree relative who also struggled with Enuresis. Another way to look at the genetic impact of the disorder is through statistics. If both of a child's parents wet the bed as a child, their child has a 77% chance of being enuretic as well. If one of a child's parents wet the bed, that child has a 42% chance. If neither of a child's parents wet the bed as a child, the odds of being enuretic drop to only 15% (Cohen, 1975). Once again, we see that the apple does not fall far from the tree.

3. What are the implications of the strong genetic component of Enuresis on treatment for the problem?
4. Given how common bed-wetting is, the odds are strong that someone in your class was a bed wetter or knows a bed wetter. How does it influence your work with people if you have personal experiences with the same problem that they do? What are the drawbacks and benefits to this situation, and do the pros outweigh the cons—or not always?

The physiological reasons for bed-wetting are complicated. Research doesn't clearly suggest that a child who wets the bed is a deep sleeper, has a small bladder, has food allergies, or had poor toilet training (Christophersen & Mortweet, 2001). Although some of these things may be a factor in the *etiology*, or cause, of Enuresis, a more likely explanation is an inability of the brain to recognize that the bladder is full, thereby preventing the child from getting to a toilet. Urinating in a toilet sounds easy enough, but in actuality, it's a complicated process. Basically, urination involves contracting the bladder detrusor muscle. Stopping urination involves contracting the muscles of the pelvic floor. But recognizing which muscles need to contract and which muscles need to relax isn't an easy task, especially if you're asleep, and if you're only an 11-year-old child whose brain is still developing.

Conceptualizing Enuresis in line with the current evidence demands that we consider the problem from two lenses, *biological* and *behavioral*. Biology and behavior interact to explain how Enuresis develops and how to treat it. For the most part, genetics and muscle contraction explain the biological etiology of the disorder. From one of his parents Tyler likely inherited a difficulty in recognizing that his bladder is full. Perhaps he also inherited some difficulty in controlling his detrusor and pelvic muscles.

While genetics and biology explain some of the etiology of Tyler's Enuresis, they don't explain it all. This is where behavioral principles can be helpful, as they can explain how behavior can be maintained. Perhaps Tyler was *negatively reinforced* by letting go of his urine in his bed, thus reducing the uncomfortable sensation of having a full bladder. *Negative reinforcement* is a tricky term. It refers to any event which increases the chances of a behavior occurring by taking away or reducing a painful, aversive, or negative experience. As anyone who has ever been stuck in a traffic jam after drinking two large cups of coffee knows, having a full bladder is an uncomfortable feeling, to say the least! But urinating, wherever we do it, reduces that uncomfortable feeling, thus increasing the chances we'll urinate again. In Tyler's case, he urinated in his bed at night. Eventually, wetting his bed became paired with the good feeling of not having to urinate anymore, thus pairing "wetting the bed" with "relief" and negatively reinforcing his behavior. Other behavioral principles besides negative reinforcement are also critical in the treatment of Enuresis, as we shall see. Key behavioral components associated with the treatment of Enuresis include overlearning, conditioned responses, and positive reinforcement. These ideas will be explained below.

5. Pair up with a partner. Explain the etiology of Enuresis in a two-minute conversation without using any fancy jargon.

6. Negative reinforcement is a difficult term to understand. Can you think of a few everyday examples to make certain that you understand it well?

7. What should be the first steps of treatment with this family, and why? Who would you involve? Would Tyler's parents be a part of treatment? What about his brothers? His grandmother?

Evidence-Based Treatment

The "best practices" treatment for nocturnal Enuresis in general, and for Tyler in particular, is the urine alarm, which is often colloquially called a "potty pager." The very name "urine alarm" can be frightening, as families may assume it means shocking a child when he wets the bed. Of course, this isn't the case. The urine alarm is a small device, about the size of a cell phone, that can be purchased online for less than $100. It's worn between two pairs of underwear, in a specially sewn pouch on the underwear, or between the folds of the frontal opening of a pair of boys' briefs. A urine alarm has a moisture-sensitive area that either vibrates, lights up, or makes a high-pitched alarm sound like a car alarm when it gets wet. When the child wears a urine alarm to bed and begins to wet the bed, the sound of the alarm startles the child and wakes him. Waking up automatically causes the pelvic floor to contract, thus stopping the urination. The child then gets up, goes to the bathroom, and continues urinating—but into the toilet. If he's a child who wets the bed two times a night, like Tyler, he can then put the urine alarm back in place (Axelrod, Tornehl, & Fontanini-Axelrod, 2014).

Using a urine alarm is a good example of creating a *conditioned response* using a *conditioned stimulus,* behavioral terms that are really useful to understand. But before we attempt to understand these terms, we need to understand what an *unconditioned stimulus* and *unconditioned response* are. The following section will define these four terms. Read the section slowly. These terms are tricky to understand but will undoubtedly be covered on an exam!

The urine alarm is a good example of an *unconditioned stimulus*, an event or stimulus that we don't need to be trained to respond to because, even without training, it naturally elicits a response. For example, when we hear an annoying, high-pitched, loud noise, like a smoke detector or urine alarm, our bodies naturally respond by activating the central nervous system, producing cortisol (stress hormone), and becoming hyper-aroused and acutely aware of the environment. We are in "Danger Mode." At such times of stress, we often forget that we need to urinate. Our pelvic floor muscles tense up, although we don't directly command them to do so. This natural response is called an *unconditioned response* because we don't have to be taught to do it. It's just our biology, or neurology, responding to what's going on around us (Brown, Pope, & Brown, 2011).

Now that we understand the unconditioned part of the equation, what about the conditioned part? A *conditioned stimulus* is a previously neutral event that, because of its pairing with an unconditional stimulus, begins to produce a conditioned response. The conditioned stimulus in the case of the urine alarm is a person's bodily cues, including having a full bladder. When a child is bed-wetting, he's unaware that his bladder is full and he needs to urinate. So, we have to teach him to associate awareness of his bodily cues (the conditioned stimulus) with the unconditional stimulus (the noise from the urine alarm). When we pair these things together, we produce a conditioned response, which is awakening in response to a full bladder just *before* the alarm goes off. Once this happens, the response to the awakening is called a conditioned response, because it occurs not to the alarm, but to the stimulus (full bladder sensations) paired with the alarm (Brown, Pope, & Brown, 2011).

A *conditioned response* is a person's physical or behavioral response to the conditioned stimulus. A conditioned response is very similar to a unconditioned response in terms of what it looks like, but the difference between the unconditioned response and conditioned response is what *causes* the behavior to happen. So, the cause of a conditioned response is the conditioned stimulus. However, the cause of an unconditioned response is the unconditioned stimulus. In the case of the urine alarm, the conditioned response is the child awakening in the night in response to the feelings of a full bladder and *before* any urine is released. A child waking up to urinate before he starts wetting the bed is our ultimate goal!

8. You just learned four difficult terms: unconditioned stimulus, unconditioned response, conditioned stimulus, and conditioned response. As a group, think of an example of each of these four terms from regular everyday life. (If you're stuck, you might think about cell phones as a starting point.)

9. What do you remember about Watson's famous experiment with "Little Albert," and how does this experiment relate to our discussion?

So, let's take a look at how this all plays out when using the urine alarm. The urine alarm wakes the child with an annoying noise when the child begins to urinate. His body responds to the high-pitched sound by activating his central nervous system. His pelvic muscles contract and he stops wetting. Night after night this same thing happens, and the child's brain pairs together two formerly disconnected things—the internal sensation of a full bladder and the loud noise of the alarm. Because the alarm creates the arousal response of the tensing of the pelvic floor muscles, eventually the internal sensations of needing to urinate become the conditioned stimulus because they have been paired with the unconditioned stimulus of the alarm. So, over time the child learns, "My bladder is full! I need to make my pelvic muscles work! I need to get up and go to the bathroom!" This message is not learned consciously, involving higher-order brain structures. Rather, it's a message that's learned on a reflexive, physiological level. Nevertheless, the child learns. The urine alarm has a fairly spectacular success rate of 75%, with treatment ranging from 5 to 12 weeks (Christophersen & Mortweet, 2001).

On its own, the urine alarm is the single most effective treatment available (Caldwell et al., 2016). However, research has shown that adding other components to the basic urine alarm can increase the chances of success. This is especially important in Tyler's case, as he and his family already attempted using an alarm system, and his Enuresis is severe given that he frequently wets the bed twice in a single night. A useful treatment package offered by Houts (2010) is called Full Spectrum Home Training, or FSHT. This training involves four main components: basic urine alarm treatment, cleanliness training, retention-control training, and overlearning. In order for treatment to work successfully, we need both the parents and child to work with the therapist. Let's take a look to see how the treatment played out with Tyler.

Roger and Maria sought help from Tyler's pediatrician, who conducted a full medical exam to rule out any health problems, as Tyler's last urinary-tract exam was several years ago. No medical problems were found, so the pediatrician referred Tyler to a child health psychologist who specializes in children, and particularly Enuresis. The health psychologist was located an hour's drive from the family home, but the Dawson family decided to commit to treatment when their pediatrician informed them that the health psychologist was the best in the area. At the first meeting, the health psychologist conducted a brief behavioral assessment, which included a thorough interview with a specific focus on Enuresis, and a broad-band instrument to assess Tyler's overall functioning from his own point of view, as well as in the eyes of his parents and his teachers. Not surprisingly, these instruments showed no behavioral or emotional problems for Tyler except bed-wetting. The psychologist then proceeded with the first step of treatment, basic urine alarm treatment including psychoeducation. The psychologist emphasized that one of the goals was for Tyler to learn to rouse himself before he wet the bed; that is, before the alarm aroused him (Caldwell et al., 2016). Maria was especially pleased that the focus of therapy would be on Tyler learning to arouse himself, as she noted that she was exhausted from not getting enough sleep.

Tyler and his parents signed an agreement to follow a series of rules around the use of a urine alarm, including such things as:

- committing to the treatment for 12 weeks,
- not scolding or punishing Tyler for wetting his bed,
- establishing a regular bedtime,
- praising Tyler when he wakes himself before the alarm,
- not restricting liquids in the evening,
- waking Tyler when the alarm goes off in the night, and
- having Tyler remake the bed every night he began to wet the bed.

The Dawson family created a chart and put it beside Tyler's bed to keep track of how he was doing every night, including if he woke before the alarm, whether he wet the bed, and whether he wore the urine alarm.

10. Which of the rules of treatment do you think will be the most difficult for Maria? For Roger? For Tyler? What would you say to each of them to keep them motivated to follow the rules?

11. Do you think the family could have just bought another urine alarm online and treated this problem themselves, so they didn't have to incur the time and financial expense of driving to see the health psychologist? Explain your answer.

12. Telehealth, where a client and service provider communicate electronically instead of face to face, is growing in popularity. Do you think this case would lend itself to treatment through telehealth? Why or why not?

For the psychoeducation component of treatment, Maria, Roger, and Tyler attended two psychoeducational sessions to learn about Enuresis. Tyler was more than eager to start treatment, as he was desperate for any solution to his embarrassing problem. The psychologist provided some background information to the family about Enuresis, including how common the disorder is and its strong genetic component. At this point in the conversation, Roger grew silent. Maria thought Roger just didn't care about what was going on with treatment since he'd be working anyway, and she asked him about his silence later. Choking back tears, Roger admitted to Maria that he wet the bed until he was in fifth grade. His parents always thought he did so intentionally, and Roger started to believe it too. He was punished and made to sleep on his bedroom floor with no sheets or blankets and came to believe what his parents said about him, that he was "just not trying hard enough." Like his son, he began to think poorly about himself and was "sorely afraid" that someone would find out about his problem. Even now, he said, he was too embarrassed to tell Tyler about his own problems with Enuresis and would discuss it with no one else besides Maria.

13. Do you think that Roger's Enuresis as a child has affected him in any way as an adult? Why or why not? What does Roger's difficulty talking about his Enuresis tell you about his culture?

14. How does Roger's history of Enuresis and Maria's lack of such a history impact treatment?

Maria was relieved to hear this, as she never understood the genetic component of Tyler's Enuresis. However, Maria knew that the bulk of the treatment work would fall on her because of Roger's work schedule. She was willing to implement the treatment that the health psychologist outlined, as she was used to waking Tyler twice a night anyway. She was especially hopeful given that the treatment focused on Tyler learning to rouse himself. The psychologist specifically asked her not to wake Tyler anymore, but to allow Tyler to wake himself or to use the urine alarm to do so. The psychologist also had the family create a behavioral chart to keep track of Tyler's wet and dry nights. When Maria and Roger tried to tell Maria's mom about the genetics of the disorder and the treatment using the urine alarm, she disregarded the explanation. Tyler's grandma continued to believe that the psychologist was misguided. She was still convinced that Tyler must have been sexually abused, because in addition to the article she read, she'd watched a daytime talk show in which an interviewee talked about her own problems with both sexual abuse and Enuresis. Maria tried to educate her mom about Enuresis and shared all the psychologist had said, but her mom would hear none of it.

15. How important is it to successful treatment that Maria's mother understands the etiology of Enuresis? How would you deal with this as a mental health provider?

After two weeks of basic urine alarm training, the family looked at the chart that kept track of the number of times Tyler roused himself and the number of wet and dry nights. The first week, he wet the bed seven of seven nights. The second week, he wet five of seven nights, sleeping right through the alarm most of the nights. The urine alarm was working, but the family had to solve the additional problem of the alarm repeatedly falling out of Tyler's boxer-briefs. Wearing the alarm between two pairs of underwear seemed to fix this problem, but other problems developed. Several nights, Maria fell asleep with her radio on and couldn't hear the alarm. Tyler didn't hear it either, and he wet the bed. One night, after several dry nights of rousing himself, Tyler begged not to wear the alarm anymore, saying he was "over it" and could manage being dry on his own. He wet the bed that night and was devastated. The health psychologist helped Tyler manage his frustration and reminded him that kids who wet the bed more than once a night have a harder job than kids who only wet the bed once a night, and that treatment often takes a little longer for them.

The family also struggled with implementing the second part of treatment, cleanliness training or dry-bed training, which involves having Tyler remake his bed every night that he started to wet it, even if the sheets are still dry. Maria felt this was unnecessarily harsh and decided not to follow this portion of treatment. Even when it was explained to her that cleanliness training improves the success rate by about 10–15% percent, she was unwilling to budge on this issue. She said that she just couldn't make Tyler change his old-but-clean dry sheets into new dry sheets in the middle of the night. She agreed to have Tyler change his sheets when they were wet, something she'd previously handled.

16. How do you think Maria's decision to forego cleanliness training with Tyler will impact the success of his treatment?

17. Do you think that if Roger were at home nights instead of Maria, he would have made the same decision as she did to forego cleanliness training? Why or why not?

Despite not complying with all of the components of treatment, Maria and Tyler developed a more regular routine with using the urine alarm. Most nights, if there were no glitches, the alarm went off at least once, Maria woke Tyler, and he got himself into the bathroom. After a month of treatment, both Maria and Tyler were waking to the sound of the alarm. Maria met Tyler in the bathroom and encouraged him for waking up to use the toilet. Although Tyler's bed-wetting had significantly improved, the alarm sounding meant that Tyler was still urinating while sleeping. It also meant that both he and Maria were losing sleep every night. By the end of the sixth week of treatment, Tyler had been dry six of seven days for two weeks straight, rousing himself each night before the alarm sounded. The family was ready to finish treatment, and they thought they were "all clear" and Tyler was cured.

The psychologist utilized a sports metaphor to help them change their minds. He said that six weeks into treatment was like half-time of a big game and it wasn't time to celebrate yet, as Enuresis was a tough opponent that could come back and win the game. He also discussed how training for Enuresis is like practicing football in that the more you practice, the better your skills will be. Roger bought into the metaphor and was motivated for the next six weeks of treatment. Maria was tired of getting up every night and wanted a vacation from Enuresis training, or at least a vacation from night duty with the kids. Tyler was just happy to wake up dry.

18. How can a child's mental health problems, and the treatment of these problems, affect the parents' marital relationship? How do you think Tyler's Enuresis is affecting Roger's and Maria's marriage?

19. Why would the psychologist use a sports metaphor with this family? What does that tell you about "mapping treatment onto the client?" If the Rudolph family didn't value sports, what metaphor could the psychologist have created to help them continue treatment?

The third phase of treatment involved retention control. Retention control training basically involves helping the child learn to postpone urinating during the day in exchange for earning money or some other reward. A reward is a good example of *positive reinforcement*, an event or item that increases the chances of the behavior that preceded it to happen again. The logic behind retention control is that children learn to strengthen the pelvic floor muscles associated with stopping urination. In retention control, kids practice delaying urination in the daytime, after they initially feel the sensation of needing to urinate, for increasingly longer intervals in order to earn money or rewards. Tyler was highly motivated to earn all the money he could and, from the beginning of this intervention, postponed urinating the full 45 minutes necessary to earn the top daily prize of $12. He asked to do this training every day, thinking that he could earn $84 a week just by delaying urination. Tyler realized that $84 could buy a number of football-related items, including multiple packs of football trading cards. Due to the potential cost, though, his family settled on once-a-week practice sessions instead of once a day. Tyler was super-motivated now. The urination-postponing activities of retention control had been a snap, and now he'd been dry—completely dry—two weeks in a row. Fourteen days without wetting the bed! Roger was ecstatic. Maria was still exhausted and hoping Roger would have a day off soon so he could take over her role in the process.

Finally, Tyler began the fourth and final phase of treatment, *overlearning*, which basically involves practicing a new skill under increasingly difficult conditions to ensure that the skill has been mastered. In the case of Enuresis, the treatment component involves having children drink an increased amount of water on consecutive nights while still staying dry. In other words, on a neurological level, it's like turning a rural route in the brain into a superhighway, connecting neurons through practice and more practice until the brain is skilled at behaving in a particular way. Overlearning is important, as the chance of relapse drops to less than one in ten if this treatment component is added, compared to one in four without this component (Morgan, 1978; Roberston, Yap, & Schuster, 2014). Overlearning also helps children get over their fears that they'll start wetting the bed again and never improve. In this last "Ultimate Challenge," as the psychologist phrased it, Tyler would go up against his toughest opponent yet. He'd drink several large glasses of his favorite drink in the evening and still not wet the bed. Tyler did very well with this phase of treatment. He had a few setbacks and wet nights, and on these nights, Maria did as instructed and gave Tyler the exact amount of liquid he had on his last dry night, thus helping him have more successful nights than unsuccessful ones.

After two weeks straight of dry nights with overlearning, and almost four weeks' dry total, Tyler was on his thirteenth week of treatment. He was ready to try to sleep through the night without his urine alarm. As often is the case with life, what should have been a momentous event was less momentous than expected. The night scheduled for Tyler to go to bed without the urine alarm for the first time, "Game on!" night, coincided with Brett's high school sectional game, which was attended by the entire family. Tyler's family got home at 1 AM, after a double-overtime win, which left the family stumbling happily into their beds, utterly exhausted. Everyone just forgot about the urine alarm.

The next night, a similar scenario occurred. Tyler had an away game and they packed in a hurry, leaving the alarm at home. Tyler thought of it at bedtime, but the alarm was hours away. After returning home two nights later, Tyler realized he'd been dry *three nights* without the alarm. Thrilled, he gave his mom a big hug, told her that she was the best mom in the world.

Tyler was dry every night thereafter and never wet the bed again. Maria finally got the uninterrupted sleep she needed. Roger never told Tyler that he wet the bed as a child but let him know that he was really proud of him for learning to be dry at night. With gentle prodding from Maria and due to Tyler's success, Tyler's grandma decided that the talk shows and articles that she'd read about sexual abuse and Enuresis must be wrong and that Tyler had probably not been abused.

Tyler also made a promise to himself. Over the years, he'd noticed that several professional athletes spoke out to support causes. Golfer Ernie Ells has a son with autism and supports autism research. Shaquille O'Neal has shared that he used to be teased for his stuttering. Lebron James encourages children to stay in school. But who's speaking up for kids who wet the bed? Tyler decided that when he goes pro and is famous one day, he'll have the courage to say that he was a bed wetter and be an advocate for all the other kids who do the same. His parents don't think he'll follow through, but they're thrilled that he's playing football and waking up dry.

20. What do you think the most important keys were to treatment, and why? Can you think of some things that the health psychologist could have done better?

References

American Psychiatric Association. (2013). *Diagnostic and statistical manual of mental disorders* (5th ed.) Washington, DC: Author.

Axelrod, M. I., Tornehl, C., & Fontanini-Axelrod, A. (2014). Enhanced response using a multicomponent urine alarm treatment for nocturnal Enuresis. *Journal for Specialists in Pediatric Nursing, 19*(2), 172–182. doi:10.1111/jspn.12066

Binderglas, P. M. (1975). The enuretic child. *Journal of Family Practice, 5*, 375–380.

Brown, M., L., Pope, A. W., & Brown, E. J. (2011). Treatment of primary nocturnal Enuresis in children: A review. *Child: Care, Health & Development, 37*(2), 153–160. doi:10.1111/j.1365-2214.2010.01146.x

Caldwell, P. H. Y., Sureshkumar, P., Kerr, M. I., Hamilton, S., Teixeira-Pinto, A., Macaskill, P., & Craig, J. C. (2016). A randomized controlled trial of a code-word Enuresis alarm. *Archives of Disease in Childhood, 101*(4), 326–331. doi:10.1136/archdischild-2015-308564

Christophersen, E. R., & Mortweet, S. L. (2001). *Treatments that work with children: Empirically supported strategies for managing childhood problems.* Washington, DC: American Psychological Association.

Cohen, M. W. (1975). Enuresis. *Pediatric Clinics of North America, 22*, 545–560.

Houts, A. C. (2010). Behavioral treatment for Enuresis. In J. Weisz & A. Kazdin (Eds.), *Evidence-based psychotherapies for children and adolescents.* New York: Guilford.

Morgan, R. T. (1978). Relapse and therapeutic response in the conditioning treatment of Enuresis: A review of recent findings on intermittent reinforcement, overlearning, and stimulus intensity. *Behaviour Research and Therapy, 16*, 273–279.

Robertson, B., Yap, K., & Schuster, S. (2014). Effectiveness of an alarm intervention with overlearning for primary nocturnal Enuresis. *Journal of Pediatric Neurology, 10*(2), 241–245. doi:10.1016/j.jpurol.2013.08.008

Weisz, J. R., & Kazdin, A. E. (2010). *Evidence-based psychotherapies for children and adolescents.* New York: Guilford.

CASE 10

Arush Patel

Arush's father, a physician from India, determines that sleepwalking is the problem troubling his gangly and awkward, yet endearing, 10-year-old son. Arush's case brings up issues of dual relationships, cross-racial therapeutic relationships, and how sleep problems manifest themselves in children.

> **ICD-10/DSM-5 Diagnosis:**
> F51.3 (307.46) Non-Rapid Eye Movement Sleep Arousal Disorder, Sleep-walking type
> F51.4 (307.46) Non-Rapid Eye Movement Sleep Arousal Disorder, Sleep terror type

Diagnostic Discussion

Sunil talked to Priti all the way home from the party. They had both enjoyed themselves, but Sunil was especially excited that he might be able to find some answers about what was going on with Arush. Priti kissed her husband and went upstairs to bed, knowing that Sunil might be up all night studying once again. Before she had washed the makeup off of her face, he had Googled "Non-Rapid Eye Movement Sleep Arousal Disorder, Sleep-walking type and Sleep terror type." He quickly navigated to reputable medical sites and found the American Psychological Association website (2016) quite helpful.

Sunil read the diagnostic symptoms for the disorder, carefully considering whether his son met the criteria. From the DSM-5 (2013) he read:

Recurrent episodes of incomplete awakening from sleep, usually occurring during the first third of the night, accompanied by either:

Sleepwalking: Repeated episodes of rising from bed and walking about. The individual usually has a blank face when sleepwalking, is unresponsive to communication, and cannot be easily awakened.

Sleep terrors: Recurrent episodes of abrupt terror from sleep, often beginning with a panicked scream. The individual seems fearful and exhibits signs of autonomic arousal, such as mydriasis, tachycardia, rapid breathing, and sweating. The individual is not easily awakened or comforted.

No, or few, dreams are recalled by the individual.

The individual has amnesia regarding the event.

257

The episodes cause distress for the individual in social, occupational, or other important areas of functioning.

The disturbance is not due to a substance (drug or medication) or to another mental or medical condition.

Sunil also read that when children experience sleep terrors, they often describe feeling a sense of overwhelming dread and report feeling an almost compulsive need to escape (APA, 2013). Sunil sent his phone a link to the APA web page that contained all of the above information. Sunil thought excitedly to himself,

That's it! That's it exactly. That's Arush. He meets the criteria perfectly. He repeatedly wakes during the night and sleepwalks. He has a blank face and is unresponsive to Priti and me when we talk to him. He absolutely cannot be wakened. None of that surprises me. I knew he was a sleepwalker. But I didn't know about this sleep terror subtype, and it perfectly describes Arush. He seems to be horrified when he screams in the middle of the night. Or technically, I should say the first third of the night— because it's usually right around midnight when he has his episodes. He screams as if he's in an absolute panic. He shows many of the examples of autonomic arousal listed on the symptom chart. He doesn't remember any bad dreams and cannot remember screaming at all. I'm sure it causes Arush distress. I suspect he'd like to go on overnights to his friends' houses but feels he can't. It certainly causes Priti and me distress! And I'm certain his problems are not due to a medical or mental condition or a drug. He has no other condition and takes no drugs.

1. People often search for medical and psychological information online. You have likely done something similar yourself. As a mental health clinician, do you view this behavior favorably or unfavorably? Explain your answer.

The next morning, Sunil woke his wife and told her that he knew what was going on with Arush. Sunil showed his wife the information he had stored on his phone.

"Sunil, you know I didn't get a medical degree. What does all this mean? What is mydriasis?" Priti asked.

"*Mydriasis* just means that his pupils are dilated," Sunil answered.

"What about *tachycardia?*" Priti wanted to know.

"Rapid heartbeat," Sunil responded.

"OK, rapid breathing and sweating . . . you don't have to define those for me, Sunil. Even we engineers are smart enough to figure out some of your medical jargon," Priti said jokingly.

As Priti looked over the list she continued, "This does look exactly like what's going on with Arush. But what are we going to do about it? Is it treatable, or is he going to wake up screaming all the time, even as a grown man?"

Sunil answered, "I'll do some more work online to look up evidence-based treatments. In the meantime, let's call Dr. Coleman and get an appointment with her."

2. Without reading the next section, what do you think is causing Arush's sleep terrors and sleepwalking?

3. This diagnostic discussion describes a father's thinking about his son's mental health diagnoses. Thus, this section is quite different from other diagnostic discussions in this book when professionals diagnose a child. What are your concerns about this? Does the fact that Arush's father is a doctor influence your answer?

Case Conceptualization

Sleep is a fascinating and interesting subject as well as a vital component of optimal health and functioning. Given the high percentage of individuals who experience regular sleep problems in our society, becoming a mental health clinician who specializes in sleep would likely enable you to help many clients in the upcoming years. Research estimates that 40% of adults experience some degree of sleep problems on a regular basis (Wilson & Nutt, 2013). Children also are prone to sleep problems. In fact, in some ways, children are more likely than adults to have sleep problems, as you will see.

The overarching diagnostic category of Sleep-Wake Disorders includes a broad array of sleep-related problems, including insomnia, breathing-related sleep problems (see Bear's problem in case 18), circadian rhythm disorder, and restless leg syndrome. *Parasomnias* are a special subcategory under the broad category of Sleep-Wake Disorders and include sleep disorders with abnormal nervous system activation during sleep, producing atypical sleep behavior (APA, 2013). Non-Rapid Eye Movement Sleep Arousal Disorders: Sleepwalking and Sleep Terrors are nested under this subcategory of parasomnias. These disorders will be referred to as Sleepwalking and Sleep Terrors in the remainder of this case study, but remember that they are non-rapid eye movement (NREM) sleep problems.

Children are more likely to exhibit parasomnias than adults (Reichenberg & Seligman, 2016). Many parasomnias occur in the transition from sleep to wakefulness, or from one sleep phase to another (Reichenberg & Seligman, 2016). The term *sleep phase* describes the stages of sleep that a person typically progresses through during a night's sleep, including light sleeping, deep sleeping or sleep that does not involve rapid eye movement (*non-rapid eye movement*), and sleep that involves rapid eye movement (*rapid eye movement*).

Non-Rapid Eye Movement sleep is commonly referred to as *NREM* sleep and rapid eye movement sleep is called *REM* sleep. We have repeated episodes of both REM and NREM sleep throughout each night. During REM sleep our brains are active and often dreaming. REM sleep is especially important to daytime alertness (National Sleep Foundation [NSF], n.d.).

NREM sleep is critical as well. It is a deep restorative sleep that causes one's muscles to relax and breathing to slow; sends increased blood to muscles; causes tissues to grow and be repaired; and releases essential hormones throughout the body that help development, growth, and healing. During NREM sleep our bodies are immobile, but our breathing and heart rates are irregular (NSF, n.d.).

Our bodies need appropriate amounts of both NREM and REM sleep to function optimally. Shortchanging yourself on sleep on a regular basis, even if you are staying up to read this book, is truly hazardous to both your short-term and long-term health (Reichenberg & Seligman, 2016).

4. Summarize the differences between NREM and REM sleep.
5. What changes do you notice in yourself when you shortchange yourself on sleep?
6. People in the United States are more likely than people in many other cultures to skimp on sleep. Why do you think this is the case?

Sleepwalking is common in children (Reichenberg & Seligman, 2016). Between 3 and 40% of children—a wide percentage range—have had at least one episode of sleepwalking and 2–3% sleepwalk often, like Arush (Mindell & Owens, 2003). Sleepwalking usually begins at around ages of 6 to 12 (APA, 2013). About one third of children who demonstrate sleepwalking problems also have problems with sleep terrors (Petit et al., 2015). This suggests that the two disorders may share a common etiology. In other words, sleepwalking and sleep terrors may be two manifestations of the same underlying disturbance.

Sleep terrors also appear to be common in children although we presently are not certain how many children are affected by this problem (APA, 2013). Determining when sleep terrors begin is tricky. In terms of the sleep terrors themselves, they usually begin around age 1½, as in Arush's case. However, the diagnosis of Sleep Terror Disorder usually is not given until a child is between 4 and 12 years old (Reichenberg & Seligman, 2016). This lag between when symptoms initially present and when parents seek treatment likely reflects a hope from parents that the disorder will go away on its own and that their child will outgrow the problem. Indeed, this often happens, as sleepwalking and sleep terrors are uncommon in adulthood (APA, 2013).

Answering the question of why parasomnias such as sleepwalking and sleep terrors occur in children is best answered by looking at genetic, developmental, and environmental circumstances. First, regarding the genetic etiology of sleep problems, genetics seem to play a role in determining which children are likely to have sleep problems. In fact, a family history for sleepwalking or sleep terrors occurs in up to 80% of people who show these problems, a very high percentage of cases (APA, 2013). This high percentage suggests a strong genetic etiology to parasomnias. In Arush's case, we do not know whether his first-degree relatives had sleep problems, but these percentages make it very likely indeed.

In addition to genetics, another reason that sleep problems occur in children is developmental. Specifically, there are differences between children's and adults' normal sleep patterns (Mash & Barkley, 2014). One reason young children have so many sleep problems is that their sleep cycles are shorter than those of adults. In fact, babies have sleep cycles of only 50 minutes (NSF, n.d.). Infants also spend more time in REM sleep than adults. Over time, young children's sleep patterns begin to look more like those of adults, with less time in REM sleep and longer sleep cycles. By middle childhood, children's cycles become closer to the 90-minute sleep cycles of adults (NSF, n.d.). Because children have shorter sleep cycles than adults, they have more transitions between one sleep phase and the next. Parasomnias are especially likely to happen during these transitional phases (APA, 2013).

Arush is 10, so his overall sleep pattern likely looks much more like to an adult's sleep than it does a toddler's. However, his problems began when he was much younger. Thus, development certainly played a role in his sleep problems. Also, even at age ten his sleep cycles are not likely as mature as that of an adult. Finally, we know that Arush is developmentally immature in many ways. Perhaps his sleep cycle is immature compared to other 10-year-old boys as well.

In addition to the genetic and developmental causes of sleep problems, environmental factors also play a role (Mindell & Owens, 2003). Common triggers for parasomnias include insufficient sleep, sleep deprivation, and changes in sleep schedule due to school, vacation, or other activities. Fatigue and stress, including both physical and emotional stress, make parasomnias more likely as well (APA, 2013). Interestingly, children are also at higher risk for parasomnias when they have high fevers (APA, 2013).

The Patel family, and Arush himself, do not demonstrate many of these environmental risk factors. The only risk factor that seems to be relevant for Arush is that his sleep terrors usually are worst during the school year. Perhaps the change in sleep schedule from the typical later wakening times of summer to the early wakening times of school in the fall is particularly difficult for Arush. Additionally, he may not adjust his bedtime to an earlier hour, even with the earlier wake time necessitated by school. Thus, sleep deprivation may also play a role in his sleep terrors. Arush is not atypical in struggling to adjust to the new sleep-wake cycle demanded as school begins for children in the fall. However, his sleep problems are worse than the average child in that they have not remitted as he has grown older. He would likely benefit from some intervention.

7. The case conceptualization section explained genetic, developmental, and environmental reasons that children develop parasomnias. Draw three columns on a sheet of paper with these three headings. Under each heading, list as many explanations you can remember.

8. Without reading ahead, what are some ideas you have about treating Arush's sleep problems? What are some "commonsense" ways you have heard about treating children's sleep problems?

Evidence-Based Treatment

At their first meeting with Dr. Norah Coleman, Sunil and Priti were both prepared—but especially Sunil. He had links and notes on his cell phone and asked Dr. Coleman pointed questions about assessment, diagnosis, and evidence-based treatment the first few minutes after the session began. Dr. Coleman had enough experience in the field not to be intimidated, but instead to appreciate the high level of motivation of the Patel family. She was a consummate professional and connected effortlessly with Sunil, Priti, and the ever-awkward Arush.

9. How would you have reacted to Sunil? Would you have been intimidated by his expertise and medical background?

Before Dr. Coleman began treatment, she addressed several important issues. She discussed confidentiality and the importance of family participation in therapy. She also directly brought up the cultural differences between herself as a black woman and the Patel family as Indian-Americans. Dr. Coleman took a broader, more contextual approach in addressing this issue instead of just asking a simple, closed-ended question that would likely discourage further conversation, such as "Will it be a problem for you that I am a black woman and you are an Indian-American family?"

Dr. Coleman began, "Therapy is always a cross-cultural relationship between a therapist and a client—or in your case, a family. I want our cultural differences to work for us, not against us. Therefore, I think it helps to begin therapy with an open conversation about race."

Priti and Sunil agreed as Arush just listened.

Dr. Coleman said, "I'm a black woman. I grew up in Atlanta and my family still lives in the city. I'm also a psychologist. I received my doctoral degree from the University of Georgia. In therapy sessions, I'm both a black woman and a psychologist—I'm not just one of these things. As a black woman, values that are important to me include fighting racism and sexism and advocating for those marginalized by society. Family and church are also important to me. As a psychologist, values that are important to me are knowing and contributing to the research, practicing psychology in an evidence-based and culturally competent way, and working to empower families and children by emphasizing their strengths. I'm interested to know what your values are as an Indian-American family."

10. How could you have improved on Dr. Coleman's cultural introduction? Do you think she self-disclosed too much?

11. Based on the ideas you suggested in answering a previous question and integrating what you know about best practices regarding self-disclosure and being an authentic relationship with a client, write an introductory paragraph for yourself as a therapist similar to what Dr. Coleman did. Does your introduction include more or less than what she shared? Why did you decide to write it as you did?

Sunil spoke first. "We're an Indian-American Hindu family. We came to the United States from India before Arush was born. Our oldest boy, Akshay, is 12. He was born in India. We're from the state of Andhra Pradesh and are a part of the Vaisyas caste. That group is composed of people like shopkeepers, traders, and farmers. We left our families to come to the United States to seek better opportunities for work and for our boys' futures. We still visit our families often and Skype with them every week. It's hard to explain what being a Hindu is all about, but we believe in many goddesses and gods, meditation, and enlightenment. We also believe in reincarnation."

Priti added, "Sunil is a doctor like you, but he's a surgeon. But you're both similar in your belief that research and evidence are important. We both think school and education are important as well and expect our boys to do well in their academics. I'm an engineer by trade but haven't worked in the States yet. I like your approach on empowering families and emphasizing their strengths. I was worried that you would tell us that Sunil and I were the problem."

Dr. Coleman summarized, "I like your honesty. Indian culture has such a rich history, with so many amazing accomplishments. I respect your focus on extended family—that's something that Indians share with black Americans like me. I also appreciate Hinduism, especially the way you see life as a continuous search for growth and enlightenment" (Pillari, 2005).

Priti nodded in agreement, adding, "Yes. We're a nation of searchers."

Dr. Coleman nodded, "That's a wonderful quality and a good way to describe a very diverse group of people."

After a pause for Sunil and Priti to speak if they wanted to, Dr. Coleman asked directly, "How will we deal with misunderstandings as they arise? My way of dealing with things is to do so directly but kindly. I'm hoping that you might deal with any confusion and misunderstandings in the same way?"

Sunil answered formally for both Priti and himself, "Most assuredly."

"Well, then, let's get to work. I'm eager to work with your family, but I need to apologize, Arush, because I haven't had much of a chance to talk with you," Dr. Coleman said smiling and looking directly at Arush.

12. What is your impression of Dr. Coleman thus far? Do you think she deserves her excellent reputation? Why or why not?

After Arush and Dr. Coleman chatted about Boy Scouts, school, cricket, and the Atlanta Braves, Dr. Coleman laid out the plan for therapy. She would begin therapy by conducting some assessment measures with Arush and the family. She asked Arush to keep a sleep diary and to specifically track what time he went to bed, what time he woke, how well he felt he had slept, and if he had any memory of awakening in the night. She asked Sunil and Priti to add information to Arush's sleep diary about his sleepwalking and sleep terrors. She noticed that all members of the family had Fitbits on their wrists, so she suggested using the electronic tracker as the perfect *actigraph*—a wearable activity monitor that tracks sleep and wakefulness. Dr. Coleman commented that so many people had some sort of fitness tracking devices that she rarely needed to prescribe actigraphs these days. Although Fitbits and similar devices do not always capture sleeping patterns exactly, they are accurate enough to determine whether Arush would awaken with night terrors or with sleepwalking in the middle of the night. Dr. Coleman also had some sleep inventories and a behavioral assessment measure that she asked Arush and his parents to complete.

Dr. Coleman explained that a good assessment is critical to treatment, as it would provide baseline data as to what was working and what was not. "These data will give us the evidence to determine what helps and what doesn't. Arush, I would like you to be in charge of collecting the data and bringing it to therapy each week. I also want you to study it, so you can be the main person who decides what's working."

Arush solemnly agreed to this task.

> 13. Do you agree or disagree with Dr. Coleman's decision to put Arush in charge of collecting data? Why or why not?

Dr. Coleman provided the family with some psychoeducation about parasomnias, but she was careful to ask the family what they had already learned in their own research before she did so. She added that sleep problems required both the parents and child to be present for sessions, and that Akshay was welcome to attend as well, but that he didn't have to do so. She was confident that Arush's problems were treatable and suggested a time frame of four sessions for treatment. Priti and Sunil were shocked that a problem that had been happening for years might take only weeks to treat.

Before they left her office, Dr. Coleman gave Priti and Sunil some important homework. She explained that trying to wake a child during a sleep terror usually makes the sleep terror last longer. Instead of being helpful, waking a child seems to make things worse (Meltzer & Mindell, 2009). She told the Patels that she understood that listening to your child cry out in anguish is horrible, as "it's the worst feeling in the world to think that your child is in pain and you aren't doing anything about it." But she reassured the Patels that Arush wasn't actually in pain. Dr. Coleman added, "When parents try to intervene out of kindness, it can make the child feel like he's being trapped, like an animal in a cage trying to escape. So, children fight more when adults intervene" (APA, 2013).

Dr. Coleman asked how soundly Priti and Sunil slept. They answered that they both slept lightly and had even installed a baby monitor in Arush's room so that they could hear him in the night in case he needed them. Dr. Coleman asked them to turn off the monitor completely. She also asked how near their bedroom was to Arush's bedroom. When she learned that the bedrooms were just separated by a short hallway, she suggested that Priti and Sunil turn on a fan or a "white noise" machine so that they could not hear Arush in the night. She reminded them that they'd taken precautions long ago to ensure that he was safe if he sleepwalked, and that he had never engaged in any dangerous behavior when sleepwalking.

"In short," Dr. Coleman summarized, "your job is to do nothing at night."

Priti and Sunil both were worried about this drastic change in how they were handling Arush's nocturnal problems.

Priti began, "I don't mean any disrespect, but I don't know if I can do that, Dr. Coleman." Priti paused and continued, "Do you have children?"

Dr. Coleman, "Yes, I do. Three of them—a boy and two girls."

Priti asked, "Could you ignore them if they were crying out in anguish?"

Dr. Coleman answered her gently, "I understand your fears. You're both just being wonderful parents. You're acting out of love for Arush. I understand that."

Sunil continued, "How do we know if he's OK in the night? What if he really needs us?"

Dr. Coleman answered, "That's a good question. Let's brainstorm it together. What do you think might work?"

Priti and Sunil considered the possibilities. Priti suggested, "Well, Akshay's room is near Arush's room, right across the hall, in fact. Perhaps we could ask Akshay to listen for his brother."

Dr. Coleman was just as careful as Priti in her response, "Do you think that would work? Because I want you to feel at ease and able to sleep through the night without worrying about Arush."

"I think it would work. Akshay's very responsible, and he's a light sleeper as well," Sunil answered. "He takes after his parents, I suppose."

"Do you want me to call Akshay and explain things to him, or do you want to explain his job?" Dr. Coleman asked.

"We can tell him. What should he do if he hears Arush screaming?" Priti wondered.

Dr. Coleman answered, "Good question. Akshay should quietly peek through the door of Arush's room, without turning on the light or saying anything. As long as Arush is not truly in danger, then Akshay should turn around and go back to bed. If Arush is in serious danger, Akshay should come get you."

Dr. Coleman asked them to try one week of not monitoring Arush's sleeping, except through his brother. Sunil and Priti agreed.

> 14. Do you think it was wise to involve Akshay in this role? Why or why not?
>
> 15. What other creative ideas can you brainstorm to solve Sunil's and Priti's concerns about worrying if Arush is OK at night?

When they returned to therapy the second time, Dr. Coleman looked at all the data that Arush had collected. Overall, the number of sleep problems that Arush was having had changed in just one short week. His parents estimated that, prior to the start of therapy, he had been having 1 or 2 nights of sleepwalking episodes per week and 2 or 3 nights of night terrors. In the past week, he had no incidents of sleepwalking and one incident of having a night terror, on Tuesday night. On Arush's sleep diary on the space that read "Tuesday night," Akshay had written in neat block writing, ARRGH!! MY BROTHER IS LOUD!

Everyone chuckled when they read Akshay's comment. Dr. Coleman asked Sunil and Priti how it was going for them, not listening to Arush sleep at night since they had turned off the baby monitor in his room. They both explained that it was very difficult the first few nights, but then they realized that they were sleeping better without the constant noises transmitted by the baby monitor. When the monitor was turned on, they were worried about every little sound they heard from Arush's room. To make sure he was OK, they sometimes went to check on him to make certain that nothing was wrong. They had never shared that information previously, and Dr. Coleman wondered if their constant checking on him was inadvertently contributing to his sleep problems. Nevertheless, she felt no need to tell them that they might actually have been affecting his ability to shift from one stage of sleep to another. Instead, Dr. Coleman just asked them how well they were doing without the reassurance of the baby monitor. Both agreed that they trusted Akshay to listen for his brother and that they were glad to be sleeping better. They laughed and added that they didn't know how lightly they had been sleeping for so many years because of their worries about Arush.

For the third week of treatment, Dr. Coleman collected Arush's data and praised him for his conscientiousness in keeping track of everything. Arush loved showing Dr. Coleman his weekly Fitbit report of the hours he logged sleeping. The weekly report from his fitness band showed that he was waking up less frequently during the night—with fewer "awake" minutes in the night—suggesting fewer episodes of sleepwalking and night terrors. Akshay again wrote on the margins of Arush's chart, I'M GOING TO USE MY HEADPHONES AT NIGHT BUT I'LL KEEP MY MUSIC QUIET. ASK DR. COLEMAN IF THAT'S OK.

Dr. Coleman asked Sunil and Priti if perhaps Akshay would consider attending a therapy session. Sunil and Priti had already asked Akshay, and he had decided he would rather not attend but would do so if necessary. Instead, Dr. Coleman wrote Akshay a note:

> Dear Akshay,
> Thank you for helping with Arush. You're a good big brother. Head-phones are fine. The best thing is to let Arush sleep unless he's seriously in danger.
> —Dr. Coleman

16. Do you think Dr. Coleman should have insisted that Akshay partic-ipate in therapy? Why or why not? Do you have any concerns about Akshay? Does it surprise you that Dr. Coleman was willing to give so much responsibility to Akshay although she had not met him?

Dr. Coleman prescribed another intervention for Arush, as she noticed that he was getting only nine hours of sleep each night. She suggested that he try to get ten hours of sleep instead. Dr. Coleman worked with Arush to fig-ure out how this might work for him, because it would mean his going to bed at 9 PM instead of 10 PM, since he had to be up by 7 AM for school. Dr. Cole-man knew that increasing sleep time, and not going to bed overtired and fatigued, can help reduce sleep problems such as parasomnias.

By the fourth week of treatment, everyone was very happy with Arush's progress. His Fitbit continued to show fewer night awakenings. Akshay wrote a final note about his brother, ARUSH DID GOOD THIS WEEK.

Sunil was embarrassed by the English mechanics of Akshay's note, explaining, "Akshay knows better than that. He should say that Arush did 'well' this week, not that he did 'good.'"

Dr. Coleman was not worried about Akshay's grammar. She was just happy that Arush was sleeping better. Sunil and Priti agreed, as did Arush.

The irony of treatment for Arush is that everyone believed treatment was 100% successful by the fourth and last week of treatment. This is not the same thing as treatment actually *being* 100% successful. However, because Priti and Sunil had turned off the baby monitor in Arush's room and turned on the ceiling fan in their bedroom, they could no longer hear if Arush were having night terrors. Akshay's decision to listen to his music made it less likely for him to hear Arush's screaming as well, if it were happening. Arush, of course, never knew if he were having night terrors as he, like most individ-uals, had amnesia for these events.

All of the right elements were present for a successful treatment, but it's hard to know what elements were the most critical to Arush's greatly improved sleep quality. Even if Arush were still having night terrors and sleepwalking episodes, he will likely eventually outgrow his parasomnias as most children do (Meltzer & Mindell, 2009). Sleeping problems in children are typically not associated with any other psychopathology (Reichenberg & Seligman, 2016). As described in the case conceptualization section, the etiology of parasomnias is more often genetic, developmental, and neurological than it is familial. Despite not knowing what factors were crucial to Arush's treatment, the Patels were more satisfied with their family life after a month of working with Dr. Coleman. Arush seemed to be sleeping better, and Priti and Sunil reported sleeping better as well. Hopefully, Akshay was sleeping better, too. Arush was happy with treatment as well. He was still his ebulliently awkward and delightfully goofy self. He said he was even feeling more energetic in the day now that he was getting better sleep. When they heard this comment, Sunil and Priti groaned in mock horror.

17. Some of the most research-supported interventions for sleep problems in children involve eliminating parent intervention at night, having children go to bed earlier (or later, depending on the problem), and eliminating naps. Why do you think these interventions are most likely to be successful given the etiology of sleep disorders?

References

American Psychological Association. (2016). Retrieved from http://www.apa.org/

American Psychiatric Association. (2013). *Diagnostic and statistical manual of mental disorders* (5th ed.) Washington, DC: Author.

Mash, E. J., & Barkley, R. A. (2014). *Child psychopathology* (3rd ed.). New York: Guilford.

Meltzer, L. J., & Mindell, J. A. (2009). Pediatric sleep. In M. C. Roberts (Ed.), *Handbook of pediatric psychology* (2nd ed., pp 491–507). New York: Guilford.

Mindell, J. A., & Owens, J. A. (2003). *A clinical guide to pediatric sleep: Diagnosis and management of sleep problems.* Philadelphia: Lippincott Williams & Wilkins.

National Sleep Foundation (n. d.). Children and sleep. Retrieved from https://sleepfoundation.org/sleep-topics/children-and-sleep

Petit, D., Pennestri, M. H., Paquet, J., Desaultels, A., Zadra, A., Vitaro, F., … & Montplaisir, J. (2015). Childhood sleepwalking and sleep terrors: A longitudinal study of prevalence and familial aggregation. *JAMA Pediatrics, 169*(7), 653–658. doi:10.1001/jamapediatrics.2015.127

Pillari, V. (2005). Indian Hindu families. In M. McGoldrick, J. Giordano, & N. Garcia-Preto (Eds.), *Ethnicity in family therapy.* (3rd ed., pp 395–406). New York: Guilford.

Reichenberg, L. W., & Seligman, L. (2016). *Selecting effective treatments: A comprehensive, systematic guide to treating mental disorders.* Hoboken, NJ: Wiley.

Wilson, S., & Nutt, D. J. (2013). *Sleep disorders* (2nd ed). Oxford: Oxford University Press.

CASE 11

Demond Jackson

Cases like Demond's are difficult because they expose us to serious issues of neglect, abuse, substance abuse, violence, and gangs. Demond's a 14-year-old black boy in Cincinnati with conduct problems as well as substance abuse problems. These problems have caused the legal system to be involved in his life as well as the mental health and Child Protective Services systems. Boys like Demond are frequently lost in the intersections of these systems. How should society intervene with children who show such complex problems given the limited resources of helping agencies?

ICD 10/DSM-5 Diagnosis:

F91.1 (312.31) Conduct Disorder, Child-Onset Type, Severe

F12.20 (304.30) Cannabis Use Disorder, Severe

F10.10 (305.00) Alcohol Use Disorder, Mild

R/O F19.10 (305.90) Other (or Unknown) Substance Use Disorder, Mild

T74.12XD (995.54) Child Physical Abuse, Confirmed

T74.02XD (995.52) Child Neglect, Confirmed

T74.32XD (995.51) Child Psychological Abuse, Confirmed

Z62.29 (V61.8) Upbringing Away from Parents

Diagnosis Discussion

Demond's behavior and history warrants a list of psychiatric diagnoses. Such a long list doesn't necessarily mean that Demond is a "bad kid." It does mean that he's experienced a great deal in his very short, 14-year-old life. Each diagnosis above is briefly discussed below.

Conduct Disorder, Child-Onset Type, Severe: Conduct Disorder is Demond's primary diagnosis and is thus listed first. The key criterion of Conduct Disorder is a persistent violation of the basic rights of others, exhibited through aggression to people and animals, property destruction, deceitfulness or theft, and serious violation of rules (APA, 2013). Regarding his aggression toward others, Demond shows aggressive behavior in the following ways. He bullies or threatens others, he initiates physical fights, he's used a weapon against others, and he's stolen while confronting a victim. Demond's legal history clearly reflects property destruction, but we don't know what property he's damaged or how badly. Regarding deceitfulness or theft, Demond has broken into someone's house, lied to obtain something he wanted, and has stolen items. Regarding serious violations of rules, we again know from his legal history that Demond has been truant and *AWOL (Absent Without Leave)* and leaves his place of residence without permission. Demond's conduct problems clearly negatively impact his life. His Conduct Disorder is considered severe because of how many symptoms he exhibits (more than three), and his behaviors cause considerable harm to others. Importantly, parenting issues are often part of the etiology of Conduct Disorder (Lorber & Slep, 2015), and this co-morbidity will be discussed further in the case conceptualization section. The specifier *child-onset* is used because Demond showed conduct disorder problems prior to age ten. As a child or adolescent meets more symptoms of Conduct Disorder, he's also more likely to show a co-morbid substance abuse problem (APA, 2013), which is the case for Demond.

Cannabis Use Disorder, Severe: Demond meets the criteria for Cannabis Use Disorder, Severe because he shows a problematic history of marijuana use (APA, 2013). To qualify for a severe substance use disorder, he must show the presence of at least six of eleven possible symptoms. Demond shows the symptom of tolerance to marijuana, as it takes increasing amounts of the drug to make him feel "high." Demond also meets other diagnostic criteria for cannabis abuse in that he uses despite having persistent social problems such as developing negative relationships with his family and foster families, uses to the extent that he can't fulfill his school obligations, spends a great deal of time trying to find marijuana, and will even steal to get money to purchase it. He also uses in physically hazardous situations, such as while breaking into a house with a gun. Finally, he spends a great deal of time using marijuana, evidenced by his reporting that he'd like to be high all the time if he could.

R/O Other Substance Use Disorder: Demond reports trying cocaine, K2 (synthetic marijuana), Spice (a different type of synthetic marijuana), PCP (a phencyclidine, which is a dissociative anesthetic drug with strong hallucinogenic properties), and sniffing a mixture of glue, paint, and fingernail polish remover (an example of an inhalant substance). Because of this heavy substance use, other substance use disorders should be ruled out. The *Rule-Out* diagnosis, written as R/O, communicates that Demond may have a variety of substance abuse disorders, but we don't have enough information to definitively diagnose this at the present time. To diagnose Substance Use Disorder with other substances in addition to alcohol and marijuana, we would need to know more about his patterns of usage, including what substances he used, how often he used them, his physiological responses to them, and how much their use displaced other activities in his life.

Child Physical Abuse, Confirmed; Child Neglect, Confirmed; Child Psychological Abuse, Confirmed: Demond's records show a long-standing pattern of child abuse, and sadly, abuse that occurred in two different families, essentially from birth to age eight. Demond's extensive history of child abuse likely played a major role in his developing conduct problems, discussed in the following section.

Upbringing away from Parents: This diagnostic category is used when a main issue in a child's life is that he's being raised not with his parents, but in the state's custody, residential treatment facilities, or a group home. After six years of being abused, Demond has essentially been bounced around from one type of living arrangement to another, including psychiatric hospitals, residential treatment centers, inpatient substance-abuse treatment facilities, therapeutic foster care, and juvenile detention. Children who move so much never have a chance to become stabilized in any one environment. As a consequence, they may develop many negative effects including behavioral, relational, attachment, psychological, educational, and medical difficulties (Ingoldsby & Shaw, 2002). Such frequent changes in placement so often is a good example of *iatrogenic effects*, which are negative, unexpected side effects caused by the treatment itself.

1. When Demond was given the above-listed diagnoses, did the diagnosing clinician miss the mark? Can you improve on the diagnoses given to him?
2. Before reading the following section, can you come up with your own coherent conceptualization of Demond?

Case Conceptualization

When a child has multiple diagnoses, we need to consider how each one impacts the development of the child in terms of his physical, psychological, and social development as well as how the diagnoses interact with one another. This *additive effect* not only makes it difficult to accurately diagnose a child but also makes it challenging to effectively treat him. However, Demond doesn't just have numerous diagnoses; he also has numerous *risk factors*—life events or demographic factors that increase the risk to develop psychopathology. Just as diagnoses interact, risk factors interact. Thus, having three or four risk factors, for example, is exponentially more difficult than having two.

From the beginning of his life, Demond had a number of significant risk factors. Risk factors are not causative. We can have many risk factors and still turn out fine, as in the case of a boy from a lower socioeconomic African American family with an abusive history who eventually goes to college, gets a good job, and becomes an attentive father and partner. But the more risk factors a person has, the more significantly his odds increase that he will struggle with mental and physical health problems. On the flip side, *protective factors*, such as positive life events, good relationships, or "lucky breaks," can enhance our *resiliency*—the ability to "bounce back" and demonstrate reasonably good functioning despite setbacks and a difficult background. Demond has few such protective factors, thus his chances of being resilient and overcoming the odds stacked against him are perilously slim.

One crucial factor missing for Demond is an adult who cares about him and develops a meaningful attachment with him. Werner (2009) noted that finding such a nurturing adult is a key environmental factor of resilient children. When children don't have such a caring adult among their biological parents, they often make efforts to recruit surrogate parents from the ranks of teachers, coaches, grandparents, older siblings, extended family members, or neighbors. Professional caregivers, such as caring foster parents, can also meet the important developmental need of attachment. These substitute parents can make a tremendous difference in helping a young person overcome difficult odds (Werner, 2009).

In Demond's case, his lack of a good attachment is a foundational problem that bodes poorly for his future. Demond's biological parents were reportedly substance abusers, possibly with mental health problems, and were involved in a violent relationship that eventually resulted in the death of his mother. His biological father was incarcerated and his mother murdered during the important years of his childhood. A grandparent can be a wonderful provider of an attachment relationship to a child. For a short period in Demond's life, it looked like his maternal grandmother, Gloria Harris, might play this role. He visited her often when he was living with his neglectful biological parents, and he presumably had a good relationship with her. He was placed in his grandmother's home for several months at age five, after his father shot his mother. However, his maternal grandmother was unwilling to change her *authoritarian* (disciplined-focused) parenting style in order to keep Demond in her home. She felt that slapping a child for talking back was justified; this is a common belief among many. Perhaps this relationship could have been Demond's primary attachment relationship, but for many reasons it didn't work out that way. We have no other mention of her having a significant relationship in Demond's life, other than that she visited sporadically.

When he was removed from his grandmother's home, he was sent to live with his aunt and uncle, the Carters. Demond lived in this home for almost two years, from the age of six to eight. The Carters, however, were physically and emotionally abusive to Demond and his siblings. What might have been a healing and ameliorating relationship ended up as a horrific and dangerous one instead. Demond, thus, had two sets of parents, his biological parents and then his aunt and uncle, who *terminated their parental rights*. Termination of parental rights is an irreversible legal decision in which a parent either voluntarily or involuntarily decides that they're no longer interested or capable of being a parent to their child (Blacker, Urquiza, Kalich, & Carmichael, 2016). Termination of parental rights, or TPR as it is often colloquially called, is often extremely difficult for a child for understandable reasons (Barone, Weitz, & Witt, 2005).

After two sets of parents terminated their rights, Demond belonged to no one. Without a relationship with a stable caring adult, a child's chances of overcoming risk factors are substantially lessened. In fact, an adult who loves a child is one of the most vital ingredients in creating a resilient child (Azar & Wolfe, 2005). Demond seemed to develop a good relationship with the Soto family, evidenced by his request to return to their care. However, the Sotos were either burned out or overwhelmed by Demond's extreme acting-out behavior. They felt that they could no longer be part of a treatment plan or provide a home for Demond following his release from the detention center. The Sotos were one of Demond's last realistic chances to develop a close attachment to someone before becoming an adult himself.

After being placed with his family, extended family, and foster homes didn't work out, Demond's life became a series of emergency placements, short-term foster homes, psychiatric hospitalizations, and residential treatment facilities. These organizations and agencies are important and offer a valuable service to children in need by providing a safe place where they cannot hurt others and others cannot hurt them. However, meaningfully attaching to adults in such short-term placements is often impossible. The merry-go-round of placements that Demond endured often plague children who are wards of the state.

A risk factor related to Demond's lack of attachment is his trauma history. Demond was a witness to domestic violence—not only to his mother's rape by his father, but also possibly to the murder of his mother by his father. During these same violent early years, Demond himself was also the target of violence as he was physically abused, neglected, and psychologically abused by his parents. Sadly, Demond's troubles didn't end when his father murdered his mother and he was removed from his biological family home. His placement with his aunt and uncle resulted in additional abuse from the ages of five to eight, which included physical abuse so severe that his arm was broken by his uncle because he was brushing his teeth too loudly. The impact of these early negative experiences is so vast and deep that it's almost impossible to overestimate. Trauma can affect how a brain is wired and neuronal connections are made, thus helping to explain persistently maladaptive behaviors later on, such as Demond shows (Stirling & Amaya-Jackson, 2008).

Demond's two most problematic risk factors, then, are his lack of attachment to a caring adult and the long history of traumatic and abusive events in his life. However, these risk factors are only two of many. In Demond's case, his risk factors are stacked precariously high, like a poorly constructed tower of children's blocks that is ready to fall because of its unstable foundation. The first of Demond's risk factors is purely demographic, as he was born into a lower socioeconomic African American family. According to Hines and Boyd Franklin (2005), society's systemic maltreatment of African Americans based on skin color demonstrates institutional racism, evidenced by blacks' higher rates of unemployment, poverty, health problems, and shortened life span as well as their low rate of home ownership. Since Demond's family struggled financially, he likely lived in substandard housing in unsafe neighborhoods and attended inferior-quality schools. Poverty is also associated with less social support and family harmony (Evans, 2004). Another risk factor is that Demond was born prematurely, weighing only 5 pounds and 1 ounce at birth with problems getting oxygen to his brain at birth due to the umbilical cord being wrapped around his neck. We also don't know if his mother used substances during her pregnancy and how this may have impacted Demond's growing brain and body. If his mother did use substances while pregnant, it would constitute another risk factor for Demond. The risk factors continue to stack up for Demond in that his parents were reportedly substance abusers, possibly with mental health problems. Thus, Demond has both a genetic and an environmental tendency to experience such problems himself.

Demond's history of problems began early, likely because the homes in which he lived were devoid of the love, security, and predictability he needed. In fact, Demond may have received attention only when he was "bad." When he was "good," he was likely just ignored. In a child's world, receiving negative attention is better than receiving no attention at all, so kids learn pretty quickly that sometimes "being bad" is the most adaptive behavior (Ahmann, 2014). Fighting and stealing are common behaviors when a child must fend for himself and is desperately trying to protect the little bit that he does own (Piotrowska, Stride, Croft, & Rowe, 2015). Once he was accepted into a gang, Demond probably felt a sense of belonging and acceptance that no adult had ever given him. It was likely no accident that Demond landed in a negative peer group: other children probably rejected him because of his acting-out behavior. In joining the gang, he almost certainly felt that someone would finally protect him and "have his back" in an argument or problem. Without his gang-member brothers, Demond would feel close to no one. Once the expectation for engaging in criminal acts and using substances is set for a peer group, the peers reward a person for participating in this behavior and punish him for not doing so. Demond's path toward a criminal life became increasingly set in stone during these early teenage years.

During these early years, Demond also began using substances, drinking alcohol beginning at age 9 and using marijuana at age 12. Early substance use is associated with more serious problems and a poorer prognosis. Youth who begin using substances earlier than their peers are more likely to be diagnosed with substance-abuse problems as an adult (Grant & Dawson, 1997). Such substance use often occurs in a complex web of antisocial behavior, lack of supervision, poor parenting, and peer substance use (MacPherson, Frissell, Brown, & Myers, 2006). Demond's family members and peers modeled substance use as a way of coping with life's stressors as well as celebrating its joys. Over time, Demond likely began to use substances as a way to manage the depression and anxiety he experienced as a result of his life situation. It's also probable that he developed positive expectations associated with his drug use, such as expecting to feel good when he was high or drunk. Over time, he increased his use as a way of managing social situations that would otherwise tax his social skills.

As a result of these experiences, Demond came to believe two discouraging life lessons: "People I love hurt me" and "I have to take care of myself because I can't rely on others to take care of me." He likely doesn't trust others—seeing the world as a dangerous place and his life as hopeless, as evidenced by his comment to Annamarie about having nothing, no body, and no reason. Demond may hold *core beliefs* (central, all-encompassing views about the world) that he can't succeed, that others can't be trusted, and that his life will never get better. This *negative triad*, or beliefs about one's self, others and the future, is difficult to change once established (Pössel & Black, 2014).

The challenge in conceptualizing Demond's case is that a clinician must balance two opposing perspectives carefully. On one hand, Demond's behavior is clearly a danger to himself and others. He's behaving in a way that's unacceptable to society, and he must stop engaging in this behavior or someone will get killed. He consistently violates the rights of others and thus goes against the very grain of what it takes to live in a pro-social and caring world. For example, he shot at a man three times while breaking and entering into his house to steal from him. So one important perspective to consider is that Demond not only must be held accountable for his behavior—he also must change it.

On the other hand, Demond's behavior must be viewed in context, with careful consideration given to the negative impact of his abusive, drug-abusing parents. Rejecting and judging Demond won't get him to change his behavior, as he already feels rejected and judged. Demond isn't deliberately trying to be "bad" just for the sake of being bad, but he sees no alternatives to getting his needs met except through violent and antisocial behavior. From his perspective, his choices are the most adaptive ones, or perhaps the only ones that he believes he can make. The key to successful therapy will be to expand his worldview so that he learns he can get his needs met if he behaves in a socially acceptable manner. This change would require some degree of hope on his behalf that his life could improve somehow, and he needs a therapist who can accept a person without accepting his behavior.

3. Do you think that Demond's grandmother slapping him across the face for talking back to her constitutes abuse?

4. What's missing from the case conceptualization that you think is important to add? How would your case conceptualization emphasize different components of Demond's life than what is written?

Evidence-Based Treatment

Demond's story now comes full circle as we return to the questions that society confronts with youths like him: What should happen to Demond? Where should he be placed, and what treatment should he receive?

When Annamarie watched Demond leave the day room, she wondered if he had any idea how profound his last statement was, writing it in the margins of his file:

"Because I got nothing. I got nobody. I got no reason for anything."

Recalling Demon's chameleon-like demeanor during their initial interview, Annamarie wasn't certain if she was being hit upon, manipulated, played with, or witnessing an earnest plea for help. All those fancy terms that she learned in college seemed much less helpful than they did before the interview, and less relevant than ever. She had hoped that when she met Demond, everything would become crystal clear and the placement recommendation for him would be obvious. She literally had no idea what to recommend to the judge regarding his placement.

Annamarie decided to consult her supervisor, a seasoned mental health worker with more than 20 years of experience working with troubled youth. Together, they decided that the best course of action would be yet another residential facility, The Challenge Center. Annamarie's supervisor was the one who suggested the center. She had placed a number of children at that residential facility over the years and was impressed with it for many reasons, including the center's willingness to hold children accountable without blaming them for their problems. The Challenge Center also utilized evidence-based treatment programs and utilized a data-driven approach to individualize treatment for each child. For example, probation officers were electronically sent monthly summaries that averaged a child's problems and progress from data collected each day, and children were provided with a comprehensive array of services tailored to their needs. Finally, as the supervisor told Annamarie, "I like the place because they don't call you and give you notice that they're going to discharge a kid within 48 hours because his behavior is too aggressive. Geez, we all knew that information when we placed these kids in the first place!"

The Challenge Center was under the jurisdiction of the Juvenile Justice Department but also provided mental health services, including a substance-abuse group based on the Seven Challenges model, an evidence-based outpatient substance abuse program for adolescents. It's designed to help teens identify the barriers to changing their substance-abuse problems, their life-skills deficits, and their situational problems (Schwebel, 2013). The research-based Seven Challenges model has demonstrated positive, significant changes in youths with backgrounds similar to Demond's.

Seven Challenges is based on the Alcoholics Anonymous 12-step model but with several crucial differences. First, it's not an abstinence model. It allows for moderate or controlled use of substances, if this fits into the teen's values and decisions. It also doesn't ask for clients to turn their lives over to God or a higher power, noting that teenagers are just beginning to determine their identities and to understand the role that faith might play in their lives. Finally, the model postulates that a teenager doesn't bear sole responsibility for his substance-abuse problems, but rather that multiple people (biological and adoptive parents in Demond's case) should shoulder some of the blame. The Seven Challenges model requires counselor training as well as ongoing support and supervision to ensure effective implementation. At the Challenge Center, all of the therapists were trained in the Seven Challenges model.

The Challenge Center also offered family therapy, group therapy, individual therapy, job placement, independent-living skills, and post-placement assistance that allowed clients to "step down" to less restrictive settings. It's an umbrella organization that offered a full range of services, including therapeutic foster care and psychiatric hospitalization, so that children could move to more or less restrictive levels of care without changing actual placements or providers. The Challenge Center prided itself on helping the most difficult children move to the least restrictive setting as soon as possible, often within weeks or months of their initial placement. The facility was several hours away, but distance was not a major barrier since Demond would have few (if any) family members visiting him anyway. Annamarie called the Challenge Center and was pleasantly surprised that they had an opening for an admission within the next seven to ten days. For the first time, she felt hopeful for Demond.

During the next few days Annamarie prepared for the placement hearing. Her supervisor would be in the courtroom as well, since Annamarie was so new to the field. Demond was present at court, but he stared at the floor so hard it looked as if he were burrowing a tunnel through the courthouse foundation. He never acknowledged Annamarie. She made a logical argument to the court about why Demond deserved a chance at treatment but also needed the structure of a residential treatment environment. She suggested the Challenge Center and discussed how they currently had an opening and had preliminarily accepted Demond based on paperwork that she'd sent.

The judge listened throughout the 15-minute hearing. Then he abruptly decided that the Challenge Center was too expensive for the already financially strapped county. He reasoned that the juvenile system had already spent a substantial amount of money trying to rehabilitate Demond, and he couldn't justify spending the county's meager juvenile justice funds on him. Instead, the judge reasoned, after quickly reviewing Demond's placement history, Demond needed to be locked up because clearly, treatment "wasn't working." He decided to send Demond to a state training school, a "boot-camp" style placement that offered essentially no treatment but was much less expensive than the Challenge Center. He ordered Demond to remain at the facility for at least two years. And with a decisive hammer of the gavel, Demond was sent to the state training facility.

In general, residential care centers such as the "boot camp" ordered by the judge haven't received much empirical support in treating adolescents with conduct disorder—in part because of the questionable wisdom of putting in one place large numbers of antisocial youths, creating a peer culture where antisocial norms are expected and rewarded (Dishion, McCord, & Poulin, 1999). Sadly, without a good treatment intervention Demond's chances of "turning his life around" are slim. Adolescents with conduct disorders often show a series of interrelated problems as they grow into adults, including psychiatric diagnoses, incarceration, health problems, and early death (Smith & Chamberlain, 2010).

An alternative model to residential facilities that has received some empirical support is multidimensional treatment foster care (Smith & Chamberlain, 2010). In this community-based model, delinquent youths live in family homes with intensive supervision, support, and skill development. Children also receive a range of mental health services, including therapy, skills training, psychiatric consultation, and daily coordination of all team members. A secondary component of multidimensional treatment foster care is intensive work with the youth's biological family, particularly his parents, with the goal of improving parenting skills and returning the child to his biological family. The program is based on a daily behavioral management system, social learning, and systems thinking, with a strong emphasis on coordination of care among all individuals. This model has shown effectiveness in decreasing delinquency in adolescent boys compared with placement of comparable children in residential facilities (Chamberlain & Reid, 1998). In Demond's case, he could have received community-based treatment foster care without services to his biological parents as he is, for all practical purposes, an orphan.

In general, best practices for treatment of children with conduct disorder share several features. First is a behavioral parenting training program, with a strong focus on *generalizability*—intentionally helping an individual demonstrate his newly learned skills across settings or across time. In this case, it means helping parents show strong parenting skills not just in the therapist's office, but at home, in the car, and in public places. It also means helping parents show such skills not only for the duration of therapy but also over a period of months and years, often through *booster sessions*, which are infrequent therapy sessions after the formal end of therapy to reinforce in clients the skills they've learned. Booster sessions also help clients brainstorm how to solve barriers preventing them from using these skills. A second component of best practices for children with conduct problems is skills training, such as teaching teenagers problem-solving skills. School-based interventions may also be helpful, and some evidence supports anti-bullying efforts (DeRosier & Marcus, 2005). A substantial problem in the mental health field remains a huge inequity between the number of programs that effectively treat children with conduct problems and the number of children in need of such services.

Did institutional racism play a factor in Demond's case? Sadly, the answer is probably yes. Black individuals are incarcerated at a much higher rate than white individuals (Leiber, Bishop, & Chamlin, 2011) even when they've been convicted of the same crimes.

From a clinical perspective, clinicians may not be aware of their own discriminatory perspectives. The best way to make sure you aren't practicing from a racist perspective is to explore your own cultural upbringing and values and thoughtfully consider how these factors affect us as clinicians. It's also helpful to recognize ethnic or racial groups who are the most difficult for us to work with and to deliberately expose ourselves to these groups to try to diminish our prejudices through the building of relationships. Exploring the idea of *privilege* is helpful, too. *Privilege* is the economic, occupational, educational, health, housing, and other benefits society provides to some people on the basis of their skin color and gender. Exploring our own cultural identity takes work, but the payoffs are worth it. Perhaps Demond's fate would have been different in a less biased world. As professionals in the field, we're constantly called upon to ask ourselves how our prejudices and stereotypes influence our clinical work. A particularly worrisome clinician is one who isn't aware of his or her own biases. Having categories and biases about human beings is normal. Failing to explore these biases is unethical.

5. What is your emotional reaction to the judge and his decision regarding Demond? After addressing your emotional reactions to the judge, think through his job of wisely managing the county's limited resources of money and time. Given the need to distribute limited resources fairly, do you agree with the judge's decision? If the money required for one year at the Challenge Center would provide services for four other children, will this influence your answer?

6. How does Demond's story connect with some of the ideas you have learned this semester through your coursework? Think of at least five important possible connections.

7. Did Annamarie's work on Desmond's case matter? Explain your answer.

Demond remained at the state training facility until he was 18, as he was unable to be discharged because of the numerous aggressive acts he committed toward other boys at the facility. On his 18th birthday, Demond was discharged with minimal aftercare services in place. He contacted his grandmother, swore that he'd changed his ways, and she warily allowed him to stay in her home. After only a few weeks, though, she kicked him out after she caught him smoking marijuana with some friends. Demond then bounced around from various friends' houses to shelters, but he never stayed in one place very long. He decided to move to Cleveland with a friend from northern Ohio whom he met in the training facility.

Within six months of the move, Demond was killed during retaliatory rival gang violence in a housing project in Cleveland. His grandmother borrowed the money to have his body sent back home to Cincinnati, and she buried him at the church cemetery beside his mother. Besides the pastor, she was the only person who attended his funeral. She wept openly, wondering what might she might have done to make a difference for her grandson.

8. The ethics code of most mental health fields (e.g., social work, psychology, and counseling) discusses self-care as an ethical obligation. Engaging in self-care requires us to assess when we're compromised in our professional work because of a variety of factors, including *compassion fatigue*, also called *secondary trauma*. It means that profes-

sional helpers may be negatively affected by the traumatic histories of their clients to the extent that it interferes with their ability to competently provide services. How do you think Annamarie has been affected by Demond and his story? What should she do, given the ethics code of your profession?

References

Ahmann, E. (2014). Encouraging positive behavior in "challenging" children: The nurtured heart approach. *Pediatric Nursing, 40*(1), 38–42.

American Psychiatric Association. (2013). *Diagnostic and Statistical Manual of Mental Disorders* (5th ed.). Washington, DC: Author.

Azar, S., & Wolfe, D. (2006). Child physical abuse and neglect. In E. Mash. & R. Barkley (Eds.), *Treatment of childhood disorders.* New York: Guilford.

Barone, N. M., Weitz, E. I., & Witt, P. H. (2005). Psychological bonding evaluations in termination of parental rights cases. *Journal of Psychiatry and Law, 33,* 387–412.

Blacker, D. M., Urquiza, A. J., Kalich, L. & Carmichael, B. D. (2016). Termination of parental rights. In T. R. Masson (Ed.), *Inside forensic psychology.* Santa Barbara, CA: ABC-Clio, LLC.

Chamberlain, P., & Reid, J. (1998). Comparison of two community alternatives to incarceration for chronic juvenile offenders. *Journal of Consulting and Clinical Psychology, 66,* 624–633.

DeRosier, M., & Marcus, S. (2005). Building friendships and combating bullying: Effectiveness of S.S. GRIN at one-year follow-up. *Journal of Clinical Child and Adolescent Psychology, 34,* 140–150.

Dishion, T., McCord, J., & Poulin, F. (1999). When interventions harm: Peer groups and problem behavior. *American Psychologist, 54,* 755–764.

Evans, G. (2004). The environment of childhood poverty. *American Psychologist, 59*(2), 71–92.

Grant, B., & Dawson, D. (1997). Age of onset of alcohol use and its association with DSM-IV alcohol abuse and dependence: Results from the national Longitudinal Alcohol Epidemiologic Survey. *Journal of Substance Abuse, 9,* 103–110.

Hines, P., & Boyd-Franklin, N. (2005). African American Families. In M. McGoldrick, J. Giordano, & N. Garcia-Preto (Eds.), *Ethnicity and family therapy.* New York: Guilford.

Ingoldsby, E., & Shaw, D. (2002). The role of neighborhood contextual factors on early-starting antisocial behavior. *Clinical Child and Family Psychology Review, 6,* 21–65.

Leiber, M., Bishop, D., & Chamlin, M. (2011). Juvenile justice decision-making before and after the implementation of the disproportionate minority contact (DMC) mandate. *Justice Quarterly, 28*(3), 460–492. doi:10.1080/07418825.2010.516005

Lorber, M. F., & Slep, A. M. (2015). Are persistent early onset child conduct problems predicted by the trajectories and initial levels of discipline practices? *Developmental Psychology, 51*(8), 1048–1061. http://dx.doi.org/10.1037/a0039421

MacPherson, L., Frissell, K., Brown, S, & Myers, M. (2006). Adolescent substance use problems. In E. Mash & R. Barkley (Eds.), *Treatment of childhood disorders.* New York: Guilford.

McMahon, R., Wells, K., & Kotler, J. (2006). Conduct problems. In E. Mash & R. Barkley (Eds.), *Treatment of childhood disorders*. New York: Guilford.

Piotrowska, P. J., Stride, C. B., Croft, S. E., & Rowe, R. (2015). Socioeconomic status and antisocial behaviour among children and adolescents: A systematic review and meta-analysis. *Clinical Psychology Review, 35*, 47–55. doi:10.1016/j.cpr.2014.11.003

Pössel, P., & Black, S. W. (2014). Testing three different sequential mediational interpretations of Beck's Cognitive Model of the development of depression. *Journal of Clinical Psychology, 70*(1), 72–94. doi:10.1002/jclp.22001

Schwebel, R. (2013). Seven Challenges Program. http://sevenchallenges.com/

Smith, D., & Chamberlain, P. (2010). Multidimensional treatment foster care for adolescents. In J. Weisz & A. Kazdin (Eds.), *Evidence-based psychotherapies for children and adolescents*. New York: Guilford.

Stirling, J., & Amaya-Jackson, L. (2008). Understanding the behavioral and emotional consequences of child abuse. *Pediatrics, 122*(3), 667–673. doi:10.1542/peds.2008-1885

Werner, E. (2009). Children of the garden island. In M. Gauvain & M. Cole (Eds.), *Readings on the development of children*. New York: Worth.

CASE 12

Lacy Davis-Woodrow

Lacy is a complex 16-year-old biracial girl who exhibits a range of significant issues, including substance use, cutting, reckless behavior, and other self-destructive behaviors. Her unusual family dynamics also contribute to her case. Lacy receives therapy from a Puerto Rican female therapist in New York City, but is the high-quality treatment she receives enough to change Lacy's dangerous behavior and improve her relationship with her parents? Lacy's case highlights themes of diagnosing personality disorders and utilizing dialectical behavior therapy with teenagers.

ICD 10/DSM 5 Diagnosis:
F12.20 (304.30) Cannabis Use Disorder, Moderate
Z63.8 (V61.8) High Expressed Emotion Level within Family

Diagnostic Discussion

After the Davis-Woodrow family left her office, Camila tapped her thumb on her desk, carefully considering a diagnosis for Lacy on the intake interview form.

Where to begin? The most obvious diagnosis for Lacy is substance use disorder due to her marijuana use. Let me double-check the criteria for Cannabis Use Disorder and see if Lacy's presenting problems warrant such a diagnosis.

Camila thumbed through her already-worn DSM-5 (APA, 2013), turning to page 509.

- Cannabis is taken in larger amounts or over a longer period of time than was intended. *We don't know this for certain, but Lacy's parents said that she's using more often.*
- Recurrent cannabis use results in a failure to meet obligations at work or school. *Lacy was suspended from school for smoking marijuana.*
- A great deal of time is spent obtaining, using, and recovering from marijuana. *Well, I know Lacy's using before school, at school, on dates, and with her friends. That suggests that she's using quite often.*
- Continued cannabis use despite having recurrent social problems that are exacerbated by use. *Lacy punched a girl at school for stealing some green, a slang term for taking her marijuana.*

- A need for markedly increased amounts of cannabis to achieve feeling high. *Lacy mentioned that it takes more than one joint to get herself high.*
- Recurrent cannabis use in situations in which it is physically hazardous. *I don't know about this criterion. If she was using the day that she rode on the motorcycle so "crazy fast," which I would guess to be true, then she certainly would meet this criterion.*

The authors of the DSM-5 have adopted a continuum approach to diagnosing substance-use disorders. Thus, a person can have mild, moderate, or severe levels of any substance problem. In Lacy's case, it's possible that she meets six criteria. A diagnosis of moderate-level substance abuse requires the presence of four to five symptoms; a severe level of substance abuse requires the presence of at least six symptoms. Because Camila isn't sure about Lacy meeting the sixth criterion, Camila decides that Lacy should be diagnosed with Cannabis Use Disorder, Moderate.

Camila sighed deeply.

OK. I don't think smoking marijuana is this girl's only problem. If she stopped using marijuana entirely, would she still be struggling? Yes, I think she would. Although I've only seen the family in one session, the Davis-Woodrow family is very—what word is the right term to describe them? Emotionally reactive.

Camila turned to the Z Codes in her DSM-5 (APA, 2013, p. 716).

High Expressed Emotion Level within Family. This is a diagnostic category that I don't particularly like. After all, my family's Puerto Rican and my white friends all think that my family's too close and too emotionally volatile! However, most families, regardless of their racial or ethnic background, wouldn't express the type of negative emotions this family does, especially during an intake interview when families are usually on their best behavior. The Davis-Woodrow family demonstrates high levels of emotional over-involvement, criticism, and reactivity, even considering the stressful situational factors of being in a therapist's office for an intake interview. They're openly hostile to each other and then instantaneously shift to seeming almost desperate for one another's love. They showed hostility and criticism, particularly Kayla towards Lacy but also Kayla towards Mark. They certainly have a great deal of energy invested in Kayla being the identified patient in the family and the one who's "sick."

After considering cultural factors that may affect symptom presentation, Camila recorded a Z-code of High Expressed Emotion Level within Family.

These qualities are going to make treatment tough.

I can't put my finger on it, but I'm wondering if substance use and family issues are not Lacy's only problems. I don't think she has depression, despite her suicidal threats and self-injurious behavior. Nor do I think she has anxiety, despite her fears—or maybe I should say alleged fears?—about being alone as the last person on the planet.

I keep returning to a diagnosis of Borderline Personality Disorder for Lacy. My clinical intuition tells me that this disorder is right, but I really don't want to diagnose this young girl with a personality disorder. Teenagers are still sorting through their personalities, and it seems unfair to diagnose them with a disorder that assumes their personalities are formed. Kids do a great deal of growing up between the ages of 16 and 18.

Camila flipped through the pages in her well-worn DSM-5 (APA, 2013) until she found what she was looking for. She read:

Adolescents and young adults with identity problems (especially when accompanied by substance use) may transiently display behaviors that misleadingly give the impression of borderline personality disorder. Such situations are characterized by emotional instability, "existential" dilemmas, uncertainty, anxiety-provoking choices, conflicts about sexual orientation, and competing social pressures to decide on careers. (APA, 2013, pp. 665–666)

Those precautionary statements sound quite a bit like Lacy, although they don't exactly capture her presentation. I think I'll wait on giving Lacy any personality disorder diagnosis and get more information so I can confirm or disprove my suspicions. I can always add a diagnosis later if she isn't making gains in therapy as I expect she should.

1. Do you think that older adolescents should be diagnosed with personality disorders if their symptoms warrant the diagnosis? Why or why not?

2. On a scale of 1 to 10, how worried are you about Lacy's substance abuse, and why? Do you think anyone else in her family is using substances? Explain your answer.

3. Camila considered her own family and cultural values when pondering the Z-code diagnosis of High Expressed Emotion Level within Family. Was this an example of good or poor clinical practice? Explain your answer.

Note to our readers: Lacy's case study is slightly different than the others presented in this book, because her full diagnosis was not apparent within the first few weeks or even months of treatment. To be consistent with the other cases presented, Lacy's first six months of treatment are described briefly, followed by an additional diagnosis section, then a case conceptualization section and secondary treatment section.

Treatment Stage One: Sessions 1–20

Camila began working with Lacy and her family in individual and family therapy, meeting three times a month for individual therapy with Lacy and once a month with Kayla, Mark, and Lacy. The focus of treatment for Lacy was her marijuana use. Camila chose motivational enhancement therapy (Miller, Zweben, DiClemente, & Rychtarik, 1999) to help Lacy better manage her decisions concerning substance use. Substance-abuse treatment has been outlined in other cases of this book and are not repeated here. In the sessions with the Davis-Woodrow family, Camila worked to help them manage their intense emotions in a healthier way. She also tried to get them to communicate more clearly and directly with one another without so much volatility, hostility, and reactivity. Both Kayla and Mark made slow but steady progress in reaching these goals after five months of therapy, although they retained some of their characteristic intensity.

Lacy was another story. Despite Camila's best efforts, therapy seemed to be going nowhere. Lacy had reduced her marijuana use to a mild level, but she still exhibited many of the problematic behaviors outlined above, including the self-injurious behavior of cutting. In working with Lacy, Camila had identified a number of new problematic symptoms as well. The two most concerning symptoms were Lacy's identity disturbance and her problems in managing her closest relationships. In terms of her self-identity problems, Lacy exhibited substantially more problems than a typical 17-year-old. The fundamental task for adolescents is to figure out who they are, an idea first proposed by Erik Erikson and supported by current research (Cote, 2009). Teenagers often change their mind about their careers, life goals, sexual orientation, and moral and political values.

Lacy's search for her identity, however, dramatically veered off course over the six months Camila worked with her. She began therapy as an overly-made-up girl with black curly hair spiraling to her shoulders, who was dating and having sex with several different boys. A month later, she decided that she was gay and had shaved her head bald, asking to bring her girlfriend to therapy. A month later, she'd dumped her girlfriend and decided that she was straight, had a new boyfriend, and was wearing a platinum wig. Her educational and career goals had changed as well. Initially, Lacy was "definitely" planning on college but, a few months into therapy, decided that she wanted to drop out of high school. Her grades began to plummet, but then she bought a "cute" pair of purple fashion glasses and decided to be a "sexy nerd," wearing the glasses (but not the wig), along with a highly visible leopard-skin print bra underneath a white blouse and a Catholic, schoolgirl-inspired, short skirt. She joined the Young Republicans group that week and begged her parents to take her to a conservative Christian church. Just two weeks later, she was marching for abortion rights and declared herself a Green Party liberal.

Most concerning of all, Lacy had begun to fear that because she hadn't found a stable boyfriend yet, perhaps she didn't exist at all. She described periods of dissociation, where she no longer felt connected to her body. Instead, she felt like she was watching herself as if in a play. At these times, she described herself as a "floating ghost" who was "totally untethered to anything or anyone in the universe."

In those first six months of therapy, Lacy also showed a disturbing inability to manage her emotions, particularly in the context of her close relationships. In every close relationship, including with her parents, her current beau, her friends, and eventually Camila, Lacy vacillated between absolute adoration of the person to extreme devaluation. One day in therapy, she cried because she'd never be the woman her mother was. The following week, she alleged to Child Protective Services that her mother had physically abused her. Lacy had scratched her own face repeatedly with the edge of a stolen diamond ring and lied that her mother had caused the scratches during an argument.

Lacy also struggled with Camila. She adored Camila the first few weeks of therapy and began dating a 21-year-old Puerto Rican solely because she thought Camila was so "cool." A month into therapy, Camila was about five minutes late to her session with Lacy because a heel broke on one of her shoes. Lacy was in the waiting room in tears, crying that Camila didn't care about her anymore. Lacy told Camila, "I can understand why you hate me. I mean, everyone does. Or at least, everyone should. But I thought my own therapist would at least be there for me. Oh my God, I can't even *pay* someone to be my friend!"

After witnessing the extent of Lacy's problems, Camila rethought her diagnosis at the six-month therapy mark. Camila had contacted Lacy's previous therapists at the onset of therapy and had read all their detailed notes. After six months of minimal progress with Lacy, Camila re-read these notes again carefully, working diligently to understand Lacy's issues from the perspective of each therapist. All of her therapists, along with the discharge summary from her hospital stays, had noted ongoing instability in Lacy's relationships, mood, and self-image, in addition to high levels of impulsive and manipulative behavior.

Camila added a new diagnosis, Borderline Personality Disorder, to Lacy's chart.

▮▮ F60.3 (301.83) Borderline Personality Disorder (provisional)

Personality disorders are enduring patterns of relating to others and the world in a way that is inflexible and maladaptive, and causes significant distress and impairment (APA, 2013). Personality disorders deviate from cultural expectations. A person must also have impairment across multiple areas, such as cognition, relationships, behavior, and mood. Although personality disorders typically begin in adolescence, clinicians should be cautious in diagnosing them prior to age 18 because, as Camila noted, teenagers are still developing their identity and interpersonal style. Teenage brains are still developing as well, and current research suggests that significant cognitive changes are occurring throughout a person's 20s (Diamond, 2002). Thus, our current diagnostic system requires that teenagers show an enduring pattern of personality problems that last for at least one year (APA, 2013).

Borderline Personality Disorder (BPD) is a specific personality disorder that has at its core a "pervasive pattern of instability of interpersonal relationships, self-image and affects, and marked impulsivity" (APA, 2013, p. 663). Another key to BPD is a fear of abandonment and an intolerance of being alone. Their fears about being abandoned lead persons with BPD to react in intense anger. Recent research has supported that borderline personality disorder can be diagnosed reliably in adolescence (Glenn & Klonsky, 2013; Speranza et al., 2012). Borderline personality disorder symptoms have been shown to be reliable across time and are correlated with lower role functioning, social functioning, and life satisfaction moving into adulthood (Winograd, Cohen, & Chen, 2008). The symptoms tend to be stronger during adolescence and early adulthood and less severe in middle age and later adulthood. Because of the severity of symptoms, BPD is considered to be both chronic and difficult to treat (McMain, Boritz, & Leybman, 2015).

Let's see whether Camila made the right choice in diagnosing Lacy with BPD. To meet the criteria for this disorder, Lacy needs to demonstrate five of the following nine APA criteria (2013) listed below, along with Camila's thoughts about how she demonstrates the symptom:

1. Frantic efforts to avoid real or imagined abandonment. *Lacy best shows her fear of abandonment when Darryl threatens to break up with her and she says she's going to kill herself. This is especially troubling, as they'd only been dating a month when she first said this. She's afraid that her parents will leave her as well, demonstrated by her fears that her parents will take off to Mexico and her constantly seeking reassurance that they love her. Lacy's behavior the day I was late due to my shoe fiasco is also typical of people with BPD, who are so afraid that others will abandon them and don't like them.*

2. A pattern of unstable and intense interpersonal relationships, demonstrated by idealization and devaluation. *Lacy shows this love/hate pattern with her friends, like her rash decision to get a tattoo of the name of a girl whom she just met, her intense but brief dating relationships, and her love/hate relationship with her mother. She also demonstrated this unstable pattern with me. She dated a guy just because he was Puerto Rican like me! Then a few weeks later, she thought I hated her.*

3. Identity disturbance, evidenced by a markedly unstable identity. *Early in therapy, I thought that Lacy's chronic lying and manipulation were most likely the behavior of a teenager acting out. However, I see these behaviors as part of a bigger puzzle now, one that includes Lacy's frantic search for who she is and what she values. She desperately clings to each reiteration of herself she creates, only to completely throw away that identity a few weeks later.*

4. Impulsivity in at least two areas that are potentially self-damaging, such as sex, substance abuse, eating disorders, reckless driving, etc. *Her marijuana use has lessened but is still a problem for her. Her riding on a motorcycle fast, especially without a helmet, is also dangerous. I know she's having sex with multiple partners, and although she's on birth control she told me that she's "not always careful" about using condoms to help protect against sexually transmitted diseases.*

5. Recurrent suicidal or self-mutilating behaviors. *Lacy cuts on her thighs and arms regularly and has threatened suicide. She has also been hospitalized twice for suicidal behavior, as her mother mentioned almost immediately in the intake session.*

6. Affective instability and a reactive mood. *Lacy clearly demonstrated her affective instability during the interview when she was so changeably hot and cold with her parents. She's demonstrated it with her parents on numerous other occasions as well. She's also been emotionally reactive with her friends and with me.*

7. Chronic feelings of emptiness. *When Lacy first came into therapy, her expressed concern about being a floating piece of nothingness demonstrates this criterion. Since then, she's said on many occasions that she lacks a purpose and meaning in life.*

8. Inappropriate, intense anger, demonstrated in temper displays, constant rage, and fights. *Lacy's been suspended from school three times this year for fighting. She regularly blows up at her parents, friends, and romantic/sexual partners.*

9. Transient paranoid ideation or dissociative symptoms. *Lacy sometimes feels like she's watching herself in a play, and she feels she isn't a person but rather a floating ghost.*

Given Lacy's presentation, she meets criteria for BPD. Lacy demonstrates nine of the nine symptoms of the disorder. Her problematic behavior has lasted for more than a year—in fact, almost two years. Camila was thoughtful in her diagnosis of Lacy and observed her behavior for six months before considering diagnosing a disorder that's often chronic and difficult to treat. She waited until Lacy's substance use was under better control and her overall family functioning was healthier. She also consulted Lacy's previous mental health providers for their clinical notes. In delaying her diagnostic decision, Camila ensured that Lacy's behavior reflected long-standing personality traits and not just a teenager's response to situational factors, such as her difficult family dynamics.

Nevertheless, Camila loathed giving any teenager a personality disorder diagnosis, fearful that Lacy's therapists in the future might judge her unfairly.

Case Conceptualization

Like most psychological disorders, BPD is caused by multiple factors. In terms of the genetic etiology of the disorder, children likely inherit a tendency to have both internalizing and externalizing problems (Bornovalova et al., 2013). For example, researchers found that the presence of ADHD and ODD in girls at the age of eight predicted the development of BPD symptoms at age 14 (Stepp, Burke, Hipwell, & Loeber, 2011). This research highlights that these disorders may share common symptoms of impulsivity and emotional dysregulation (Stepp et al., 2011). If these genetically vulnerable children are raised in a negative family environment, the risk of developing BPD increases. Specifically, family interactions of children with BPD have been found to be invalidating, conflicted, critical, or highly negative (Blizard, 2009; Linehan, 1993a). Disruptions, interpersonal trauma, and problems interacting with primary caregivers are common among people diagnosed with BPD. In fact, 57% of those diagnosed with BPD have a history of parental loss through death or divorce (Walsh, 1977).

A vicious cycle can develop quickly in that children feel rejected or invalidated by their families. This invalidating environment sets off a primitive alarm system in the child's attachment to her caregivers. The child feels at some level that she's unloved, or perhaps unlovable, or in danger of not being taken care of. The child's response to this situation is to seek proximity and reassurance from her caregivers. This desperate clinginess and attention-seeking behavior drives the caregiver away from the child—the opposite effect of what the child intended (Bleiberg, Rossouw, & Fonagy, 2011).

Imagine that this vicious cycle plays out multiple times a day over several years. Both the child and the caregiver become more and more distressed. The child ups the ante and tries to increase her proximity-seeking and attention-seeking behavior, perhaps by eventually using substances, engaging in self-harm, gambling, or engaging in other self-destructive behavior, such as eating disorders. These self-defeating behaviors create their own vicious spiral. The negative effects of these behaviors cause their own bad consequences, but the worst consequence is how negatively a person begins to feel about herself. Sadly, this self-destructive behavior continues to drive other people away, including both family and friends.

Let's put these ideas to work for Lacy. We don't know how her biological parents, Kayla and Charles, related to Lacy her during first six years of life. Camila likely will explore this area early in the therapeutic process. We know that Lacy's biological father died in a traumatic way when she was six. His untimely death may have contributed to her irrational fear of abandonment. Perhaps bringing Mark into the family was a stabilizing influence; perhaps it was a destabilizing choice that happened too soon after Charles' death. The timing of the remarriage, and Lacy's relationship to Mark when he began seriously dating Kayla, are critical. We don't know the mental health history of either parent, but mental health problems in Kayla, Charles, or Mark are likely to contribute to Lacy's problems. We know that the parents relate to each other, and to Lacy, in a bitter, almost caustic manner.

Lacy's response to this invalidating environment is evident in her attention-seeking and manipulative behavior. These daily "tests" allow Lacy to assess her mother's and stepfather's love and presence, which she's perpetually afraid of losing. Perhaps Lacy fears the death of her mother. This fear comes across as *emotional lability* (unpredictable or erratic feelings and displays of emotion) and frantic manipulative clinginess in order to keep people attached. For example, in the intake interview she used her stepfather's anger to control her mother's reaction, leading to a loving embrace that was then reinforced by Lacy stating how much she loved her mother. Though sincere, this emotional manipulation serves to lessen Lacy's fear of abandonment and keep Kayla attached to Lacy, allowing Lacy to feel more secure in her environment.

Lacy is at high risk to escalate her drug use as another way to "test" her parents' love for her. Lacy's marijuana use is a way to decrease the intensity of her emotions while also helping her to identify with peers. Developmentally, peer groups are critical during adolescence (Nawaz, 2011). Adolescents with any sort of psychopathology may report increased levels of identity distress, which clearly affects Lacy as she struggles to understand who she is (Klimstra, 2013). Not only does substance use tend to increase in adolescents, but so do the symptoms of BPD. In fact, BPD symptoms tend to be particularly severe in late adolescence when self-identity is such an important developmental task (Crowell, Beauchaine, & Lenzenweger, 2008). Substance abuse is one of the most common co-morbid problems of people with BPD (Reichenberg & Seligman, 2016).

From a family systems perspective, Mark and Kayla also play a role in Lacy's presentation. Her stepfather is emotionally expressive, as exhibited by his hand gestures and angry outbursts. Her mother, on the other hand, is overly controlling. Both parents are highly reactive to each other and to Lacy. These family dynamics create a confusing environment for Lacy to learn about emotional expression. Mark may inadvertently provide Lacy with confusing messages because of his anger. He may tell her he loves her but does so in an angry tone or when behaving angrily. This is called a *double bind,* a family therapy term that describes when an individual receives conflicting messages about how to act and feel. This may result in Lacy feeling like she'll be punished no matter how she behaves. Kayla also provides mixed messages about how Lacy is expected to behave, whether her acting-out behavior is acceptable, and what the best ways are to earn parental attention. In short, communication dynamics within the Davis-Woodrow family create an unstable environment for Lacy and likely contribute to her manipulative behavior being effective.

Additionally, Lacy will have to consider how being biracial fits into her overall identity (Moss & Davis, 2008). Identity development may be difficult because of the different pressures placed on biracial or multiracial individuals (Poston, 1990). Identity development may be more complicated for individuals who are bi- or multiracial because of pressure from society to "choose" a culture to identify with based on one's heritage. Many modern identity models for individuals who are biracial or multiracial focus on "choosing" a heritage in early identity stages before integrating aspects of multiple races (Renn, 2008). Furthermore, integrating different parts of one's identity may take significant work and can happen over a long period of development (Rummens, 2003).

For Lacy, her biracial identity may lead her to internalize prejudice she perceives in her environment, leading her to engage in further substance use or to try different behaviors in order to fit in. People in her environment may increase Lacy's stress through *microaggressions,* brief, often unintentional exchanges that send denigrating messages to certain people because of their identity (Liao, Weng, & West, 2016). Issues surrounding race seem to be a hot-button topic in the Davis-Woodrow family, evidenced by their reactivity and abrupt departure from their first therapy session. For example, when

Lacy was trying to provoke her mother into an argument in their first session, Lacy accused her mother of not liking her boyfriend because he was black, suggesting that the family has unresolved conflicts about race. While the case study presents no evidence that Lacy has been directly criticized for being biracial, she's likely very sensitive to her parents' strong feelings and may be interpreting their negativity as rejection of herself. She may also be receiving negative messages from peers at school. These sorts of confusing messages would lead to Lacy feeling invalidated and not understood by others at the developmentally sensitive time of adolescence, when feeling understood by others is both paramount and elusive. Understanding what race means to each individual will be critical for Camila to explore in therapy. Helping Lacy find the freedom to explore her own identity in a family that can be reactive and critical will be a crucial component to successful treatment.

When working with people with BPD, it's crucial to remember that they don't "choose" to be the way they are. No one chooses to be an alcoholic or diabetic, but sometimes these problems arise anyway due to a combination of genetic and environmental factors. A key element of BPD is anger, but the anger really occurs because of the fear of being abandoned. Another key element of BPD is an unstable identity and sense of self, causing a person to seek constant reassurance from others. Imagine how lost and alone a person diagnosed with BPD must feel. No one wants to feel that way.

4. Many therapists choose not to work with people diagnosed with BPD because of the *countertransference* issues, meaning that they have an emotional reaction to the client's behavior that can interfere with their ability to provide treatment. What would your reaction to Lacy be, and how would you deal with it in therapy sessions?

5. Consider how microaggressions have likely impacted the Davis-Woodrows as a mixed-race couple, and Lacy because she's biracial.

6. Treatment in Lacy's case will be a multiracial experience on many layers. How do you think this will affect treatment?

7. What challenges do you anticipate in treating the Davis-Woodrow family, and how would you handle these challenges? Family dynamics have clearly contributed to Lacy's problems, yet she's the one who receives a diagnosis. What do you think of this reality?

Evidence-Based Treatment

Several treatment options have proven effective for the treatment of BPD symptoms, including dialectical behavior therapy (DBT) (Linehan 1993a, 1993b), mentalization-based treatment (MBT) (Laurenssen et. al., 2014), schema therapy (Kellogg, 2006), transference-focused therapy (TFP) (Yeomans, Levy, & Caligor, 2013), and emotion regulation training (Schuppert, 2009). Research suggests high levels of *commonality*, or shared treatment components across these various treatment options (Biskin, 2013; Bliss & McCardle, 2014). However, DBT is one of the most well-researched treatments for BPD and is helpful with decreasing suicidality and self-harming behaviors (Kliem, Kröger, & Kosfelder, 2010). DBT has also been recommended for adolescents (Fleischhaker et al., 2011) and for adolescents with substance abuse problems (Linehan et al., 1999).

DBT is a form of cognitive behavioral therapy designed by Marsha Linehan (Linehan, 1993a, 1993b). *Dialectical* is a word not commonly used in everyday conversations, but it means to accept an idea and also to accept its opposite. In short, it means to see both sides of an argument, behavior, position, or idea. In DBT, the therapist utilizes dialectical thinking to accept the person being treated, but not the person's behavior. In other words, the therapist works to challenge the behavior but not the person. A skillful balance of accepting and challenging is extremely difficult, but Camila liked to be tested.

DBT is designed to be delivered across four main modalities: individual therapy, skills training (typically group therapy), as-needed consultation between the client and therapist outside of sessions, and therapist consultation meetings for feedback and support (Rizvi, Steffel, & Carson-Wong, 2013). Overall, DBT focuses on increasing emotional regulation, adaptive coping skills, and interpersonal functioning (Swales, Heard, & Williams, 2000).

Treatment Stage Two: Sessions 21–45

Let's return to Lacy's case study to see how Camila chose to implement DBT with the Davis-Woodrows. Unlike some other treatments for childhood psychopathology, DBT is not a brief intervention and usually takes about 12 months. After six months of Lacy being in therapy with only marginal progress, Kayla and Mark expressed concern, not at the length of treatment, but about the mounting cost of the co-pays required by their insurance company. Camila addressed these concerns openly and stated, "It sounds like money is a big concern for your family. I know how stressful it can be to worry about money. Handling money-related stress is something we can talk about in therapy. Regarding the co-pay, I know from dealing with insurance companies that it's something that you'll just have to pay. You need to decide whether therapy for Lacy is worth the expense of the co-pays." Mark and Kayla both agreed that they'd look into it, but they said they were concerned enough about Lacy that they would scrape together the money somehow. They were also happy with Camila's work and trusted her. And they were quite pleased that Lacy's marijuana use had lessened, although Camila warned them not to share their excitement with Lacy, or she might increase her use again as a way to test her parents' love.

Camila was hoping to enroll Lacy in a DBT therapy group for young adults, but it didn't work out. The local psychiatric hospital, which offered the group, was unwilling to take Lacy as a member of the group until she was 18 years old. Camila was disappointed but instead worked to teach Lacy the critical skills of DBT in individual therapy. Camila continued to meet monthly with Mark, Kayla, and Lacy to help the family learn some of the fundamental DBT skills. The goal of these family sessions was to help Mark and Kayla provide the appropriate support for Lacy and to better understand BPD. Camila watched hopefully as Lacy's parents used some of the skills they were learning to help create a more validating and supportive family environment overall.

During the family therapy sessions, both Mark and Kayla shared a great deal of information about themselves and their family situation. First of all, Lacy's comments in the intake interview about her family's financial situation were spot-on. Despite outward appearances, the Davis-Woodrow family was teetering on the edge of bankruptcy. They had a nice house and drove nice cars, but their consumer debt, not including the reverse loan on their house mortgage, was twice their family income. Their debt consisted mostly of high levels of credit card charges from both Mark and Kayla, each hiding expensive purchases from the other. The facade didn't end with finances, however. Mark had several disciplinary warnings at work because of losing his temper with hotel guests and was on the verge of being fired. Kayla's real estate business was extremely unsuccessful, and she was struggling to sell houses in the highly competitive New York market. In fact, she'd sold only one house in the last two years.

The family secrets didn't end with finances and careers. In the second family therapy session Mark shared that his marriage to Kayla was his fourth marriage and that he had grown children and now grandchildren from his previous marriages. Kayla also shared a complicated history of her own. When she was four, her mother died of a voracious, cancerous brain tumor that had progressed from diagnosis to death in less than six months. Kayla also had a substantial mental health history of her own and had been in and out of psychiatric hospitals for suicidal threats, eating disorder problems, and problems managing her emotions. Kayla reported that she'd been diagnosed Bipolar Disorder and BPD in the past. Kayla married her first husband at age 18. They tried to get pregnant for years, and Lacy was conceived only after years of expensive fertility treatments. From the time Lacy was 6 (when Charles was killed) to when she was 10 and Kayla married Mark, Kayla reported that she "drank like a fish." She also abused prescription pain medication. Kayla had been in treatment for substance use but had been clean and sober since Lacy was 10. Kayla wasn't in treatment at the present time, nor was she taking any psychotropic medication for psychological problems, because she felt that she was managing them "pretty well overall."

8. How does Mark and Kayla's family history help you understand Kayla's situation?

9. What approach would you take in the family therapy session if you were Camila? Specifically, what would your priorities be, and why would you prioritize these things?

Therapy with Lacy was uneven and, occasionally, exasperating. It seemed at times to be a giant game of bunny hop, with one step forward and two steps back.

In individual therapy, Camila taught Lacy some important coping skills that are fundamental to DBT. Camila began therapy by focusing on decreasing Lacy's self-harming behaviors. Lacy and Camila worked together to draft and sign an agreement for Lacy to engage in appropriate coping skills instead of self-harming through cutting. A critical treatment element in DBT is *mindfulness practice,* in which an individual learns to become more conscious of her feelings and thoughts by paying attention to her bodily sensations. For example, Lacy learned to accept such distressing thoughts as, "I need to go cut myself," without acting on the thought. Relaxation and deep breathing are key components of mindfulness, and Camila worked with Lacy on these skills as well. Lacy also learned *replacement behaviors,* or alternative behaviors, such as putting ice on her wrist instead of cutting her wrist. The coldness of the ice would help Lacy achieve the physical sensation she used to get when she'd cut but without actually harming herself.

Camila was glad that she taught Lacy these skills, because Lacy repeatedly utilized them. Lacy used mindfulness practice to cope when she and Darryl had ended their relationship. (Lacy broke up with Darryl because he'd shared his marijuana with his buddy Mason instead of her.) She also used deep breathing, mindfulness, and replacement behaviors to manage her intense feelings after the numerous short-lived sexual and romantic relationships that had imploded during the course of therapy. After breaking up with her girlfriend, Lacy came to the next session devastated, despite being the one who initiated the break-up. She arrived with superficial cut marks down her legs and arms. Once she calmed down, Camila reminded Lacy of her replacement behaviors, and Lacy agreed to try the "ice idea" the next time she felt like cutting herself. Lacy left the therapy session calmly, although with trails of mascara down her face from her crying.

Lacy learned *distress tolerance,* in which an individual is taught to accept events nonjudgmentally as they happen. For Lacy, distress tolerance was used in situations she finds upsetting, such as family dinners that often dissolved into arguments about money. Camila taught her to just *notice* the argument between her parents—not to judge it as good or bad, but just to observe it, as one might watch a play. Lacy had numerous chances to practice these distress tolerance skills, as her home life seemed to be designed to evoke pathos.

These DBT skills all served to help Lacy develop better emotional regulation, so that she felt more in control of her emotions rather than at the mercy of them. DBT includes repeated homework outside of sessions, and Camila taught Lacy to keep a simple daily diary card to learn to self-assess her emotions, understand events, and use skills outside of treatment. For example, Lacy and Jay, her boyfriend at the time, fought about him texting another girl. Lacy recorded in her diary card that she hated Jay and that he was absolutely worthless, thus completely devaluing him. Camila helped Lacy realize that her opinion of Jay was either that he was ideal or awful. She encouraged her to find a middle ground that more objectively considered both his weaknesses and strengths. In short, she encouraged her to think dialectically.

The diary card also helped improve Lacy's understanding of her emotional experience and of what triggered her emotional dysregulation. Camila worked with Lacy to conduct a *chain analysis* of a situation, helping her break down sequential events into micro-steps. Lacy slapped Jay as a result of the texting situation, and Camila encouraged her to see how different actions could have led to different outcomes. For example, instead of slapping Jay, Lacy could have walked away.

Therapy was often a series of crises. After a month of dating Jay, Jay and Lacy broke up "for good" at his insistence. Camila and Lacy processed the break-up in a dialectical and nonjudgmental way. Initially, she was hurt and he was "a jerk" for breaking up with her, but Camila taught Lacy to see that Jay didn't feel the same way and was simply doing what he thought was best for both of them. In this way, he was just being honest—a positive quality, though his honesty hurt Lacy. Lacy and Camila experienced this sadness together in session, with Lacy still hurting from the break-up and sitting in session ferociously biting her fingernails. However, Lacy was able to handle her pain from the break-up without resorting to cutting herself.

After almost a year of therapy, Camila noticed additional positive changes in Lacy. She had no cut marks on her arm or legs. Instead, she kept an elastic hair band on her wrist at all times. The ice idea hadn't worked consistently, but Lacy had been trying to snap the hair tie on her wrist when she felt like cutting. She'd chosen an elastic hair tie instead of a rubber band so that nobody questioned why she had a rubber band around her wrist. This had been a success for Lacy, and her scars had even begun to fade. Lacy's marijuana use was only occasional, and she had begun to question her own reasons for hanging out with people who were pressuring her to smoke pot.

After a year and a half in therapy Lacy was continuing to make progress, but at the same uneven pace. On the positive side, Lacy hadn't cut herself or smoked pot in six months. She also began participating in a free barre class, a ballet-inspired workout offered through her school. Lacy was learning to appreciate her body through mindful acceptance. On the negative side, she still struggled to manage her emotions. For example, on the way to her senior prom, her date told her that she looked "so exotic." She slapped him across the face and refused to go to prom.

Lacy's parents continued their once-monthly session, but their initial gains in therapy plateaued. Meaningful changes in their chronically toxic family relationships were hard-won and infinitesimal. Freeing Kayla and Mark from their long-standing patterns of relating to one another and Lacy through hostility and contempt proved a tall order, despite everyone trying to hold on to newly learned patterns. After a year of family therapy, a transcript from a session would have looked almost identical to the first.

Camila and Lacy agreed to continue to work together for at least another six months. Camila was hoping that Lacy would find a more supportive and validating environment as she left home to attend college after her senior year.

10. What do you think Lacy will be like in college? What challenges will she face?

11. How will Lacy's parents' marriage change if she goes away to college?

12. What's your prognosis for Lacy? What would your treatment plan be for Lacy if you were Camila? Consider your long- and short-term goals over the next six months of therapy and the interventions you would select to help Lacy reach these goals.

References

American Psychiatric Association. (2013). *Diagnostic and statistical manual of mental disorders* (5th ed.). Arlington, VA: Author.

Biskin, R. S. (2013). Treatment of Borderline Personality Disorder in youth. *Journal of the Canadian Academy of Child & Adolescent Psychiatry, 22*(3), 230–234.

Bleiberg, E., Rossouw, T., & Fonagy, P. (2011). Adolescent breakdown and emerging Borderline Personality Disorder. In A. W. Bateman & P. Fonagy (Eds.), *Handbook of mentalizing in mental health practice* (pp. 463–509). Arlington, VA: American Psychiatric Publishing.

Bliss, S., & McCardle, M. (2014). An exploration of common elements in Dialectical Behavior Therapy, mentalization based treatment and transference focused psychotherapy in the treatment of Borderline Personality Disorder. *Clinical Social Work Journal, 42*(1), 61–69. doi:10.1007/s10615-013-0456-z

Blizard, R. A. (2009). The role of double binds, reality-testing and chronic relational trauma in the genesis and treatment of Borderline Personality Disorder. In A. Moskowitz, I. Schafer, & M. J. Dorahy (Eds.), *Psychosis, trauma and dissociation: Emerging perspectives on severe psychopathology.* Hoboken, NJ: John Wiley & Sons.

Bornovalova, M. A., Huibregste, B. M., Hicks, B. M., Keyes, M., McGue, M., & Iacono, W. (2013). Tests of a direct effect of childhood abuse on adult Borderline Personality traits: A longitudinal discordant twin design. *Journal of Abnormal Psychology, 122*, 180–194.

Cote, J. E., (2009). Identity formation and self-development in adolescence. In R. M. Lerner & I. Steinberg (Eds.), *Handbooks of adolescent psychology Vol. I. Individual bases of adolescent development* (3rd ed., pp. 266–304). Hoboken, NJ: John Wiley & Sons.

Crowell, S. E., Beauchaine, T. P., & Lenzenweger, M. F. (2008). The development of Borderline Personality Disorder and self-injurious behavior. In T. P. Beauchaine & S. P. Hinshaw (Eds.), *Child and adolescent psychopathology* (pp. 510–539). Hoboken, NJ: John Wiley & Sons.

Diamond, A. (2002). Normal development of prefrontal cortex from birth to young adulthood: Cognitive functions, anatomy, and biochemistry. In D. T. Stuss & R. T. Knight (Eds.), *Principles of frontal lobe function* (pp. 406–503). Oxford: Oxford University Press.

Fleischhaker, C., Böhme, R., Sixt, B., Brück, C., Schneider, C., & Schulz, E. (2011). Dialectical Behavioral Therapy for Adolescents (DBT-A): A clinical trial for patients with suicidal and self-injurious behavior and borderline symptoms with a one-year follow-up. *Child & Adolescent Psychiatry & Mental Health, 5*(1), 3–12. doi:10.1186/1753-2000-5-3

Glenn, C. R., & Klonsky, E. D. (2013). Reliability and validity of Borderline Personality Disorder in hospitalized adolescents. *Journal of the Canadian Academy of Child & Adolescent Psychiatry, 22*(3), 206–211.

Kellogg, S. E. (2006). Schema therapy for Borderline Personality Disorder. *Journal of Clinical Psychology, 62*(4), 445–458.

Kliem, S., Kröger, C., & Kosfelder, J. (2010). Dialectical Behavior Therapy for Borderline Personality Disorder: A meta-analysis using mixed-effects modeling. *Journal of Consulting and Clinical Psychology, 78*(6), 936–951. doi:10.1037/a0021015

Klimstra, T. (2013). Adolescent personality development and identity formation. *Child Development Perspectives, 7*(2), 80–84. doi:10.1111/cdep.12017

Laurenssen, E. P., Hutsebaut, J., Feenstra, D. J., Bales, D. L., Noom, M. J., Busschbach, J. V., & Luyten, P. (2014). Feasibility of mentalization-based treatment for adolescents with borderline symptoms: A pilot study. *Psychotherapy, 51*(1), 159–166. doi:10.1037/a0033513

Liao, K. Y., Weng, C., & West, L. M. (2016). Social connectedness and intolerance of uncertainty as moderators between racial microaggressions and anxiety among black individuals. *Journal of Counseling Psychology, 63*(2), 240–246. http://dx.doi.org/10.1037/cou0000123

Linehan, M. M. (1993a). *Cognitive behaviour therapy of Borderline Personality Disorder.* New York: Guilford.

Linehan, M. M. (1993b). *Skills training manual for treating Borderline Personality Disorder.* New York: Guilford.

Linehan, M. M., Schmidt, H., Dimeff, L. A., Craft, J., Kanter, J., & Comtois, K. A. (1999). Dialectical Behavior Therapy for patients with Borderline Personality Disorder and drug-dependence. *American Journal on Addictions, 8*(4), 279–292. doi:10.1080/105504999305686

McMain, S. F., Boritz, T. Z., & Leybman, M. J. (2015). Common strategies for cultivating a positive therapy relationship in the treatment of Borderline Personality Disorder. *Journal of Psychotherapy Integration, 25*(1), 20–29. http://dx.doi.org/10.1037/a0038768

Miller, W., Zweben, A., DiClemente, C., & Rychtarik, R. (1999). *Motivational enhancement therapy manual: A clinical research guide for therapists treating individuals with alcohol abuse and dependency.* Rockville, MD: US Department of Health and Human Services.

Moss, R. C., & Davis, D. (2008). Counseling biracial students: A review of issues and interventions. *Journal of Multicultural Counseling & Development, 36*(4), 219–230. doi:10.1002/j.2161-1912.2008.tb00084

Nawaz, S. (2011). The relationship of parental and peer attachment bonds with the identity development during adolescence. *FWU Journal of Social Sciences, 5*(1), 104–119.

Poston, W. (1990). The Biracial Identity Development Model: A needed addition. *Journal of Counseling & Development, 69*(2), 152.

Reichenberg, L. W., & Seligman, L. (2016). *Psychosis, trauma and dissociation: Emerging perspectives on severe psychopathology.* Hoboken, NJ: John Wiley & Sons.

Renn, K. A. (2008). Research on biracial and multiracial identity development: Overview and synthesis. *New Directions for Student Services, 123,* 13–21. doi:10.1002/ss.282

Rizvi, S. L., Steffel, L. M., & Carson-Wong, A. (2013). An overview of dialectical behavior therapy for professional psychologists. *Professional Psychology: Research and Practice, 44*(2), 73–80. doi:10.1037/a0029808

Rummens, J. (2003). Conceptualizing identity and diversity: Overlaps, intersections, and processes. *Canadian Ethnic Studies, 35*(3), 10–25.

Schuppert, H. H. (2009). Effectiveness of an emotion regulation group training for adolescents—a randomized controlled pilot study. *Clinical Psychology & Psychotherapy, 16*(6), 467–478.

Speranza, M., Pham-Scottez, A., Revah-Levy, A., Barbe, R. P., Perez-Diaz, F., Birmaher, B., & Coreos, M. (2012). Factor structure of Borderline Personality Disorder symptomatology in adolescents. *Canadian Journal of Psychiatry, 57*(4), 230–237.

Stepp, S. D., Burke, J. D., Hipwell, A. E., & Loeber, R. (2011). Trajectories of Attention Deficit Hyperactive Disorder and Oppositional Defiant Disorder symptoms as precursors of Borderline Personality Disorder symptoms in adolescent girls. *Journal of Abnormal Child Psychology, 40,* 7–20.

Swales, M., Heard, H. L., & Williams, J. G. (2000). Linehan's Dialectical Behaviour Therapy (DBT) for Borderline Personality Disorder: Overview and adaptation. *Journal of Mental Health, 9*(1), 7–23. doi:10.1080/09638230016921

Walsh, F. (1977). The family of the borderline patient. In R. R. Grinker & B. Werble (Eds.), *The borderline patient* (pp. 158–177). New York: Jason Aronson.

Winograd, G., Cohen, P., & Chen, H. (2008). Adolescent borderline symptoms in the community: Prognosis for functioning over 20 years. *Journal of Child Psychology & Psychiatry, 49*(9), 933–941. doi:10.1111/j.1469-7610.2008.01930.x

Yeomans, F. E., Levy, K. N., & Caligor, E. (2013). Transference-focused psychotherapy. *Psychotherapy, 50*(3), 449–453. http://dx.doi.org/10.1037/a0033417

Index